Civic Responsibility and Higher Education

Edited by
Thomas Ehrlich

AMERICAN COUNCIL ON EDUCATION
ORYX PRESS
Series on Higher Education
2000

The rare Arabian Oryx is believed to have inspired the myth of the unicorn. This desert antelope became virtually extinct in the early 1960s. At that time, several groups of international conservationists arranged to have nine animals sent to the Phoenix Zoo to be the nucleus of a captive breeding herd. Today, the Oryx population is over 1,000, and over 500 have been returned to the Middle East.

Library of Congress Cataloging-in-Publication Data

Civic responsibility and higher education / edited by Thomas Ehrlich.
     p. cm.—(American Council on Education/Oryx Press series on higher eduation)
Includes bibliographical references and index.
ISBN 1-57356-289-0 (alk.)
     1. Citizenship—Study and teaching (Higher)—United States. 2. Education, Higher—Aims and objectives—United States. I. Ehrlich, Thomas, 1934- II. Series.

LC1091.C5289 2000
378'.01'5—dc21   99-057257

CONTENTS

PREFACE

I n the book *Democracy and Education*, Dewey proposed two radical insights about American society. One was that most citizens, not just the elite, can have a life of the mind. The other was that a life that is only of the mind is inadequate to the challenges of American democracy. Our society requires civic engagement to realize the potential of its citizens and its communities. And, he argued, education was the key to that engagement.

Higher education faces many challenges these days. None is more important than to meet the mandate that Dewey posed for all of American education. Students and their parents are asking what *is* the "value added" from a college education and what *are* the outcomes they can expect? All too often, those outcomes are stated solely in terms of economic success. Too many institutions of higher education have adopted what William Sullivan labels, in Chapter 2 of this volume, "a sort of default program of instrumental individualism. This is the familiar notion that the academy exists to research and disseminate knowledge and skills as tools for economic development and the upward mobility of individuals." The result, he laments, is that leadership in both the private and public sectors is increasingly dominated by "narrow careerism and private self-interest." For-profit universities are expanding to deliver job training that is often cheaper and more targeted to employment needs than is the curriculum offered in traditional nonprofit colleges and universities. Unless the former institutions can not only promise but also deliver something more than job training, their role in society will decline. That "something more" must include, as Dewey taught us, a focused concern on the civic responsibility of colleges and universities, to and within their communities, and on the civic capacities of the students whom they are educating.

What does civic engagement mean and what can colleges and universities do to promote it? At the core of the issue, civic engagement means working to make a difference in the civic life of our communities and developing the combination of knowledge, skills, values, and motivation to make that difference. It means promoting the quality of life in a community, through both political and nonpolitical processes. How should these civic virtues be taught? What are good models of the engaged campus? There are no easy answers to these pressing questions.

Dewey wrote that "a democracy is more than a form of government; it is primarily a mode of associated living, of conjoint communicated experience." Dewey's "Democracy and Education" contains no civic curriculum and no list of specific courses or skills to promote civic virtues. Rather, when one considers the book as a whole, it is about how leaders of a school or educational system should shape all programs and arrangements, curricular and extracurricular, toward the goal of democracy.

Dewey did not give concrete examples or even many hints about how this "mode of associated living" should best be learned, but clearly he had in mind that a school should be a microcosm of society, structured in ways that enhance the learning environment by simplifying and organizing. He stressed two "conditions" as key. First, "the school must itself be a community life in all which that implies." Second, "the learning in school should be continuous with that out of school." How best to meet those conditions? Again, Dewey did not give details, and like most of us in higher education, he did not practice much of what he preached.

The essays in this volume should be of significant interest to everyone troubled about American democracy and its future, as well as about the future of higher education in this country. The authors have written with particular attention to college and university faculty and administrators and what they can do to educate their own students to be responsible citizens. No less important, these essays provide important insights on how campuses themselves can be engaged citizens of their communities. But the volume is also written for a larger audience of those concerned about how to reverse the decline of civic engagement in the United States. The authors not only diagnose the reasons why higher education has been primarily on the sidelines during this decline, but also propose concrete steps to change that reality.

Inevitably, the authors raise many more issues than they resolve. As Jane Wellman makes clear in Chapter 18, higher education as a whole has not been clear even about what is meant by civic responsibility, let alone how to assess effectiveness in preparing students or their campuses for the exercise of that responsibility. These are issues that must be addressed if higher education is to be a significant force in dealing with what many have termed a crisis in our democracy.

"Crisis" may seem too strong a term, and perhaps it is. Nonetheless, as Linda Sax notes in Chapter 1, it is exactly the term used in a 1985 Carnegie Foundation report by Frank Newman: "If there is a crisis in education in the United States today, it is less that test scores have declined than it is that we have failed to provide the education for citizenship that is still the most important responsibility of the nation's schools and colleges." And Sax provides powerful evidence that the problem of political involvement has intensified in the intervening years since that report. Although community service by college students has increased significantly, "interest in politics has plummeted." She even suggests that the two may be related—students may be turning to community service as a way to help their communities without having to engage in political processes, which they view with deep suspicion at best, cynicism at worst.

The Introduction to this volume is an essay by Anne Colby and me, together with three research colleagues. We are working together on a project to examine American undergraduate education in terms of programs to enhance the moral and civic responsibility of students, and we are also seeking to encourage colleagues and universities to strengthen those programs. Our introductory essay explains what we mean by both moral and civic responsibility and gives an overview of the ways in which committed colleges and universities are helping to prepare their graduates for responsible citizenship.

Part 1 of this volume examines the deep concerns that led to the creation of this work. The section opens with two essays; one by Linda Sax and one by William Sullivan. Together with the third essay, by Harry Boyte and Nancy Kari, Part 1 presents the problems in enhancing civic responsibility that are facing higher education. Sax focuses particularly on students and what they think. Sullivan and Boyte/Kari look more generally at the institutions of higher education. Boyte makes the case that the great innovation of American democracy is its tie to work, and the task of renewing colleges and universities as agents of democracy requires a return to a tradition of public work.

Part 2 gives an overview of what colleges and universities are doing about the problems raised in Part 1. It includes three essays that were originally drafted for a conference sponsored by the American Council on Education and hosted by Florida State University in Tallahassee. That conference brought together about 100 educators and students from across the country to consider ways to enhance the roles of colleges and universities as engaged citizens of their communities and as educators of future civic leaders. The discussions were illuminating and intense, and this volume stems from one of the recommendations that emerged from the sessions. Another recommendation was that colleges and universities listen carefully to civic leaders in their communities; as a result, the American Council on Education has sponsored a series of meetings in various cities, and other similar sessions are planned for the future.

In the first of the three conference essays, Nancy Thomas surveys an impressive range of programs aimed at promoting civic responsibility. They provide an important set of good practices for replication. In the second conference essay, Carol Schneider points out that the dominant model of academic preparation for civic responsibility depends on developing essentially value-neutral analytic skills, and urges that this model is "deeply insufficient" for our society. She proposes an approach that focuses more directly on the needs of our society. Finally, Alexander Astin argues in Chapter 6 that the most important single step colleges and universities can take to meet their own civic responsibilities is to concentrate time, attention, and resources on the least-prepared students. Instead of rejecting the role of remediation, as seems to be the trend across the country, he urges the reverse.

The four essays in Part 3 which focus on the ways that issues of higher education and civic responsibility intersect with other social sectors. David Mathews relates the challenges to higher education directly to the atrophy of citizen interest and engagement in politics, and proposes steps to meet those challenges. Jay Rosen turns to the impact of the media and ways in which the media and higher education can work together. In this work, he draws on his efforts to shape a concept and practice of public journalism. Lee Benson and Ira Harkavy focus on what they view as the most important public problem of our society—the decline of primary and secondary education. They relate their own work at the University of Pennsylvania to the larger issues of what higher education can do to enhance public schooling. Finally, Penelope Eckert and Peter Henschel consider the new opportunities and challenges that the digital age poses to the ways in which colleges and universities meet their civic responsibilities. In the face of concerns that "the virtual campus" will further erode the civic engagement of both students and their institutions, they suggest ways in which technology can enrich the exercise of civic responsibility by institutions of higher education.

Part 4 offers a wonderfully rich array of six essays that describe how different types of colleges and universities struggle with the challenges of civic responsibility. Paul Elsner begins with an examination of community colleges. He focuses particular attention on his own institutions, the Maricopa Community Colleges, which have long been civic leaders under his presidency. Judith Ramaley follows with a look at comprehensive universities, drawing on her own background at Portland State University, where she made that institution into a model of the engaged campus, and at the University of Vermont, where she is now president. Greg Prince examines the opportunities and obligations of liberal arts colleges from his vantage point as president of Hampshire College in Amherst, Massachusetts. Gloria Scott considers the special roles of historically black colleges, including her own insights drawn from Bennett College in Greensboro, North Carolina, where she is president. William Byron examines the roles of religious-based colleges and universities, drawing on his background as president of The Catholic University of America in Washington, D.C. And Mary Walshok analyzes the hurdles facing research universities in this arena. She uses her experience at the University of California at San Diego to explore how institutions of higher education can connect to the communities around them. She particularly stresses the role of those institutions as convenors in helping to resolve or ease community concerns.

Three essays on themes that cut across all types of institutions are included in Part 5. Disciplines are still at the heart of the academic enterprise in higher education, and Ed Zlotkowski discusses the ways that civic responsibility can be integral to the work of many disciplines. He draws on his remarkable work in organizing a series of monographs on service-learning in various disciplines. His essay, along with others, reveals that service-learning is a key tool for promoting the civic responsibility of students. Jane Wellman's essay starts with the stark judgment that higher education does poorly in assessing and accounting for its civic teaching and community service roles, and proposes some important steps to deal with that failing. Elizabeth Hollander and Matthew Hartley raise related concerns in their essay, which focuses on the need for a national network to assist campuses as engaged citizens and enhance the civic responsibility of their students. Finally, Zelda Gamson offers some insights in her Afterword drawn from the essays viewed as a whole and from her own experience in promoting the involvement of various campuses in the civic activities of their communities.

This volume as a whole adopts the view of John Dewey that American democracy and education are inexorably intertwined. This is not simply because our citizenry must be educated to choose responsibly its political leaders and to hold them accountable. Much more important, a democratic society is one in which informed citizens interact with each other, learn from each other, grow with each other, and together make their communities more than the sum of their parts. Dewey urged that a community of learners is the primary mechanism through which this democratizing process occurs. To be successful, the educational community must be both interactive and collaborative, a place where the processes of decision making are more important than the decisions themselves. And it must be a diverse community, reflecting the diversity of the larger communities into which students will move upon graduation.

To translate this mandate into an institutional program, many questions still need to be asked and answered. The essays in this volume seek to do just that. They approach the challenge of Dewey's premise that a learning community is one in which no single member of the community knows everything, in which every member can contribute something, and in which there is a clear vision of a better future combined with a healthy skepticism about the abilities of anyone to know all the answers, whatever the questions. This was the democratic society that Dewey sought and for which he posited a powerful role for higher education. These essays are important steps in showing the ways to realize that role.

Hundreds of wonderful faculty members and students from scores of colleges and universities contributed ideas and insights for this volume—too many to acknowledge by name. But I owe special thanks to the American Council on Education, and its president, Stanley O. Ikenberry, who sponsored a program that includes this book, and to my partners in leading that program, Zelda F. Gamson and Jane Wellman. My gratitude is due as well to colleagues at San Francisco State, and particularly its president, Robert Corrigan, who heads a model of a civically engaged urban campus, and Brian Murphy, director of its Urban Institute. The Carnegie Foundation for the Advancement of Teaching has been an extraordinarily collegial home for me in working on issues of civic and moral responsibility and higher education. Anne Colby, another senior scholar at Carnegie, is a superb collaborator, and we have both learned a great deal from the three research associates who work with us, Elizabeth Beaumont, Jennifer Rosner, and Jason Stephens. Throughout this project, Ruby Kerawalla has handled with skill and good humor innumerable details of shepherding ideas to manuscripts and manuscripts to print. Finally, and most important, my wife Ellen, who has been not only a perfect partner for more than four decades but also an exemplar of civic responsibility.

Thomas Ehrlich
The Carnegie Foundation for the Advancement of Teaching

CONTRIBUTORS

Alexander W. Astin is Allan M. Cartter Professor of Higher Education at the University of California, Los Angeles, and director of the Higher Education Research Institute at UCLA. He has served as director of research for both the American Council on Education and the National Merit Scholarship Corporation. He is the founding director of the Cooperative Institutional Research Program, and has authored 18 books and some 300 other publications in the field of higher education. He has been the recipient of 10 honorary degrees and 14 research awards from national educational associations. A 1990 study in the *Journal of Higher Education* identified him as the most frequently cited author in the field of higher education.

Elizabeth Beaumont graduated from Pomona College with a B.A. and is currently a Ph.D. student in political science at Stanford University.

Lee Benson served in the United States Army, 1942–46, and holds a B.A. from Brooklyn College, an M.A. from Columbia University, and a Ph.D. from Cornell University. Professionally trained as an American historian, he has taught at Columbia University, Wayne State University, and, since 1964, the University of Pennsylvania (professor emeritus, 1991 to present). A distinguished fellow of the Center for Community Partnerships at Penn, he collaborates with Ira Harkavy on action-oriented research and teaching designed to exemplify their conviction that the primary mission of American universities is to work in practical ways to help bring about an optimally democratic society and world. He is author of six books.

Harry C. Boyte is co-director of the Center for Democracy and Citizenship at the University of Minnesota, a senior fellow at the Humphrey Institute, and a graduate faculty member of the College of Liberal Arts. From 1993–95, he served as national coordinator of The New Citizenship, a broad, nonpartisan coalition of civic and educational groups that worked, in association with the White House Domestic Policy Council, to analyze the gap between citizens and government and to develop strategies and recommendations for the strengthening of citizenship in the United States. Boyte served as a senior advisor to the National Commission on Civic Renewal and to the "State of the Union" public television series, and represented the United States at the 1996 International Conference on Civic Education in Seoul, South Korea. For the last 10 years, he has helped to organize action research projects at the Humphrey Institute; these projects were aimed at developing effective practical theory to reengage citizens with public life and to revitalize the public culture of mediating institutions such as schools, government, and higher education. He is author, co-author, and editor of eight books. His writings have appeared in more than 70 publications, including *The New York Times, The Wall Street Journal, Democracy,* and *Policy Review.* His doctorate from The Union Institute is in political and social thought. In the 1960s, he was a field secretary for the Southern Christian Leadership Conference in the southern civil rights movement.

William J. Byron is distinguished professor of the practice of ethics in the McDonough School of Business at Georgetown University, where he also served as rector of the Jesuit Community. He was formerly president of The Catholic University of America and of the University of Scranton, and dean of arts and sciences at Loyola University in New Orleans. He was a founding director of Bread for the World and a member of the original Board of Directors of the Federal Commission on National and Community Service (now the Corporation for National Service). A past member of the Board of Commissioners of the Joint Commission on the Accreditation of Healthcare Organizations, Father Byron is a current trustee of Loyola College in Maryland and of the University of San Francisco. He has published nine books.

Anne Colby is a psychologist whose work centers on adult development, with special reference to the development of character and values. She joined The Carnegie Foundation for the Advancement of Teaching as a senior scholar in 1997. Her work at the foundation focuses on professional education and on the role of undergraduate education in developing students, civic engagement, and moral commitment. She was previously director of the Henry Murray Research Center of Radcliffe College, a longitudinal studies data archive and social science research center. Colby completed a B.A. at McGill University and Ph.D. in psychology at Columbia University. She is the principal author of *A Longitudinal Study of Moral Judgement* (1983), *The Measurement of Moral Judgement* (1987), and *Some Do Care: Contemporary Lives of Moral Commitment* (1992); and co-editor of *Ethnography and Human Development: Context and Meaning in Human Inquiry* (1995) and *Competence and Character through Life* (1998).

Penelope Eckert is a research scientist and professor in the Department of Linguistics at Stanford University. She is a sociolinguist and ethnographer whose research centers around the role of language and other symbolic systems in the negotiation of social identity. She has done ethnographic and sociolinguistic work in high schools, focusing on adolescent social categories and on the reproduction of social class in the schools. She is currently studying the construction of gender in preadolescence and early adolescence under a grant from the Spencer Foundation. She earned her B.A. from Oberlin College and her Ph.D. from Columbia University.

Thomas Ehrlich is a distinguished university scholar at San Francisco State University and a senior scholar at The Carnegie Foundation for the Advancement of Teaching. He was formerly president of Indiana University, provost of the University of Pennsylvania, and dean of Stanford Law School. He also served as the first director of the International Development Cooperation Agency and the first president of the Legal Services Corporation. He is chair-elect of the American Association of Higher Education, a director of Bennett College, a director of the Corporation for National Service, a director of the National Center for Public Policy and Higher Education, a director of the Public Welfare Foundation, and the former chair of the Campus Compact Executive Committee. He is author or editor of eight books.

Paul A. Elsner has spent 40 years in community college leadership positions. Recently, he became chancellor emeritus of Maricopa Community Colleges (Arizona) where he served for 22 years. Dr. Elsner currently chairs the Board of Trustees for ETS (Educational Testing Service) at Princeton and was an original member of the Executive Committee of Campus Compact. Dr. Elsner was a Kellogg Fellow at Stanford where he received his doctorate. As chancellor emeritus of the Maricopa Community Colleges, Dr. Elsner is currently employed half-time at Mesa Community College where he is involved with the teaching and development of international programs. Dr. Elsner is also currently working on a book on community building and development.

Zelda F. Gamson is a sociologist who has devoted her career to the study and critique of the academy. A founding director of the New England Resource Center for Higher Education (NERCHE) and the doctoral program in higher education at the University of Massachusetts in Boston, she currently serves as a senior associate with NERCHE. She spent more than 20 years as a researcher and faculty member at the University of Michigan in the Survey Research Center, the Center for the Study of Higher Education, and the Residential College. She has served on the boards of Antioch University, the Center for Campus Organizing, and the American Association for Higher Education. She is also editor of several professional journals, including *Change* magazine. Her books include *Academic Values and Mass Education*, *Liberating Education*, *Higher Education and the Real World*, and *Revitalizing General Education in a Time of Scarcity*.

Ira Harkavy is associate vice president and director of the Center for Community Partnerships, University of Pennsylvania. A historian, Harkavy teaches in the departments of history, urban studies, and city and regional planning. The West Philadelphia Improvement Corps (WEPIC), a 14-year partnership to create university-assisted community schools that connect the University of Pennsylvania and the West Philadelphia community, emerged and developed from seminars and research projects he directs with other colleagues at Penn. Harkavy is executive editor of *Universities and Community Schools* and an editorial board member of *Non-Profit Voluntary Sector Quarterly*. He has written and lectured widely on the history and current practice of urban university-community partnerships and strategies for integrating the missions of teaching, research, and service. He is chair of the Coalition for Community Schools and co-chair of the Philadelphia Higher Education Network for Neighborhood Development (PHENND).

Matthew Hartley is an advanced doctoral student at the Harvard University Graduate School of Education. He is a board member and co-chair of the *Harvard Educational Review*. His research interests are in organizational change in higher education and civic education. Before pursuing his doctorate, he was the founding director of Bradford College's Office of Community Service-Learning.

Peter Henschel came to the Institute for Research on Learning (IRL) in April 1991, after nearly three years in Britain as managing director of "Business in the Cities"—a public-private partnership program to revitalize inner cities in the U.K. Led by Prince Charles, the project was designed to build long-term alliances between local business and political leaders in the service of common goals for distressed communities. Immediately prior to his work in London, Henschel served as deputy mayor for management and programs for the city and county of San Francisco. His career has centered on public sector management, human resources management, and the creation of lasting partnerships and alliances in various settings. He comes to the world of learning research and development with a lifelong dedication to the reform of

K-12 education and to the creation of major improvements in the quality of work-life and the workplace. Trained in classical music, Henschel is an avid concert and opera fan. He also maintains a keen interest in wilderness travel, kayaking, volunteer civic duties in San Francisco, and all things Chinese. He earned a B.A. from Harvard University and an M.P.P. from the University of California at Berkeley.

Elizabeth Hollander is the executive director of Campus Compact, a national coalition of 630 college and university presidents who support the expansion of opportunities for public and community service in higher education and the importance of integrating service into academic study. Hollander was the executive director of the Monsignor John J. Egan Urban Center at DePaul University, which works with the university to address critical urban problems, alleviate poverty, and promote social justice in the metropolitan community through teaching, service, and scholarship. She was also the president of the Government Assistance Program in Illinois and the director of planning for the city of Chicago under Mayor Harold Washington. While in Chicago, Hollander worked as a mentor in the Harris School for Public Policy at the University of Chicago and as a member of the Truman Regional Scholarship Committee. She also served on the boards of trustees at Chicago State University and the Illinois Institute of Technology. She now serves on the boards of the Woodstock Institute in Chicago, the American Association of Colleges & Universities Diversity Web, and the American Committee of the International Consortium on Higher Education.

Nancy N. Kari is director of Program and Faculty Development for the Higher Education Consortium of Urban Affairs. She is co-author, with Harry Boyte, of *Building America: The Democratic Promise of Public Work*. Her writings on public work, civic professionalism, and democracy have appeared in *The New Democrat, Policy Review, Dissent, Commonwealth, The Wall Street Journal*, and other publications. She is a co-founder of the Jane Addams School for Democracy.

David Mathews, who is president of the Kettering Foundation, was secretary of health, education, and welfare in the Ford administration and, before that, president of the University of Alabama. He received a Ph.D. in philosophy from Columbia University and taught American political and social history for nearly 20 years. As chair of the Council on Public Policy Education and one of the organizers of the National Issues Forums, he has worked to revive the tradition of the American town meeting and the practice of deliberative democracy. He has written extensively on such subjects as education, political theory, southern history, public policy, and international problem solving. His most recent books are *Is There a Public for Public Schools?* and a second edition of *Politics for People*.

Gregory S. Prince, Jr. is the fourth president of Hampshire College, a four-year independent liberal arts college in Amherst, Massachusetts, with an enrollment of 1,100 students. Prince is also a professor in the School of Social Science and currently teaches a course entitled "Conflict Resolutions and Historical Analysis." Among his numerous leadership roles in civic and community activities, Prince served as chairman of the board of the Association of Independent Colleges and Universities of Massachusetts (AICUM) and was president of Five Colleges, Inc. He has served on boards as diverse as the International Association of Chiefs of Police (IACP), the Montshire Museum of Natural Sciences, the Vermont Institute of Natural Science, the Yale-China Association, and the University Press of New England. He currently serves on the board of directors of the Washington Campus, the National Inventive Thinking Association, Mass Ventures, the New England Association of Schools and Colleges, and the Nature Conservancy.

Judith A. Ramaley is president of the University of Vermont. Prior to coming to UVM, she was president and professor of biology at Portland State University in Portland, Oregon. Dr. Ramaley has served as a member of the board of the Association of American Colleges & Universities (AAC&U) and is currently a member of the board of the American Council on Education (ACE), a vice chair of the board of Campus Compact, a member of the National-Work-Advisory Board, chair of the steering committee of the National Forum on Civic Responsibility, chair of the subcommittee on College Drinking of the Advisory Council of the National Institute on Alcohol Abuse and Alcoholism (National Institutes of Health), and a trustee of Wilmington College in Wilmington, Ohio. Dr. Ramaley received her bachelor's degree from Swarthmore College and conducted her graduate studies at the University of California, Los Angeles, where she earned a doctorate. In 1982, Ramaley became the chief academic officer at the State University of New York at Albany. She also served as executive vice president for academic affairs and as acting president for one semester at SUNY-Albany. Ramaley was also the executive vice chancellor at the University of Kansas.

Jay Rosen is associate professor of journalism at New York University. From 1993–97, he was the director of the Project on Public Life and the Press, funded by the Knight Foundation. Since 1990 he has been a leading figure in the reform movement known as "public journalism," which calls on the press to take an active role in strengthening citizenship, improving political debate, and reviving public life. His book, *What Are Journalists For?*, was published in 1999 by Yale University Press. Rosen is also an associate of the Kettering Foundation.

Jennifer Rosner graduated from Columbia University with a B.A. and from Stanford University with a Ph.D. in philosophy.

Linda J. Sax is assistant professor in-residence in the Graduate School of Education and Information Studies at UCLA. Dr. Sax is director of the Cooperative Institutional Research Program (CIRP) and associate director of the Higher Education Research Institute (HERI). In that capacity, she is responsible for CIRP's annual survey of incoming freshmen, as well as an annual survey of continuing college students, and a triennial survey of college faculty. Dr. Sax recently directed a national evaluation of student participants in President Bill Clinton's Learn and Serve America Higher Education (LSAHE), a project sponsored by the Corporation for National Service. Dr. Sax has authored book chapters and monographs, and has published more than a dozen articles in journals such as *Research in Higher Education, The Review of Higher Education, The Journal of Higher Education, The Journal of College Student Development,* and *Educational Record.* She also serves on the editorial boards for *The Review of Higher Education* and *Research in Higher Education.*

Carol Geary Schneider was named president of the Association of American Colleges & Universities (AAC&U) in 1998, after serving as executive vice president since 1988. Dr. Schneider has directed AAC&U's major initiative on higher education and U.S. pluralism, titled "American Commitments: Diversity, Democracy and Liberal Learning." With support from the Ford Foundation, the National Endowment for the Humanities, and several other foundations, the American Commitments initiative assists colleges and universities on ways of educating students for a diverse democracy. She also has led a series of projects on revitalizing general education and reforming college majors. At the University of Chicago, she directed the Midwest Faculty Seminar and founded both the Consortium on Quality in educating nontraditional students and the University of Chicago Institute on Teaching and Learning. She has published extensively on purposes and practices in undergraduate liberal education. She holds a B.A. from Mount Holyoke College and a Ph.D. in history from Harvard University, and has taught at Boston University, Chicago State University, and the University of Chicago.

Gloria Dean Randle Scott is president of Bennett College for women. She was formerly vice president at Clark College, director of Educational Planning and Evaluation and professor of higher education at Texas Southern University, director of Institutional Research and Planning at North Carolina Agricultural and Technical State University, dean of students at Knoxville College, instructor at Marian College, and research associate in genetics at Indiana University. She is a founder of Africa University. She served as national president of Girl Scouts of USA; trustee of Wilson College; and director of boards for the American Association of Higher Education; American Association of Colleges; Women's College Coalition; National Association of Independent Colleges and Universities; National Association of Schools, Colleges and Universities; National Association of Schools, Colleges and Universities of the United Methodist Church; and the University Senate of the United Methodist Church. She served as commissioner of the national commissions on the International Women's Year and on the International Year of the Child and the Environment, and as chair of the Defense Advisory Committee on Women in the Services. She is chair of the Council of Presidents of the Black College Fund of the United Methodist Church. She is executive producer of *Community Journal*.

Jason Stephens graduated from the University of Vermont with a B.A., received an M.Ed. from Vanderbilt University, and is currently a Ph.D. student in psychology at Stanford University.

William M. Sullivan is a senior scholar at The Carnegie Foundation for the Advancement of Teaching and professor of philosophy at La Salle University. He holds a Ph.D. in philosophy from Fordham University. He has been an active researcher in the areas of political and social theory, the philosophy of the social sciences, ethics, the study of American society and values, the professions, and education. He publishes and lectures widely in these areas. He is co-author of *Habits of the Heart: Individualism and Commitment in American Life* and *The Good Society*. He is author of *Reconstructing Public Philosophy* and *Work and Integrity: The Crisis and Promise of Professionalism in American Life*. He serves on the editorial board of *The Responsive Community*, the national journal of the Communitarian Network.

Nancy L. Thomas directs the American Council on Education's *Listening to Communities*, a series of regional forums that explore higher education's civic role. She also serves part time as special assistant for legal affairs to the president at Western New England College. She is a senior associate at the New England Resource Center for Higher Education, a fellow with the Society for Values in Higher Education, and a member of the National Association for College and University Attorneys.

Mary Lindenstein Walshok is associate chancellor for Extended Studies and Public Programs and adjunct professor in the Department of Sociology at the University of California, San Diego. She received her B.A. from Pomona College and her M.A. and Ph.D. in sociology from Indiana University. She has been associated with UCSD since 1972 and has remained active as an industrial sociologist, authoring numerous book chapters and articles on education and the world of work, as well as the book *Blue Collar Women,* published by Anchor/Doubleday. Her second book, *Knowledge Without Boundaries: What America's Research Universities Can Do for the Economy, the Workplace, and the Community*, was published by Jossey-Bass in 1995.

Jane V. Wellman is a senior associate with The Institute for Higher Education Policy in Washington, D.C., where she conducts research and analysis on policy, planning, and finance in higher education. She is the co-director of the "New Millennium" project, a national study of higher education renewal strategies funded by the Ford Foundation. She also provides consulting advice in higher education finance, planning, and governmental relations to institutions and associations. Wellman has worked for more than 20 years in higher education and government relations, at both the federal and state levels, and with public and private institutions.

Edward Zlotkowski is a professor of English at Bentley College, a senior associate at the American Association for Higher Education (AAHE), and a senior faculty fellow at Campus Compact. In 1990, he founded the Bentley Service-Learning Project, an institution-wide program that has involved in its work all the college's undergraduate academic departments, more than a quarter of its full-time faculty, and several thousand students. In 1995, he was named a senior associate at AAHE and in that capacity has served as general editor of a monograph series exploring the relationship between service-learning and academic disciplines/disciplinary areas. The first 10 volumes in that series are currently in print. His book, *Successful Service-Learning Programs: New Models of Excellence in Higher Education,* was published by Anker in 1998. Dr. Zlotkowski has acted as a consultant to the Corporation on National Service, the Council of Independent Colleges, the Pew Charitable Trusts, and regional/state service-learning associations from Maine to Hawaii as well as to more than 100 individual colleges and universities.

INTRODUCTION

Higher Education and the Development of Civic Responsibility

Anne Colby, Thomas Ehrlich,
with Elizabeth Beaumont, Jennifer Rosner, and Jason Stephens

T he essays in this volume are rooted in the common concerns of the authors about the increasing public disdain for civic engagement, particularly political involvement, in this country, and their common beliefs that higher education should have important roles in reversing those trends. We share those concerns and beliefs. In a project under the auspices of the Carnegie Foundation for the Advancement of Teaching, we are analyzing the American undergraduate scene in terms of campus efforts to promote both the moral and civic responsibilities of students. We are also working to encourage colleges and universities to strengthen those efforts.

Although this volume focuses on civic responsibility, we include moral responsibility in this chapter, as well as in our project, because we believe the two are inseparable. Our democratic principles, including tolerance and respect for others, procedural impartiality, and concern for both the rights of the individual and the welfare of the group, are all grounded in moral principles. Likewise, the problems that the civically engaged citizen must confront always include strong moral themes—for example, fair access to resources such as housing, the moral obligation to consider future generations in making environmental policy, and the conflicting claims of multiple stakeholders in community decision-making. None of these issues can be adequately resolved without a consideration of moral questions. A person can become civically and politically active without good judgment and a strong moral compass, but it is hardly wise to promote that kind of involvement. Because civic responsibility is inescapably threaded with moral values, we believe that higher education must aspire to foster both moral and civic maturity and must confront educationally the many links between them.

WHAT ARE THE PROBLEMS?

Many commentators have chronicled a widespread lack of public interest in civic affairs, especially political affairs, and a general lack of trust in and respect for American democratic processes. This trend is manifested in an overall decline in civic and political participation and in the ascendence of superficial sloganeering over thoughtful, substantive, and honest public debate. Demographic data indicate that political disaffection is especially pronounced among youth. Americans growing up in recent decades vote less often than their elders and show lower levels of social trust and knowledge of politics.[1] On college campuses, political discussion has declined: Data from annual freshman surveys indicate that the percentage of college freshmen who report frequently discussing politics dropped from a high of 30 percent in 1968 to 15 percent in 1995.[2] Similar decreases were seen in the percentages of those who believe it is important to keep up to date with political affairs or who have worked on a political campaign. This mounting political apathy bodes ill for the future of American democracy, unless these generations of young people come to see both the value of and necessity for political participation.

In addition to political disengagement, contemporary critics have also decried a closely related phenomenon—the excessive individualism of contemporary American culture and its negative implications for our society.[3] The consequences of this cultural climate include a growing sense that Americans are not responsible for or accountable to each other; a decline in civility, mutual respect, and tolerance; and the preeminence of self-interest and individual preference over concern for the common good. Goals of personal advancement and gratification dominate our culture, frequently at the expense of broader social, moral, or spiritual meaning. Though this emphasis on individual success has some social benefits, it can also entail high social costs by promoting a world view in which there is no basis for enduring commitment beyond the self. The most visible alternative to this focus on self-interest is a kind of orthodox and intolerant moralism. Ironically, each of these opposing moral approaches contributes to the same result: a society which is increasingly polarized and fragmented, with little sense of being united by shared values, or of participation in a common enterprise.

Many authors (e.g., Barber, 1984)[4] have written eloquently about these problems and the need for moral and civic renewal if we are to move toward a more cohesive and humane society. A number of national reports have been issued in recent years proposing steps to promote these social goals as well as diagnosing the hurdles in the way of achieving them. We have been struck, however, by the fact that many of these reports (e.g., National Commission on Civic Renewal, 1998; Council on Civil Society, 1998)[5] pay minimal attention to the role of higher education in helping to shape the moral and civic lives of students and American culture more generally. Moreover, when higher education is discussed, it is sometimes considered part of the problem rather than part of the solution, a critical perspective that is shared by some writing within the field as well as some outside.

The humanities have traditionally been viewed as the academic arena in which moral and civic issues should be central as well as being considered the core of a liberal arts education. In the past, many considered moral philosophy and literature to be prime tools to aid students in developing their own values, prompting the creation of "Great Books" programs like that adopted by the University of Chicago in the 1930s. The emphasis in these courses, in which students read the Greek philosophers, the Hebrew and Christian Bibles, along with the Enlightenment philosophers, was on the power of reason in working through complex moral issues, on the need for civic virtues in grappling with public issues, and on the importance of individual liberty. Similarly, literature courses have long used texts that exemplify moral struggles—one definition of a great literary work is the degree to which it exposes human struggles with moral quandaries. Understanding of those quandaries and their possible resolutions can be gained in powerful ways through studying works such as *Crime and Punishment* and *Jude the Obscure*.

Despite the strong tradition of moral engagement in the humanities, our sense today is that most students are not exposed in their philosophy, literature, or other humanities classes to the kinds of analysis of moral and civic questions that provide a central rationale for a liberal arts education. We have heard innumerable anecdotes about teachers of moral philosophy who, in discussing the moral theories of Plato, Aristotle, Hobbes, Locke, Hume, Kant, and others, point out the shortcomings of these theories without aiding students in the process of developing principles for moral reasoning that they may live with and demonstrate. This approach, combined with the fact that teachers often conceal their own values and commitments, is ultimately corrosive for students seeking their own moral compass. Students may be led to believe that all systems of moral justification are fundamentally flawed and therefore that moral positions can be no more than matters of personal preference. This interpretation can be as dangerous as dogmatic approaches that inculcate moral and civic values without tolerating legitimate questioning or recognizing conflicts among those values. Though much of our evidence remains anecdotal at this point, it appears that in the humanities, as in the sciences and social sciences, the dominant mode of teaching is to examine and analyze without helping students develop the means to anchor their own experiences, past and future, in moral and civic lessons from complex texts.

We recognize the difficulties and potential pitfalls educators face when discussing moral and civic values in a society as strongly pluralist as our own, in which tolerance and respect for difference are held as fundamental values in themselves. Yet we also believe that democratic pluralism is not to be equated with moral skepticism or relativism, but rather with ongoing and public moral discourse in which citizens are encouraged to express, revise, and refine their own ethical commitments. Relativism undermines democracy if all values are seen as merely expressions of personal preference, with no interest in engaging in a thoughtful dialogue about the reasons for holding a particular view, or its ability to withstand thoughtful criticisms.

Educational institutions can respect diversity of opinion on particular ethical questions and avoid both illegitimate indoctrination and moral relativism if they are explicit about their commitment to those moral values that are fundamental to a democracy, while being careful not to foreclose open-minded consideration of multiple solutions to moral dilemmas in which fundamental values conflict. By their very nature, it is also appropriate for educational institutions to foster values such as mutual respect, open-mindedness, and intellectual integrity.

Belief in the need for ongoing, public discussion and teaching of values is illustrated by Jaroslav Pelikan's address for the 1986 Woodrow Wilson Center Conference, titled "King Lear or Uncle Tom's Cabin?"[6] in which he considered alternative methods for teaching values. Pelikan discussed Tolstoy's argument in *What Is Art?*, in which Tolstoy argued that art's highest purpose is to inculcate moral values. Tolstoy lauded Harriet Beecher Stowe's novel, *Uncle Tom's Cabin*, for achieving this goal, but he criticized Shakespeare's *King Lear* for its failure on this count. While sharing Tolstoy's vision of the moral purpose of art, Pelikan maintained that both works promote moral values, but do so through different artistic methods. Pelikan then argued that just as these two works exemplified different approaches to moral problems, when teaching values multiple paths should be taken to enable students to gain sound moral purchase on complex issues.

We concur strongly with Pelikan's view. Those of us who teach materials that particularly lend themselves to raising moral issues have an obligation to do so in ways that help students wrestle with their own moral dilemmas as well as with larger social and political concerns. It is not enough simply to show that any moral framework built by reason can be criticized by reason, but rather we must also take on the much more difficult task of helping students to think through for themselves which moral perspective is best able to answer their intellectual, personal, and social needs. Moral inculcation is not what we have in mind—that is the province of the pulpit. The moral and civic learning that we urge is totally integrated with substantive knowledge and intellectual reasoning, and works to allow students to develop their own frameworks of judgment.

Like Socrates and Thoreau, we expect our students to avoid the unexamined life, and to do so requires not only intellectual, but moral and civic virtues. We as teachers need to provide multiple means for students so that they consider values in the context of their own actions or inactions. And the social sciences and the natural sciences each have important contributions to make to this educational process, though they may seem less obvious than those of the humanities. Our project has revealed many ways in which issues of moral and civic responsibility can be addressed powerfully in fields such as engineering, biology, and economics—domains that are often viewed as "value free" or morally neutral. Donald Moon (1991)[7] has argued that contemporary liberal education must pay attention "to the ways in which knowledge might be used in practical life" (p.204), and that we must be more thoughtful about the relationship between technical or substantive knowledge gained through higher education—expert knowledge—and moral values and democratic practices. This approach speaks to a central concern of our analysis: the need for higher education to connect the intellectual or academic content of learning to the development of moral and civic goals.

What do we mean by "moral" and by "civic"? For the purposes of our project, we consider "morality" to be concerned with prescriptive judgments about how one ought to act in relation to other people. As we use the term, "morality" is not confined to a specific sphere of life or action, nor is it necessarily tied to religion. In advocating that education should foster moral engagement, we are not suggesting that educational institutions should promote any particular ethical viewpoint, except a commitment to democratic ideals, such as procedural fairness, respect for persons, and a willingness to engage in reasoned discourse. Instead, we believe that education should foster the development of moral reasoning and the adoption of viewpoints and commitments that emerge from reasoned consideration and democratic principles. We believe that higher education should encourage and facilitate the development of students' capacities to examine complex situations in which competing values are often at stake, to employ both substantive knowledge and moral reasoning to evaluate the problems and values involved, to develop their own judgments about those issues, and then to act on their judgments.

We consider "civic" to range over all social spheres beyond the family, from neighborhoods and local communities to state, national, and cross-national arenas. Political engagement is a particular subset of civic engagement that is required for sustaining American democracy. We are not promoting a single type of civic or political engagement, but instead urging that the effective operation of social systems and the successful achievement of collective goals demand the time, attention, understanding, and action of all citizens. Institutions of higher education have both the opportunity and obligation to cultivate in their graduates an appreciation for the responsibilities and rewards of civic engagement, as well as to foster the capacities necessary for thoughtful participation in public discourse and effective participation in social enterprises.

In general terms, we believe that a morally and civically responsible individual recognizes himself or herself as a member of a larger social fabric and therefore considers social problems to be at least partly his or her own; such an individual is willing to see the moral and civic dimensions of issues, to make and justify informed moral and civic judgments, and to take action when appropriate.

We believe that moral and civic development is enhanced by mutually interdependent sets of knowledge, virtues, and skills. Because they are interdependent, no simple listing of attributes is adequate. Such a listing may imply that the elements involved have precise definitions and parameters that might be gained through a single course or even from reading a few books. We have come to understand through studying various colleges and universities that this is not the case. Instead, enriching the moral and civic responsibility of all members of the campus community is best achieved through the cumulative, interactive effect of numerous curricular and extracurricular programs, within an environment of sustained institutional commitment to these overarching goals.

By listing important representatives from these sets of knowledge, virtues, and skills, we do not mean to assert that they are either necessary or sufficient for all situations or circumstances. We focus on those that we believe are central to moral and civic development and integral to a sound undergraduate education. This should not be understood to imply that one cannot be a morally and civically responsible person without attending college, but only that a college education can and should enhance these attributes and capacities.

Included in the core knowledge we consider integral to moral and civic learning is knowledge of basic ethical concepts and principles, such as justice and equity, and how they have been interpreted by various seminal thinkers. Also included is a comprehension of the diversity of American society and global cultures, and an understanding of both the institutions and processes of American and international civic, political, and economic affairs. Finally, deep substantive knowledge of the particular issues in which one is engaged is critical.

This core of knowledge cannot be separated from the virtues and skills that a morally and civically responsible individual should strive to attain. The virtues and skills we have in mind are not distinct to moral and civic learning but are necessary for active engagement in many personal and professional realms. Among the core virtues are the willingness to engage in critical self-examination and to form reasoned commitments, balanced by open-mindedness and a willingness to listen to and take seriously the ideas of others. Moral and civic responsibility also requires honesty in dealings with others, and in holding oneself accountable for one's actions and inactions. Without a basis of trust and habits of cooperation, no community can operate effectively. Empathy and compassion are also needed, not only for relating to those in one's immediate social sphere, but for relating to those in the larger society as well. Willingness to form moral and civic commitments and to act on those is a core virtue that puts the others into practice.

Finally, the core skills of moral and civic responsibility are essential for applying core knowledge and virtues, transforming informed judgments into action. They include the abilities to recognize the moral and civic dimensions of issues and to take a stand on those issues. But they also include skills that apply to much broader arenas of thought and behavior, such as abilities to communicate clearly orally and in writing; to collect, organize, and analyze information; to think critically and to justify positions with reasoned arguments; to see issues from the perspectives of others; and to collaborate with others. They also include the ability and willingness to lead, to build consensus, and to move a group forward under conditions of mutual respect.

HOW CAN HIGHER EDUCATION HELP ADDRESS THE PROBLEMS?

The primary purpose of the first American colleges and universities was the development of students' characters, no less than their intellects. Character was defined in terms of moral and civic virtues. The founding charters are clear. The following excerpt from the founding documents of Stanford University, for example, is typical: The objectives of the university are "to qualify students for personal success and direct usefulness in life and to promote the public welfare by exercising an influence on behalf of humanity and civilization. . . ." Similar goals can be found in the mission statements of most higher education institutions across the country, which almost universally give at least formal recognition to the institutions' responsibility for fostering the moral and civic maturity of their students. But few campuses have a coherent institutional strategy to implement those statements. We recognize that the development of student character as a primary institutional purpose may have been more an aspiration than a reality at many colleges and universities, even in earlier times.

We also realize that higher education is very different today than when most of those founding documents were written. The student bodies served are far more diverse than at any time in our history, in terms of age, race, gender, and socioeconomic status. This diversity can be a powerful agent of moral and civic learning, but it can also make the development of a cohesive campus community, which is the most likely environment for that learning, more difficult. The dominant template for pre-World War II higher education was private institutions, educating full-time students from affluent families in residential settings. This is now the model for only a small minority of

American undergraduate education institutions. Currently, more than three out of four undergraduates attend a public institution, and almost that same share are commuter students.[8] A near-majority of undergraduates today do not come to college or university directly from high school. They are older than their predecessors, they work part time and are part-time undergraduates, many are married, and many are parents. Many do not view themselves as members of "a community of learners," but rather as consumers who seek to get what they want as rapidly, as easily, and as cheaply as possible. This may mean attending two or three different institutions in the course of an undergraduate career, over a six- or eight-year period. At the same time, nearly 40 percent of undergraduate credit hours today are taught by adjunct faculty, and they often find it difficult to develop relationships with their students or to influence them outside the classroom.[9] Further, many full-time faculty members view themselves more as independent contractors than members of an academic community. Their loyalties are often stronger to their disciplines than to their campuses. These are just a few of the forces pressing on institutions of higher education, from within and without, which cause attention to the development of students' moral and civic responsibility to be more difficult than ever before.

Partly in spite of these forces and tensions, and partly because of them, we believe that higher education has the potential to be a powerful influence on reinvigorating the democratic spirit in America. Virtually all political and professional leaders are products of higher education, and the general public is attending college in ever higher numbers. This extensive reach places colleges and universities in a strong position to help reshape the culture. American higher education has a long and distinguished tradition of serving democracy, upholding the ideals of public service and intellectual integrity, and stimulating students' reexamination of questions of value and meaning. Research over many decades has shown that, in fact, the undergraduate experience does have a significant socializing effect on political beliefs and other values, and that outcomes such as maturity of moral judgment, racial and religious tolerance, and civic and political participation are positively associated with educational attainment.[10]

Not only can higher education have a significant impact on students' moral and civic development, but taking these outcomes seriously has the potential to strengthen and enrich other educational goals. We are convinced that when thoughtfully pursued, academic, moral, and civic goals will be mutually enhancing. Moral, civic, and political development involve, among other things, the achievement of a more sophisticated and conceptually advanced understanding of complex social and ethical ideas, and thus are integral to intellectual growth. The goal of higher education should not be a database of facts, but the competence to act in the world and the judgment to do so wisely.

A full account of competence, including occupational competence, must include consideration of judgment, the appreciation of ends as well as means, and the broad implications and consequences of one's actions and choices. Education is not complete until students not only have acquired knowledge, but can act on that knowledge in the world; thus, the scope of learning outcomes must include these values-based aspects of competence, broadly defined. Furthermore, the liberal academic enterprise depends on some core moral values for its very *raison d'être*. In fact, the academic enterprise would be fatally compromised if intellectual integrity and respect for truth ceased to guide scholarship, teaching, and learning.

Our inquiries have shown us that some American colleges and universities do take very seriously their mission statements' references to the moral and civic education of their students. For a few of these institutions, such commitment shapes many or most aspects of the educational experience and constitutes an intentional and holistic approach to moral and civic, as well as academic education. For other institutions, strong programs designed with moral and civic development in mind exist within an overall campus environment that does not place a comprehensive emphasis on these goals.

The colleges and universities that explicitly address the moral and civic development of their students are extraordinarily diverse. They include every category of higher education institution—community colleges, four-year colleges, comprehensive universities, and universities with many graduate and professional programs. Some are residential, others are nonresidential; some are public, others are private; some are large, others are small; some are religiously affiliated; some are military academies; some are single-sex; and some are primarily for members of a minority group. These and other institutions are represented among those that treat their students' character and citizenship as central to their mission. We have found that while such diverse institutions all take seriously the goals of moral and civic responsibility; they understand those goals differently and concern themselves with different aspects of these broad domains.

Against this background, it may be helpful to outline our working conceptions of moral and civic responsibility and point to general pedagogical tools and strategies that may contribute to their enhancement. We are concerned with the development of the person as an accountable individual and engaged participant in society—local, state, national, and global. Responsibility includes viewing oneself as a member of a shared social structure and a fair target of reactive attitudes, such as praise and blame. Virtues such as honesty, trustworthiness, fairness, and respect contribute to the development of personal integrity, fostering fair dealing and concern for how one's actions affect others. These are the kinds of virtues that are often the focus of university honor codes, which deal particularly with an individual student's academic integrity and respect for the rights of others.

Social conscience, compassion, and commitment to the welfare of those outside one's immediate sphere are important matters of moral development that go beyond the level of personal integrity addressed by honor codes. Some institutions of higher education seek to enhance a sense of social concern among their students through course work that focuses on important social or moral issues, while others use programs of community service or pedagogies of active engagement, such as service-learning, and still others use a combination of approaches.

Partially overlapping these two dimensions of personal integrity and social conscience is a civic component: coming to understand how a community operates, the problems it faces, and the richness of its diversity, as well as fostering a willingness to commit time and energy to enhance community life and to work collectively to resolve community concerns. Colleges and universities try to promote civic responsibility through both curricular and cocurricular programs, including service-learning programs and problem-based learning courses.

Finally, constructive political engagement, defined in terms of democratic processes, is a particular subset of civic responsibility which has been the focus of substantial concern in recent years. While there is overlap between them, we believe that it is important to distinguish the political domain from nonpolitical civic participation, since psychologically they can be quite independent of one another. For example, even as community service among young people has increased in recent years, for example, political interest and participation have dramatically decreased.[11] While some institutions of higher education are seeking ways to stimulate political engagement as well as other kinds of civic participation and leadership, thus far we have found that this is the aspect of civic responsibility that is least attended to in higher education, even among schools with strong commitments to moral and civic learning.

Within each of these four main areas, there are skills and capacities that are required for mature functioning. Within the domains of individual integrity, social responsibility, civic responsibility, and constructive political participation, a fully developed individual must have the ability to think clearly and in an appropriately complex and sophisticated way about moral and civic issues; the moral commitment and sense of personal responsibility to act, which can also include moral emotions such as empathy and concern for others; moral and civic values, interests, and habits; and knowledge and experience in the relevant domains of life.

Moral judgment or reflection has been the most widely studied moral capacity. Different aspects of the development of moral reflection have been described by a number of theorists, most notably Lawrence Kohlberg (1969).[12] These theorists have described the formal features of individuals' thinking about moral issues and conflicts and the developmental changes in moral thinking that occur over time, leading to more sophisticated approaches to moral issues as development proceeds. While Kohlberg's theory of moral judgment has been criticized on a number of grounds, there is broad consensus, even among those critics,[13] that moral judgment and an intellectual understanding of moral issues are essential features of moral maturity and appropriate goals of education.

Mature moral judgment, though important, is not in itself a guarantee of morally responsible conduct, however broadly judgment is defined. Moral conduct requires moral commitment, a sense of personal responsibility to act on one's beliefs. A critical mediator between moral understanding and moral commitment is the place of moral values in people's identities. Several studies (e.g., Blasi, 1993)[14] have shown that this integration of morality with the self is the key to understanding moral conduct. In one such study,[15] we found that a close integration of self and morality formed the basis for the unwavering commitment to the common good exhibited by "moral exemplars" who had dedicated themselves for decades to fighting against poverty or for peace, civil rights, and other aspects of social justice. While moral behavior depends in part on moral understanding and reflection, it also depends on how and to what extent the individuals' moral concerns are important to their sense of themselves as persons; higher education can help to foster students' understanding of themselves as morally committed and civically engaged citizens.

Likewise, Youniss and Yates (1997), Flanagan and Gallay (1995), Verba, Schlozman, and Brady (1995),[16] and others have written about the development of political or civic identity in a way that parallels this conception of moral identity. For example, Youniss and Yates present data showing that the long-term impact of youth service experience on later political and community involvement can best be explained by the contribution these service experiences make to the creation of an enduring sense of oneself as a politically engaged and socially concerned person. In their view, civic identity—which entails the establishment of individual and collective senses of social agency, responsibility for society, and political and moral awareness—links certain kinds of social participation during adolescence and young adulthood with civic engagement by these same people later in adulthood. It is for this reason that we have been particularly interested in examining the ways in which service-learning and community-based learning can be used by higher education to promote students' civic engagement.

Yet another reason we cannot rely wholly on sophisticated moral thinking as sufficient for moral and civic maturity is that not all moral or socially responsible conduct is preceded by deliberation or conscious reflection. Most moral and ethical action, in fact, is habitual. Whereas moral reflection is closely tied to intellectual competence, moral habits are embedded in emotional and behavioral systems that are bolstered by the cultural context and years of practice. The content of one's values and interests, and the nature of one's routine practices derive from socialization within the family, the community, the peer group, the schools, the cultures of these institutions, and the ways in which those cultures are transmitted. This, too, suggests an important role for higher education, pointing to the need for schools to create a campus atmosphere that supports a concern for others and for the common good. Few would dispute that universities ought to represent and embody not only the values of intellectual integrity and concern for truth, but also tolerance and respect for others, interest in civic and political issues, concern for equity and other aspects of social justice, and civil discourse as a means for resolving differences. While some colleges and universities make an institutional priority of these moral and civic goals, approaching them in an intentional and broad-based way, others have taken approaches that are less comprehensive, more mixed, and that sometimes send conflicting messages to students about these issues.

In addition to a mature understanding of moral and civic issues and personal commitment to act on those beliefs, people who are truly effective in their moral and civic engagement also need substantive expertise in the complex issues with which they are grappling. An emotionally driven concern for the environment, or for international human rights, for example, is unlikely to lead to effective action unless the actor is knowledgeable as well as concerned. But being informed about important social and political issues is not as simple as reading the right books or taking careful notes in class. Although much of students' content knowledge clearly comes from books and lectures, it also comes from class discussions and extracurricular or cocurricular experiences outside the classroom. For example, experience living and working with people from diverse backgrounds can yield a kind of expertise and knowledge that is particularly useful for effective moral and civic engagement, and many programs at the college level include efforts to provide this kind of experience.

There is a full body of developmental theory and research about the conditions under which moral capacities develop (e.g., Turiel, 1997).[17] These studies show that intellectual engagement and challenge around moral issues and dilemmas lead to the development of more sophisticated judgment. Participating in political or community service activities often entails such moral challenges and can also expand the range of people for whom one feels empathy and responsibility, thereby fostering the capacity to understand others' perspectives. This kind of active learning experience can also lead to a change in the way students see themselves, with moral values becoming a more central part of their self-definitions. This change, in turn, can generate a greater willingness to take action on moral and civic issues. Empirical studies of service-learning and other service activities show that, for the experience to have this kind of developmental impact, there must be a "reflection" component in which participants think about and discuss the meaning of their service experiences, connecting it with broader social issues and personal values.[18]

Another powerful influence on one's moral development is identification with people one admires, which can influence one's ideal self. Efforts to bring one's actual self more in line with one's ideal may lead to changes in identity and character over time. Many schools with a strong commitment to the moral and civic development of their students emphasize mentoring relationships— peer, faculty, or staff. Finally, participation in a community, with strong norms of contributing to the good of the whole, and coherence among the messages about moral and civic issues that are conveyed by the various members of the community, help develop a sense of personal responsibility and a tendency to act in accordance with one's beliefs. A clear institutional statement about the importance of moral and civic learning, which is widely publicized and generally understood by students, faculty, and staff, can provide a powerful framework for the campus community. We have observed that, working together, these various processes underlie all the educational programs seeking to nurture moral and civic development.

WHAT STRATEGIES ARE CAMPUSES USING?

There has been a groundswell of interest in returning higher education to its broader public mission, which includes preparation of students for responsible citizenship. Many colleges and universities have made very serious commitments to this kind of work. Most of those campuses, however, have focused their efforts on particular programs or activities that do not affect most undergraduates, and the institutions usually do not centrally coordinate those efforts. Examples of these programs include academic centers and institutes, freshman seminars, and senior capstone courses. While major research universities are least likely to embrace a comprehensive approach to these student outcomes, many of them do have significant programs, designed to foster moral and civic development, that reach at least a part of their student bodies.

In contrast, relatively few colleges and universities have made broad institutional commitments to the development of all students' moral and civic development. We have sought to document the work of some of these campuses with comprehensive and intentional approaches to moral and civic learning.[19] All of the campuses we have visited have shared several important institutional features. First, these schools' public statements of institutional purpose stress the importance of personal integrity, social responsibility, and civic and political engagement and leadership. Second, the upper levels of the administration in both academic and student affairs endorse the importance of these educational goals and allocate resources to programs designed to promote them. Third, multiple, overlapping approaches are used in each setting, and there are mechanisms in place to facilitate communication among the different programs to strengthen the coherence of the student experience.

Although the campuses we chose for site visits are a diverse group and represent a range of unique adaptations to a common task, they share a number of assumptions, programmatic elements, and challenges. For example, they share some assumptions about what kinds of educational approaches are likely to make a difference, assumptions which are consistent with recent developmental theory and research. Their programs target many of the moral and civic capacities we outlined earlier in this essay. In particular, they address the cognitive or intellectual dimension of moral and civic development, and seek to connect general capacities for sophisticated and analytical judgment with substantive issues of real moral and social significance. Finally, they attempt to create a shared culture of concern for moral issues; they offer opportunities for engagement and action; and they provide a variety of means for shaping the positive development of students' moral and civic identities.

At all of these campuses, we saw widespread incorporation of moral and civic issues into academic teaching and learning. For most campuses, though not all, this integration was deliberately planned as a part of the curriculum and often included both interdisciplinary courses and courses within a large cross-section of disciplines. The consideration of moral, civic, or political issues in course work was often tied with efforts to foster critical thinking and effective communication, since these are widely recognized as important features of civil discourse. As one faculty member said, "Students in my class are encouraged to express their opinions on political issues, whatever those opinions are, just as long as they back up their claims with arguments and are respectful of others' points of view."

Most of the campuses we visited also placed strong emphasis on the processes of teaching and learning, and many of them had teaching and learning centers which provided help with curriculum development and course assessment, sponsoring such programs as interdisciplinary faculty reading groups and seminars on technology in the classroom. In addition to the emphasis on teaching and learning, and often in conjunction with it, service-learning is used on all the campuses we visited and is prevalent on most of them. The idea behind service-learning, also called community-based learning, is that academic study can be linked to community service through structured reflection so that each enriches the other. Service-learning courses are now offered at virtually every college and university in the country, and cover almost every academic discipline in the sciences, social sciences, humanities, and professions. Some of the schools we visited require all students to take at least one service-learning experience. Many more encourage, but do not require, such an experience.

Many faculty teaching these courses expressed the belief that their students' learning of the course material was significantly enhanced by tying it to community service. As reported by Eyler and Giles (1999) in *Where's the Learning in Service-Learning?*,[20] service-learning is an important means of enhancing critical thinking skills. This was confirmed by the students with whom we spoke, many of whom told us how much their service-learning experience had enriched their learning of the course content as well as changed their perspectives on moral issues or on groups of people they had encountered for the first time during these courses. As Eyler and Giles conclude, "one of the things that jumped out at us was that almost irrespective of the type, intensity, or quality of the service or service-learning experience, students report that involvement in community service has a powerful impact on how they see themselves and others."[21]

Other programs of volunteer community service, such as alternative spring break, in which students perform service work either in their home community or in a community to which they travel, were also ubiquitous. These programs varied, however, in the extent to which they included opportunities for reflection and integration with course work and other intellectual endeavors.

Student leadership programs were important on all of the campuses, providing opportunities for sustained collaboration with faculty and participation in student government, campus judicial systems, and student involvement in campus and community issues. The students who participated in these programs often mentioned their opportunities for leadership as among the most powerful of their college experiences, leading to a strong sense of their own capacities to effect change and to obtain a wide range of civic skills, including negotiation, consensus building, public speaking, fiscal management, and the like. For example, on most campuses, student leaders provided critical logistical support and teaching assistance to faculty who were teaching service-learning courses by establishing and maintaining relationships with community organizations. Students also gained leadership skills at many of these schools through peer mentoring programs, in which students who were more advanced in their academic careers provided guidance and support to their peers. These mentoring programs provide a powerful experience for students on both sides of the mentoring relationship.

In addition to peer mentoring, on every campus we have seen a conscious effort to provide other types of mentoring relationships and positive role models for students. Often faculty whose research has integrated important social issues serve this function in informal ways, inspiring students through their own commitment to socially responsible work and often involving their students in that work. Students who have taken leadership roles also provide admired models. On many campuses, there have been special programs to bring speakers to campus with compelling stories of moral courage, integrity, or commitment to social justice. For example, a recent conference at the U.S. Air Force Academy included two Vietnam veterans who had been present at the My Lai massacre and were among the few to disobey orders to shoot civilians, orders which were later determined to be unlawful. At the College of St. Catherine, the Core Convocations program brings to campus a series of speakers and events that focus on social justice.

We also found that on every campus we visited, issues of diversity and multiculturalism were closely linked to concerns for student moral and civic development. While most of these schools have faced challenges in this area, either with attracting a diverse student body or faculty, or with promoting full integration of the student body, they all expressed strong commitment to the ideal of diversity, and recognized explicit linkages between living in a diverse society and the strength of our civic and democratic ideals. Developing increased understanding of cultural traditions other than one's own and promoting respectful engagement across differences were central goals for both academic programs and student affairs. Often these goals were incorporated into the core curriculum, and they were almost always central to community service and service-learning experiences. In many cases, efforts to foster mutual respect across racial, ethnic, religious, and other differences were joined with efforts to develop a global perspective on social issues. The conviction that students must be educated for participation in a pluralistic and multicultural society and a world that extends beyond the boundaries of the United States was present on every campus.

Another challenge we have seen at all of these campuses is the problem of developing, funding, staffing, and maintaining such ambitious programs. Mounting programs of this sort is institutionally difficult, given the many other challenges colleges and universities are facing. Limited resources make it hard for most to support the team-teaching that interdisciplinary courses require, and faculty often see an elaborated core curriculum as draining resources from the disciplinary departments. Generally, this kind of work is labor intensive, and faculty time is a scarce resource on all campuses.

While teaching for moral and civic as well as intellectual development can be extremely demanding, the impact of these efforts on faculty morale seems to be very positive. On several campuses, faculty who are taking on this challenge said that it has led them to be more reflective about their teaching and to talk with their colleagues more about teaching. They also said that this work, which is often collaborative across departments, has helped to create a stronger sense of intellectual community and has added new challenge and meaning to their professional lives. Faculty report that they are also rewarded by their students' greater engagement and deeper understanding of the subject matter. Many faculty, however, have also expressed some concerns about whether their own participation in service-learning courses and other time-intensive and nontraditional programs will negatively affect their ability to win promotions and tenure from departments and administrations that continue to measure academic worth largely, if not entirely by scholarly publication.

Many campuses have centers that assist faculty who are attempting some of these new approaches to teaching, such as service-learning and problem-based learning, and coordinate the range of other activities designed to promote student moral and civic development. These centers differ greatly from one campus to the next but in most cases they provide a focal point of activity and a means of communication across disparate programs. They include the Center for Character Development at the U.S. Air Force Academy, the Center for Academic Excellence at Portland State University, the Service Learning Institute at California State University at Monterey Bay, and the Center for Social Concerns at the University of Notre Dame.

At each of the campuses we have visited, as in higher education as a whole, assessment of student outcomes is the least developed component of the overall effort to foster student moral and civic development. Adequate assessment instruments do not exist for most of the desired outcomes, and costly experimental and longitudinal designs would be required to control for program selection bias and to evaluate whether programs have any long-term impact. Research using self-report questionnaires, interviews, and focus groups has documented the positive effect of service-learning on attitudes, civic behaviors, and academic performance (e.g., Eyler and Giles, 1999),[22] but very little research has been done on the effectiveness of the other kinds of programs we observed.

If we are to go beyond participation rates and student self-assessments, we will need to develop observation procedures that document the processes of influence and instruments that capture more fully the important but less tangible psychological constructs such as moral identity and commitment, and performance variables such as critical thinking, negotiation, and effective communication.

Among the campuses we have visited, the one that has done the most work on assessment is Portland State University (PSU), which has been developing methods for the assessment of community-based teaching and learning. Their assessment project attempts to document the impact of teaching that includes partnerships with community organizations on students, faculty, partner organizations, and the university. Instruments include interviews, focus groups, surveys, observations, student journals, contact logs, and faculty syllabi and curricula vitae. At this point, most of the indicators of student development are self-reports, but work to develop more direct indicators of outcomes is underway.

Most campuses lack the resources to do any assessments of their moral and civic education programs beyond student evaluations of teaching in particular courses. In the absence of such evaluations, we can get some baseline sense of the programs' potential effectiveness by talking with students and faculty about their impressions of the work. It is fairly easy to distinguish between programs and courses that students see as poor quality and do not take seriously and those they describe as deeply engaging and, in their view, transformative. We have found both students and faculty on the campuses we have visited were quite willing to point out programs that did not seem to be working well, as well as to recognize those that were.

Although the work being done on these campuses is impressive in its scope, quality, and apparent impact on students, the programs are all very much "works in progress." Developing courses and other programs that are both intellectually rigorous and personally transformative is extremely difficult, and the programs we have seen both within and between campuses varied in the extent to which they were able to achieve their goals. Many of the offerings we have observed will be revised and improved as experience accumulates and better assessment tools are developed.

Beyond these general conclusions, our campus visits revealed the distinctive approaches of the particular institutions we observed. These unique approaches reflect each institution's mission, goals, history, and student body. The particularities are of interest because each is a seed-bed of new ideas that can be adapted for use in different contexts.

PRELIMINARY RECOMMENDATIONS AND CONCLUSIONS

We are convinced that there is a strong and growing movement in this country to reinvigorate higher education's civic and democratic mission. Increasingly, many colleges and universities are taking seriously their responsibilities to their local communities and developing community-university partnerships around schooling, discourse about public issues, programs for youth and families, land use, and the like. Within individual campuses, many colleges and universities have made serious commitments to programs of moral and civic education of their students, as we have seen in our campus visits.

We are now beginning to see growth in efforts to coordinate and foster communication about this work and to enact change on a wider scale. Campus Compact, an organization of college and university presidents, has been particularly successful in this role. It was begun in 1985 by a small group of college and university presidents who thought that while the "me generation" was an unfair label for their students, those students nevertheless needed active encouragement to engage in community service. The organization initially focused on service generally, but by the beginning of the 1990s the focus shifted to service-learning as it became clear to the Campus Compact leadership that important advantages are lost unless community service is linked to academic study through structured reflection. Without that reflection, community service often has little lasting impact on students, and community service that is unconnected to the curriculum is often viewed by faculty members as simply one more extracurricular activity, like sports, not central to the educational mission of the institution. As a result, Campus Compact shifted its attention to providing materials and other support for community service-learning programs throughout the country. More recently, Campus Compact has expanded its attention to the whole array of concerns related to higher education and civic engagement. It sponsored an Aspen Institute invitational conference of more than 50 college and university presidents, who issued a bold declaration of responsibility for enhancing civic engagement on the part of their campuses, and an assessment tool to measure success. A number of other higher education organizations are also active in this arena, including the American Association for Higher Education, the American Council on Education, and the Association of American Colleges and Universities.

In addition, regular conferences on college student values and moral development, such as those sponsored by Florida State University and Duke University, provide opportunities for people who are working on moral and civic education at the college level to meet and share information with others about their experiences. Some of these meetings also provide opportunities for cross-fertilization between people working at the college level and those working in elementary and secondary schools, which have been pursuing moral and civic education for a long time. This is of obvious importance, since students entering college will be differentially receptive to activities such as service-learning, depending on their previous school experiences. In fact, community service has become widespread in elementary and high schools in the past several years, and this has important implications for programming at the college level.

Efforts to respond to the kinds of critiques of higher education that we reviewed in the first section of this essay are even beginning at research universities. For example, representatives from major research universities met twice in the last year at Wingspread Conference Center in Wisconsin. One result is a "Wingspread Declaration for Renewing the Civic Mission of American Research Universities." The declaration urges research universities to prepare their students for engaged citizenship "through multiple opportunities to do the work of citizenship today through real projects of impact and relevance, learning the skills, developing the habits and identities, and acquiring the knowledge to contribute to the general welfare." The declaration is accompanied by a set of planning documents to further its goals.

New approaches to institutional accreditation are also highlighting the moral and civic development of undergraduate students. A trend toward greater emphasis on outcomes-based accreditation criteria is reflected in the recent report by the National Project of the American Academy for Liberal Education, "The Re-visioning of Accreditation in the Liberal Arts." This report lists "civic virtue" as one of the five categories of student achievement that should be provided in liberal education. "Civic virtue" is defined to include interest in and consideration of the public good, a tangible concern with the moral implications of technical knowledge and the ability to think critically and empathically.

Recommendations

Our project is still underway, but we do have some preliminary insights based on our work to date.

1. A high degree of institutional intentionality in fostering moral and civic responsibility is the hallmark of those colleges and universities that lead in this arena. The campuses not only have mission statements that include this goal, but the statements are well known and understood by most students, faculty members, and staff. The administrative leadership speaks and acts in ways that promote the goal, as does faculty leadership.
2. A wide range of programs can contribute to moral and civic learning—both curricular and extracurricular. Without limiting those programs, campuses should build conscious connections among them with the goal of making the campus a whole more than the sum of its parts. Those connections should be documented, publicly discussed, and open to review and revision.
3. An effective program in this arena needs a clear conceptual framework, and too often program developers fail to make explicit the theoretical assumptions and educational philosophies underlying their approaches. This framework should pervade the campus, operating not merely as institutional rhetoric, but as a genuine guide for long-range planning, faculty and staff hiring and development, curricular and cocurricular program design, and student admission and orientation.
4. Active pedagogies that engage students in the practice of grappling with tough moral and civic issues, as well as examining them in theory, are essential to the full development of informed, committed, socially responsible, and politically engaged citizens.
5. A network of scholars is needed to take leadership in assessment and research concerning undergraduate moral and civic education. Longitudinal studies on programs being developed are important if we are to learn what kinds of educational approaches are most effective and have long-term impact. A coordinated effort in the area of instrument devel-

opment would be extremely beneficial since adoption of some common measures would allow for comparison across programs. It is not necessary or even desirable for each campus to develop its own measures. The development of assessment tools will be a very challenging task, however, and we need to be very cautious about trying to capture complex and subtle developmental phenomena with superficial instruments.

6. Additional mechanisms are needed through which campuses can learn from each others' experiences, even across very different kinds of institutions. These mechanisms could include visits to each others' campuses, regional and national conferences, as well as Web-based communications systems.

7. More inter-institutional efforts, such as the Aspen and Wingspread Conferences referred to above, are needed. Ideally, in our view, the success of colleges and universities in promoting moral and civic responsibility should be a part of the higher education accreditation processes.

Conclusions

It has become commonplace to bemoan a loss of moral and civic responsibility, particularly among young people, and to urge increased attention to moral and civic education among students at every level. If the issue is viewed solely as one of information transfer, the role of higher education is inevitably a modest one. This is no less true if the issue is seen solely as proselytizing students not to cheat or to pay attention to politics. Like John Dewey, we have much more in mind. We believe that democracy and education, like moral, civic, and cognitive learning, are inexorably intertwined. This is not simply because our citizenry must be educated to deal honestly with each other and to choose responsibly our political leaders and hold them accountable. Much more important, a democratic society is one in which citizens interact with each other, learn from each other, grow with each other, and together make their communities more than the sum of their parts. Dewey (1916)[23] urged that a community of learners is the primary mechanism through which this democratizing process can best occur. To be successful, the community must be both interactive and collaborative, a place where the processes of decision-making are at least as important as the decisions themselves. And it must be a diverse community, reflecting the diversity of the larger communities into which students will move on graduation.

To translate this mandate into effective institutional programs, we must attend to many questions. What are the essential elements of moral and civic character for an American in the next century? What specific knowledge, skills, and values contribute to those elements, recognizing that there may be a range of different ways to be a good citizen? What contribution can higher education make in developing these qualities in sustained and effective ways?

What evidence is there about the types of civic educational efforts that are most effective in preparing for responsible citizenship? What are the problems that confront colleges and universities which attempt to engage in sustained civic education, and what are the best strategies to help overcome them?

These are the kinds of issues that are addressed in the essays that follow as well as in our project for the Carnegie Foundation for the Advancement of Teaching. They are issues at the heart of democracy's future in America.

NOTES

1. R.P. Putnam, "Tuning In, Tuning Out: The Strange Disappearance of Social Capital in America," *PS: Political Science and Politics,* 28 (1995): 664–83; S.E. Bennett and E.W. Rademacher, "The 'Age of Indifference' Revisited: Patterns of Political Interest, Media Exposure and Knowledge About Generation X," in *After the Boom: The Politics of Generation X,* ed. S.C. Craig and S.E. Bennett (Lanham, MD: Rowman & Littlefield, 1997).

2. L.J. Sax and A.W. Astin, "The Development of 'Civic Virtue' Among College Students," in *The Senior Year Experience: A Beginning Not an End,* ed. J. Gardner and G. Van der Veer (San Francisco: Jossey-Bass, 1997), 196–227; A.W. Astin, S.A. Parrott, W.S. Korn, and L.J. Sax, *The American Freshman: Thirty Year Trend* (Los Angeles: Higher Education Research Institute, 1997).

3. R.N. Bellah, R. Madsen, W.M. Sullivan, A. Swidler, and S.M. Tipton, *The Good Society* (New York: Vintage Books, 1991); R.P. Putnam, "Bowling Alone: America's Declining Social Capital," *Journal of Democracy,* 6 (1995): 65–78; R.P. Putnam, "Bowling Alone Revisited," *The Responsive Community,* 5, no. 2 (1995): 18–33; R.P. Putnam, "The Strange Disappearance of Civic America," *American Prospect,* 4 (1996): 24.

4. B. Barber, *Strong Democracy: Participatory Politics for a New Age* (Berkeley: University of California Press, 1984).

5. National Commission on Civic Renewal, *A Nation of Spectators: How Disengagement Weakens America and What We Can Do About It,* Final Report (College Park, MD: University of Maryland, 1998); Council on Civil Society, *A Call to Civil Society: Why Democracy Needs Moral Truths, A Report to the Nation from the Council on Civil Society* (New York: Institute for American Values, 1998).

6. J. Pelikan, "King Lear or Uncle Tom's Cabin?" (paper presented at the Teaching of Values in Higher Education Conference, Woodrow Wilson Center, Washington, DC: 1986).

7. J.D. Moon, "Civic Education, Liberal Education, and Democracy," in *Higher Education and the Practice of Democratic Politics,* ed. B. Murchland (Dayton, OH: Kettering Foundation, 1991), 196–207.

8. U.S. Bureau of the Census, *Statistical Abstract of the United States: 1998,* 118th ed. (Springfield, VA: National Technical Information Services, 1998).

9. Ibid.

10. E.T. Pascarella and P.T. Terenzini, *How College Affects Students: Findings and Insights from Twenty Years of Research* (San Francisco: Jossey-Bass, 1991).

11. A.W. Astin et al., *American Freshman.*

12. L. Kohlberg, "Stage and Sequence: The Cognitive-Developmental Approach to Socialization," in *Handbook of Socialization Theory and Research,* ed. D.A. Goslin (Chicago: Rand-McNally, 1969).

13. C. Gilligan, "In a Different Voice: Women's Conception of Self and Morality," *Harvard Educational Review,* 47 (1977): 481–517; N. Noddings, *Caring: A Feminine Approach to Ethics & Moral Education* (Berkeley: University of California Press, 1984); R.A. Shweder, M. Mahapatra, and J. G. Miller, "Culture and Moral Development," in *The Emergence of Moral Concepts in Early Childhood,* ed. J. Kagan and S. Lamb (Chicago: University of Chicago Press, 1987).

14. A. Blasi, "The Development of Identity: Some Implications for Moral Functioning," in *The Moral Self,* ed. G.G. Noam and T.E. Wren (Cambridge, MA: The MIT Press, 1993), 99–122.

15. A. Colby and W. Damon, *Some Do Care: Contemporary Lives of Moral Commitment* (New York: The Free Press, 1992).

16. J. Youniss and M. Yates, *Community Service and Social Responsibility in Youth* (Chicago: University of Chicago Press, 1997); C. Flanagan and L.S. Gallay, "Reframing the Meaning of 'Political' in Research with Adolescents," in *Perspectives in Political Science: New Directions in Political Socialization Research,* ed. M. Hepburn (New York: Oxford University Press, 1995), 34–41; S. Verba, K.L. Schlozman, and H.E. Brady, *Voice and Equality: Civic Voluntarism in American Politics* (Cambridge, MA: Harvard University Press, 1995).

17. E. Turiel, "The Development of Morality," in *Handbook of Child Psychology: Vol. 4, Social, Emotional, and Personality Development,* 5th ed., series ed. W. Damon, volume ed. N. Eisenberg (New York: John Wiley & Sons, 1997), 863–932.

18. J. Eyler and D. Giles, *Where's the Learning in Service-Learning?* (San Francisco: Jossey-Bass, 1999).

19. At the time of this writing, we have visited or planned to visit the following campuses: The Air Force Academy, Alverno College, Bennett College, California State University at Monterey Bay, College of St. Catherine, Diné College, Emory University, Kapi òlani Community College, Messiah College, Notre Dame University, Portland State University and Tusculum College. In addition, we will visit one or more community colleges and Native American Tribal Colleges.

20. Eyler and Giles, *Where's the Learning in Service-Learning?*

21. Ibid., 24.

22. Ibid.

23. J. Dewey, *Democracy and Education* (New York: Macmillan, 1916).

PART 1

· · · · · · · · · · · ·

What Are the Problems:
Higher Education
and Its Students

CHAPTER 1

Citizenship Development and the American College Student

Linda J. Sax

INTRODUCTION

The development of citizenship among college students is a long-standing goal of higher education in the United States.[1] More than 200 years ago, education for citizenship was seen as essential to the development of a well-informed and critically thinking society (Morse, 1989). Although civic education was somewhat de-emphasized during the industrialization and educational specialization of the nineteenth century, citizenship reappeared as a priority of higher education through the general education movement of the early twentieth century. For many years, general education was seen as a means of safeguarding civic education from curriculum overspecialization.

By the mid-1980s, however, many educators sensed that higher education was not effectively meeting the challenge of nurturing students' sense of civic responsibility. As noted in a Carnegie Foundation report, "If there is a crisis in education in the United States today, it is less that test scores have declined than it is that we have failed to provide the education for citizenship that is still the most important responsibility of the nation's schools and colleges."[2] As we embark on the twenty-first century, F. Newman's remarks continue to ring true, and colleges are increasingly being asked to reevaluate their civic functions.

This chapter examines the issue of citizenship development by focusing specifically on the college students themselves. How does the commitment to civic life among today's college students differ from students in the past? How does students' sense of civic responsibility change during the college years? How can colleges best prepare students for lives as caring and involved citizens?

These questions are examined through the use of data on college students collected by the Cooperative Institutional Research Program (CIRP) at the Higher Education Research Institute, University of California, Los Angeles. Established at the American Council on Education in 1966, the CIRP is the nation's largest and oldest empirical study of American higher education, involving data on more than 9 million college students at over 1,500 colleges and universities.

Student trends are examined primarily through student responses to the Freshman Survey, the CIRP's annual nationwide survey of incoming college students. The Freshman Survey, completed each year by over 300,000 freshmen at more than 600 colleges and universities nationwide, profiles the background characteristics, attitudes, values, educational achievements, and future goals of students entering colleges and universities in the United States.

Changes in students' civic values and behaviors are examined through longitudinal data collected on college students at three points over a nine-year period. Specifically, the sample includes 12,376 students from 209 four-year colleges and universities who completed the CIRP Freshman Survey in 1985 and were followed up four and nine years after college entry. The four-year follow-up survey, conducted in 1989, includes information on students' college experiences, their perceptions of college, as well as post-tests of many of the items that appeared on the 1985 freshman survey. The nine-year follow-up survey, conducted in 1994, provides information on graduate school and early career experiences, involvement in community service/volunteerism, as well as post-test data on many of the attitudinal and behavioral items appearing on the 1985 and 1989 surveys.

FRESHMAN TRENDS

This section addresses how college students today compare with students in the past with respect to two aspects of civic responsibility: (1) involvement in volunteerism and community service; and (2) interest in politics.

Volunteerism and Community Service

Data from the Freshman Survey show that volunteerism has been on the rise over the past decade, with a record high 74.2 percent of college freshmen in 1998 performing volunteer work during their last year in high school (see Figure 1). For many students, volunteering represents more than just a token

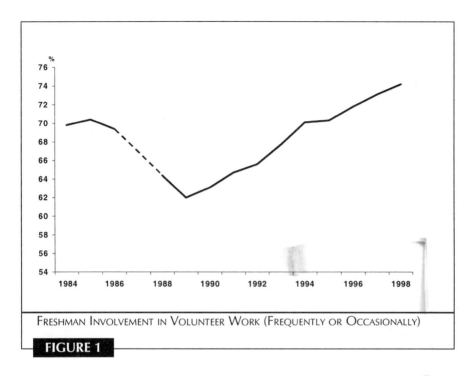

FRESHMAN INVOLVEMENT IN VOLUNTEER WORK (FREQUENTLY OR OCCASIONALLY)

FIGURE 1

day at a soup kitchen or a brief visit to a children's hospital. In fact, more than half of students who volunteer do so on a weekly basis.[3]

Several factors have contributed to the rise in volunteerism among incoming college students over the past decade. First is the increasing number of service programs supported by federal and state governments.[4] Legislation such as the National and Community Service Act of 1990 and President Bill Clinton's National Service Trust Act of 1993, as well as numerous city and statewide initiatives around the country, have helped to connect more students with service opportunities in the community.

Second is the increasing number of service-learning opportunities available at the elementary and secondary levels.[5] An outgrowth of experiential education, service learning is a pedagogical tool that uses community or public service to enhance the meaning of traditional course content. Its connection with specific courses is what distinguishes service learning from other forms of volunteer work. Recent research has documented that, at least among college students, course-based service has a stronger effect on promoting students' sense of civic responsibility than does service conducted independently or through the cocurriculum.[6]

A third factor promoting student involvement in community service is the growing number of high schools requiring community service for graduation.[7] Many skeptics assume that the rise in student volunteerism is due primarily to such requirements. However, the fact is that only one in four students who volunteered during their last year in high school attended schools that required community service for graduation.[8] It appears, therefore, that the majority of students who engage in volunteer work do so of their own volition.

Interest in Politics

Despite young people's growing interest in volunteerism and community service, their interest in politics has plummeted. For example, only 32.4 percent of the 18 to 24 age group voted in the most recent general election, compared with 50.9 percent in 1964. Further, while voter turnout has also declined in the general population, the proportionate decline for the 18 to 24 age group is 50 percent larger than that of all registered voters.[9]

An examination of trends from the CIRP Freshman Survey provides further evidence of political disengagement. For example, the percent of incoming college students who feel that it is important for them to keep up to date with political affairs dropped from 57.8 percent in 1966 to a record low 25.9 percent in 1998 (see Figure 2). Similarly, only 14.0 percent of freshmen say they frequently discuss politics, compared with 29.9 percent back in 1968. Political disengagement is also apparent when it comes to student government: A

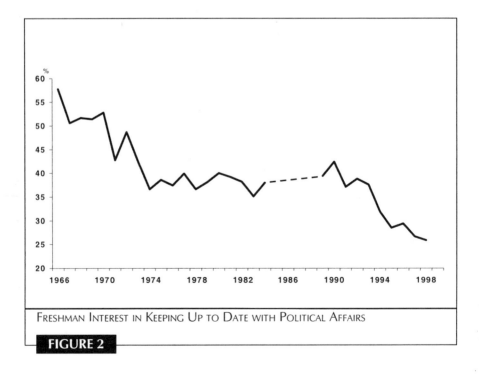

FRESHMAN INTEREST IN KEEPING UP TO DATE WITH POLITICAL AFFAIRS

FIGURE 2

record low of 21.1 percent of entering freshmen regularly voted in student elections at their high school, compared to a high of 76.9 percent in 1968.

What might account for the increasing sense of political disengagement among today's college students? One explanation relates to students' negative perceptions of politics and politicians, and a sense of skepticism that has no doubt been fueled by extensive media coverage of political scandals, negative campaigns, and government gridlock. In a study released by the Kettering Foundation, interviews of college students found that "most everything they have learned about politics, most everything they see and hear involving politics, makes them believe that it is not about solving problems; instead, it is individualistic, divisive, negative, and often counterproductive to acting on the ills of society."[10]

Second, students today are unlikely to view politics as an effective vehicle for change.[11] As a result, many see no particular benefit to getting involved in the larger political system. Instead, as revealed in the volunteerism trends described above, students are trying to make a difference by taking action in their local communities.

Finally, many of today's college students feel a sense of disconnection or alienation from the political issues themselves.[12] Unlike students who attended college in the 1960s and 1970s, whose interest in politics was stimulated by issues such as the Free Speech movement, Civil Rights movement, and Vietnam War, many of today's college students feel that today's political issues are simply not relevant to their daily lives.

Further analysis of CIRP data provides additional perspectives on students' political disengagement. The first relates to students' left/right political orientation. Since the question of political orientation was first introduced on the Freshman Survey in 1970, the number of students identifying as "middle of the road" has risen from 45.4 percent to 56.5 percent. During the same time period, there has been a net decline in identification with "liberal" or "far left" political labels (from 36.6 percent in 1970 to 23.5 percent in 1998). "Conservative" or "far right" orientations have shown only a modest change over the last three decades, rising from 18.1 percent in 1970 to 20.1 percent in 1998.

While an increasingly moderate political orientation does not by itself imply "disengagement" from the political process, the data do in fact show that students who consider themselves "middle of the road" are significantly less likely to talk about politics than those who identify with either liberal or conservative orientations (see Figure 3). What this suggests is that the politically "moderate" student is also the more politically disengaged student.

The likelihood of discussing politics also varies by several other student characteristics, most notably students' socioeconomic status and intended college major. For example, 21.9 percent of students whose mother or father holds a graduate degree discuss politics on a frequent basis, compared with 9.6

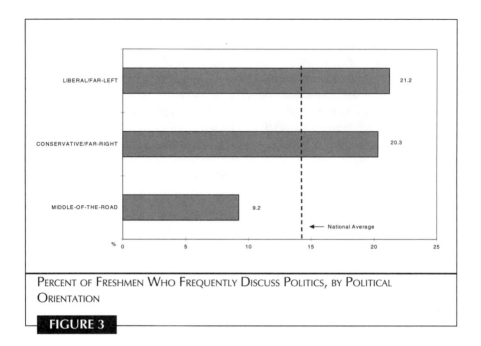

PERCENT OF FRESHMEN WHO FREQUENTLY DISCUSS POLITICS, BY POLITICAL
ORIENTATION

FIGURE 3

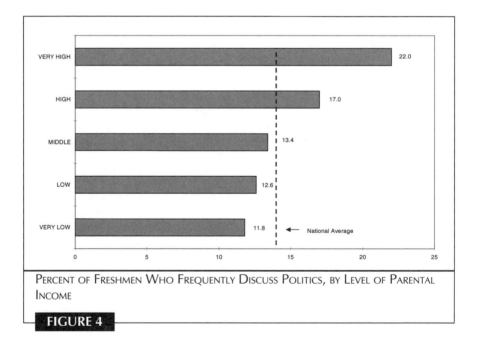

PERCENT OF FRESHMEN WHO FREQUENTLY DISCUSS POLITICS, BY LEVEL OF PARENTAL
INCOME

FIGURE 4

percent among students whose parents never graduated high school. Similarly, students from families in the top 20 percent of family incomes are nearly twice as likely to discuss politics frequently than are students from families falling in the lowest 20 percent of income (see Figure 4).

The most dramatic disparities in political interest relate to students' major (see Figure 5). Not surprisingly, students majoring in political science or history show the highest frequency of discussing politics (55.5 percent)—four times more likely than the average college student. Students majoring in English or the humanities also discuss politics at significantly higher than average rates (29.7 and 23.2 percent, respectively). The lowest rates of political discussion occur among those freshmen majoring in the health professions and agriculture (8.5 and 9.3 percent, respectively).

Somewhat more surprising—and disturbing—is the relatively low frequency of political discussion occurring among students majoring in education. Only one in ten education majors (9.7 percent) discusses politics on a frequent basis. Clearly, it will be very difficult to reverse these trends toward disengagement, and to spark students' interest in politics, when America's future teachers are some of the most politically disengaged students of all.

IMPACT OF COLLEGE ON CIVIC VALUES AND BEHAVIORS

The trends highlighted above suggest clearly that we have two simultaneous—and somewhat contradictory—trends among incoming college students: a

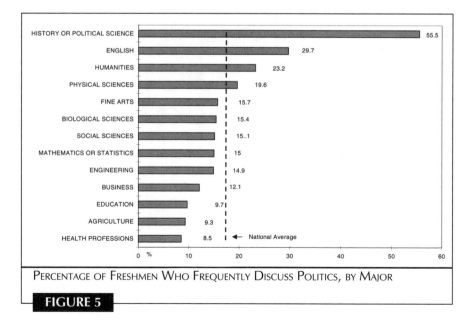

PERCENTAGE OF FRESHMEN WHO FREQUENTLY DISCUSS POLITICS, BY MAJOR

FIGURE 5

growing orientation toward community service paralleled by a declining interest in politics. An important question is what happens to these students when they attend college? How do the college years further influence students' civic values and behaviors, particularly their interest in and commitment to their communities and the larger society? These issues are addressed through an examination of the following research questions:

1. How do students' civic values and behaviors change during and after the college years?
2. How are students' civic values and behaviors affected by characteristics of the college environment (e.g., institutional size, type, and control; faculty and peer group attributes)?
3. How are civic values and behaviors affected by students' involvement in the college experience (e.g., courses taken and time spent on various curricular and extracurricular activities)?

In addressing these questions, the study focuses on the following three outcome measures, chosen to reflect both the attitudinal and behavioral aspects of citizenship:

1. Commitment to social activism
2. Sense of empowerment
3. Community involvement

Commitment to social activism is defined in terms of the personal importance the student assigns to each of the following life goals: participating in community action programs, helping others who are in difficulty, influencing social values, and influencing the political structure. Sense of empowerment is derived from students' level of disagreement with the statement, "Realistically, an individual can do little to bring about changes in our society." Students who disagree with this item (i.e., are more "empowered") can be seen as exhibiting greater potential for involvement in civic life. Finally, community involvement is a behavioral measure reflecting the number of hours per week respondents report engaging in "volunteer work/community service" during the past year.

Change During and After College

This section addresses the first research question by describing how students' civic values and behaviors change during and after the college years. Changes in the four components of "social activism" are shown in Table 1. At the point of college entry (1985), 57.3 percent of students considered helping others in difficulty a "very important" or "essential" life goal. During the college years, students' commitment to this goal grew markedly to 68.1 percent. However, nine years after entering college, this level of commitment dropped to 60.8 percent, representing a net gain in the commitment to helping others of only 3.5 percent over nine years. Similar changes occur for two of the other social activist goals: to influence the political structure and to participate in a community action program. Students show substantial increases in both of these goals over the four years after entering college, and in both cases the gains almost entirely disappear in the years after college.

TABLE 1						
COMMITMENT TO SOCIAL ACTIVISM: CHANGE OVER TIME						
					Change	
	1985	1989	1994	85-89	89-94	85-94
Help others who are in difficulty	57.3	68.1	60.8	+10.8	-7.3	+3.5
Influence social values	27.6	45.9	44.6	+18.3	-1.3	+17.0
Participate in a community action program	20.4	29.5	21.3	+9.1	-8.2	+0.9
Influence the political structure	13.0	18.0	13.1	+5.0	-4.9	+0.1

Results thus far suggest that the increase in commitment to social activism during the college years may in fact only be temporary. However, there is one measure of social activism for which gains made during the college years are retained in the years after: the commitment to influencing social values. In this case, the dramatic increase in students' commitment to this goal seen during the college years (an increase from 27.6 percent to 45.9 percent) is followed by a post-college decline of only 1.3 percent.

The second outcome measure, sense of empowerment, exhibits very little change during the nine years after college entry. As freshmen, 63.2 percent of students believe "somewhat" or "strongly" that an individual has the ability to change society. This figure increases only slightly—to 66.0 percent—after four years of college. Little change is seen five years later, with 67.5 percent of students reflecting a sense of empowerment. Therefore, unlike commitment to social activism, which grows significantly during college, students' confidence in their ability to make actual changes in society appears largely unchanged during college and the years after.

Turning now to our behavioral measure of citizenship, community involvement, Table 2 shows rates of volunteerism among students at three time points during the nine-year period. Involvement in volunteer service is greatest during high school (1985), with 72.1 percent of freshmen reporting participation in volunteer work during their senior year. Participation declines markedly to 35.7 percent during college (1989), and increases to 46.1 percent in the years after college (1994).

TABLE 2

RATES OF VOLUNTEER PARTICIPATION: HIGH SCHOOL, COLLEGE, AND POST-COLLEGE

Level of participation	Percentage
High School (1984-85)	
Frequent	17.4
Occasional	54.7
Not at all	27.9
College (1988-89)	
3 or more hours per week	11.4
1-2 hours per week	14.0
Less than 1 hour per week	10.3
Never	64.3
Post-College (1994)	
3 or more hours per week	15.0
1-2 hours per week	10.7
Less than 1 hour per week	20.4
Never	53.9

The fluctuation in rates of volunteerism leads to the question of how much the pool of volunteers actually changes over time. Table 3 illustrates the issue of "consistency" by showing the relationship between prior volunteer experience and volunteerism conducted during and after college. Clearly, having been a volunteer in the past increases one's likelihood of volunteering again in the future. Frequent volunteering during high school more than doubles the likelihood that a student will be a frequent volunteer (more than three hours per week) both during and after college. Similarly, those who volunteered three or more hours per week in college were more than twice as likely as noncollege volunteers to frequently engage in volunteer work after college.

While Table 3 suggests some degree of consistency in the volunteer force over time, it also demonstrates a high degree of inconsistency in who volunteers, since many students who volunteer at one time choose not to volunteer later. For example, among frequent volunteers in high school, more than half (54.7 percent) report having done no volunteer work in college, and 46.5 percent report doing no volunteer work after college. Similarly, 43.9 percent of those who reported spending three or more hours per week volunteering in

| TABLE 3 |

CONSISTENCY IN VOLUNTEERISM OVER TIME
(1985 FRESHMEN FOLLOWED UP IN 1989 AND 1994)

Level of participation	Level of college (1989) participation (in hours)				Level of post-college (1994) participation (in hours)			
	3+	1-2	<1	None	3+	1-2	<1	None
High School (1985)								
Frequent	21.4	13.5	10.5	54.7	26.1	13.1	14.2	46.5
Occasional	9.8	17.3	12.2	60.7	13.5	11.5	27.3	47.8
Not at all	8.9	8.7	6.2	76.3	10.8	8.0	11.8	69.3
College (1989)								
3 or more hours per week	—	—	—	—	21.9	16.5	17.7	43.9
1-2 hours per week	—	—	—	—	26.7	17.2	33.6	22.5
Less than 1 hour per week	—	—	—	—	8.4	14.8	34.1	42.6
Never	—	—	—	—	12.3	7.3	15.9	64.4

college report spending no time volunteering after college. This marked disappearance of the volunteer force suggests that the habits of volunteerism that are fostered in high school and in college are very unstable over time.

The Impact of College

While the previous section establishes that students' civic values and behaviors change during and after college, it does not explain why such changes occur. This section addresses the second and third research questions by summarizing how college influences each of our three dimensions of citizenship—commitment to social activism, sense of empowerment, and community involvement—in the years after college (as measured by the 1994 follow-up survey). In particular, how are these outcomes affected by characteristics of institutions, curricula, faculty, and peer groups? What role is played by place of residence, choice of major, and various forms of involvement?[13]

Commitment to Social Activism

How does college influence students' commitment to social activism in the years after college? Among the characteristics of the college environment, two appear to be particularly influential. First is the positive effect of a commitment to social activism among the student body at the institution. This suggests that regardless of students' pre-college commitment to social activist goals such as helping others in difficulty and influencing the political structure, they tend to become even more committed to these goals if they attend a college where other students espouse a social activist mentality.

The second environmental influence on students' commitment to social activism is the negative effect of majoring in engineering. Students who major in engineering are less likely to develop a personal commitment to social activism. This effect is consistent with Astin's[14] finding that majoring in engineering is associated with increases in materialism and conservatism and declines in concern for the larger society. Findings in the present study suggest that these deleterious effects of engineering persist in the years after college.

Additional effects on the commitment to social activism include the positive effects of time spent attending religious services, performing volunteer work, attending classes and labs, and exercising or playing sports. Students who spend more time watching television, on the other hand, are less likely to develop a commitment to social activism. This latter finding is consistent with earlier research showing that watching television is associated with the development of materialistic values and a decline in concern for the well-being of others.[15]

Sense of Empowerment

The second citizenship outcome—sense of empowerment—is significantly influenced by only one characteristic of the college environment. That is, the positive effect of the socioeconomic level of the student's peer group. In other words, attending a college that enrolls students from wealthier and more highly-educated families tends to promote students' post-college belief that individuals have the ability to change society.

Students' sense of empowerment is also positively influenced by several measures of involvement, including socializing with people from different racial and ethnic backgrounds, discussing political and social issues, and attending religious services. Conversely, declines in empowerment result from feeling depressed while in college as well as by the perception that college administrators do not care about student concerns.

Community Involvement

With respect to the behavioral measure of citizenship—community involvement—only one measure of the college environment has a significant influence: the commitment to social activism among the students' peers. In other words, attending a college where other students are highly committed to social activism tends to encourage students' own involvement in their communities in the years after college.

Several measures of student involvement during college appear to promote post-college volunteerism: attending religious services, attending racial/cultural awareness workshops, socializing with students of different racial/ethnic groups, working full-time, performing volunteer work, and talking with faculty outside class. Together, these measures reflect the critical role of personal interaction, either with students, faculty, co-workers, or employers. Interestingly, college students who smoke cigarettes are less likely to volunteer after college.

SUMMARY AND DISCUSSION

This chapter has focused on the development of citizenship in higher education as reflected in the college students themselves. Citizenship development was addressed through an examination of trends among successive cohorts of entering freshmen, as well as by assessing how students' sense of civic responsibility changes during college and the years after.

The trends in data revealed that while students today volunteer in record numbers, they are more politically "disengaged" than ever. At first glance this contradiction seems odd, since one might suspect that greater involvement in volunteer work would parallel a growth in political awareness. However, it is quite possible that students are simply placing their energies where they feel they can make a difference—by getting involved in issues such as education, crime, the environment, and homelessness in their local communities. Given their frustration with political scandals and negative political campaigns, students simply may not perceive politics as an effective vehicle for positive change. Indeed, "students care deeply about the issues of the day, and they wish that politics gave them a way to act on their concerns."[16]

Next, longitudinal analyses described in this chapter have shown that college is associated with increases in many measures of civic responsibility. In particular, during the college years students become more committed to helping others in difficulty, influencing social values, influencing the political structure, and participating in community action programs. Such findings are consistent with earlier research showing college to be associated with gains in altruism and civic responsibility.[17] However, findings presented in this chapter show that many of these gains disappear in the first several years after college, suggesting that the effects of college on students' altruistic or community orientations may in fact only be temporary. Further, although the majority of students' are involved in volunteer work or community service before starting college, the likelihood of volunteering is significantly lower during college and the years immediately after.

Finally, this chapter examined the ways in which colleges promote students' sense of civic responsibility after college. As described in the section above, many different aspects of the college experience serve to influence students' commitment to social activism, sense of empowerment, and community involvement. Among those, three stand out as being particularly effective. First is the amount of time students spend in religious services or meetings, which positively influences all three citizenship outcomes. The role of religious involvement is not surprising, given the emphasis on altruism and philanthropy inherent in most religions.

Second is the effect of performing volunteer work during the college years, which enhances students' commitment to social activism and involvement in the community after college. Clearly, forming a habit of volunteerism is critical to the long-term development of citizenship. Nevertheless, findings also show how the pool of volunteers changes dramatically from high school to college, and again from college to the years after. Together, these findings suggest that to build and maintain a volunteer labor force, efforts to promote volunteerism in college should focus as much on retention as they do on recruitment.

A third common theme influencing citizenship development is socializing with students from different racial/ethnic groups, which influenced both the sense of empowerment as well as students' involvement in their communities after college. Further, students' likelihood of community involvement was also enhanced by attending racial/cultural awareness workshops. While positive effects of "diversity" activities have been reported in four-year longitudinal research,[18] this study has demonstrated that interacting with and learning from people different from oneself have effects that last beyond the college years.

Lastly, college experiences that tend to discourage citizenship development include smoking cigarettes, watching television, and feeling depressed. As a group, these experiences suggest that engaging in relatively isolated or antisocial behaviors will tend to inhibit the development of civic responsibility in college students.

In sum, it appears that the development of civic responsibility during the college years is enhanced by students' degree of involvement during college—mainly, interacting with students and faculty through curricular and cocurricular activities. These findings are consistent with previous research describing involvement as a key predictor of altruistic values or behaviors.[19]

It is interesting to consider the dynamics of the relationship between involvement and civic responsibility. On the one hand, citizenship development is enhanced by the nature of specific activities, such as attending religious services, socializing across racial/ethnic lines, and discussing political and social issues. On the other hand, students who become involved in such activities are likely forming a habit of involvement; it is this habit that carries over into students' lives in the years after college.

Therefore, the message to institutions is to provide a wide variety of opportunities for student involvement, particularly in ways that expose students' to a diversity of people and issues. The more involved and connected students become during college, the more likely they will seek out forms of involvement in their communities after college. In other words, "civic education" is more than simply teaching students "civics." Instead, education for citizenship can be accomplished more broadly by encouraging students to become active and proactive participants in the learning process by pursuing their own interests and making meaningful connections with students and faculty. In this way, colleges can contribute to the development of good citizenship among individual college students while at the same time investing in the long-term welfare of the larger society.

NOTES

1. E.L. Boyer and F.M. Hechinger, *Investment in Learning: The Individual and Social Value of American Higher Education* (San Francisco: Jossey-Bass, 1980); B. Finkelstein, "Rescuing Civic Learning: Some Prescriptions for the 1990s," *Theory into Practice, 27,* no.4 (Fall 1988): 251–56; R. Ketcham, "A Rationale for Civic Education," *Educational Record, 73,* no. 2 (Spring 1992): 19–22; S.W. Morse, "Renewing Civic Capacity: Preparing College Students for Service and Citizenship," *ASHE-ERIC Higher Education,* Report No. 8 (Washington, DC: School of Education and Human Development, The George Washington University, 1989); W.H. Newell and A.J. Davis, "Education for Citizenship: The Role of Progressive Education and Interdisciplinary Studies," *Innovative Higher Education, 13,* no. 1 (1988): 27–37.
2. F. Newman, *Higher Education and the American Resurgence* (Princeton, NJ: Carnegie Foundation for the Advancement of Teaching, 1985), 31.
3. L.J. Sax, A.W. Astin, W. Korn, and K.M. Mahoney, *The American Freshman: National Norms for Fall 1998* (Los Angeles: Higher Education Research Institute, University of California, 1998).
4. J. Kahne and J. Westheimer, "In the Service of What? The Politics of Service Learning," *Phi Delta Kappan, 77,* no. 9 (May 1996): 592–99; N.Z. Keith, "Introduction: School-based Community Service: Answers and Some Questions," *Journal of Adolescence, 17,* no. 4 (1994): 311–20; A. Levine, "Editorial: Service on Campus," *Change, 26* (July/August 1994); E.M. O'Brien, "Outside the Classroom: Students as Employees, Volunteers, and Interns," *Research Briefs,* no. 4 (Washington, DC: U.S. Department of Education, Division of Policy Analysis and Research, 1993).
5. D.J. Eberly, "National Youth Service: A Developing Institution," *NASSP Bulletin, 77,* no. 550 (1993): 50–57.
6. A.W. Astin and L.J. Sax, "How Undergraduates Are Affected by Service Participation, *Journal of College Student Development, 39,* no. 3 (May/June 1998): 251–63.
7. Keith, "School-based Community Service"; Eberly, "National Youth Service."
8. Sax et al., *American Freshman.*
9. U.S. Bureau of the Census, Current Population Reports, *Voting and Registration in the Election of November 1996* (Washington, DC: U.S. Government Printing Office, 1998): 20–504.
10. Harwood Group, *College Students Talk Politics* (Dayton, OH: Kettering Foundation, 1993), 5.
11. D. Mathews, "Why Students Hate Politics," *The Chronicle of Higher Education, 39* (7 July 1993): A56; C.A. Rimmerman, "Teaching American Politics through Service," in *Education for Citizenship: Ideas and Innovations in Political Learning,* ed. G. Reeher and J. Cammarano (Lanham, MD: Rowman & Littlefield Publishers, 1997).

12. G. Reeher and J. Cammarano, *Education for Citizenship: Ideas and Innovations in Political Learning* (Lanham, MD: Rowman & Littlefield Publishers, 1997).

13. To examine these college effects, it was important to exert as much control as possible over self-selection (that is, over potentially biasing entering-student characteristics). Preliminary analyses showed that key predisposing factors include a pre-college commitment to social activism, prior volunteer experience, and being female. Once these and other early predictors were controlled, the net effects of college were examined.

14. A.W. Astin, *What Matters in College? Four Critical Years Revisited* (San Francisco: Jossey-Bass, 1993).

15. Ibid.

16. Mathews, "Why Students Hate Politics," 1.

17. A.W. Astin, *Four Critical Years* (San Francisco: Jossey-Bass, 1977); H.R. Bowen, *Investment in Learning: The Individual and Social Value of American Higher Education* (San Francisco: Jossey-Bass, 1980); H.H. Hyman and C.R. Wright, *Education's Lasting Influence on Values* (Chicago: University of Chicago Press, 1979); P.E. Jacob, *Changing Values in College* (New York: Harper & Brothers, 1957); E.T. Pascarella, J.C. Smart, and J. Braxton, "Postsecondary Educational Attainment and Humanitarian and Civic Values," *Journal of College Student Personnel, 27,* no. 5 (September 1986): 418–25; E.T. Pascarella and P.T. Terenzini, *How College Affects Students* (San Francisco: Jossey-Bass, 1991).

18. Astin, *What Matters in College?*; A.W. Astin, "Diversity and Multiculturalism on the Campus: How Are Students Affected?" *Change, 25,* no. 2 (April 1993): 44–49.

19. Astin, *What Matters in College?*; Pascarella and Terenzini, *How College Affects Students*; E.T. Pascarella, C.A. Ethington, and J.C. Smart, "The Influence of College on Humanitarian/Civic Involvement Values," *Journal of Higher Education, 59,* no. 4 (July/ August 1988): 412–37.

CHAPTER 2

Institutional Identity and Social Responsibility in Higher Education

William M. Sullivan

T
o act responsibly in higher education, we must know who we are. If higher education today is uncertain about its social responsibilities, as seems manifestly the case, then this suggests that the American academy is unsure about its institutional identity. For organizations as well as individuals, responsibility follows from relationships. But relationships grow out of our purposes, just as how we relate to others helps to shape our aims. Vital and successful institutions stand out by their ability to maintain their direction and sense of meaning even amid significant shifts in the social landscape. They can aid in providing direction for other institutions, keeping them true to their purposes. Now, however, as major economic and social change shakes American society, higher education is facing serious tests of its resourcefulness: Can the academy reinvigorate its central mission amid difficult and confusing conditions?

Higher education has shown such resourcefulness in the past, reshaping itself in response to new challenges and opportunities. A century ago the academy reinvented itself through the creation of an innovative group of new universities such as Cornell and Chicago, along with the metamorphosis of some older private and state colleges, such as Harvard and Yale, and the universities of Wisconsin and California. These new institutions attempted to combine the European idea of research with the traditional American collegiate emphasis on teaching and the formation of citizens. The most creative among them tried to mediate the inherent tension between disciplinary

Note: This essay was originally published by the Council on Public Policy Education.

specialization and curricular coherence by emphasizing the integrative nature of their public mission.

Higher education entered the twentieth century by announcing its dedication to bringing the powers of cultivated intellect to bear on the economic, social, and cultural life of American democracy. Its sense of mission was often rooted in reform-minded liberal Protestantism, yet at its best, aspirations soared beyond the parochial sectarian as well as the purely national. The universities proclaimed themselves in service to great, panhuman ideals. Those aims were almost immediately compromised by the prejudices of class, race, sex, and religion, as well as by the imperious patronage of "captains of industry." Still, in the popular mind, the mission of the academy remains distinctly public and philanthropic. To reinterpret this earlier sense of public purpose for our time could help reestablish the academy's identity, sparking renewed efforts to clarify what higher education is responsible for and to whom.

During the past half-century, higher education has cooperated with national initiatives to provide educational opportunity to a larger segment of the population than has been true in other industrial nations. At its best, today's academy, diverse in form and descending from many traditions, illustrates the American ability to derive collective strength from social diversity and institutional pluralism. For example, the liberal arts institutions continue to have a distinctive and vital mission: to bring the humane and civic arts to bear upon the problems and concerns of the present. The religious traditions of service and prophecy go on spurring new forms of engaged learning and scholarship in many institutions. Community colleges are showing new vitality by reclaiming their role as innovators in expanding educational opportunity and as a site for civic development. As advocates of civic engagement remind us, campuses educate their students for citizenship most effectively to the degree that they become the sites for constructive exchange and cooperation among diverse groups of citizens from the larger community. All these traditions have importance. Moreover, by engaging with the needs of the communities which often lie just beyond the campus, institutions formed by the values of their past often are able to gain new energy from the creative sparks of fresh dedication to their defining mission.

Yet at the same time it is far from evident that the historic defining purposes of higher education remain sufficiently alive to guide the academy through the difficult time it is entering: a time of reorganization. When the issue of purpose is raised within higher education, it is as often a source of division as it is a rallying point. Conflicting influences from various external patrons such as industry, philanthropy, and government, as well as dissension within, have pushed academic leadership to simply shelve the whole issue of identity and purpose, instead getting by on bland managerialism. But that strategy seems less and less viable. The academy has come under a good deal of skeptical scrutiny of late, to say nothing of serious attack from hostile critics. But we also get a powerful clue that something is importantly wrong from the sense of drift and demoralization that seems all too common in the world of higher education.

THE DESTRUCTIVE DOMINANCE OF THE DEFAULT PROGRAM

Despite its great size and prestige, much of American higher education today suffers from a sense of demoralization and decline. In part this problem is political and financial, as critics within state governments and elsewhere have mounted serious attacks on the integrity of the enterprise as a whole. Higher education today is a "mature industry," rather than the growing sector it was for most of this century. It is also a remarkably diversified and decentralized sector, ranging from elite research universities, both private and public, to private liberal arts colleges, religious schools, state comprehensive systems, and two-year institutions. This makes generalization risky.[1] Fundamentally, however, there is a common problem afflicting this "mature industry." This is the question of identity. Higher education seems to have lost an animating sense of mission. There is much talk of reform, but mostly of an administrative and financial nature, with little attention to content and purpose. Yet, it is precisely the neglect of the question of purpose that has robbed the academy of collective self-confidence at just the moment it most needs to defend itself in increasingly bitter arguments about educational policy and finance.

In the absence of an updated version of its founding conception of itself as a participant in the life of civil society, as a citizen of American democracy, much of higher education has come to operate on a sort of default program of instrumental individualism. This is the familiar notion that the academy exists to research and disseminate knowledge and skills as tools for economic development and the upward mobility of individuals. This "default program" of instrumental individualism leaves the larger questions of social, political, and moral purpose out of explicit consideration. These things, if considered at all, are simply assumed to follow from the "real" business of the higher education "industry." So, for example, the nation's leading research universities are touted as the "best in the world" as evidenced by the number of foreign students flocking to them. It's noteworthy, however, that this is a market measure—i.e., the "value added" by U.S. degrees to internationally competitive professionals.

The consequences of the default program are indirectly evident in the type and quality of social leadership in the United States today. The leaders in business, government, the professions, the media, and religious and cultural institutions are, nearly without exception, graduates of higher education and, usually, of the most prestigious institutions. Moreover, the academy can count as its alumni and alumnae most of the top socioeconomic stratum in America, the upper 20 percent whom Robert Reich has dubbed symbolic analytic workers and whose outlook J.K. Galbraith has described as a "culture of contentment." This is the leadership core of the middle class. It is also the class which continues to benefit, as most Americans have not, from the current period of economic change sometimes called "globalization."

The most successful of this fortunate fifth of the American population have joined the wealthy in increasingly separating themselves from their fellow citizens by where they live, where they educate their children, the medical care they receive, and the retirement they can expect. They have helped guide, or at least acquiesced in, the development of an increasingly divided and unequal society during the current period of self-proclaimed national economic success. Collectively, this comfortable minority has in fact if not in intent abdicated social responsibility for a narrow careerism and private self-interest. It is as if they have forgotten that they are members, and highly privileged ones at that, of the national society. In the absence of a sense of belonging to a larger moral entity, the most successful of Americans have in effect seceded from the shared responsibilities of citizenship.[2] Far from serving as a counterbalance, higher education, in the grip of the default program of instrumental individualism, has often promoted or colluded with this socially destructive process.

There are even more direct indications of the implications of the default paradigm of instrumental individualism for the future of academe itself. One might think of the University of Phoenix as the purest example to date of such a model of academe: a for-profit, expanding educational institution that grants degrees to adult learners in a variety of fields, all of immediate value to business and business careers. It is successful. And, notably, it operates without the expensive overhead "frills" of traditional academic institutions. The University of Phoenix has no permanent campus, no organized student life, and no permanent faculty.

How has the American academy arrived at this juncture? Ironically, perhaps, today's default program is the direct descendent of the celebrated post-World War II expansion of higher education. During the postwar decades, as Derek Bok has pointed out, American higher education came to enjoy an unprecedented level of prestige and public support. This was because of the key roles higher education came to play during the era of the cold war. In effect, higher education took responsibility, with government help, for advancing two major tasks then seen as essential to the national interest: technological progress, especially in defense-related areas such as the silicon chip and the Internet, and the skill and status upgrading of an expanding middle class.[3] Higher education became an important partner with government and industry in the shaping of the postwar American order.

This second objective, the upgrading and expanding of the middle class, became the rationale for a series of federal initiatives, beginning with the G.I. Bill and continuing through affirmative action for women and minorities. These programs greatly expanded higher education while helping to make American society more democratic and inclusive than it had been before World War II. However, these efforts were as much a part of the logic of waging cold war as the rapid development of military technology. If the United States was to compete ideologically with the ideological appeal of communism abroad, so ran the rationale, its prosperity had to be visibly spread throughout the population, if only to refute the communist claims that capitalism inevitably bred sharp inequalities and class tyranny.

With the end of the cold war, the pursuit of greater social and economic equality no longer carries the same strategic importance. In the absence of ideological competition and external strategic threat, political support for increased economic and social equality has waned, especially among the already successful. As the political fortunes of concerns about social equality, already under attack from powerful social groups, have declined, so has government involvement in promoting access to higher education. As government effort has receded, the forces of the market have been allowed a larger role in determining the shape of the American academy, with the result that wealth has come to ever more completely determine both educational access and priorities. Business and industry, after all, are often the direct beneficiaries, as well as patrons, of much academic research and training.

It is important to note then, as Bok does not, that the postwar projects of higher education were heavily tilted toward instrumentalism from the start. They aimed at particular strategic outcomes thought critical to winning the geopolitical struggle with the Soviet Union. The relation of the means chosen to the purposes of higher education as an institution was a much less important issue. By focusing so relentlessly on contributing to external goals, the academy gradually lost the inclination to address these ends from the point of view of its own intrinsic responsibilities. In its most generous aspects, the postwar spirit imagined an academy that would take a creative role in improving the quality of democratic life in the American polity, including more open access to higher education. The aim was both to foster greater economic and social equality and to enlist for the nation previously ignored talents. Actual practice, however, emphasized immediate individual and institutional self-interest at the expense of both long-term democratic values and the academy's distinctive contribution to society's self-reflective capacities. Science was emphasized because it had proved to be the indispensable source of that technological advance which conferred military superiority, while access to higher education was promoted to spur economic growth by providing a skilled, more socially integrated professional workforce. Federal interventions insured that academic institutions structured themselves to facilitate this strategic program. These governmental efforts simultaneously provided a massive push toward increasing disciplinary specialization, as the lion's share of resources poured into scientific and engineering fields. For their part, academic institutions were often quick to seize these often extravagant opportunities to advance their wealth and prestige, even changing their own identities and characters in the process.[4]

Just as federal largesse underwrote vast enterprises of research, subsidies, grants, and loans promoted college degree programs that allowed individuals to grasp their opportunity by learning the skills currently in demand. Any other aims of higher education became peripheral. The long-term result was the withering within the academy of certain habits of thought crucial for its own integrity as well as for the wider good of democracy. Academic leaders stopped asking what effects the new purposes were having on the character and identity of their faculties, their students, or on their institutions themselves. In the drive for cold war supremacy, virtually anything could be exploited to serve the ends of national security and economic growth. Even at the time, this could seem a troubling maxim to guide public policy in a democracy. After all, this was the principle which underlay the unprincipled use of propaganda by totalitarian regimes. Its adoption by the United States threatened to undermine public trust in government—a threat which was finally realized in the 1960s, with continuing consequences. The widespread use of these tools of expedience, given intellectual structure in the form of instrumental rationality, shaped not only state propaganda but much of commercial advertising and entertainment, even the public relations of the academy itself. It is hardly surprising, then, that within higher education, as throughout the nation, little thought was applied to inquiry into what institutional structures would be needed to ensure that the technologies—and the newly credentialed middle class professionals—would contribute to the goals of democratic life.

Under the pressure of cold war imperatives, there seemed little need to make conscious efforts at weaving these developments into the requirements for a self-reflective and mutually responsive nation. With the cold war now over, higher education lacks even this instrumental rationale for connecting its functions of research and credentialing to larger public purposes. Academic spokespeople increasingly describe their enterprise in purely market terms, depicting it as a business much like any other, as they worry out loud about how to cultivate and expand their "customer base," especially business and consumers of educational services. They seem to assume that a kind of invisible hand will ensure that their single-minded pursuit of institutional growth and prestige will enhance the general welfare. However, the consequence of this embrace of the totems of the marketplace is that the American academy is losing its public mandate. It is thus no accident that despite the nation's manifest needs for investing in knowledge and skills in many areas of social importance, the academy has done so little to take the lead in proposing new public purposes to address these needs.

Various public figures have imagined candidates for such public efforts, such as the needs of the young and the poor in education, health care, and employment. We might add the strengthening of the nonprofit sector which provides so much essential social infrastructure, to say nothing of attention to improvement of democratic skills of public discussion. But these goals only make sense if one has first recognized the university as serving some larger public purpose as a citizen within civil society rather than simply as a self-aggrandizing creature of the market. This is the perspective that is currently missing from the frequently anguished debates about what to do about higher education.

TROUBLE IN THE PROFESSIONS

The malaise in the academy finds resonance in the sense of decline and drift within the ranks of the professions as a whole. The professions, after all, have grown out of the academy. The teachers of all professionals are themselves members of the professoriate. The professions remain further linked to the academy through the common value of professionalism, the guiding ideal throughout higher education as well as professional fields of all kinds. Moreover, both the professions as a whole and higher education in particular have been relatively privileged and successful institutions in the United States during the past half-century. It is noteworthy, then, that many professional fields have, like the academy, come to accent the marketability of their technical skills while de-emphasizing their contribution to civic life. In other words, the professions today do not typically seek to gain legitimacy by stressing the social importance of the knowledge they provide and the functions they perform for the community. Rather, they emphasize the specialized, expert knowledge and skills they provide in the market.

The importance of their social contribution is increasingly measured, in the world of both the professions and higher education, by the market value of their specialized skills, without serious reference to how these functions relate to any broader social well-being. Movement in this direction has greatly intensified in recent decades, further eclipsing the civic as opposed to the purely technical understanding of professionalism. The dominant view of professional knowledge has accordingly shed aspects of a more socially embedded conception of knowledge, with its concomitant ideas of social authority accruing on the basis of social responsibility, while displaying an increasingly instrumental and detached understanding of professional expertise.

This shift in perspective has accompanied and helped to justify an increasing degree of specialization in professional fields. But this development has also so separated knowledge from social purpose that expertise and skill appear as simply neutral tools to be appropriated by successful competitors in the service of their particular ends. This is, of course, an instrumental view of knowledge. It finds its natural complement in an individualistic and libertarian moral attitude which favors laissez-faire in most areas of social life. Since the professions have continued to importantly define middle class aspirations, however, this emphasis has had important effects beyond the professional ranks. These developments in the culture of professionalism not only reflect but have helped foster an aggressively individualistic understanding of society. An important corollary to this conception of knowledge, however, has been the narrowing of the idea of responsibility, both individual and collective.[5]

This perspective of instrumental individualism has become dominant in much professional and academic opinion. On the one hand, it has seemed to release individuals and institutions from much unwanted moral responsibility. All they need to do is obey the impersonal dictates of market forces. And, in fact, the change in attitude has progressed along with a shift in the allocation of rewards, talent, and vocational interest during the past 25 years. That is, there has been a conspicuous movement within the educated workforce away from teaching and public and social service occupations toward more market-oriented, private-sector professional employment. Within the professional ranks, moreover, the past two decades have seen the ominous growth of increasing gaps in prestige and income between a few "stars" at the top of the heap over their erstwhile peers.[6] However, this retreat from social responsibility has not produced enhanced freedom or fulfillment, even for most professionals. Nor has it much improved the moral quality of American life. Rather, the consequences could be said to have been widespread vocational demoralization on the part of professionals—a demoralization evident in a need to compensate through getting as much material reward as possible in the short term, within a society grown meaner, fiercer toward losers, and less hopeful about its collective future.

For higher education, the consequence of these developments has been a diffusion of identity, the loss of direction and defining purposes amid the pull of extraneous but enticing lures to professional and institutional self-interest. Academic institutions have sought to follow market trends unreflectively— much as they have followed government funding trends—with often negative consequences for their long-term commitments and defining values and purposes. The results have been growing divisions of all kinds within and among institutions of higher learning as well as within professional ranks.

With this has come the weakening of concern with public responsibility. Perhaps these trends explain the paradox of finding so many of the "world's best universities" amid conditions of urban decay and social neglect. This is indeed an instance of the detachment of knowledge from responsibility carried to an extreme degree.

These unhappy outcomes reflect a profound tension within the academic enterprise, a tension which can be healthy for the enterprise but which, if unnoticed or ignored, can wreak havoc, as it now threatens to do. Consider an analogy from a related, though very different, professional enterprise: journalism. Like higher education, journalism is in the business of shaping its public as well as responding to it. Both institutions play crucial roles in making democratic societies viable: their activities are critical if public deliberation is to work at all under modern conditions. The way journalism and higher education conceive and carry out their purposes—the way they understand themselves—is integral to their ability to function as responsible institutions.

Today, journalism, especially in the traditional core institution of the metropolitan newspapers, finds itself under heavy pressure to reform itself into an adjunct of a strictly commercial enterprise, to become one more part of the emerging global "info-tainment" industry. Yet, as Tom Rosenstiel of Columbia University's Project for Excellence in Journalism argues, this remains, as it has proven in the past, a self-defeating strategy for newspapers. It is worth considering Rosenstiel's argument since it provides an illuminating analogy to the current controversies in higher education.

Newspapers have often wanted to turn their reporting into directly profit-driven functions. The problem, according to Rosenstiel, has always been that readers resist and resent news reporting that they suspect has been concocted to please or manipulate them. As a result newspapers—and television as well—have repeatedly found that the route to economic survival leads, paradoxically, toward investing heavily in news gathering and editorial independence. Building audience loyalty takes years. It also requires giving people information that may at first attract only a small following, just because it is new. "What journalism companies are selling," writes Rosenstiel, "is their authority as a public asset. And that depends, especially with an ever more skeptical public, on proving you're in it for more than a buck."[7]

In other words, journalism succeeds commercially only when it actually acts as a citizen, when it places public service and concern for the integrity of its professional standards ahead of immediate profit. But it is equally important that the "professional standards" as well as the identity of both academe and journalism have been historically publicly focused in a strong sense. The identity of these occupations and their institutional homes only makes sense in reference to what is common to a whole community, to a general, diverse, pluralistic constituency all of whom must nonetheless manage to cooperate.

For both professions, truth must be publicly arrived at and publicly argued, while the most important truths under investigation concern not just what is happening or how things work but how we are to live as a nation.

The movement for public or civic journalism has galvanized much attention while also serving as a rallying point for efforts at reform in the media. The movement contends that journalism can find its full significance only by seeing itself as a critical partner in the "public sphere" of opinion and acting accordingly. The public sphere refers to the diffuse set of connections through which members of a democratic society try to understand and guide their affairs by active participation.[8] Part of the appeal of the public journalism perspective derives from recognition on the part of important segments of the newspaper industry that its future depends upon cultivating a readership interested in its product. That readership turns out to have a peculiar configuration, as compared with other "market segments." Newspaper readers overwhelmingly turn out to be persons who describe themselves as concerned with public affairs, not just consumers of news. They are also disproportionately active in the life of the larger society and likely to want a share in shaping the news as well as reading it. Thus, material interests bolster the ideal aim of building a more active and cooperative relationship between journalists and the public.

Something similar describes higher education in relation to its "market." Support for the academy in its integrity also depends upon persons who see themselves not just as consumers of services but as participants in a larger public realm. These are persons, often themselves graduates of higher education, who are interested in it not just for its instrumental value in enhancing their own and their offspring's economic marketability, but because they respect the contribution higher education makes to the society through promoting intellectual activity and making it more available to citizens generally. There is a naturally reciprocal relationship between academic institutions and this public. This public values higher education as a force for improvement and democracy, while the academy finds its meaning through trying to expand and build up this public. The big question is whether it is possible to give this understanding of higher education a formulation that is at once intellectually sound and generally comprehensible. To attempt this today is to enter an important debate. This debate is an ongoing national process of sorting out not only intellectual differences but rival principles of cultural authority and social organization as well.

RECOVERING FROM DEFAULT: INQUIRY AS PRACTICAL REASON

The default program of instrumental individualism rests upon a conception of rationality variously denominated as technocratic or scientific. This conception in its several forms has assumed dominance within much of the academy. Its core tradition and values are those of positivist empiricism, a cultural movement descending from the nineteenth century that generalizes into a total cultural program and certain interpretation of the natural sciences. Positivism insists that because natural scientific research succeeds by straining evaluative judgment out of observation of phenomena, therefore the larger truth must be that facts can be understood independently of value. The conclusion positivists have drawn is that while factual knowledge can be objectively verified, all questions of ethics and meaning are merely matters of taste and subjective judgment. Hence the affinity of positivistic understandings of research for "applying" knowledge to the social world on the model of the way engineers "apply" expert understanding to the problems of structure, logistics, or communication. While increasingly outdated as an interpretation of how natural science in fact has developed, this epistemology is firmly entrenched as the operating system of much of the American university, as we have seen. It provides an important intellectual warrant for the legitimacy of the instrumental individualism of the default paradigm.

Just as the currently ascendant default program contains at its core an epistemology—a conception of knowledge and its purpose—so the alternative of socially responsive higher education grows out of a counter ideal of knowledge and its purposes, together with the kind of social relationships this ideal entails. The alternative to the socially detached, positivist conception of knowledge and learning emphasizes the fusion of fact and value in practical experience, the interconnection of means and ends. Without denying individual talent or insight, this alternative model insists that knowledge grows out of the activities of a "community of inquirers," in the terminology of American pragmatist C.S. Peirce. For this alternative understanding of the life of the mind, the common core of all processes of investigation is a kind of reasoning which is essentially social and in which there is always a purpose at work. Grasping and articulating this purpose is crucial because, whether acknowledged or not, such purposes in fact shape the practices of investigation and teaching. These purposes are themselves fundamentally rooted in the identity of the inquirers and their community, expressive of their common commitments and relationships.

The animating idea of this alternative conception of investigation and learning is that rationality is finally always practical, rooted in the practices of some social group. Knowing is an aspect of the overall effort by members of a society to orient themselves within the world. At its root, that is, reason is essentially "communicative," as knowledge is part of an ongoing conversation among inquirers about their world. Though not simply something manufactured by social processes, even knowledge of nonhuman nature is always mediated by the norms and aims of some social group. In modern societies, that group, or groups, has become institutionalized in the professional inquirers who staff the academy. As distinguishing aspects of human historical existence, rationality and knowing have moral and ethical dimensions. Knowledge and the process of inquiry bear upon the quality of life and the nature of relationships among people. So, knowledge is finally a public value and concern, while those institutions which specialize in its discovery and interpretation exist within the framework of a modern society's overall goals and values.

This alternative understanding has in recent years begun to make significant impact on opinion within higher education. This has been due in part to the efforts of its contemporary spokespersons. Donald Schon's notion of "reflective practice," for example, has brought home the insufficiency of the received positivist model of "applied science" in a variety of fields, both professional and academic. There is also the growing body of largely academic criticism of positivism sometimes called the post-positivist philosophy of science.[9] Interestingly, these recent developments echo the founding ideas and program of the one indigenous American philosophical school, the classic pragmatism of Peirce, James, Royce, and Dewey.

The significance of this tradition of thought for higher education and its contemporary problems has been worked out by Charles W. Anderson.[10] Anderson has provided the useful clue that pragmatism can provide a needed coherence in discussion of these issues through its approach. This might be called an inductive synthesis by means of critique. It is critical in the sense that it traces out the assumptions of the dominant model while also showing its often unintended consequences. It is an inductive method because it begins inquiry with the practices at hand and then directs that inquiry toward comparing those actual methods of the disciplines with their aims as these have been revealed and interpreted over time. By asking what particular practices are good for, this approach is also synthetic and integrative. It points beyond the current state of professional fields and institutions toward possibilities for cooperation often only half-recognized by practitioners. Very importantly, it is an approach which reveals the public significance of the intellectual enterprise.

The kind of inquiry through practical reasoning urged by Anderson articulates a strong alternative to the presently dominant default program. The perspective opened up by the pragmatist account of practical reasoning suggests a way to rethink, and ultimately, to reconstruct all three aspects of the identity of the American university: its aims as a setting for inquiry; its formative educational function; and the social responsibilities which follow from its civic identity.

PRACTICAL REASON AND THE IDENTITY OF HIGHER EDUCATION

The way in which social relationships are conceived and lived out importantly influences how knowledge develops. This is because every intellectual enterprise, as it develops its distinctive practices and lore, shapes its participants' sense of identity and their notions of what is important in the field. While the internal life of a field is the most basic determinant of the values of its practitioners, the worlds of professional activity remain, to varying degrees, importantly open to influence from other institutions, not least from their patrons and critics. Who the members of a field imagine the audience or supporters of their enterprise to be matters significantly when it comes to deciding what sorts of questions will gain priority and who will be recognized as significant partners in the process of learning.

The development of postwar science and technology, for example, was significantly shaped by the imperatives first of national defense and then of corporate profitability. These social influences pushed research in the direction of devices which are increasingly complicated (and expensive) to design, build, and maintain. In contrast, other dimensions of technical and engineering excellence, such as ease of use, repair and replicability, or simplicity of design, received far less attention. This largely tacit process of purpose-driven inquiry has had fateful consequences in many areas. Think of the growth of the huge institutional research and engineering complex, much of it university based, which has been developed at an enormous expense to support today's high-tech, acute care medicine. Yet, this form of health care mostly benefits the affluent. There has been far less support for research and applications in public health, advances that benefit the public more broadly and may be as effective, as experience suggests in Europe and elsewhere, if not more effective, in improving the overall well being of the population than the more expensive developments of medical high technology.

By this standard, the record of the postwar university has been a very mixed report. As we have seen, the postwar era saw higher education deliver prodigious advances in scientific knowledge and its applications while opening professional status to wider segments of the population. At the same time, however, higher education has allowed external patrons to set priorities without engaging in much scrutiny of the larger point and value of these priorities. And the academy has rashly embarked on projects out of an unreflective self-interest. Typically, higher education has not been self-reflective about its own organization and the effects on its identity and aims of the practices of the disciplines. Despite protestations of its dedication to disinterested research, the positivistic separation of the rationality of technique from thought about value and purpose has made such omissions academic matters of course.

It is precisely this narrowness of aim that a focus on practical reason promises to overcome. Practical reason views epistemic practices, like those of every human institution, as ultimately guided by partly implicit ideal aims. So understood, inquiry becomes a self-reflective process of investigating and appraising the quality of the performance, measured against some interpretation of its fundamental purpose. Of course, conceptions of purpose are always themselves open to question and challenge, and indeed the glory of the academy is that it is an institution which has tried to find ways to sustain just this process of ongoing scrutiny of practice and its aims. Yet, the academy has been as embarrassingly resistant as any other organization to applying its skills of inquiry to its own activities. The turn to practical reasoning is motivated by the desire to do just that.[11]

Once this process of inquiry develops, however, new implications emerge. The questioning and appraising of specific practices within disciplines requires practitioners to become more self-aware about their function within their "community of inquirers." They typically come to adopt a stance toward their field that is at once critical and yet loyal to the basic aims of the enterprise, seeking to improve its aim at its essential purposes as they come to see them. Such a stance toward one's field obviously has strong affinities with the responsibilities of participation in an ongoing social enterprise. It becomes, as Charles Anderson has reminded us, an enhanced kind of citizenship, pertaining "not just to public affairs but to our performance in every realm of life."[12] Once seriously involved in such inquiry, Anderson suggests, the inquirers become progressively more aware of the importance of quality of performance and how crucial self-reflective loyalty to purpose is in more and more areas of the life of their institutions, including how the disciplines and practices mesh or fail to mesh with each other in promoting the larger aims of knowledge which lead into the public realm.

Inquiry, properly understood, leads its participants into questions about the overall coherence and mutual import of their many specialized endeavors. It awakens responsibility by revealing how participants are already engaged in loyalty to matters of public import and bearing. In this way, citizenship enters ever more seriously into the "job description" of academic professionals, not as an externally imposed "add-on" but as a defining feature of the very activities of inquiry and discourse themselves. Practical reason leads toward a collaborative search for practices that meet common purposes reliably and well. While this does not mean that the university loses its distinctive aims and organization, it does entail a more self-aware and deliberate relationship between the specialized concerns of academe and the problems and controversies of societies, such as our own, which are struggling to institute a fully democratic way of living.

REVITALIZING THE MISSION OF HIGHER EDUCATION

We can only speculate what difference it might have made to the evolution of higher education during the postwar decades had such a conception of practical reason played a major role in academic thinking and administration. But the postwar record confirms, even if ambiguously, that the link between the way knowledge is organized and institutional identity is real and important. Today's default program certainly fits much of the present organization of the academy. Yet other efforts are underway to connect higher education with the society in ways consistent with the democratic implications inherent in the notion of inquiry as practical reason.

The notable upsurge of interest among students in social service volunteer programs, as well as the growth in institutional support for such efforts at every level of higher education, is testimony to the breadth of the sense that there is need for a change of direction, that academe must do more to educate for civic leadership and service. This movement is now very widespread, ranging from the national organization Campus Compact, founded by university presidents in the 1980s, to a plethora of indigenous efforts in rural as well as metropolitan institutions. Within the curriculum, the appearance of the movement for "service learning" or "experiential learning," while not uncontroversial, has opened up discussion and sometimes fierce debate on the place of social service in academic practice, as well as the question of the nature of investigation and its relation to practical experience and self-reflection.

There are other experiments even more directly engaged in the task of reorienting the focus of the academy, in its research as well as its educational function. These have been projects to connect the intellectual and technical resources of higher education with the problems of surrounding communities, sometimes conceived as whole metropolitan regions and sometimes as the immediate, often poor, urban neighbors of the academy. This is a more complex movement, still very much in process. Some have developed as interinstitutional partnerships, sometimes with philanthropic support. These projects have built linkages among schools, including whole school systems, and various academic institutions from community colleges to research universities. Others have proceeded in a more "grass roots" way, relying on the initiative of groups of faculty, students, and administrators working with groups outside the academy.

It is noteworthy that the more successful efforts to redefine university identity around service and citizenship share a certain family resemblance rooted in the practice of inquiry as practical reason. First, such efforts consciously conceive their purpose to be changing the university's understanding of research and teaching, along the lines of critical practical reason, toward a much greater focus upon social service and improvement. "Participatory action research" is one such methodological innovation. Second, these efforts have typically sought to develop this change in attitude by establishing enduring partnerships with institutions, such as schools, social service agencies or businesses, and health care providers, with which the academy already shares aims, practices, and often personnel, at least in the form of apprentice teachers and health care professionals. Third, such projects seem to succeed best in actually becoming institutionalized as standard academic procedure when they develop as genuine partnerships in which knowledge and practices evolve cooperatively rather than proceeding in a one-directional way from experts to outsiders.[13]

The success of these efforts at changing the dominant tendencies within the American academy depends partly on how clearly the participants understand what they are doing—and how effective they can become at persuading others of the significance of what they are engaged in accomplishing. To become more self-aware is the first step toward awakening to one's responsibility. The second step is to recognize that serious self-scrutiny often leads to changes in identity, to growth in self-discovery and a broadening of one's aims and loyalties. Identity receives important shape from social relationships and the way they are organized. In the positivist scheme, researchers "produce" knowledge, which is then "applied" to problems and problematic populations, by varying forms of design and engineering. On the other hand, if knowledge is developed through inquiry, the identity of the participants in the process will have bearing on the kind of knowledge discovered. These experiments suggest that academic institutions, like professionals, can realize their public responsibilities by becoming self-aware partners in addressing the needs and weaknesses of the nation's shredding social fabric. Once established over time by good faith on both sides, however, cooperation becomes self-sustaining as it manifestly produces an enlarged sense of identity and purpose for both the academy and its partners.

These practical experiments, and the theory of practical reason, also have important bearing upon the directly educational mission of higher education. Today, as for some time, higher education remains a powerful formative institution. It exerts profound social and cultural influences in shaping expectations about what skills and knowledge are valuable, what career aspirations are reasonable and admirable, what kind of society Americans want to have, and what kind of people they want to be. Much of college experience, the "hidden curriculum," consists of "anticipatory socialization." That is, universities and colleges link vocational preparation with personal aspirations by creating the social and cultural context within which individuals choose and shape their goals and skills. The environment and ethos of higher education, the values and purposes which are seen by students to matter among faculty, staff, alumni, and administrators are among the most powerful shaping forces in American society. To the degree that this environment reflects only or mostly the values of the current default program, higher education will simply reinforce the tendencies toward social disengagement so evident among successful Americans.

Because of its great influence not only as a source of innovation but as a shaper of outlooks, higher education is a preeminently public—though nongovernmental—institution. Everyone has a stake and an interest in what it does. It is a critical participant in the democratic public sphere. We in the academy need to connect seriously with our actual social position, both as an institutional sector within the national society and as particular organizations living with often very different neighbors in our local communities. But we cannot do this without serious reflection and discussion about our identity and purposes. And this requires social vision. A more responsible and connected institutional life requires that we think of our institutions as distinctive participants in a public sphere, a member of democratic civil society, with important responsibilities to the nation and to the wider world. And not just as knowledge-producing entities or service providers (the industrial-market conception), but as important shapers of identity (including our own), as explorers and conservators as well as critics of values and goals.

This is not a wholly novel approach in American life. Within the tradition of what could be called developmental democracy, earlier leaders, such as the philosopher John Dewey, warned of the perpetual American tendency to collapse the aspirations to democracy into the straight jacket of what I have called the default program of individualism and instrumentalism. The price for this, these pioneers warned, is not more freedom but diminished possibilities for us all. On the other hand, democracy promises associated living. This means a fuller life for individuals as well as a more just and cohesive society. Individuals can develop a strong and confident sense of selfhood only as members of a society in which they can believe and invest their energies, one in which they can trust and know they are trusted. Higher education, too, finds its best self through contributing to such a society. This civic perspective can provide the leaders in academe with some direction for developing a democratic yet reflective public. Such a public is the best guarantee that higher education will have a future in which it will be worthwhile to participate.

NOTES

1. A. Levine, "How the Academic Profession Is Changing," *Daedalus, 126,* no. 4 (Fall 1997): 1–20; B.R. Clark, "Small Worlds, Different Worlds: The Uniqueness and Troubles of American Academic Professions," *Daedalus, 126,* no. 4 (Fall 1997): 21-42.

2. R.C. Reich, *The Work of Nations: Preparing Ourselves for 21st Century Capitalism* (New York: The Free Press, 1991); J.K. Galbraith, *The Culture of Contentment* (Boston: Houghton Mifflin, 1992); Michael Lind has used the term "White Overclass" to describe this stratum in *The Next American Nation: The New Nationalism and the Fourth American Revolution* (New York: Simon and Schuster, 1995).

3. D. Bok, "Reclaiming the Public Trust," *Change* (July/August 1992): 18.

4. For example, R.S. Lowen, *Creating the Cold War University: The Transformation of Stanford* (Berkeley and Los Angeles: University of California Press, 1997).

5. W.M. Sullivan, *Work and Integrity: The Crisis and Promise of Professionalism in America* (New York: HarperCollins, 1995); S. Brint, *In an Age of Experts: The Changing Role of Professionals in Politics and Public Life* (Princeton, NJ: Princeton University Press, 1994).

6. D. Bok, *The Cost of Talent: How Executives and Professionals Are Paid and How It Affects America* (New York: The Free Press, 1993): 89 ff.

7. T. Rosenstiel, "Investing in Integrity Pays," *New York Times* (20 October 1997).

8. For example, see J. Rosen, "Making Things More Public: On the Political Responsibility of the Media Intellectual," *Critical Studies in Mass Communication, 11* (1994): 362–88.

9. See the discussion of these authors and themes in Sullivan, *Work and Integrity,* 159–90.

10. C.W. Anderson, *Pragmatic Liberalism* (Chicago: University of Chicago Press, 1991); C.W. Anderson, *Prescribing the Life of the Mind: An Essay on the Purpose of the University, the Aims of Liberal Education, the Competence of Citizens, and the Cultivation of Practical Reason* (Madison: University of Wisconsin Press, 1993).

11. Anderson, *Pragmatic Liberalism,* 3–22.

12. C.W. Anderson, "Democracy and Inquiry," *The Good Society, 7,* no. 2 (1997): 16–19.

13. For accounts and interpretation of some of these projects, see L. Benson and I. Harkavy, "School and Community in the Global Society: A New-Deweyan Theory of Problem-Solving Schools and Cosmopolitan Neighborly Communities," *Universities and Community Schools, 5,* no. 1–2 (1997): 16–71; L. Benson and I. Harkavy, "De-Platonizing and Democratizing Education as the Bases of Service-Learning" in *Service-Learning: Pedagogy and Research,* ed. R.A. Rhoads and J. Howard (San Francisco: Jossey-Bass, forthcoming).

CHAPTER 3

Renewing the Democratic Spirit in American Colleges and Universities
Higher Education as Public Work

Harry C. Boyte and Nancy N. Kari

> I know of no safe repository of the ultimate powers of the society but the people themselves; and if we think them not enlightened enough to exercise control with a wholesome discretion, the remedy is not to take it from them, but to inform their discretion by education.
>
> Thomas Jefferson, *The Works of Thomas Jefferson* (1903)

American colleges and universities were founded with a strong civic mission. They aimed at producing public leaders that were, in Thomas Jefferson's terms, examples "of talent and virtue."[1] Jefferson combined democracy and education in his affirmation, expressed in the founding of the University of Virginia.

As the twentieth century began, American higher education continued to be infused with a lively sense of civic mission. The German system emphasized detached scholarship. The English sought to prepare an aristocratic elite. In contrast, Charles Eliot, president of Harvard, wrote as follows in 1908: "At bottom, most of the American institutions of higher education are filled with the democratic spirit. Teachers and students alike are profoundly moved by the desire to serve the democratic community." Even as late as 1947, the President's Commission on Higher Education entitled its report, *Education for Democracy*.[2]

Since World War II, universities have exploded in influence, in numbers of students, and in fields of study. There have been many advances from the standpoint of making higher education a more just and inclusive system—

greater diversity in student bodies; curricula that take account of different cultures and ways of knowing; most recently, stirrings of a new movement in higher education to reconnect with surrounding communities through initiatives such as service learning. Yet few today would make Eliot's claim. What would it take for higher education to be once again filled with democratic spirit and broad public purpose? That is the question we take up in this essay.

From America's founding, the interdependence of education and democracy has posed distinctive challenges to colleges and universities. The democratic imperative of the early Republic was the establishment of an enduring popular government on a continental scale; higher education sought to cultivate public leaders of "talent and virtue." After the Civil War, the nation, taking up the task of generating "useable" knowledge for the needs of an emerging industrial democracy, created land grant colleges. Mid-twentieth century America harnessed science and technology in the struggle of the "free world" against communism, creating the "multiversity" to that end.

None of these moments in higher education has been without contradictions. Thus, to cite only one example, higher education's veneration of science in the cold war weakened aspects of democracy, even as it sought to preserve freedom. It shifted authority from citizens and placed it in the hands of experts who saw themselves as a class outside the people. Recognizing the full ambiguity of this history is important as we renew the democratic project.

America's democratic challenge at the end of this century—widespread productive re-engagement of the citizenry in public life—calls institutions of higher education to return to Thomas Jefferson's original formulation, with a twist. When Jefferson pointed to the lapses in "wholesome discretion" among the general public, he assumed a tutoring of the people by the educated class. Today, the distancing of American academics from identification with other citizens, a pattern observable in many professions, is part of democracy's crisis. Yet there is an urgent need to form a more "public" citizenry in this time of civic disaffection, widespread feelings of powerlessness, and a popular culture that roils with rancour on the one hand and false intimacies on the other. How do we become a people who see our individual self-interests embedded in the general welfare, who have more faith in each other and in our public institutions, who can act together with poise and boldness?

These questions call for a broad, many-sided democratic politics that grounds authority among the citizenry. Such a politics is founded on respect for the capacities and intelligence of citizens while it refuses to romanticize "the people" or to trivialize the hard work it takes to develop public habits, build power relationships, and develop identities as "producers" of democracy, not simply its consumers. It aims to free the powers and public spirit of people to contribute to our common world. Democratic politics requires a place in which to acquire civic skills—none more important, in the information age, than a college or university.

Mediating institutions of many kinds—media, schools, unions, political parties, settlements, YM and YWCAs—once provided a rough and tumble but powerful education in democracy. They were environments in which people learned to deal with others different than themselves, developed interest in public affairs, and came to see connections between everyday efforts and larger arenas of policy and decision making. As institutions have redefined themselves as service providers and as citizens have come to be customers and clients, we have seen such education erode, and we are less effective and less confident as a citizenry. Institutions of higher education that become mediating institutions will be central to renewed civic confidence.

The project of renewing colleges and universities as agents of democracy has far ranging implications. It calls for broadening our understanding of the aims and processes of knowledge creation. It requires attention to the craft of teaching and to the many sources of learning. It will mean sustained effort to expand professional identities to include civic dimensions, and also reworking structures that detach professionals from public life.

Ideas in an information age are a key form of power. We argue that the current map of democracy needs redrawing if we are to address these challenges.

DEFINITIONS OF DEMOCRACY AND EXPECTATIONS OF CITIZENS

To develop the politics and democracy education needed in our time will require a Copernican-type shift in views of democracy, how it is practiced, and where it is sustained. Democracy understood as the ongoing (and thus ever unfinished) work of the people, simple as it seems, is such a shift.

American history can be told in terms of the struggles of its people for inclusion in the definition, rights, and responsibilities of citizenship, as a story about conflict on a fundamental question—who are citizens? Education has been central to this struggle to define civic membership. A *Petition to the State Legislature of the Commonwealth of Massachusetts,* delivered by a group of African-American leaders in 1787, the year of the nation's Constitutional Convention, declared: "We are of the humble opinion that we have the right to enjoy the privileges of free men, but that we do not will appear in many instances and we beg leave to mention one out of many." The right in question was "the education of our children which receive no benefit from the free schools in the town of Boston . . . for no other reason [than] they are black."

Similarly, the Philadelphia Working Men's Committee in 1830, after conducting an investigation on schools, declared itself "constrained to believe that, until the means of equal instruction shall be equally secured to all, liberty is but an unmeaning word, and equality an empty shadow." In place of the existing system which schooled children of the wealthy, it declared itself in favor of "common schools" extended "throughout the Commonwealth, placed "immediately under the control and suffrage of the people," and open "to all classes . . . supported at the expense of all."[3]

Issues of inclusiveness have been widely debated on campuses through the storms of controversy surrounding questions like multiculturalism, even if such debates do not usually address the class dimension of the question suggested by the Philadelphia Working Men's Committee. Yet the other dimension of citizenship has scarcely been addressed at all. We debate *who* is a citizen. We rarely ask, *what* is a citizen? What does a citizen *do*? How do we educate people for the work of citizenship? The answer flows from how we define citizenship.

Three main conceptions of citizenship thread throughout American history, each tied to a corresponding understanding of democracy. They overlap and mingle in the real world, yet each is distinct enough and tied to broad traditions, institutions, and practices that it is useful to distinguish among them. Each, moreover, shapes approaches to civic education (how we "inform the discretion of the people," in Jefferson's terms) and appear in current practices in higher education. Citizens have been understood as:

1. Rights-bearing members of a representative political system who choose their leaders through elections. This "civics" view of citizenship stems from a view of democracy mainly as representative government and the rule of law.
2. Concerned members of communities who share common values and are responsible to each other and for their community. This rendering of citizenship, defined by the "communitarian" philosophy, is also regularly associated with ideas of "civil society."
3. Public problem solvers and co-producers of public goods. This perspective is based on a work-centered philosophy of democracy, which views authority for the commonwealth residing among the citizenry. It is associated historically with the political idiom of commonwealth in American history.

Currently, the first two perspectives dominate. The civics view (or what is called in political theory, the "liberal view") defines democracy as primarily a system of representative political institutions and political and civil rights. The center of attention is on formal governmental institutions: division of powers, how a bill becomes law; how to vote; how to make one's views known to legislators. The point of politics and government is fair distribution of goods and services. From a government-centered perspective, citizens are individuals with rights guaranteed under law. Liberty is understood in largely negative terms: the right to protection from unwarranted interference, harassment, or unjust imprisonment. Duties of citizens include voting, paying taxes, obeying the law, and responding to periodic civic tasks such as jury duty or service in the armed forces in times of national emergency. From this perspective, the crisis in democracy resides in the flawed machinery of government and citizens' view of government as alien, or worse, an enemy to be dismantled. The Clinton administration's focus on reinventing government for more efficient, customer-friendly services operates from this diagnosis.

This first outlook holds important insights, and describes the main workings of the world. It is a kind of everyday conventional wisdom. In higher education, efforts to strengthen citizenship from this perspective take the form of voter registration efforts, programs to enhance student knowledge of public affairs, student government, and political internships, among others.

Contrasted with (and also complementing) the government-centered approach, a second view of citizenship emphasizes shared values and strong communities. Those who promote this perspective stress a balance between responsibilities and individual rights, and thus highlight the importance of character education. Above all, the purpose of politics should be to pursue the "common good." Responsibility, mutual regard, and understanding of differences are important outcomes. Voluntarism is sometimes advanced as the exemplary civic activity. The 1998 Presidential Summit on Volunteerism illustrated this perspective. Community service and service learning developed as a national movement largely to advance this view, as a broader and deeper version of citizenship than simply a focus on government.

Neither view is wrong. Educating students who are knowledgeable about civics is worthwhile. Values of personal responsibility and concern for others are elemental ingredients of any functioning civic culture.

Communitarians in particular have reintroduced concepts of participation and civic values which are vitally important. The problem is that communitarian versions of citizenship tend to separate ideals like community, the common good, and deliberation from the messy, everyday process of getting things done in a public world of diverse interests. This separation is embodied in the neglect by communitarian theorists of the civic dimensions of work roles in a number of settings. Indeed, the conventional definition of citizenship in communitarian theory, locating it in the "voluntary sector" of civil society separated from work and government, explicitly reifies this separation. Citizenship detached from work, whether paid or unpaid, strips people of sources of authority and power. Moreover, without a focus on work, or productive, sustained, often hard and demanding activity, there is no real way to counter the pervasive identities of "consumer" and "victim" that now shape our political culture.

Unless political ideals are combined with awareness of the multiplicity of interests and purposes that characterize serious politics and public projects of all kinds, and unless ideals are connected to real work, they all too easily become sentimental or a clamor of competing moral claims. Thus, for instance, seeing community service as about teaching caring and concern feeds the thin associations of citizenship in "a thousand points of light," and the imagery of the heart, symbol of the volunteer. In political terms, communitarians argue that people should appeal to each other in a "moral voice." In reality, however, the problem is not the *lack* of moral speech but rather *contending* moral frameworks. Jeffrey Bell, Ronald Reagan's former speechwriter, argues for a politics of morality in terms strikingly similar to progressive communitarians. For Bell, "the setting of a society's standards is, in the final analysis, what politics is about."[4]

Of direct relevance, the limits of the communitarian framework are suggested by the recent array of commissions and calls for civil society, civic renewal, and civility in American public life. The neglect of higher education as a serious site for the project of civic renewal and democratic reconstruction is a dramatic feature of almost all such calls.

Yet civic commissions have produced resources that can be drawn upon for the work of democracy in higher education. For instance, the National Commission on Civic Renewal, directed by William Galston, co-chaired by William Bennett and former Senator Sam Nunn and including many of the nation's leading intellectuals in its advisory groups, omits explicit attention to higher education. Yet after two years of detailed research into America's civic practices, it did detect "stirrings of a new movement of citizens acting together," through which people are taking public action on problems and tasks, a movement "largely unnoticed, unappreciated, and unsupported" by official policies. Moreover, the commission itself, representing a wide range of political viewpoints, came to a definition of democracy far ranging indeed in our age when marketplace language reigns supreme. The distinctive feature of the definition is that it goes well beyond either liberal or communitarian views: Democracy is neither a consumer good nor a spectator sport but rather the work of free citizens, engaged in shared civic enterprises.

Finally, the commission's diagnosis of "the problem" in the nation's civic life had a richer and more political approach than most others, which have tended to highlight the purported moral failings of citizens and ignore questions of power, politics, and even democracy. The commission focused on widespread feelings of powerlessness and loss of citizen authority: "Too many of us lack confidence in our capacity to make basic moral and civic judgements, to join . . . to do the work of community, to make a difference . . . rarely have we felt so powerless."[5] Such feelings of powerlessness are glaring in higher education. The graduate school experiences of most faculty members generate little confidence in collective action.

The sense that the fundamental contours of our institutions are largely fixed and immutable is widespread, even in the midst of radical and rapid change. It is an enormous challenge for those of us in higher education to put ourselves back on "the map." But it is an essential, vital task. It is one that requires refocusing on work itself, individually and collectively, as potentially a profound resource of democratic renewal.

THE PUBLIC WORK TRADITION

The limits of both liberal (civics) and communitarian versions of citizenship point to the need to unearth a third understanding, the commonwealth or public work tradition. This tradition highlights the great innovation of the American tradition of democracy, its tie to work.

As new scholarship has begun to emphasize, the distinctive feature of the American Revolution was neither a Lockean focus on rights nor a classical republican concern with virtue. Rather, America's revolution produced a political culture that was practical, down-to-earth, work-centered, and energetic. As Gordon Wood put it in his recent work, *The Radicalism of the American Revolution*, "when [classical ideals of disinterested civic virtue] proved too idealisitic and visionary, [Americans] found new democratic adhesives in the actual behavior of plain ordinary people."[6]

Thus, in America's early years, citizenship had a practical dimension. It focused on the development of people's capacities for work together through civic problem solving. Education was seen as the foundation for democracy. Thomas Jefferson's quote about the tie between education and popular sovereignty found counterparts in the views of many others.

Civic education entailed practical, generalist training. Thus, Benjamin Franklin argued that any man might have to do anything in an open, fluid society. The point of his model school, the Philadelphia Academy, was to train male children to deal with unanticipated situations. It was to be a school out of which boys "will come . . . fitted for learning any Business, Calling, or Profession."[7]

In the nineteenth century, a flowering of institutions developed in the civic space between private life and the state—often called "civil society"—including institutions of higher education. These associations taught the skills of practical citizenship. Alexis de Tocqueville was surprised again and again in his travels across the country in the 1830s to discover that the public substituted its own activity for that of officials or government. In America, he observed that 100,000 citizens had declared their intention to refrain from alcohol; in Europe, he said, they would have sent a petition to the king.

Citizen-centered politics came under assault with the growth of institutions, transcontinental communications, and technocratic ways of thinking in the twentieth century. Yet the rise of professional politics was never a clear-cut process. Democratic politics continued to flourish in what might be best called "mediating institutions." These, in turn, were sustained by diverse strands of the public work tradition for the first decades of the twentieth century.

The tradition views citizens as producers of public goods that contribute to society's material and social culture. Public work of significance—in offices and schools, factories and farms, government agencies or in higher education—has been the way diverse people have forged connections with each other and addressed the nation's problems. Through public work people gain visibility, authority, and larger intellectual horizons. In the process, they become creators of their communities and stakeholders in the country. This frame highlights the work-centered philosophy of democracy suggested by Abraham Lincoln, whose idea of government of the people and by the people remained vibrant well into the 1940s.

Citizenship as public work has several strands that weave together a broad tradition of "productive citizenship." The concept "public work" draws from the idea of building the commons; it is associated with democratic movements; and it highlights traditions of "catalytic" professional practice in the twentieth century.

Creating the Commons

In the eighteenth and nineteenth centuries and through the 1930s, democratic citizenship in America was indelibly tied to a commonwealth perspective—a popular republicanism informed by the experiences of many immigrant groups whose work "built the commons." From voluntary fire departments to the "common school movement," from public arts to the Civilian Conservation Corps (CCC) of the 1930s and 1940s, the commons tradition accented the work of citizens joined in projects which shaped communities and, ultimately, the nation. Often, such experiences were transformative. Veterans of the CCC, for instance, recount their youthful work in building parks, planting forests, and doing other conservation work as shaping a civic identity that lasted throughout their lives.[8] Thus citizenship was understood in terms of the down-to-earth labors of ordinary people who created goods and undertook projects of public benefit, not mainly as the high-minded, virtuous and leisure activity of gentlemen. This kind of civic identity helped create an important balance between pursuit of individual wealth and the creation of public things.

Democratic Movements

Citizenship as public work also had an insurgent edge which lent dynamism and spirit to American democracy. It accorded honor and authority to those, whatever their birth or educational status, who were builders of the commonwealth. Those excluded from public life, such as slaves, women, and the landless poor, found in the practices of public work resources for democratic action and the potential to claim full participation based on their contributions.

Throughout American history, democratic movements have gained power as marginalized groups that have claimed authority based on public contributions. It is important to distinguish this point from the democratic potential of work made by theorists of workplace democracy. Workplace democracy focuses on the power relations and decision-making patterns in work settings. It is a widely known concept in democratic theory that stresses habits and skills developed through workplace decision making. Public work as a concept draws attention to the civic claims that powerless groups can make on the basis of their contribution to the commonwealth regardless of the internal structure of their workplaces.

The effort to claim democratic authority based on ordinary people's labor is a central theme in the African-American freedom movement. The bookend events of Martin Luther King Jr.'s public career—the Montgomery bus boycott, sustained by the dignity of maids who walked to work, and the Memphis garbage workers' strike—find resonance in the great poem by Langston Hughes, *Freedom's Plow*, which eloquently links the struggle for democracy to work and freedom. Anticipating Martin Luther King Jr., Langston Hughes's poetry situated the history of the African-American struggle within the American tradition. At the heart of this tradition, he saw an ongoing movement toward freedom, built on work. "Out of labor—white hands and black hands," he wrote, "came the dream, the strength, the will, to build America. . . ."[9] For Hughes, the "built" nature of America was an endless source of hope, even in the hardest times because it created a space for the contributions of the common people to become visible.

Similarly, women used the claims based on their civic work, challenging the distinction between work paid and unpaid, as the foundation for suffrage. This claim also included a view of freedom as public contribution. Thus, Frances Willard, leader of the largest women's association of the nineteenth century, believed that "the larger liberty for women" lay in the freedom to develop individually and to contribute to the social welfare. She titled her book, *The Work and Workers of the Women's Christian Temperance Union*.[10]

Willard's perspectives flow into yet a third strand of the public work tradition, the idea of professional practice that catalyzes civic effort and collaborative problem solving rather simply applying expert intervention.

Catalytic Professions

In the philosophy articulated well by Jane Addams, professional work was conceived as "freeing the powers" of people for public creation and contribution. In her 1902 volume, *Democracy and Social Ethics*, Addams argued that the educator has a role beyond simply informing the student:

> We are gradually requiring of the educator that he shall free the powers of each man and connect him with the rest of life. We are impatient to use the dynamic power residing in the mass of humankind, and demand that the educator free that power. . . . Every man is a creative agent, a generator of fine idealism. But we are skeptical of the moral idealism of the few, and demand the education of the many that there be greater freedom, strength, and subtlety of intercourse, and hence an increase in dynamic power.[11]

This approach to professional practice continued and spread in rich, if now largely unknown streams of practice, through the twentieth century. In catalytic practice the point is not to shape or normalize clients, but rather to provide tools and occasions for people and institutions to discover their distinctive spirit, traditions, and public work. Catalytic practice can help to "build" publics, as well as contribute to public life.

Few professionals articulated the essence of catalytic professional practice as clearly as Jane Addams, but some sense of the civic dimensions of work influenced many professional traditions through most of the twentieth century. Teachers, social workers, clergy, youth workers, journalists, public health professionals, union organizers, settlement workers, civil service employees, and many others often understood themselves as citizens first. They were "public workers" in common projects with other citizens. These work identities, in turn, helped to sustain public cultures and practices in many mediating institutions which connected people's everyday experiences to larger arenas. For instance, as late as 1940, the YMCA in America had as its central mission "education for democracy."[12]

Mediating institutions, even at their best, were full of contradictions and exclusions. Nonetheless, they powerfully helped to sustain a public culture well into the 1940s that shaped people's understandings of democracy and of themselves as citizens. Much of this history has yet to be unearthed, but it will provide resources for democratic action in the next century.

The current crisis, from a public work perspective, results from the widespread disengagement of the citizenry from public life, from the pervasive sense that we as a people do not have the will or the collective ability to address society's complex problems, and from the shift in elemental civic identities from "producers" (or co-creators) to "consumers" of democracy.

Higher education both reflects and exacerbates these trends, but there are earlier traditions to draw upon for renewing its democratic traditions.

EDUCATING FOR DEMOCRACY

Jane Addams' public work conception of the purpose of education—to free people's talents and powers for contribution to the commonwealth—holds possibilities for a renewed vision for higher education today. In the first decades of the twentieth century, her philosophy of a broadly based education for democracy, in fact, was woven into many facets of higher education (even if it was never the dominant theme). Public and land-grant colleges formed vivid examples.

Land-grant institutions grew out of the Morrill Act, signed by President Lincoln in 1862. The Morrill Act promoted "the liberal and practical education of the industrial classes in the several pursuits and professions of life." It resulted in a number of new colleges, open to wider constituencies. Land-grant colleges had a practical inclination. They aimed to develop a science that would be relevant and useful to the challenges of agriculture and rural life. This period was a time of remarkable scientific developments in farming: artificial fertilizers, the Babcock milk test, new knowledge about the transmission of diseases, and the control of crop and animal diseases all made a dramatic appearance.

Rhetoric about the democratic purposes of land-grant colleges was widespread. For instance, the Trustees of the Ohio Agricultural and Mechanical College declared in 1873 that they desired not "to educate those confided to them simply as Farmers or Mechanics, but as men, fitted by education and attainments for the greater usefulness and higher duties of citizenship." In some states, civic concerns in land-grant education were shaped by reform agitation among students and faculty involved with farmer and labor movements. In other states, citizenship training was often simply equated with the addition of social sciences into the curriculum. Still others had a larger civic vision. Andrew White, president of Cornell University, stressed the need to teach and cultivate an ethos of public service in all students."[13]

By the 1890s, the civic mission of land-grant education was expressed through extension work. Extension work at its best was reciprocal. It recognized knowledge gained from experience, and it provided a vehicle for blending scientific knowledge and local knowledge. Farmers themselves often challenged the idea that university-based research and science was the only appropriate knowledge. They organized their own institutes to convey and legitimize "craft based" knowledge, views of what crops were best and strategies for taking care of farms that came from "collecting and systematizing" experiences of farmers themselves.[14]

Early twentieth-century leaders such as Liberty Hyde Bailey helped to formulate a philosophy of education for democracy through what he called "public work." Bailey, the pioneering dean of the newly created New York State College of Agriculture at Cornell, was perhaps the most influential philosopher of land-grant schools at that time. He saw land grant rural work as parallel to urban settlements. And like Addams, he tackled difficult and critical questions—the relationship between science and public knowledge, the pedagogies of democracy, and the public meaning and democratic possibilities of students' training in technical and professional fields. These are questions centrally relevant today.

Liberty Bailey, with support from farming communities across New York state, helped Cornell to become known as a "people's college" and the world's preeminent agricultural school. Bailey's philosophical focus was well illustrated by his contrast between technical education—which he argued any despotism could provide—and education for a democracy. Bailey's approach was to integrate specialized knowledge about agriculture into a much more comprehensive vision. "Students in agriculture are doing much more than fitting themselves to follow an occupation," he wrote. "They are to take part in a great regeneration. The student in agriculture is fitting himself for a great work."[15]

College-based rural extension workers, for instance, could play pivotal roles if they helped communities develop their own problem-solving capacities. Bailey continued:

> Real leadership lies in taking hold of the first and commonest problems that present themselves and working them out. I like to say to my students that they should attack the first problem that presents itself when they alight from the train on their return from college. It may be a problem of roads; of a poor school; of tuberculosis; of ugly signs along the highways.

The significance of this work was not simply the specific problem. Rather, it was the fact that the public work of problem solving created opportunities to develop community capacity for self-action.[16]

Bailey's example of catalytic practice is instructive for professionals of all kinds. For Bailey, "farming is a philosophy, not a mere process." He saw the specialization of disciplines, while bringing some benefits, as endangering the mission of rural work unless the larger point of democracy was constantly stressed. "The farmer is not only a producer of commodities," he argued, "He is a citizen of the commonwealth."

Bailey had a shrewd political sense. This proved essential for his success because his philosophy directly confronted the rising conventional wisdom which held that academic knowledge, developed in environments detached from practical experience, was the most valid.

Bailey's voice, prominent as it was, became gradually marginalized as a positivist theory of knowledge based on the model of "objective," scientific research increasingly shaped higher education. Nonetheless, echoes could still be found well into midcentury.

As late as 1951, Lewis Mumford, the distinguished philosopher of higher education, proposed that public work experiences be required of all young men and women. Mumford too warned about the rise of a bureaucratic, technical society and the corresponding loss of an ethos of citizenship based on public work. He believed a public work corps could counter such trends.

Yet overall, Mumford's was a lonely voice in a society that increasingly ceded authority to scientific knowledge and to experts. The particular social, political, and economic forces at midcentury became intertwined in a way that constricted public life and eroded both the explicit language and the everyday experiences of public work.

All of these changes influenced institutional cultures, including higher education. The civic-minded understandings of the core purposes of higher education gave way to a far more disciplinary, expert culture, evident in conventional conceptions of "public service" itself. Thus in her 1989 "David Dodds Henry Lecture," Donna Shalala, then chancellor of the University of Wisconsin, combined an emphasis on responsibility and service with a starkly expert model. She upheld "the ideal of a disinterested technocratic elite" fired by the moral mission of "society's best and brightest in service to its most needy." She said the imperative was "delivering the miracles of social science" to fix society's social problems just as doctors "cured juvenile rickets in the past."[17]

Shalala's perspective reflects a culture which developed over time and is characterized by focus on disciplinary identities and separation of the professoriate from public life. The consequences of this professional culture are poignantly evident in a series of interviews conducted over the last year with senior faculty at the University of Minnesota. At a critical time when faculty and administrators believe the university is in transition, many faculty feel overworked, underappreciated, and caught by conflicting demands.[18]

Among the worries expressed, faculty note two themes repeatedly. Many feel that the university's institutional culture and communal sense has changed radically. "People look out for their individual self-interests. You don't look out for the college, or the interdisciplinary group, or in some cases, even the department now," said one senior faculty who has been at the university for many years. Others described their experience of loss of connection with the university as "living in a balkanized community" and noted a "circle the wagons mentality." Charles Backstrom, a professor of political science who retired in 1987, put it poignantly:

When I came to the University of Minnesota in 1959, the political science department gave students credit for working in the community and on political campaigns. We had what some said was the finest internship program in the country. I thought of my job as including work with communities. I believed in the "Wisconsin idea" of public universities: the borders of the U were the borders of the state. I worked with the extension service in a rural public leadership program. But there was a war of cultures at the U then. I felt pressure to focus on research and publication. At the same time, I also had examples of 'rising stars' who were working with communities.

A second theme is the fear that marketplace values are overwhelming others. "We feel the need for a more moral tone in the university. A sense of overall integrity," observed an English professor. "Our values are getting inverted, with things that should be central now on the periphery. We need to regain a balance between responding to market pressures and liberal and civic values."

For all the discouragement, many faculty also express a desire for deeper public engagement, and a sense that rewards and norms should be aligned to make this possible. There is strong agreement that "for our own sake," faculty must take leadership on such questions. "If we don't do the mission, it will be done to us." This realization among the professoriate is helping to fuel the stirrings of widespread change in higher education.

RENEWING HIGHER EDUCATION AS AN AGENT OF DEMOCRACY

Signs exist of a growing ferment in higher education expressed in terms of public mission and civic renewal. In a recent volume on public work in the humanities, for instance, Jamil Zainaldin, president of the Federation of State Humanities Councils, argued that there is a new "public humanities movement" with deep civic implications. "The lifeblood of the work of the humanities councils [is] to help expand in society that realm of seriousness, that space for the pursuit of meaning, and in this work to invite the scholar to join with the public in a common search," Zainaldin proposed.[19]

Zainaldin's description of a public humanities movement finds parallels in other settings. For instance, higher education associations are increasingly taking up themes of "democracy," "civic renewal," and "civic mission." The Kettering Foundation has developed a wide network of partners in higher education interested in topics of democracy, deliberation, and civic renewal. The Association of American Colleges and Universities has had a project for several years on democracy and diversity, and it made civic renewal a central theme throughout its 1999 annual meeting. The American Association for

Higher Education's Project on Faculty Roles and Rewards made civic engagement a central question in its most recent meeting. A new "Wingspread Declaration," issued from a December 1998 conference of college presidents and leading faculty in higher education concerned with these questions, calls for a far deeper and more work-centered approach to democratic renewal. The topic was the major issue for a presidents' meeting of Campus Compact in late June 1999.

Recasting civic education as the public work of higher education holds potential to move the collective efforts in civic renewal to a new stage. But this will entail reexamination of traditional pedagogy, scholarship, the public traditions of disciplines, and systems of reward, among other things. As public cultures are recreated within institutions, the culture itself becomes a kind of overall pedagogy for such work.

If work with public purpose is the heart of a democratic people, then democracy education has to tap the interests, talents, and energies for such work, and cultivate lifelong civic habits and skills. These include the arts of public argument, civic imagination, the ability to evaluate information critically, the curiosity to listen constantly, interest in public affairs, and the ability to work with others far different from ourselves on projects that recognize multiple contributions. This is different from simple acquisition of information. Higher education viewed as dissemination of knowledge increasingly will be accomplished by the "virtual university," linked to the idea of information as commodity and student as customer. In contrast, a conception of higher education as preparing students for public life through work by diverse publics, in public, for public purposes offers an alternative to education that sees the radical erosion of its interactive dimensions, the spectre now haunting our futures.

We do not suggest that such a transformation will be easy or without turmoil. But we are convinced, on the basis of our on-the-ground experiments, our historical research, and our analysis of the current crisis, that there are large possibilities beginning to appear for public work approaches in higher education.

SHAPING INSTITUTIONAL CULTURES: THE COLLEGE OF ST. CATHERINE

Civic renewal efforts at colleges and universities hold possibility for reframing work identities, understandings of knowledge, definitions of teaching and learning, and relationships with communities. Such an experiment has been underway at the College of St. Catherine (CSC), a Catholic women's college in St. Paul, Minnesota. Although it remains a work in progress, significant lessons emerge from eight years of experience.[20]

The work has been based on the conviction that an institutional culture rich with complexity and difference is itself a key element in education for citizenship. The college has witnessed important successes, although many obstacles and challenges have emerged along the way.

The renewal effort has not been created or directed in top-down fashion by the college administration, nor has it been named as an "official" institutional initiative. The process of change is not linear. Rather, the work is organic in nature, rooted in the college's core values. It is multifaceted and has focused thus far more in the "mid-layer" of the institution. Faculty and staff have been the main initiators, with students as important players. Broad political concepts and a vision that higher education's deepest purpose is the education of citizens for full participation in democracy have guided the overall work of cultural change.

A striking outcome is a change in work patterns among faculty and between faculty and staff. For instance, in the recently revised core curriculum, a group of faculty representing each academic department and some staff members designed two interdisciplinary "bookend" courses, taught by faculty of all disciplines and required of all graduates. The curriculum design stretches teachers and students in multiple ways. It challenges reliance on the expert model for teaching and learning. Because each course is interdisciplinary and discussion-based, it calls for new ways to ensure intellectual rigor and to assess learning outcomes. Most important, the curriculum casts teaching as a public activity, not a private domain.

When faculty worldviews expand, they imagine new possibilities, including the connection of their work at the college to a broader public world. Thus, in a recent assessment forum for the capstone course, the "Global Search for Justice," Neil Elliott, a theology professor, reflected:

> We could envision this course not only as a "common experience" for students but as a common experience of CSC faculty, who are doing important work outside the college. We should think of our activist work not [as] separate from our teaching, but [as] tied to it. This course gives us the opportunity to invite students to journey with us for one semester—to share the questions we ask about social change, to join our networks, and see how we and others work for justice in a variety of areas.

Other changes are evident as well. Faculty have rethought structures and practices of self-governance. Educators have explored the dynamics of reciprocal learning relationships both within the classroom and in neighborhood settings. A group of faculty and staff is developing a structure that redefines students' paid work (work-study) as "public work," with ties to learning goals and course work.

We have seen at the college that learning is not simply an intellectual process. Common work can be a powerful catalyst for rethinking learning. The concept of work tied to learning has prompted the college to expand its understanding of where learning takes place and what it involves, and it has helped to reframe the nature of the partnerships it forms with communities. One project where this has become vivid is the Jane Addams School for Democracy (JAS), a community-based education and action initiative on the West Side of St. Paul, Minnesota.

The school is located in Neighborhood House, a 102-year-old settlement on the West Side, a longtime immigrant community. It was created as a partnership among Hmong and Latino residents, Neighborhood House, the College of St. Catherine, the Center for Democracy and Citizenship at the Humphrey Institute (University of Minnesota), and the College of Liberal Arts, also at the university. JAS is itself a mediating institution in important respects, connecting new immigrants to arenas of public policy and public life, while also serving as a space where people can learn skills of common work and express and cultivate identities of productive citizenship. For the College of St. Catherine, the Jane Addams School has provided a remarkably rich context for learning about immigrant cultures and the civic possibilities of different disciplines and professions.

The founding vision was to develop a community-located site through which college, high school students, and immigrants alike could effectively learn and work together. Inspired by Jane Addams' work at Hull House, its vision is "to free and cultivate the talents, cultures, and interests of people from diverse backgrounds and traditions in order to add their energy and wisdom to the common wealth." A guiding principle at JAS is that everyone is a learner, everyone is a teacher.

As a mediating institution, JAS catalyzes a range of public work efforts. Immigrants and their children partner with high school and college students in learning about citizenship and democracy (as well as studying for the citizenship test), language, and culture. After two and a half years, approximately 50 Hmong adults have passed the test, a remarkable achievement for the hill people of Laos who come from a nonliterate culture. Nearly 200 people are involved in various projects. Hmong veterans, college students, and faculty have worked to get congressional recognition for the contributions of Hmong veterans during the "Secret War" in Laos. A cross-cultural initiative to promote health education among Latinas and Hmong women is currently underway. The Jane Addams School has initiated an annual "Freedom Festival" on the West Side, celebrating diverse contributions to freedom and democracy. Young people and adults have undertaken farming projects, community gardens, plays, work on teen pregnancy, and issues of racism and gang violence in the high school.

JAS provides a space for immigrant families to build upon the strength of their cultures while learning about and incorporating aspects of American culture. As Aleida Benitez, one of the architects of the school and herself an immigrant from El Salvador puts it, "It is important to find common ground between the traditional values my parents instilled in me and the larger world in which I find myself."

For the College of St. Catherine, Jane Addams School provides a remarkable laboratory for cross-cultural work and civic learning, while generating opportunities for public scholarship and validating diverse forms of knowledge. For instance, the school was the setting for a seminar course, "Sociocultural Components of Clothing." Two Hmong women partnered as "community faculty" with a college professor to teach students traditional Hmong clothing and the roles of women in an agrarian culture. In other contexts, the seminar students taught Hmong immigrants U.S. history and citizenship. When college students and Hmong women created a public display of traditional costumes to show how women contribute to and sustain the culture, it became clear to all that the outcome could not have been as successful without the diverse knowledge and talents of all participants. The Hmong women taught students about women's roles and the old methods of clothing construction used in traditional Hmong life. The students (many of whom were fashion majors) shared approaches to professional display and discussed women's roles in contemporary culture.

When concepts of public work frame education, it provides a different lens. New ideas are sparked. New questions arise. For instance, using the example above, how could a professional major, such as fashion design, think about its civic dimensions? What would this mean in practical work settings? Could professional departments of all kinds include in their history and methods courses a retrieval of earlier civic practices and traditions? At a broader level, pedagogical experiments such as those at Jane Addams School that move beyond the expert model of teaching and learning bring into view central assumptions about knowledge creation. Civic renewal calls for a critical examination of epistemology.

PUBLIC ACHIEVEMENT

The projects of the Center for Democracy and Citizenship at the Humphrey Institute of Public Affairs over the last decade also suggest the possibilities of a public work approach to education (in both K-12 and higher education). For a little over a decade, the center has sought to work with many partners in democratic experiments within institutions to develop the democratic potential of work especially in professional traditions and practices.

The premise of the center's work came from a strategic analysis that many mediating institutions, which had once provided civic muscle for citizens to hold to account corporations and government, had become service delivery operations, dominated by a culture of efficiency and customer service. At the same time, we judged that professional cultures experience a crisis of meaning and practice.

The largest effort at the Center for Democracy and Citizenship is Public Achievement, a youth initiative now working with more than 25 partner schools, in seven communities and, most recently, in Northern Ireland. In Public Achievement, teams of young people ages 8 to 18 are "coached" by older teens and adults. They undertake public work projects around substantial issues that express their values and interests. We have seen the potential of such work to begin to change the basic culture of schools, including approaches to teaching and identities of students and teachers. Perhaps most importantly, as young people engage in visible, significant work, over time they develop a sense of power and confidence.

Public Achievement has taught important lessons about civic renewal and work. In the first instance, the heart of education for democracy needs to "free the powers" for public creation, as Jane Addams put it. This is one reason why the concept of public work is useful. Attention to both process and product of work is key. The education that takes place as people gain skills of working strategically in real-world settings equips them for public life and frequently leads to a transformed sense of self. "Adults won't take us seriously unless we take ourselves seriously," said Kaitlyn, a seventh grader. "What Public Achievement does is teach us about how to deal with the real world." Joe Groves, a teacher active in Public Achievement, describes what he has seen in inner-city schools. "Our kids generally come into Public Achievement feeling hopeless about the tremendous problems they see in their communities—drugs, crime, prostitution. Public Achievement unleashes hope in kids that they can actually take action to change things."

Second, attention to products, the actual creations of work for which people are accountable, in which people take pride, and through which they gain a sense of stake and ownership in their environment, adds depth and accountability to the process language associated with helping, deliberating, and serving. "I feel like I'm writing my signature on the neighborhood, so that everyone can see," said one young woman. Public products can include the material and tangible—buildings, parks, murals, and other public art, all contributions to restoring the environment. At St. Bernard's school, located in a working class neighborhood of St. Paul, a group of fifth and sixth graders created a safe neighborhood playground in an area that was thought to be too dangerous because of gangs. The students negotiated use of a lot from the parish, worked with the city for rezoning and street changes, and raised more than $60,000 to create the park. Public products also can include social or cultural creations. At the same school a group of seventh-grade girls designed a curriculum about sexual harassment that has influenced the culture of the neighborhood.

Third, public work is a way to highlight the identity shifts and the practical, organizing dimensions involved in democratic renewal. In public work, professionals (including academics) take part and lend their real skills, but they do not "fix things," or dominate. Rather they are part of a broad effort that taps diverse public talents and contributions. James Farr, a political theorist who helped to form Public Achievement's educational partnership model, explains that involvement in Public Achievement has changed his teaching and his work. "I went into political science because I liked politics," Farr recounts. "But political theory was about as close as it got. Political science seemed very distant from public life. I felt a great gap between why I went into the field and what I was doing." Public Achievement offered new strategies for teaching. "It gave my students a great opportunity to try out theories of democratic education and citizenship in real-life settings." It also provided Farr opportunities for communicating in more public ways. "In a university setting, you become used to speaking a language of political theory or social science," Farr explained. "But you are not challenged to speak in ways that engage the real world. Here, suddenly when you have to speak with teachers, principals, parents, community leaders, and kids, it becomes a whole different thing." It wasn't abstract. "Talk follows work. You learn to communicate with people as you are engaged in real projects, not the other way around. This is much more real than a focus on 'learning to communicate' in the abstract."

Farr's experiences find parallels with Hmong women who serve as community faculty in the course on culture and clothing design at the Jane Addams School. Such common work offers multiple spaces and occasions for shifts in power relationships, because it focuses on what different groups have to offer to the common product—not what position they occupy.

Finally, Public Achievement suggests a kind of "craft" approach to power where the point is not mobilization or advocacy but rather freeing the distinctive spirit and developing the public aspects of schools. In several of the Public Achievement school sites teachers and staff, with effective organizing, have undertaken substantial change in teaching and institutional cultures. When this happens, the public culture itself becomes both product of and context for learning democratic skills. The institution comes to see its role in new terms. In the spring of 1999, St. Bernard's had organized a lecture and discussion series of national leaders, as part of its intention to be a visible national leader in "Catholic education for democracy and social justice."

St. Bernard's school and the College of St. Catherine indicate what a public work framework offers for institutional renewal and education for democracy.

The framework moves the current conversation of civic education to a new stage with broad political possibilities.

The democratic potential of the politics of public work lies in its capacity to enlist a variety of ideological positions. A public work approach does not eliminate the fierce debates about distributive justice or questions of values, but it allows people with great differences on such issues to work together on public tasks of large significance. Thus it constitutes a politics that is simultaneously full of diverse voices and also transformative and far-ranging in its potential impact.

CONCLUSION

At a recent conference on the world democracy movement hosted by the Kettering Foundation involving democracy activists from around the world, Juan Antonio Blanco, a former official in the Cuban Mission at the United Nations now heading an international civil rights effort, argued that we stand at a pivotal moment.

> We once assumed there was one possible future—whether it was Marxism, Christianity, or liberal capitalism. No longer. It is now clear that humanity is at an historical crossroads. How the future develops depends upon us. And it depends especially on whether we articulate a compelling vision of democracy that is an alternative to the versions that now predominate around the world, which people know are not working.[21]

In the information society developing at the threshold of a new millennium, we once again are faced with the necessity to choose how we understand democracy and ourselves, in a fashion analogous to the nation's founding. This is not to minimize the obstacles. Like our ancestors who could scarcely conceive of themselves other than as loyal British subjects, many today find it hard even to imagine a future different than the current expert-dominated, consumer society. Yet as in that age when people created a new map for their society and new identities for themselves within it, alternative ideas of democracy and of ourselves as public actors can help us to imagine the future we want to build.

It is time to move from theory about what is wrong to action that builds such a future. All of us associated with higher education—faculty, students, administrators, staff, boards of trustees, and community partners—must rise to the occasion. We can reshape our institutions. We can build a future that is not fragmented or dominated by the values of the marketplace.

Institutions and leaders who take up this challenge of public creation can reshape our age. Higher education is positioned in unique fashion. We hold the power to be midwives of democracy's rebirth.

MODELS OF DEMOCRACY, CITIZENSHIP, AND HIGHER EDUCATION			
	Civics	**Communitarian**	**Commonwealth**
What is democracy?	Representative institutions, the rule of law	Representative government and civil society	Democracy as the work of the people, building public institutions and other public goods
What is the aim of politics?	Distribution of goods, services (who gets what, how, when)	Spirit of community	Creating the commons
Citizenship	Voter, consumer	Community member, volunteer	Civic producer, "public worker"
Government role	"For the people": to provide services, guarantee rights (exemplar: LBJ)	"Of the people": to express and promote civic values, common understanding (exemplar: WJC)	"By the people": to catalyze public work; provide tools for public work (exemplar: FDR)
Higher education	Creation of expert knowledge; career preparation	Cultivation of character through moral education, service-learning	Development of public imagination, capacities for public work through multiple public work experiences and reflection

This table describes approaches to citizenship and higher education based on three ways democracy and citizenship are understood: 1) The "civics" approach in which citizenship is mainly the act of voting; and the citizen is an individual bearer of rights (with a few other responsibilities such as paying taxes) and a consumer of benefits; 2) the "civil society or communitarian" approach in which the model citizen is the volunteer, citizens are responsible members of a community and citizenship education focuses on teaching character and habits of voluntary involvement; and 3) the "commonwealth" approach in which citizens do public work and are producers of public things. None of the approaches is "wrong"—but the common- wealth approach develops a much more robust understanding of civic agency, points to the challenges of civic renewal (tapping the powers and energies of people for public tasks) in a variety of institutions, not simply "community"; and develops an identity of "civic producer" that is clearly different than consumer and victim.

NOTES

1. Jefferson quoted from S. Morse, *Renewing Civic Capacity: Preparing College Students for Service and Citizenship* (Washington, DC: Association for the Study of Higher Education, 1989): 27; Morse points out that early colleges and universities had three aims: the promotion of common culture, the teaching of moral philosophy which was to guide students, and the production of civic leadership.
2. Quoted from I. Harkavy, "School-Community Partnerships" (Paper presented to the Joint Forum of the U.S. Department of Education and HUD, 8 January 1998).
3. Petition quoted from R. Kluger, *Simple Justice: The History of Brown v. Board of Education* (New York: Vintage, 1977), 2; Working Men's Committee quoted from *Humphrey Institute Leadership Program Essays* (Minneapolis, MN: Humphrey Institute, 1989), 305.

4. J. Bell, quoted in D. Broder, "GOP Replays Refrain on 'Values'," *Minneapolis Tribune* (23 May 1992).

5. Quoted from the final report of the National Commission on Civic Renewal, *A Nation of Spectators: How Civic Disengagement Weakens America and What We Can Do About It* (College Park: University of Maryland, 1998): 8–9.

6. As Wood observed, this "was momentously radical in the long sweep of world history up to that time." G.S. Wood, *The Radicalism of the American Revolution* (New York: Vintage Press, 1991), ix; for an extensive treatment, see H. Boyte and N.N. Kari, *Building America: The Democratic Promise of Public Work* (Philadelphia: Temple University Press), chapter two.

7. Quoted from C. Greer, *The Great School Legend* (New York: Basic Books, 1972), 15.

8. For discussion of these experiences and interviews, see Boyte and Kari, *Building America* (Philadelphia: Temple University Press, 1996), chapter five; F. Green, *The Civilian Conservation Corps: Building a Legacy* (Minneapolis, MN: Center for Democracy and Citizenship, 1999).

9. Excerpted from L. Hughes, "Freedom's Plow" in *Selected Poems of Langston Hughes* (New York: Random House, 1987), 293.

10. E. Foner, *The Story of American Freedom* (New York: Norton, 1998), 110.

11. J. Addams, *On Education* (New Brunswick, NJ: Transaction Publishers, 1994), 98–99.

12. S. Peters, *The Promise of Association: A History of the Mission and Work of the YMCA at the University of Illinois, 1873–1997* (Champaign, IL: YMCA, 1997).

13. E.D. Ross, *Democracy's College: The Land Grant Movement in the Formative Stage* (Ames: Iowa State College, 1942), 22. This discussion draws from Scott Peters's groundbreaking research into the largely forgotten public work history of land grant and public universities and cooperative extension when he was a graduate researcher at the Center for Democracy and Citizenship from 1993–1997. For further discussion, see S. Peters, "Extension Work as Public Work: Rethinking Cooperative Extension's Civic Mission (Ph.D. diss., University of Minnesota, 1998).

14. For a discussion of these contending currents and the craft-based approach favored by farmers, see G.W. Stevenson and R.M. Klemme, "Advisory/Oversight Councils: An Approach to Farmer/Citizenship Participation in Agenda-Setting at Land-Grant University," *American Journal of Alternative Agriculture*, 7 (1992): 111–17.

15. L.H. Bailey, *York State Rural Problems* (Albany, NY: J. B. Lyon Co., 1913), 11–12.

16. Ibid., 29–30, 133.

17. D. Shalala, "Mandate for a New Century: Reshaping the Research University's Role in Social Policy," (Eleventh David Dodds Henry Lecture, Urbana-Champaign, IL: University of Illinois, 1989), 9, 16.

18. These interviews were conducted by H. Boyte and E. Fogelman from September 1997–December 1998 as part of a planning process to develop a "civic mission project" at the University of Minnesota.

19. J. Zainaldin, "The Realm of Seriousness," in *Standing with the Public: The Humanities and Democratic Practice*, ed. J.F. Veninga and N. McAfee (Dayton, OH: Kettering Foundation Press, 1997): 97–98.

20. The St. Catherine experiences are described at length in N.N. Kari, "Political Ideas: Catalysts for Creating a Public Culture," in *The Power of "Big Ideas": Conceptual Organizing, Education for Democracy and Public Work*, ed. H.C. Boyte, et al. (Dayton, OH: Kettering Press, forthcoming).

21. Quoted from transcribed discussion, International Civil Society Exchange, sponsored by the Kettering Foundation, Fort Lauderdale, FL (3 February 1999).

PART 2

· · · · · · · · · · · ·

What Are Colleges and Universities Doing about the Problems: An Overview

CHAPTER 4

The College and University as Citizen

Nancy L. Thomas

T he 1980s was an era of public disenchantment and cynicism toward nearly all government activities. The ripple effect of these attitudes on colleges and universities was hardhitting. Higher education "took it on the chin" for many alleged failings: for maintaining "Ivory Tower" aloofness and indifference; for producing abstract research unconnected to real-life problems; for abandoning the humanities, the classics, and "core" curriculum; for yielding to the political sensitivities of "60s radicals" who resisted traditional Western beliefs and values; for allowing, if not commanding, faculty members to research to the detriment of their teaching; for catering to "victims' groups" at the expense of constitutional rights of free speech and equal protection; and for producing poorly educated students who are not only unprepared for work life but who also have no "souls."

Institutions responded with a flurry of activity, much of it aimed at fostering values through curricular and cocurricular activities. Responses included introducing or expanding "values education" courses, interdisciplinary curricula, first-year programs, and capstone courses for graduating seniors; restoring required ethics and philosophy courses; examining the "core curriculum"; establishing community service requirements for students; and incorporating service-learning in isolated courses.

Despite these changes, public disenchantment persisted and higher education leaders continued to call for change. Ernest Boyer of the Carnegie Foundation for the Advancement of Teaching expressed his concern as follows:

> [W]hat I find most disturbing . . . is a growing feeling in this country that higher education is, in fact, part of the problem rather than the solution. Going still further, that it's become a private benefit, not a public good. Increasingly, the campus is being viewed as a place where students get credentialed and faculty get tenured, while the overall work for the academy does not seem particularly relevant to the nation's most pressing civic, social, economic, and moral problems.[1]

Proposing a new paradigm for the role of the academy, Boyer spoke of expanding higher education "more productively into the marketplace of ideas." He challenged the academy to broaden the scope of scholarship and to pursue what he called a "scholarship of engagement." He explained

> At one level, the scholarship of engagement means connecting the rich resources of the university to our most pressing social, civic and ethical problems. . . . Increasingly, I'm convinced that ultimately, the scholarship of engagement also means creating a special climate in which the academic and civic culture communicate more continuously and more creatively with each other. . . . Scholarship has to prove its worth not on its own terms, but by service to the nation and the world.[2]

Reaching out to local, national, and global communities is not new to higher education. Colleges and universities have historically supported many activities—including cooperative extension programs, continuing education, clinics, faculty consulting, and student volunteerism—that contribute to their outreach missions. Yet despite these longstanding activities, colleges and universities continue to be criticized as "disconnected from" public life or "unresponsive to" society's pressing problems. Why has public discontent persisted? Why did Ernest Boyer, a leader in higher education, call for the higher education community to reexamine its priorities?[3]

Colleges and universities are not ignoring their civic responsibilities, but perhaps they could be taking them more seriously internally and externally. Common outreach and public service activities generally occupy a marginal status on campus. They tend to be isolated units or projects, disconnected from rather than integral to academic functions. Commensurate with this peripheral status is modest support, recognition, planning, evaluation, and understanding internally. Externally, colleges and universities simply do not appear to be deeply immersed, as citizens, in problem solving and collaboration with local or regional communities.

This may be changing. Many institutions, particularly in urban areas, are reexamining how they fulfill their public service, outreach, and civic missions, and are struggling with the question, "what works?" They are rewriting mission statements; implementing innovative strategic plans; reforming curricula to incorporate themes of civic, social, and moral issues; partnering with community groups; forming and supporting centers, institutes, centralized coordinating offices, and partnerships; encouraging individual and collective entrepreneurial faculty activity; revising promotion and tenure standards; and increasing visibility and support for civic activities. The projects vary in scope, leadership, mission, structure, and even reception on campus. And while each initiative resulted from a unique confluence of individual passions, community needs, political influences, and special circumstances, common themes nonetheless emerge.

This chapter examines how colleges and universities use their resources to contribute to the civic mission of the institution. Specifically, it examines 10 historical and contemporary institutional activities relating to civic engagement and education:

1. curriculum reform and pedagogy;
2. cooperative extension and continuing education programs;
3. clinical programs and field-based learning opportunities for students in professional programs;
4. top-down administrative initiatives;
5. centralized administrative-academic units with outreach missions;
6. academically based centers and institutes;
7. faculty professional service and academic outreach;
8. student initiatives;
9. institutional initiatives with an economic or political purpose; and
10. access to facilities and cultural events.

The chapter then examines elements essential to developing and sustaining these initiatives.[4] A primary goal of this chapter is to review how higher education can renew and enhance its civic mission, not to the detriment of, but *in connection with* its traditional academic mission.

A COMMENT ON SCOPE AND TERMS

What is meant by the "civic mission" in higher education? Some educators link higher education's civic responsibilities to academic functions—teaching and research—while others highlight "outreach" or "public service" activities. Michigan State University links these functions by recognizing academic outreach (defined as "knowledge made available and accessible to external audiences," Fear and Sandmann, 1995).[5] Do well-run academic outreach programs fulfill, even partly, an institution's civic mission? If an institution provides a "service"[6] to an external community—through research, a volunteer project, or access to its facilities—does that advance the institution's civic mission? Or should the discussion center on student development and how higher education can produce graduates who harbor a deep understanding of and commitment to "the arts of democracy—dialogue, engagement, and responsible participation."[7]

At the risk of oversimplifying the discussion and for the purpose of this chapter, the short answers are, "yes, yes, and yes." The "engaged campus" involves multiple constituencies and programs of the institution. It employs new approaches to democratic learning that emphasize citizenship in the context of social, sexual, ethnic, and racial differences. Higher education's civic mission should be reflected in an integrated approach to fostering students' citizenship skills through both educational and cocurricular programs and activities and conscious modeling of good institutional citizenship through external partnerships and activities. The typologies reviewed in this chapter reflect these approaches.

RESPONSIVE CURRICULA

From its historical mission rooted in training religious and civic leaders, higher education sought to address societal needs and values through academic programs. Yet current societal demands, global problems, local needs, and demographic changes make curricular design simultaneously more complex, challenging, innovative, and energizing than ever before. Arguably, courses and programs provide the primary forums for enhancing students' understanding of and commitment to the principles of democracy and engaged citizenship.

Higher education has come a long way from the traditional "Western Civilization" requirement. Initiatives that educate students for citizenship include:

- Civic themes and issues—that prepare students to live and work in a culturally diverse society—across the curriculum
- Courses and programs—often interdisciplinary—on ethics, moral reasoning, and professional responsibility that stress practical application and problem solving
- For-credit programs during spring breaks, winter recesses, and summer vacations that send students abroad, to developing countries, or to poor American communities where students can simultaneously learn and serve
- First-year programs that link academic and residential life to studies on pressing civic, societal, and moral issues
- Capstone courses and senior seminars, often requiring team work, that include civic projects or themes

- Interdisciplinary majors or minors in environmental studies, urban studies, women's studies, cultural or ethnic studies
- Service-learning, community-based learning, and experiential learning that link traditional learning experiences with service to a non-profit or community-based organization or initiative
- Learning communities, curricular clusters that link two or more disciplines in the exploration of common—often civic—themes
- Collaborative learning across the curriculum
- Portfolio projects through which students demonstrate their civic skills and community contributions

This section looks at some innovative examples of these curricular methods.

Core Curricula

Most colleges and universities underscore social issues and problem-solving through courses, minors, or concentrations. Some institutions, however, stress civic themes in a significant percentage of the general education requirements. At St. Edward's University in Austin, Texas, 18 of the 57 credit hours in general education are devoted to a program called "Cultural Foundations," a curriculum designed to help students develop an understanding and appreciation for multiple cultures. Students take six team-taught courses in four years. The courses are interdisciplinary and consider Western and non-Western societies, third-world cultures, and global issues. Faculty members emphasize multicultural viewpoints, individual and public responsibility, notions of "the common good," and strong writing and participatory discussion skills.

Cultural Foundations

This includes a community-based learning component. Students work with community agencies and nonprofits to identify local problems and solutions. They then write about the problem and present the solution to the town council or mayor orally.

In their senior year, all students must complete a capstone project. Focusing on a local, national, or global issue, students must write a significant ("potentially publishable") paper that reflects their best critical thinking and problem-solving efforts.

Community-Based Learning

Educators agree that students should be able to connect theory with practice. Community-based learning (and related pedagogies of service-learning, experiential learning, active learning, and internships) enables students to link theory and practice while they also learn important lessons in civic responsibility. How community-based learning is incorporated into courses varies, but common denominators include traditional academic study (reading assignments, class discussions and lectures, writing assignments, and evaluation), community service that is linked to the academic component of the course ("volunteering" in a relevant community organization or agency, acting as a consultant by conducting research, or managing a project) and structured reflection (journals, papers, and/or presentations) to link the academic and service components.[8]

Some examples of community-based learning include:

- Students in two courses—psychology and creative writing—work in pairs to make weekly visits throughout the semester to homebound elderly persons. Their task is to write a short biography.
- Students in literature classes run book club sessions for high school teachers, residents of long-term care facilities, or student athletes at local schools.
- Students in two separate courses—one on environmental studies and the other in political science—serve as a team of researchers (collecting historical data and interviewing community members likely to be affected) for a town struggling with the decision to place a desperately needed new middle school on a town park.[9]
- Students work closely with faculty members to design a leadership program for residents of a nearby housing authority.

Service-learning does not belong in every course, nor should faculty members try to incorporate it into courses with a "one size fits all" approach. Robert Bringle, director of the Center for Public Service and Leadership at Indiana University-Purdue University at Indianapolis (IUPUI) cautions, "I don't have the idea . . . that service-learning solves all problems and everybody should do it. Just as not every course will involve a laboratory, for example, or has to require a term paper." Nonetheless, he believes that service-learning can bring about a certain kind of learning, reflected in IUPUI's flyer to students: "Tell me and I forget. Teach me and I remember. Involve me and I learn." [10]

Learning Communities

Wagner College in New York integrates what Provost Richard Guarasci calls "relational learning" [11] with community-based learning to stress civic and democratic participation, writing, interpretive reading, and persuasive argument. As part of the core curriculum, all students must complete 3 of 16 team-taught learning communities offered. Examples from the 1998–99 academic year include:

- "Politics and Business: An Analysis of 20th Century Scandals" (examining scandals such as toxic-waste dumps, political corruption, the Challenger space-shuttle disaster, and sexual harassment)
- "Changing the Rules of the Game: Power, Wealth, and Societal Response" (an examination of economic policies and distribution of scarce resources in society)
- "Social and Moral Perspectives on Contemporary Issues" (applying concepts of moral reasoning to societal issues such as affirmative action, welfare, date rape, and bilingual education)
- "Literature and Politics: Reading/Writing America" (with a focus on cultural diversity, a comparison—based on the views of novelists and political scientists—between mainstream and minority visions of citizenship)

Students conduct field work at community sites such as hospitals, schools, government agencies, and neighborhood organizations. They write on their experiences by keeping journals or writing in-depth analytic papers.

First-Year Programs

Many institutions offer first-year programs or courses designed to increase student attention to issues of racial, ethnic, or sexual diversity; environmental issues; and interdisciplinary approaches to solving pressing social problems. At St. Lawrence University in Canton, New York, faculty members tackled several perceived internal problems on campus as well: an "anti-intellectual" attitude among students, a powerful Greek system and the associated overuse of alcohol and student misconduct, and a curriculum that failed to stress society's pressing needs, particularly concerning race, class, and gender. They sought ways to engage students, enhance the intellectual climate, and support students in balancing their academic and social lives.

The result was a two-semester, team-taught, interdisciplinary course required of all first-year students called the First Year Program ("FYP"). Groups of 45 students live in "residential colleges" where they work closely with three faculty members who stress "the interconnection of community and personal development" as well as research, writing, and oral skills. Program-wide requirements include a significant research paper, extensive faculty and mentor advisement, a science experiment, and common themes of responsibility to society and community, distribution of resources, and the environment, gender, and race.

The university committed significant financial and human resources to the FYP. It renovated dormitories to accommodate classrooms and faculty offices. Faculty members take leaves from their departments for a three-year commitment to the program. The college hires new faculty members to replace members of departments who rotate into the FYP. The student judiciary code was revised to give the residential colleges the autonomy and opportunity to address student grievances and transgressions through their own "social contracts." Graduate student resident assistants are specially trained to participate in the program. A mentoring program provides first-year students with upper class role models in residence.

Capstone Experiences

Around the turn of the century, it was not unusual for seniors to take a culminating course on ethics or leadership skills, often taught by the president of the university. The contemporary version is a senior project within the student's major, usually involving a significant research paper.

Some institutions require students to participate in a senior experience that involves the pedagogies reviewed in this section. Portland State University requires all students to complete a senior capstone before graduating. Students must select from pre-designed learning communities. Students work collaboratively. The capstones vary in length and intensity. For example, the capstone "Outdoor Education/Recreation for the Handicapped" is an intensive, two-week, live-in capstone course for seniors interested in careers in human services. Students teach and care for children and adults with severe disabilities. In the "Social Capital in Portland Neighborhoods" capstone, students work in area neighborhoods to develop a plan for citizen participation in local affairs.

To summarize, pedagogical trends include the following points:

- What and how students learn is being reframed to fulfill higher education's civic mission in a diverse democracy
- Colleges are linking and reorienting curricular, cocurricular, and residential life to address issues of community and citizenship
- Courses and programs place less emphasis on specific disciplines and more emphasis on problem-based learning [12] (e.g., "real-world" problems and solutions, current issues, cultural pluralism, global issues, and democratic concepts)
- Team taught, multidisciplinary approaches—particularly in the form of learning communities—are growing
- Collaborative and cooperative learning techniques are replacing individual projects and assignments
- The focus is on learning rather than teaching
- Linking academic study, community service, and reflection—community-based learning—is receiving widespread support

- Courses or programs along these lines are required, providing commonality to all students' learning experiences on campus
- While these pedagogies were once reserved for liberal arts programs, many professional schools and institutions are revising their curricula to produce competent professionals who have a corresponding civic commitment
- Efforts to engage students begin in the first year, but continue in upper classes, sometimes culminating in multifaceted capstone courses involving community-based learning or community projects, team work, and real-world problem solving

SERVICE STEMMING FROM AN EARLY MISSION: THE LAND GRANT/COOPERATIVE MODEL

While nearly all colleges and universities can point to their civic roots, land-grant universities are the foremost institutions established specifically to ground higher education within a public context. Through the Morrill Act of 1862, the federal government awarded funds to states to create universities with open access and a curriculum grounded in practical and applied research and teaching. As the nation shifted from a rural, agricultural society to a more industrial and urban one, so did the focus of public service activities in land-grant institutions. In most recent years, continuing education and cooperative extension programs are directed to adult learning and professional development.

Most land-grant universities are organized so that extension programs and continuing education are separate units, at the fringe of traditional academics. They are separately funded and administered. They draw from a pool of instructors—the "service" professionals, sometimes called "instructors" or "staff"—who are not on a tenure track, not part of an academic unit, and are often adjunct or one-time teachers.

Some institutions integrate cooperative extension and continuing education programs with traditional academic units. One such institution is Oregon State University (OSU). Concerned by competing interests regarding state forests (particularly the spotted owl verses the logging industry), institutional leaders developed a new initiative for "dependent communities." Both extension and traditional faculty were invited to attend a meeting on the initiative. The interest level was high and represented a broad cross-section of disciplines. After enthusiastic discussion on what each discipline could contribute to the initiative, one faculty member observed, "Yes, but I cannot afford to pursue this. It will not be recognized as valid scholarship." "*That*," observed OSU's Vice President for Academic Affairs Roy Arnold, "got everyone's attention." A task force was formed and charged with examining whether

OSU's reward structure aligned with its mission. After a year-long series of discussions, the conclusion was that it did not. In response, the institution amended its promotion and tenure standards based on Boyer's *Scholarship Reconsidered*. OSU's most ambitious adjustments include integrating the cooperative extension and continuing education programs into the mainstream campus and realigning extension field staff with academic colleges and departments. All extension faculty members are part of academic departments where they hold full faculty status, undergo annual evaluation as faculty, and can achieve tenure. Promotion and tenure guidelines were revised. The traditional approach of rewarding teaching, research, and service was replaced by a system that recognized four forms of scholarly activity: discovery, integration, the application or development of knowledge, and creative artistry. Peers evalutate scholarly achievement "based on its quality, originality, and impact on or significance to the public beyond the University."[13]

Arnold reports that the new guidelines "are working," but he cautions that changes of this kind must be accompanied by training, orientation, discussion, and a particular focus on departments (where scholarship is assessed). He stresses, "The challenge is to bring external needs to the attention of the faculty, and let them loose on a problem. This is best accomplished at the academic unit level."

The University of Georgia at Athens (UGA) offers an interesting comparison. There, public service is noteworthy because the program is extremely large and comprehensive. In its Public Service and Extension Annual Report for 1995–96, UGA reported that "Citizens from all walks of life in every community and nook and cranny of the state were the recipients of outreach educational activities.[14] In 1995–96, faculty members secured $31,356,959 in contracts and grants to support public service initiatives.

At UGA, a centralized office for public service is responsible for planning and promoting a university-wide agenda for public service, overseeing cooperative extension, continuing education, and institutes and centers; maintaining statistics; and publishing reports and data. Each school on campus has a position of "outreach director," whose office is responsible for linking the university's public service mission with academic units. Outreach directors report to the deans who then file reports with the vice president for service on outreach projects.

Like most land-grant institutions, UGA offers separate tracks for university professors and extension instructors. Some faculty members carry joint status. The public service rank is designed for public service professionals who have "only an indirect relation to research in the pure sense and [whose work] may or may not lend itself to publication in traditional academic journals."[15] Although not tenured, public service faculty members have an expectation of continued employment. Their contracts are twelve-month agreements (rather than nine).

Public service remains a criterion for promotion at the professorial rank. As part of their written requirements, faculty members in academic units are expected to engage in service, defined in the promotion and tenure guidelines as "the integrated application of knowledge through research, teaching and technical assistance to solve problems confronting an ever-changing and increasingly complex society." The guidelines also stress that "the University distinguishes between routine performance [of service] and service that draws upon the breadth and depth of scholarship." Tenure-track faculty members with service responsibilities deliver it at a quality level reflecting scholarship.

Michigan State University's (MSU) approach to its cooperative extension and continuing education functions is evolving. Structurally, it looks like most land-grant institutions. Centralized leadership comes from the Office of the Vice Provost for University Outreach. What is unique is the institution's effort to shift mindsets—both on campus and nationally—regarding "academic outreach." "The essence of our thinking about outreach," according to MSU spokespeople, is in the following definition: "Outreach is a form of scholarship that cuts across teaching, research, and service. It involves generating, transmitting, applying, and preserving knowledge for the direct benefit of external audiences in ways that are consistent with university and unit missions."[16]

This view of outreach as a crosscutting enterprise seems to be taking hold. Respected outreach efforts by faculty members include redesigning courses to include service-learning for students; applied and action research; consulting (undertaken with an academic unit's program or mission in mind); and redesigning the public's accessibility to knowledge through distance, time, place, format, and approach changes in how knowledge is transmitted (e.g., offering a course at a convenient time and place given the subject matter and constituency).

Beyond treating outreach as a crosscutting enterprise, MSU refined how it responds to external constituencies. Like most land-grants, MSU formerly aimed programs at interest groups (e.g., farmers or aspiring politicians or teachers), offering pre-designed courses with established curricula. MSU calls this "instructional" outreach (emphasis on transmitting knowledge). MSU's new approach adds "problem-focused" outreach (emphasis on generating and applying knowledge) efforts. For "problem-focused" outreach, MSU asks, first, what problems does the external community face, and second, drawing from all of the institution's resources and expertise, what partnerships and collaborative efforts can be formed to address those pressing problems (Fear and Sandmann, 1995, p.119)? [17, 18]

The results? In a 1995 survey of the 2,000 MSU faculty members, more than 65 percent reported that they were involved in outreach activities to a moderate degree; more than 40 percent said that their involvement was considerable; and 90 percent stated an intention to become involved within three years. Those numbers are growing, reports Lorilee Sandmann, MSU's director of Community Outreach. Perhaps more significant, Sandmann says attitudes are changing. Although cooperative extension and field faculty members continue to follow a separate promotion track and are still called "staff," "outreach scholarship" is becoming more respected among tenured and tenure-track faculty members. Some, Sandmann reports, are "really excited" about the notion of outreach scholarship.

To summarize, contemporary models of extension programs and continuing education at land-grant institutions share these features:

1. The lines between cooperative extension services/adult education and the traditional academic units are being blurred, but for the most part, not dissolved.
2. Attitudes are changing. At some institutions, tenure is available to qualified "service staff," and "academic outreach" or "outreach scholarship" are recognized as valid forms of scholarship for traditional faculty members.
3. Centralized offices for public service and outreach are being complemented by academic outreach offices in schools and colleges.
4. "Instructional outreach" remains the primary form of outreach activities, however, more outreach is "problem-focused." Such interdisciplinary, cross-cutting efforts are tailored to address pressing, identified problems.
5. Courses are designed to be more responsive to community needs in terms of time, place, format, and approach.
6. Outreach activities are being evaluated and reviewed for their quality, impact on a community, and scholarly contribution.

OUTREACH AT PROFESSIONAL SCHOOLS

All medical schools run clinical programs through their own or affiliated hospitals so that students can obtain the requisite hands-on training after their course work. Law schools offer optional clinical programs for students, generally with themes such as environmental law or landlord-tenant clinics. Engineering schools link students with agencies or businesses to provide field-based learning opportunities. Schools of education collaborate with school districts to design and implement reforms. Business schools involve students, either through courses or voluntary cocurricular opportunities, in economic development programs designed to promote urban renewal. These programs traditionally focus on student learning and, like cooperative extension and continuing education, serve a peripheral status on most campuses. Faculty members are usually involved only as advisors/teachers.

Institutions nationally are reexamining their professional schools' clinical programs in recognition of the significant impact they can have on a community. The Center for Healthy Communities at Wright State University in Ohio, for example, involves a partnership between the Schools of Medicine, Nursing, Professional Psychology, and Social Work at Wright State University, the Kettering Medical Center, the Allied Health Division at nearby Sinclair Community College, Dayton Public Schools, public housing, health, and hospitals in the area, and local volunteer and action groups. Unlike traditional models, the center's clinical experiences occur not only in the hospital but also in area ambulatory units, schools, community walk-in clinics, housing projects, churches, the area YMCA, homeless shelters, and through visiting nurse associations and volunteer care providers.

The center also solicits grants for faculty applied research, sponsors faculty development, compiles statistics, publishes a newsletter and quarterly reports, and serves as a liaison to the community. The faculty reward system was restructured so that professional service and applied research are recognized forms of scholarship.[19]

In New Haven, Connecticut, a city plagued by high violent crime and death rates in the late 1980s, local police officers, state child welfare workers, and neighborhood activists work with the Yale School of Medicine Child Development and Community Policing Program. CDCP offers a 24-hour hotline, seminars for police officers on basic concepts of child development, training of faculty members (through in-services and "ride-alongs") on police practices and perspectives, and consulting on demanding cases. If a child witnesses a violent crime, a psychologist and a social worker from Yale come immediately to the crime scene. Clinicians follow up by providing families with in-home services and optional assessments and psychotherapy. Police referred more than 1,000 cases to the CDCP between 1991 and 1997. The program is now reaching beyond Connecticut. With financial support from the U.S. Department of Justice, CDCP offers a replication program and is establishing programs in 10 cities nationally and one internationally.

Outreach efforts through professional schools are not limited to urban institutions. In West Virginia, the state's most pressing problems exist in rural areas. In the 1980s, West Virginia University's School of Medicine organized a two-way audio system, called the Medical Access and Referral System (MARS). MARS gave rural physicians access to university medical experts at any of the statewide system's 10 locations. Seeing a need for visual presentations, the university expanded MARS to form "MDTV," a two-way video communication network that enables specialists at major medical centers to see and talk with patients and their local physicians throughout the state. MDTV also offers continuing education programs in medicine, nursing, pharmacy, microbiology, radiology, dentistry, social work, psychiatry, and other subjects. Because clinical conferences such as grand rounds in pediatrics and emergency medicine are also offered, MDTV has become an integral training tool for medical residents and interns in rural settings.

To summarize, contemporary trends regarding outreach at professional schools include:

1. Activities that are both problem-centered *and* instruction-centered. Problem-centered outreach is responsive to an identified community need rather than a broadly defined group.
2. The time, place, and manner of the outreach activity that are tailored to address identified community needs.
3. Projects that consist of partnerships between outside government agencies, private interest groups, community organizations, and multiple academic units of the institution.

TOP-DOWN ADMINISTRATIVE INITIATIVES

Institutional leaders, including trustees, academic affairs officers, deans, and particularly presidents, can play an important role in a community. They serve on local boards, speak at public and private events, host parties or provide a forum for addressing particular issues, and comment for the media about current events. Sometimes, however, institutional leaders assume an entrepreneurial, if not activist, role. And when institutional leaders at the very top are involved with a community, the result can be transformational, externally and internally.

When Paul Elsner started as chancellor of the Maricopa Community College District (MCCD) in Phoenix, Arizona, in 1977, he envisioned his institution as a set of community-focused learning centers. Within one year, he opened the Rio Salado campus, a "college without walls" that focuses on partnerships with businesses, government agencies, nonprofit organizations, and other educational organizations. Most courses are offered on site. Elsner developed "Fast Forward," a nationally recognized training program in labor relations, and then set up "Visions," an internship program for staff interested in exploring career alternatives. He built fitness and wellness centers open to neighboring communities, not simply faculty, staff, and students.

In 1997, to enhance his emphasis on outreach as central to MCCD's mission, Elsner created the Office for the Community Agenda and placed it next to his office. In 1997, the Office for the Community Agenda took an inventory of community outreach programs and partnerships system-wide. The inventory revealed hundreds of examples of community outreach efforts stemming from its 10 colleges. Too many to list, some examples include community partnerships (e.g., youth training programs, summer youth programs, school-to-work initiatives); literacy and adult learning programs, many with multicultural themes; one-day service events (e.g., Clean Up Day, "cyclefests"); and the "Chair Academy," a nationally attended training program for department chairs.

MCCD offers an unusual employee development program. Called "Creative Pathways," all employees may take a paid "sabbatical" to pursue an interest or enhance skills. Placements must be "intellectually stimulating, academically rigorous, community relevant, and/or philanthropic." Most placements are with nonprofit organizations, community service groups, or government agencies. To illustrate, a bookkeeper on campus (and a horse owner off campus) obtained a leave one day a week so that she could volunteer at South Mountain Park, the largest urban park in the United States. Among the park's attractions are many ancient American Indian ruins. The employee rides to these obscure areas, checking them weekly.

Another dynamic leader is Evan Dobelle at Trinity College in Hartford, Connecticut. Selected by Trinity's board of trustees to implement an "urban strategy," Dobelle (a former politician and community college president) seemed like an unusual choice for this traditional liberal arts college. His well-publicized "neighborhood revitalization plan" (a collaborative venture involving area hospitals and the local public radio station) involves transforming 15 neighboring blocks into an educational, business, and residential community with science, medical, and technology themes. The plan runs the gamut from the significant (raising more than $200 million for schools, job training, mortgage assistance, family services, and physical improvements), to the practical (turning a nine-acre abandoned bus station/yard into three new schools), to the symbolic (removing previously locked gates to the outside community). The plan includes a Learning Corridor Campus; Boys and Girls Clubs on campus; a family resource center; child care facilities; a job training center; "Streetscape Improvements" such as improved street lighting, new landscaping, and attractive fencing; a Health and Technology Center; a community-based arts program; and a new police station. The college buys dilapidated buildings, renovates them, and then sells them back to local residents with reduced-rate mortgages. Trinity provides housing subsidies to those who also take advantage of the plan's educational or vocational opportunities.

Not surprisingly, change on campus has not kept up with the frenetic pace set by Dobelle, but faculty members and administrators report a shift in attitude and institutional culture. The urban theme envisioned by the board of trustees and the link between the neighborhood revitalization and Trinity's academic program is gaining strength. Raymond Baker, the dean of the faculty, is "rethinking" liberal arts. Calling it "the second part of the plan," Baker speaks of his vision of "liberal arts . . . with a difference." About 15 (of

150 campus-wide) faculty members already produce what he calls "seamless" work that integrates research, teaching, and community service.

Trinity's efforts are unique in many respects. First, they are trustee-generated, although the obvious catalyst is its unusual president. Second, while many other institutions are reaching out to their communities, few have been as comprehensive or imaginative. According to former Secretary of Housing and Urban Development Henry Cisneros, Trinity's plan for urban renewal "is simply the best example." Dobelle, he asserts, "is doing it better than anyone." [20]

One reason Dobelle may be "doing it better than anyone" is that the plan is founded on mutual respect for and involvement by local residents. Trinity is not the legendary "white knight" rescuing the local community. Rather, through an internal office of community affairs run by a local resident and a reciprocal and genuine partnership with a neighborhood organization, Trinity does more than "involve" the local community in revitalizing the area. It empowers the neighborhood to assume a leadership role in planning and implementation processes.

Leaders such as Dobelle and Elsner raise several questions. For example, will their efforts be sustained after they leave? How do they ensure that their efforts are institutionalized? Another concern voiced about strong external presidents is, are they "keeping their internal house in order?" Highly visible presidents should be mindful of these concerns.

To summarize, college and university leaders can provide entrepreneurial leadership for effective community change. The challenge is to remain attentive to their internal, and respectful of their external, constituencies.

CENTRALIZED ADMINISTRATIVE-ACADEMIC UNITS WITH OUTREACH MISSIONS

Most urban institutions have offices of community affairs. Traditionally, these offices manage public affairs, the media, and town-gown relationships. They provide press releases on the hopefully infrequent crisis. They handle sometimes delicate negotiations between campus security and local police. They schedule the president to speak at local events. They arrange for the occasional faculty member to comment publicly about a current event. Historically, they have played little role academically.

Similarly, many institutions have offices or centers designed to develop or enhance community-based learning opportunities for students. Generally, these offices are led by a director, often a faculty member. They run training programs for faculty members and look for appropriate community partners for student learning opportunities. Some evaluate programs or student learning experiences. Some coordinate student (and even faculty) volunteer programs as well.

A contemporary model combines these two functions (community liaison and community-based learning director) and adds a few more. Staff members perform a variety of tasks: they serve as community liaison, perform field requests, broker partnerships, coordinate efforts, propose innovative solutions, draft grant proposals, raise funds, and oversee assessment and evaluation of external partnerships. Staff members describe themselves as "brokers," "catalysts," "facilitators," "innovators," "coordinators," "liaisons," "partners," and "advocates." Two fortunate byproducts are heightened institutional morale and favorable public relations opportunities. These offices are increasingly more visible and respected internally and externally.

New titles symbolize their new-found status. At some institutions, they are no longer called offices of "community affairs" or "service-learning," but rather centers or offices for "academic excellence," "civic leadership," "academic outreach," or a combination of themes.[21]

Founded in 1992, the Center for Community Partnerships at the University of Pennsylvania (UPenn) began when institutional leaders "removed their blinders" and realized that UPenn's surrounding neighborhood needed to be transformed from an area suffering from poverty, crime, violence, physical deterioration, population decline, and poor schools into a reasonably safe, attractive, and cosmopolitan urban community.[22] Founded on the premise that UPenn could play a leadership role in revitalizing West Philadelphia, the center draws on the university's wide range of resources and expertise to serve as a catalyst for change. Some projects include:

- A citywide higher education coalition and a West Philadelphia coalition of institutions, governmental agencies, community groups, and businesses that are developing a business corridor bordering the university
- Seminars, studies, and symposiums on urban renewal and planning
- Academically based community service, where students and faculty engage in service to local schools, families, and community (the center coordinates internships for students)
- A multiyear replication project
- A national network of colleagues interested in this work through a journal (Universities and Community Schools), a newsletter, an online database, and a series of national conferences
- A program whereby UPenn's purchasing department helps create opportunities for minority and female employment and business ownership in West Philadelphia through purchasing contracts

UPenn's center clearly impacts the local community, but is it institutionalized on campus? According to the center's director, Ira Harkavy, the programs "are not mainstream, but they are not marginalized either. It is a significant component of UPenn's intellectual life."

The Indiana University-Purdue University at Indianapolis (IUPUI) Center for Public Service and Leadership offers a somewhat different model of the academic center for outreach. Having evolved from a center for service learning, its six goals are to increase:

1. the number of service-learning courses
2. faculty leadership in service-learning
3. the scholarship of professional service
4. campus participation in public service
5. the number of programs in student leadership
6. the number of broad-based university-community partnerships

The center's director, Robert Bringle, stresses that the purpose of centralizing outreach and public service activities on campus was not to "take them over," but to provide "coherence and coordination." For example, the center provides one-on-one consultation with faculty members, runs 10 faculty development workshops, and offers 16 course development stipends for service-learning courses. In 1995, the center ran a three-part workshop on documenting professional service. It raises funds for an annual Professional Service Award, recognizing exemplary faculty applied research.

To summarize, some important distinctions exist between the former "office of community affairs down the hall from the office for community-based learning" model and the current "offices for academic excellence and outreach." The goals of the newer models are to:

- identify and facilitate projects, partnerships, and activities that are problem-focused (responsive to the pressing needs of the external community) and provide good learning opportunities for students
- support faculty and students by helping organize, fund, publicize, and gain recognition and visibility for outreach efforts
- take academic outreach seriously by offering guidance on assessment of outreach scholarship and student learning opportunities

ACADEMICALLY BASED CENTERS OR INSTITUTES

Throughout the country, centers and institutes provide an organizational structure and support for outreach activities relevant to a specific field or problem. Generally, they coexist with an academic unit (e.g., a resource center for higher education within a university's school of education or institute for economic development within schools of public administration or business). Usually, institutes and centers result from the entrepreneurial thinking of an individual or group of people in one or more academic units. Institutes and centers tend to be problem-centered (e.g., dedicated to addressing the needs of at-risk children), interdisciplinary (e.g., drawing from faculty members with expertise in education, law, social work, and the health professions), collaborative (e.g., working with communities to identify problems and then convening experts to generate solutions), and varied in their delivery (e.g., funding applied research projects, offering workshops and think tanks, running seminars and programs, consulting for a fee, initiating community-based learning opportunities for students, matching needs relating to a specific problem with experts on campus who can provide a solution).

In 1991, faculty members from Lesley College's School of Education noted teacher and parent concerns generated from television broadcasts of the Gulf War. Sensing the teachers' feelings of inadequacy about how to discuss war and conflict with young children, these faculty members invited teachers and activists to join them in developing projects where the skills of nonviolent conflict resolution could be practiced in the context of systematic change. Theses views evolved into The Center for Peaceable Schools, a coalition of national and Boston-based educators and youth workers who envision schools as learning communities where conflict resolution and diversity flourish. The center's activities include a cable television series; teacher training workshops; consulting; a five-day summer institute; internships and a community service-learning program for students; a network for teachers and youth workers to continue the center's work; a volunteer program in the schools; research on effective classroom practices; and a master's program for teachers. Because it grants degrees, the center is integral to traditional academic units at the college.

Many new centers are interdisciplinary. Tulane University with nearby Xavier University is home to the National Center for the Urban Community, a multidisciplinary initiative that grew from Tulane's well-publicized "experiment" in public housing. (Working with the federal government, the city, the public housing authority, and housing authority residents, Tulane is working to revitalize New Orleans' public housing and the local institutions that affect lower-income areas—schools, physical plant, safety, and employment.) Described as "interdisciplinary and intra-disciplinary," the center supports:

- faculty outreach scholarship
- student community-based learning
- applied and participatory research opportunities for faculty
- the redesigning of courses to incorporate community-based learning

- the training of residents of public housing complexes—both for jobs and for leadership within the complex
- professional development for government agency employees

Centers and institutes do not always receive widespread support. Centers are sometimes viewed as elite entities where faculty members carry reduced or nonexistent teaching loads, earn higher salaries (often funded through grants), skim scarce resources, and have little or no responsibility for student advising or service to the institution. Often, center directors report to the chief academic affairs officer rather than the dean of a college. Center faculty are usually not accountable to an academic unit. Center faculty may face resentment or jealousy by faculty who teach full loads, advise students, serve on committees, and must undergo traditional peer review. Centers may face uncertainty as to their future as well. Sometimes, finances dictate their longevity. In others, the center's work is so closely linked to one individual that if that individual relocates, the center folds. While their autonomous existence on campus might make centers and institutes more efficient and effective, unencumbered by administrative duties and restraints, it can also exacerbate their already marginalized existence on campus.

To summarize, centers and institutes are a result of the creative and responsive thinking of one or more individuals about an identifiable external need; both instructional and problem-focused units; sometimes isolated from academic units and peripheral to the work of the institution as a whole; and supported by external grants (therefore, their continued existence can be precarious because it is dependent on future sources of funding).

INDIVIDUAL FACULTY MEMBERS' PROFESSIONAL SERVICE AND PROFESSIONAL OUTREACH

Many, if not most, faculty members are "good citizens." They serve on institutional committees, in their local communities, and for their national professional associations. Many also use their expertise to benefit external communities. But it is only in recent years that educators examined how faculty members perform "service" and whether their involvement impacts their students, teaching, research, publications, chances for promotion and tenure, compensation, and work benefits. This was the focus of a research project at the New England Resource Center for Higher Education (NERCHE) at the University of Massachusetts at Boston. NERCHE researchers studied how faculty members use their professional expertise beyond the walls of the campus, how others on campus view those activities, and how they impact professional lives. NERCHE discovered an enormous amount of activity—groups of faculty members doing service (defined as: "work based on the faculty member's knowledge and expertise that contributes to the outreach mission of the institution") in the community. NERCHE also concluded that faculty professional service and outreach is not generally recognized as part of the legitimate work of the academy. It is, rather, an "add-on," often the result of individual interest and initiative.[23] Many faculty members interviewed opined that service projects should be reserved for after the award of tenure in view of the strong pressures to publish or perish.

> NERCHE calls faculty service activity *"service-enclaves."* Service-en-claves are groups of faculty and staff working on service initiatives in the community. . . . [They] support the outreach activities of the faculty within them but are, for the most part, perceived as parenthetical to the academic enterprise. . . . When we refer to academic units as enclaves, we are referring to the status of their service work—work which remains marginalized on most campuses.[24]

How faculty members get started and then sustain their projects vary. Most follow their instincts and interests, start small, run pilot projects, and then hope their projects grow. Seed money is easier to find than sustained institutional support. Faculty members often worry that once the grant money is spent, the project will need to fight for survival.

At IUPUI, Patricia Keener, a professor and associate dean of the Department of Pediatrics, is widely respected for her creative and significant outreach efforts. "It all began," she says, when she was working in an emergency room, and the daughter of a friend was brought in unconscious due to a choking accident. The child, who was in the care of a sitter when the incident occurred, died. Later that day, still extremely distraught, Keener confided in a friend. Rather than sympathize, the friend responded, "Well, what are you going to do about it?" In response, Keener founded and now directs "Safe Sitter," a course for adolescents on medically responsible babysitting. Since its start in 1980, the program has trained more than 150,000 adolescents. She serves as the director while holding her academic positions at the university.

Keener did not stop with this program. From 1989 to 1992, the university "lent" her to the city of Indianapolis to work with the city to reduce infant mortality rates. With her involvement, they reduced infant mortality rates from a record high to the lowest in recent history. Other innovative projects she designed include: "Supershot Saturday," an urban immunization program; "Spring House Calls," where students from the medical school and philanthropy departments join to clean up and beautify a local community; computer literacy programs linking senior citizens, parents, and preschoolers; and a 24-hour child care center for hospitals to accommodate the needs of parents who work the night shifts. Recently, IUPUI gave her a joint appointment with the Department of Philanthropy where she teaches a graduate course.

The institution, she says, has been "incredibly supportive" of her activities. It provides money and allows her the flexibility to do professional service. She feels no pressure to publish, either. She said candidly, "I do not publish. The way I see it is 'you can do it, or you can write about it.' I *do* it."

Most institutions, however, maintain a "publish or perish" requirement. Faculty members struggle to reconcile the pressure they feel to publish based on theoretical research, to teach well and often, and to become involved in community partnerships. At some institutions, faculty engaged in academic outreach feel isolated to the point where they do not even tell others about their activities. At most institutions, reward structures focus on research first, teaching second, and service to the institution a distant third, while academic outreach may not even be part of the equation.

Some institutions, including Oregon State University, Michigan State University (both profiled above) and Portland State University (PSU), have revised their standards for promotion and tenure following Boyer's "scholarship of engagement." Faculty members are evaluated based on their demonstrated "discovery," "integration," "interpretation," and "application" of knowledge. PSU's guidelines state: "Faculty engaged in community outreach can make a difference in their communities and beyond by defining or resolving relevant social problems or issues, by facilitating organizational development, by improving existing practices or programs, and by enriching the cultural life of the community." More faculty members are engaged in "action research," "applied research," or "participatory research," and those forms of research are gaining respect. They remain, however, the exception rather than the rule.

Faculty can integrate their research, teaching, and public service, and they should be recognized and rewarded for doing so. Sociology professor Mark Chesler at the University of Michigan is dedicated to many projects. He studies the psychosocial impact of cancer, particularly childhood cancer, and serves as president of an international cancer organization and a board member for a childhood cancer foundation. He runs the university's program on conflict management alternative (conducting both research and service projects). He also directs the sociology department's service-learning program. In recognition of his work, Chesler was awarded the 1997 Ernest A. Lynton Award for Faculty Professional Service and Academic Outreach.

STUDENT INITIATIVES

Most institutions coordinate student volunteers through student affairs offices. They recognize and support "service clubs." Some student volunteerism comes directly from student groups (e.g., Greek houses) and is not administered by the administration. Student volunteerism varies from long-term commitments (e.g., tutoring in local schools for the year) to one-time events (e.g., "Clean Up the Neighborhood Day").

Students can serve as powerful catalysts for civic activities that the institution then embraces. One program, known as HIPHOP (Homeless and Indigent Population Health Outreach Project) offers an example. In 1992, a group of medical students at the University of Medicine and Dentistry of New Jersey/ Robert Wood Johnson Medical School organized to address the health needs of the New Brunswick community. Organizing students, faculty, and staff into teams, HIPHOP tackled perceived barriers of language, culture, financial concerns, and time limits that seemed to prevent local citizens from finding primary and preventive health care options. HIPHOP projects include clinic/ home visits; monthly seminars on subjects such as immunizations, lead poisoning, and home safety; HIV prevention; and sexual health and responsibility. Community partners include three primary health-care clinics, social service system directors, school administrators, local city officials, and a local soup kitchen. Organizationally, the program is unique in that it is administered by a steering committee of nine second-year medical students. The students hire their own staff. A governing board of faculty and students links HIPHOP to the university and ensures its continued existence.[25]

Students can provide institutions valuable creative problem-solving energy, but only when their views are welcome, respected, and acted upon. Presenting a problem to students and inviting them to respond can yield powerful results. Open lines of communication and expections that faculty and staff will take seriously student-community partnership initiatives will enhance their chances of success.

INSTITUTIONAL INITIATIVES DESIGNED TO HAVE AN ECONOMIC OR POLITICAL IMPACT

Colleges and universities have significant buying power. They sometimes use that power to advance political goals (e.g., to protest companies with ties to the tobacco industry or, in the 1980s, to protest apartheid in South Africa), to support local businesses (by contracting with local vendors), or to support minority-owned companies. The University of Maryland Medical System in Baltimore invests the system's economic and human resources in the surrounding low-income, predominantly African-American community. Approximately 30 percent of its purchasing contracts go to minority-owned businesses. To the extent practicable, the hospital hires from the local community and forms business relationships with local, minority-owned construction and medical supply companies. Similarly, UPenn's Buy West Philadelphia Program (profiled above) increased the university's West Philadelphia purchasing from $2.1 million in 1987 to $15 million in 1994.

Many institutions offer low-interest mortgages to faculty members and staff, primarily as an incentive to attract them to the institution. Yale University, however, offers a different model. Yale's Employee Homebuyer Program is designed to entice university employees to live in local neighborhoods. Yale pays $25,000 over 10 years to each employee who buys a home in one of the specifically identified neighborhoods around the university. Two hundred and eighty faculty and staff have purchased local homes under the plan. There is no cap on the number of participants, their income, or the purchase price of the homes.

Enticing university employees to live locally is beneficial beyond economically impacting a community: It increases the likelihood that employees will be interested in the long-term success of the local community and, therefore, is supportive of launching and sustaining university-community partnerships. It generates good will with the community and good publicity for the institution. And it increases the likelihood that employees will be available for and participate in campus events and institutional service activities "after hours," before and after classes are scheduled.

ACCESS TO FACILITIES

Providing public access to events on campus and use of facilities is an almost-taken-for-granted service most colleges and universities provide. It includes access to and use of facilities (e.g., athletic fields and equipment, the library, banquet halls and food services, on-campus chapels, classrooms, bus service, and computer and telecommunications systems), invitations to events (e.g., film festivals, theater productions, and musical events), and public invitations to longstanding traditions on campus (e.g., museums and symphony halls). Usually institutions charge for public access, but sometimes they make facilities and activities available free of charge to underserved populations, local communities, public schools, or to support specific causes (e.g., a United Way campaign). Similarly, colleges and universities sometimes take cultural activities, theater productions, musical events, and the like, into communities by performing in local schools, nursing homes, businesses, community centers, or theaters. For example, law school students might join with drama students to write and produce an enlightening skit on sexual harassment that they then perform in area businesses, nonprofit organizations, and government agencies.

David Mathews, president of the Kettering Foundation, urges colleges and universities to "reposition themselves in public life, in part by creating more public space on their campuses, more places for people to do the work a democratic citizenry must do." [26] Among his suggestions, Mathews urges institutions to assume a convening role by making room for deliberative processes on critical issues facing every community—drug abuse, welfare, affirmative action, and economic development, for example. Participants would include civic leaders, government employees, neighborhood associations, program directors, religious leaders, local businesspeople, and media representatives. "Creating public space" would require an institution to commit physical and human resources, but it will also enhance external relationships, create positive public relations opportunities, and be a positive step to solving divisive social problems.

STRATEGIES FOR ENHANCING CIVIC EDUCATION AND ENGAGEMENT

At the institutions profiled, and many others not discussed due to space constraints, it is clear that faculty members and institutional leaders are committed—at some level—to enhancing the institution's civic role. Nearly all of the institutional representatives interviewed describe their efforts as "works in progress." They are still struggling to find the most effective ways to enhance their civic education and engagement.

Many barriers exist to enhancing civic life on campus. Faculty members complain that they do not have enough time to work with communities due to demands that they publish based on theoretical research, a heavy teaching load, their advisory role with students, and their service on internal committees. Institutional leaders and faculty members complain of the scarcity of funding to support a project's start or continuation once seed money is exhausted. Staff and physical space inadequately support projects. And perhaps most significantly, those involved with civic initiatives complain that their work is not adequately valued either in formal (e.g., peer review) or less formal settings (e.g., department functions).

This section focuses on the following specific strategies and elements to overcome the barriers:

- *leadership* at many levels
- ideas and projects should *"fit"* existing or tranformed institutional culture
- ideas and projects should *"fit"* with community needs
- institutional *support* for projects and individuals associated with them
- extensive *collaboration*
- political *savvy*

Leadership

In her review of successful outreach initiatives, Walshok (1995) noted that intellectual and political support from institutional leaders were important elements. The NERCHE study categorized leadership further by noting that

effective leaders can assume three roles: entrepreneurial, advocacy, and symbolic. [27] For civic initiatives to flourish, more than one form of leadership is
necessary, although sometimes one individual or the same individuals serve
multiple leadership roles.

Entrepreneurial leadership exists at the most basic level of a program,
project, or partnership. All the projects profiled above resulted from the
creative thinking, expertise, and energy of one or more faculty members or
institutional leaders. The Center for Peaceable Schools at Lesley College,
discussed above, offers an example of how several faculty members, sensing
that parents and teachers were concerned about the impact of the Gulf War
on elementary school students, created a responsive solution. Sometimes, the
need is identified by the board of trustees, as with the deteriorating neighborhood surrounding Trinity College, and the entrepreneur leading change
efforts is the president. Students, too, can serve as the entrepreneurs, as
illustrated by the HIPHOP program profiled above.

The entrepreneurs need the support of advocacy leaders. Advocacy leaders
might be department chairs, deans, or chief academic affairs officers. Michigan
State University (MSU) recognizes the pivotal role department chairs can play
as advocates for civic engagement. MSU's Model Unit Leadership Training
Initiative (MULTI) offers management training and financial support for
department chairs to support collaborative academic outreach. Resulting
partnerships include an urban planning group in local communities, a summer
institute for high school teachers, the provision of work space for artists, a
student-run "Science Theater" in the Physics Department, and an emphasis
on applied and participatory research methods for graduate students. Centralized offices or individuals can also play a crucial role as brokers, catalysts,
liaisons, facilitators, and proponents of innovative projects. In the most
effective structures reviewed, advocacy leaders existed in both central administration and in academic units.

Finally, symbolic leaders, usually the president or chief academic affairs
officer, can reinforce an institution's civic mission by "marshaling resources for
change." [28] At the University of Hartford, President Humphrey Tonkin worked
to reestablish the institution as "*the* university" serving Hartford. To underscore his commitment, he offered Hartford high school graduates half-price
tuition. He personally serves on many community boards and initiatives.
Symbolic leaders are crucial because they take action and challenge others to
do the same.

Initiatives That "Fit": Enhancing or Transforming Culture

A commitment to civic education and engagement will be "an easy sell" when
it is consistent with the institution's history and faculty culture. At IUPUI,
Robert Bringle said of the campus-wide acceptance of his Center for Public

Service and Leadership, "This institution consists of 17 academic units, most of which are professional schools. We had an advantage. The faculty had already established community connections." Similarly, Thomas Dyer at the University of Georgia at Athens explained, "Service is an ethos here. We have a long history of a commitment to it. It is in our roots."

At most institutions, however, engaged faculty members struggle to validate and sustain their civic initiatives which are often viewed as inconsistent with more "appropriate" faculty roles and responsibilities. Sometimes, faculty members or administrators question the value and relevance of community-based scholarship at their institution. "After all," said one faculty member at an elite, liberal arts college, "*this* is not a community college." Another recalls a faculty member at a meeting mocking, "So does this mean that if I serve as a Boy Scout leader, I will be awarded tenure?" Or the claim is that while external partnerships "belong" with clinical programs, cooperative extension and adult learning, and student volunteer efforts, they are extraneous to the traditional academic enterprise overall. A representative of one prestigious research university stated that, despite the institution's multimillion dollar commitment to revitalize local neighborhoods, there is simply no discussion among faculty on revising promotion and tenure standards to reflect Boyer's scholarship of engagement.

Gamson[29] has challengeed colleges and universities to rethink their approach to valuing scholarship.

> We need to get over the traditional research culture that has sapped the vitality of most of our colleges and universities by drawing faculty away from commitment to their institutions and communities. The denigration of applied research and problem-solving has further eroded higher education's connection to the world. . . . [T]he domination of research and publications in tenure and promotion decisions has had a chilling effect even on those faculty members who wish to engage as citizens outside of their institutions.

Institutions that lack the historical commitment to and existing culture of engagement will need to pursue strategies for institutional transformation. There are many places to start, but among them should be a review of mission statements and strategic plans and a comparison of desired and real practices. Another place to start is with the community itself and a meaningful exchange of ideas and needs. Institutions should encourage faculty members to think creatively about how they teach; about how the audiences for their research, whether applied, participatory, community-based, or action research should be consistent with their research goals; and about how to integrate teaching, research, and outreach. Emphasis should be placed on faculty development and faculty roles and rewards.

Attitudes *are* changing, albeit slowly and most effectively in places that attract and support the "already converted." For those who embrace new models of research and new forms of university-community relationships, the results are exciting and rewarding. In 1997, Ansley and Gaventa wrote

> [W]e have been heartened by our experiences in working to bring more democratic research principles to our own practice and to our institution. Time and again, we have seen how excited faculty, administrators, and community members become when they are provided with the space and time to work together on real problems.[30]

Partnerships Need to be Mutual, Responsive, and Flexible

Mutuality is a crucial element. Problem solving "for" communities (sometimes inferred in the term "outreach") is an outdated and elitist view. Successful projects are founded on a sense of shared responsibility and genuine community participation rather than institutional "take over." Centers or centralized administrative structures formed to enhance an institution's civic mission should be guided in part by a citizen's board that consists of civic and neighborhood leaders, agency representatives, school teachers and officials, local clergy, law enforcement officers, the media, and business and philanthropic leaders. For institutions just "getting started" or trying to enhance existing relationships, a series of "town meetings" or "study circles" (forums at which external and internal constituencies can meet and exchange ideas) can open lines of communication, identify community needs, and propel the process of collaborative problem solving. A collaborative approach might generate the welcome byproduct of enhancing an institution's internal sense of community as well.

Civic partnerships should be responsive to identified problems or needs. The previously profiled Center for Healthy Communities at Wright State University illustrates how important this is. The center resulted when leaders realized that offering health services through existing clinics and hospitals was not enough. To be effective, health care providers had to go to the community rather than force the community to come to them.

Similarly, effective projects provide quick responses rather than work off an academic calendar or semester schedule. St. Lawrence University, in upstate New York, reacted quickly in January 1998 when six local counties were declared federal disaster areas due to a massive ice storm. Although the institution lost power for eight days, it purchased generators and established emergency shelters for local residents in the dorms, provided housing and meals for some 300 emergency workers called into the region to restore power, housed 80 soldiers relocated to provide general assistance, broadcast vital information on available assistance over the campus radio, coordinated university employee and student volunteers in areas needing help, and even provided child care for local parents. The institution absorbed the costs of these prompt efforts. Responsive projects are also flexible. Consider the professor who teaches a political science course on the state legislature. Several state representatives hear about the course and ask to audit it. The professor, sensing a broader need, agrees to run an abbreviated version of the course, open to students, state legislators and their staff, on site at the state capitol 60 miles away. The course will be offered on seven consecutive Friday afternoons for longer class periods. Students from the institution will receive half-credit for the course. The professor agrees to offer a second half-course on campus to students so that they can receive full credit. This example illustrates how faculty members can redesign their courses in response to identified external needs, problems, and institutional resources, and start the process of collaborative problem solving.

Institutional Support

Support for faculty and staff interested in developing courses, programs, or community partnerships can take many forms, including the following:

- funds and release time for professional development
- release time for faculty and staff
- endowed chairs
- promotion and tenure standards that reward outreach scholarship
- research and graduate assistants
- seed money
- grant-writing support
- development office support
- marketing and public relations support
- internal publicity such as awards, recognition ceremonies, newsletters, and forums to present service activities
- office space
- telephone and computer access
- support staff

Absent faculty commitment, institutional efforts to address social needs will remain marginalized. Institutional support can generate faculty support by financing, encouraging, and rewarding faculty development initiatives, such as sending faculty to conferences and workshops on applied and action research and on community-based learning, paying consultants to work with faculty on restructuring the reward system, collaborating with other institutions interested in seriously committing to civic education and engagement, and hiring facilitators to lead internal workshops on democratic principles and their relevance across the curriculum.

Support is not easy to come by. Money and time are scarce resources. Even at the most established projects, directors and faculty members complain that they have to "scramble" or "fight" to get more than seed money. Underlying many civic activities is the nagging feeling of impermanence.[31] "Giving lip service to community-university partnerships while failing to devote significant resources to support them may hurt more than help the effort in the eyes of the crucial community allies."[32]

Collaboration

At many levels, collaboration is a critical element. Interdisciplinary collaboration enhances creativity and responsiveness. It decreases feelings of resentment from those not involved and increases feelings of permanence for those involved. Collaboration with administrative offices or units that will support a project and provide advocacy leadership is also important. This form of collaboration is crucial for eliminating duplication, sharing scarce resources, generating publicity and support, assessing effectiveness, and sustaining projects beyond the pilot stage. Collaboration with external communities assures that projects are responsive and effective. This collaboration should be at all phases of a project, including start-up, implementation, and assessment.

Because ownership would be shared, cross-cutting, collaborative initiatives are more likely to be institutionalized.

Political Savvy

Entrepreneurial, advocacy, and symbolic leaders need a high level of skill and political acumen. The NERCHE researchers found that, "Time after time we noted instances of faculty knowing when to initiate a project, with whom to collaborate, and what offices and individuals to avoid . . . successful enclaves were attuned to their institutional cultures and know how to take advantage of their elements."[33]

CONCLUSION

Consider this hypothetical situation. A fourth-grade teacher is troubled by the nature and extent of personality conflicts among her students. She is interested in learning more about conflict resolution so that she can work with her students to resolve personal problems and generate a spirit of collaboration and cooperation in the classroom. Under the traditional model (instructional outreach), she might look to schools of education (their summer programs or teacher development programs) for a course or program on the subject. Under a more contemporary model (problem-focused outreach), however, she contacts a local university's Office of Community Involvement. She explains her problem. The coordinator for that office serves as the "broker" by recruiting two people, a faculty member in the department of communications in the School of Arts and Sciences who teaches an undergraduate course on mediation and a graduate student researching early childhood education and development. The communications professor assigns to her students the task of developing and implementing an age-appropriate program for elementary school students on mediation and conflict resolution. With a small stipend from the university, the graduate student provides expertise in child development. The teacher's classroom is used for the pilot program. After the pilot ends, the program is refined and then duplicated the next year school-wide, with the support of a grant jointly awarded to the school and the university. The faculty member publishes on the project and presents her findings at national conferences.

This example illustrates how problem-focused learning differs from the more common instructional learning involving courses on predetermined subjects. Problem-focused learning is not practiced in lieu of instructional learning but in addition to it. It draws from all institutional resources rather than ancillary instructors and staff. It is flexible and responsive to identified issues and problems. Problem-focused responses to external constituencies are put together in different ways, through collaboration with entrepreneurial and advocacy leaders and community representatives.

Of course, this is a "best-of-all-worlds" scenario. It can only work if all of the elements are in place: entrepreneurial leaders who can respond with a plan; advocacy leaders who can field the call and link the collaborators; financial resources to support the graduate student; free time on the part of the faculty member to respond; internal structures to support each element; and recognition on the part of the university community that this is a valuable activity consistent with the mission of the institution. Underlying each element is the need for political savvy—people who know how to employ leaders, create links, generate financial support, and respond efficiently and effectively.

In 1997, Zelda Gamson wrote: "[M]ost of the commitment to community service on the part of colleges and universities is lip service. The conditions that would encourage more than just the very committed people—who can be counted on even in the most discouraging circumstances—do not exist on most campuses." [34] This essay was not designed to document the extent of public service activities at colleges and universities. Nonetheless, Gamson's statements ring true. Despite their stated commitment to community service, most higher education institutions are not structured in a way that the scenario described above would occur.

This chapter describes educational programs and institutional public service and academic outreach activities that share these characteristics: they are innovative and responsive to real-world problems and issues; they integrate teaching, research, and public service missions; they are both interdisciplinary and cross-cutting; they are collaborative; they are respectful of community needs and views; and they recognize and embrace the unique challenges posed by a democratic society of diverse citizens. Institutions trying to revitalize their civic education and engagement can use these models as sources of reflection for forming their own practices.

In that reflective process, each institution should consider whether it has its own "democratic community" in order as well. At many colleges and universities, the typically hierarchical governance structures fail to follow democratic principles. Institutions might consider conducting an internal review of their decision-making processes, with particular attention to faculty and student roles, written policies vis-a-vis actual practices, and institutional values. They should face issues and problems squarely, invite diverse opinions and dissent, discuss how to balance competing interests, and encourage collaborative decision-making authority and responsibility. In short, colleges and universities should practice, not just teach, the "arts of democracy—dialogue, engagement, and shared participation."

Mobilizing institutional resources to help address social needs, although difficult, is worthwhile. Civic initiatives—through courses and programs, community partnerships, volunteerism, and public access—generate external good will and respect, internal excitement and high morale, meaningful social change, *and* positive role models and learning opportunities for students.

NOTES

1. E. Boyer, "The Scholarship of Engagement," *Journal of Public Service & Outreach, 1,* no. 1 (Spring 1996).
2. Ibid.
3. E. Boyer, *Scholarship Reconsidered: Priorities of the Professoriate* (Princeton, NJ: The Carnegie Foundation for the Advancement of Teaching, 1990).
4. This chapter does not measure the *extent* of civic initiatives in higher education, nor does it draw any conclusions regarding the *effectiveness* of the projects discussed.
5. F.A. Fear and L.R. Sandmann, "Unpacking the Service Category: Reconceptualizing University Outreach for the 21st Century," *Continuing Higher Education Review, 59,* no. 3 (Fall 1995).
6. The term "service" can be clarified. "Service" at colleges and universities can mean several things, including the following:
   a. *Service to the department or institution:* Faculty members and administrators are commonly asked to serve on countless committees, ranging from task forces on special issues to promotion and tenure review teams.

b. *Service to students:* Advising, mentoring, helping with special projects, and even hand-holding through personal crises are common roles faculty members and administrators play. In some cases, the relationships are connected to course work or study plans, but in some cases they are co-curricular or even beyond the call of duty.

c. *Service to a profession:* Faculty members and administrators often serve as officers or committee members for their national professional organizations or editors for professional journals. In many cases, the national recognition results in career enhancement and is appreciated, if not required, at the time of peer review.

d. *Service to a local community organization:* Many academics are good-hearted by nature and serve as state legislators, school board members, fund raisers, Boy Scout leaders, Big Sisters or Brothers, etc. In doing so, they are not, generally, drawing on their academic expertise. They are simply being good citizens.

While these types of service are important and reflect the overall committed values of most faculty members, they are not the focus of this paper.

7. R. Guarasci and G.H. Cornwell, *Democratic Education in an Age of Difference: Refining Citizenship in Higher Education* (San Fransisco: Jossey-Bass, 1977), xiii.

8. T. Ehrlich, "Civic Learning: Democracy and Education Revisited," *Educational Record, 78,* no. 3–4 (Summer/Fall 1997): 57–65.

9. R.L. Sigmon and Colleagues, *Journey to Service-Learning* (Washington, DC: Council of Independent Colleges, 1996).

10. T. Marchese, "Service-Learning in the Disciplines: An Interview with Monograph Series Editors R. Bringle and E. Zlotkowski," *AAHE Bulletin* (March 1997).

11. Guarasci and Cornwell, *Democratic Education.*

12. Ehrlich, "Civic Learning."

13. *Promotion and Tenure Guidelines,* Oregon State Unversity (1995), 3.

14. The University of Georgia, *Public Service and Extension Annual Report 1995–1996* (Athens: University of Georgia, 1996), 4.

15. The University of Georgia, *The University of Georgia Guidelines for Appointments and Promotion, Public Service and Outreach Rank* (Athens: University of Georgia, May 1997).

16. *Points of Distinction: A Guidebook for Planning and Evaluating Quality Outreach* (East Lansing: Michigan State University, October 1996).

17. Fear and Sandmann, "Unpacking the Service Category," 119.

18. Another unique aspect to MSU's approach is its commitment to evaluating faculty and unit outreach efforts. In 1996, MSU published *Points of Distinction: A Guidebook for Planning and Evaluating Quality Outreach.* It provides tools for evaluating outreach projects and planning guidance for institutions interested in reexamining their outreach mission and activities.

19. S.D. Seifer and K.M. Connors, *Community-Campus Partnerships for Health: A Guide for Developing Community-Responsive Models in Health Professions Education* (San Francisco: Center for the Health Professions, 1997), 129.

20. J. Gross, "Trinity College Leads Effort to Create Hartford Renewal," *New York Times* (14 April 1997): B5.

21. At smaller institutions, such as Clark University in Worcester, Massachusetts, this role might be served by an assistant to the president. At Tulane University in New Orleans, recently hailed by *Time* for assuming management responsibilities for 10 public housing projects city-wide, the university attorney serves in this capacity. S.C. Gwynne, "Miracle in New Orleans," *Time* (9 March 1998): 74.

22. I. Harkavy, "Organization Innovation and the Creation of the New American University: The University of Pennsylvania's Center for Community Partnerships as a Developing Case Study," in *Outreach Scholarship for Youth and Families: Building University-Community Collaborations for a Twenty-first Century,* ed. R.M. Lerner and A.T. Simon (New York: Garland Publishers, 1998).

23. S. Singleton, D. Hirsch, and C. Burack, *Organizational Structures for Community Engagement,* NERCHE Working Paper #21 (1997), reprinted with permission from *Universities as Citizens,* ed. R. Bringle and E. Malloy (Boston: Allyn & Bacon, 1998).

24. Ibid.

25. Seifer and Connors, *Community-Campus Partnerships for Health.*

26. D. Mathews, "Creating More Public Space in Higher Education," (Washington, DC: The Council on Public Education, 1998), 1.

27. Singleton, Hirsch, and Burack, *Organizational Structures for Community Engagement,* 10–11.

28. R. Heifetz, *Leadership without Easy Answers* (Cambridge, MA: Harvard University Press, 1994).

29. Z. Gamson, "Higher Education & Rebuilding Civic Life," *Change* (January/February 1997): 10.

30. F. Ansley and J. Gaventa, "Researching for Democracy & Democratizing Research," *Change* (January/February 1997): 46.

31. Singleton, Hirsch, and Burack, *Organizational Structures for Community Engagement,* 19.

32. Ansley and Gaventa, "Researching for Democracy," 53.

33. Singleton, Hirsch, and Burack, *Organizational Structures for Community Engagement,* 22.

34. Gamson, "Higher Education & Rebuilding Civic Life," 13.

FURTHER READING

Bender, Thomas. *Intellect and Public Life: Essays on the Social History of Academic Intellectuals in the United States.* Baltimore, MD: Johns Hopkins University Press, 1993.

Bloom, Allan. *The Closing of the American Mind: How Higher Education Has Failed Democracy and Impoverished the Souls of Today's Students.* New York: Simon and Shuster, 1987.

Clemance, Roger, William Donohue, Bud Webb, and Oak Winters. "Fulfilling Higher Education's Covenant with Society: The Emerging Outreach Agenda," at the Capstone Symposium of the W.K. Kellogg Foundation—MSU Lifelong Education Grant, April 1996.

Fear, Frank A., Lorilee R. Sandmann, and Mark A. Lelle. "First Generation Outcomes of the Outreach Movement: Many Voices, Many Paths," a presentation at "21st Century Campus Culture," Washington, DC, June 5, 1997.

Heller, Rafael. "Learning Communities: What Does the Research Show?" *AAC&U Peer Review* (Fall 1998): 11.

Humphreys, Debra. *General Education and American Commitments: A National Report on Diversity Courses and Requirements.* Washington, DC: Association of American Colleges and Universities, 1997.

Lynton, Ernest A. *Making a Case for Professional Service.* Washington, DC: American Association for Higher Education, 1995.

Matthews, Roberta, et al. "Creating Learning Communities," in J. Gaff and J. Ratcliff (eds.) *Handbook of the Undergraduate Curriculum.* San Francisco: Jossey-Bass, 1997.

Maurana, Cheryl A., and Kim Goldenberg. "A Successful Academic-Community Partnership to Improve the Public's Health." *Academic Medicine* vol. 71, no. 5 (May 1996): 425–31.

Portland State University. The Capstone Capsule, Spring/Summer 1997.

Promotion and Tenure Guidelines. Oregon State University, 1995.

Provost's Committee on University Outreach. *University Outreach at Michigan State University: Extending Knowledge to Serve Society,* October 1993.

Rudolph, Frederic. *The American College and University.* New York: Knopf, 1962.

Tinto, Vincent. "Reconstructing the First Year of College." *Planning for Higher Education* vol. 25 (Fall 1996): 1.

Votruba, James. "Strengthening the University's Alignment with Society: Challenges and Strategies." *Journal of Public Service and Outreach* vol. 1, no. 1 (Spring 1996): 30.

Whiteley, John M. *Character Development in College Students* (foreword by Nevitt Sanford). Schenectady, NY: Character Research Press and the American College Personnel Association, 1982, xiii.

CHAPTER 5

Educational Missions and Civic Responsibility
Toward the Engaged Academy

Carol Geary Schneider

As the United States moves into a new century, calls abound for a renewal of civic engagement and social responsibility. From campus to community, in proposals from educational leaders, foundations, national associations, and grass-roots organizations, a broad consensus seems to be forming: We must renew the public sphere, revitalize our associational life, and reinvest in those civic activities that are the nursery of citizenship and civic vitality.

Political scientist Benjamin Barber speaks for many in describing the challenge that now confronts American society. The first priority for our own as well as new democracies, he writes, must be "the reconstruction of civil society as a framework for the reinvention of democratic citizenship. . . ." Civil society, he goes on to explain, is a "mediating third domain between the overgrown but increasingly ineffective state governmental and the metastasizing private market sectors. . . ." As such, civil society "needs a habitation; it must become a real place that offers the abstract idea of a public voice a palpable geography somewhere other than in the twin atlases of government and markets."[1]

Havard philosopher Cornel West provides a more impassioned call for a renewed engagement with the public sphere. Assessing the palpable estrangements across race and class that continue to deface American democracy, West warns:

As a people—*E Pluribus Unum*—we are on a slippery slope toward economic strife, social turmoil, and cultural chaos. If we go down, we go down together. . . . The paradox of race in America is that our common destiny is more pronounced and imperiled precisely when our divisions are deeper. . . .

What is to be done? . . . First, we must admit that the most valuable sources for help, hope, and power consist of ourselves and our common history. . . . Second, we must focus our attention on the public square —the common good that undergirds our national and global destinies. The vitality of any public square ultimately depends on how much we *care* about the quality of our lives together. . . .

Last, the major challenge is the need to generate new leadership. . . .

We need leaders . . . who can situate themselves within a larger historical narrative of this country and world, who can grasp the complex dynamics of our peoplehood and imagine a future grounded in the best of our past, yet attuned to the frightening obstacles that now perplex us. Our ideals of freedom, democracy, and equality must be invoked to invigorate all of us, especially the landless, propertyless, and luckless.[2]

As this entire volume makes clear, the concept of a reinvigorated public sphere plays a large role in contemporary strategies for reviving civic engagement, leadership, and commitment to the solution of public problems. The public sphere in turn is to be animated through the work of mediating institutions which, proponents argue, must provide a meaningful space for public discourse and action.

Mediating institutions are those voluntarily formed organizations—independent of both the government and the market sphere—that express aspirations for community, for voice and visibility, and for actions to pursue an intended good in concert with others. These civic organizations include, for example, schools, foundations, voluntary associations, religious communities, activist movements, and the media. What binds such disparate entities together in a common category is their ethos of voluntarism and social purposefulness. As John Dewey famously observed, democracy is, among other things, a design for "associated living." The mediating institutions that constitute civil society are the spheres in which this associated living is both enacted and tied to goals that matter to discrete communities and to the society as a whole.

While the role of mediating institutions in general has been much discussed in the contemporary literature on civic vitality, there has been surprisingly little attention to the role that higher education institutions in particular might play in the renewal of civic engagement. There is, of course, a robust and widely encouraged movement in support of campus-based community service, which proponents see as a primary contribution to the revitalization of our civic life. But community service initiatives, worthwhile though they are, typically remain extracurricular and elective on most campuses. There remains a crucial need for exploration of potential connections between the core missions of colleges and universities as educational institutions and the quality of our civic life.

This chapter explores those connections between the core educational missions of colleges and universities and civic vitality. It revisits one of the most hallowed purposes of academe: the expectation that higher learning contributes substantially to learners' preparation for citizenship. In brief, this chapter argues that the higher education community's sense of *how* it addresses this espoused purpose is in need of fundamental reconceptualization. The chapter further contends that resources for such a renewal are already developing at many colleges and universities, in a set of programs and reforms I describe here as "engaged academy."

In making this argument that we need a renewed vision, for which resources are already at hand, I explore four issues: (1) the recent history of higher education's understanding of the connections between education and civic responsibility; (2) what I suggest is the exhaustion of our most recent approaches; (3) experiments emerging across higher education that embody a new direction; and (4) a specific proposal for reengaging democratic principles and practices.

CHANGING CONCEPTIONS OF HIGHER LEARNING AND PREPARATION FOR CITIZENSHIP

Until the early decades of the twentieth century, higher learning was limited, in the United States as elsewhere, to an elite of the well-born, the spiritually dedicated, and (a small percentage of) the professionally enterprising. From the colonial era through the early twentieth century, higher education's contribution to civic vitality was indirect, accomplished primarily through the intellectual and moral development of a small but significant group of people for leadership roles, whether in their own communities, the professions, or the society as a whole.

If the pre-twentieth-century American academy was indirect in its contribution to the public weal, it was nonetheless forthright about its methods, which mixed healthy doses of Christian piety and classical culture in the service of individual and public virtue. The classics that dominated study in the colonial and nineteenth century colleges were never understood as an end in themselves. Rather, in a tradition that echoed back to the ancient Greco-Roman world, studying the classics was viewed as a direct source of moral instruction and character development as well as valuable learning.[3]

In this vein, the discipline of mastering grammatical and linguistic constructions from a bygone era was recommended as much for its beneficial effects upon the wayward will as for the resulting linguistic competence. Moreover, once achieved, knowledge of ancient languages opened to the educated the spiritual truths of the Scriptures as well as the enduring insights of philosophers, epic poets, and statesmen. The pre-twentieth century classical curriculum, in short, developed moral fibre even as it fostered mental discipline. Both were viewed as a contribution to the civic health of the young republic.

It is easy to see, when one looks at the colonial and nineteenth century academy, the extent to which essentially Christian values and assumptions were woven into both educational practice and civic life. What is too easily forgotten is that this vigorous fusion of Christianity and higher learning persisted in intellectual cultures until well into the twentieth century.

Even as the research university began to emerge from the classical college, many advocates offered a religious justification for the significance of the new scientific disciplines—and of the new curricula to which they gave rise. For centuries, Christians had believed and taught that the world was governed both by a moral law and by the laws or workings of nature. Human liberty consisted in understanding and embracing the claims of these laws and in adjusting the heart, will, and mind to their requirements. The moral promise of the new physical and social sciences, early proponents argued, was that these disciplines would lead the educated to a deeper understanding of the divine plan and to new capacities to align the heart and will with the intentions of providence.

Henry King, then president of Oberlin College, depicted this understanding of an intimate connection between scientific disciplines and moral development in a featured presentation to a gathering of college presidents at the 1915 first annual meeting of the then newly formed Association of American Colleges:

> [I]f the Christian college is honestly to fulfill the aim of education in this age, it must make possible to its students some personal sharing in the scientific spirit and method. . . . [This] implies wide and patient and systematic study of the facts, and insight into laws—natural, economic, political, social. Without such insight, and the obedience which should follow from it, there can be no true discipline of education. Huxley's definition of education has permanent truth: "Education is the instruction of the intellect in the laws of nature . . . and the fashioning of the affections and will into an earnest and loving desire to move in harmony with those laws." . . . And this attitude has a genuine moral quality that is unmistakable, and that the Christian college must clearly recognize and distinctly teach."[4]

This fundamentally Christian world view remained deeply embedded in United States academic culture, not only in the many colleges with denominational origins or active affiliations, but in the land grant institutions and new research universities as well. Faint echoes of this founding vision resonate even today in assertions that a liberal education does or should result in higher levels of moral development and ethical insight.

THE ACADEMIC REVOLUTION

Nonetheless, as historian Thomas Bender has amply documented, this once confident linkage between Christian values and academic culture was broken after World War II. From 1945 on, the academy entered into an era of roaring growth and increasing self-assurance about its centrality in a world newly pervaded by the triumphs and terrors of science and technology. In this context, American intellectual culture was cut loose from its Christian ethical moorings and rapidly secularized.[5]

Increasing knowledge, not virtue, became the raison d'etre of both the research university and the undergraduate college, with knowledge celebrated both as valuable in itself and as a powerful engine of productivity and economic and social progress. A new cosmopolitanism emerged, founded on enlightenment values of reason, science, democracy, and a presumed universality. American scholars began to focus on "the end of ideology," the emergence of consensus, value-free analysis, and the development of ever-more sophisticated methods of disciplinary inquiry.

An important consequence of these developments in the academy was a move away from overt involvement in civic themes and issues. As Bender observed:

> In retrospect it appears that the disciplines were redefined over the course of the half century following the war: from the means to an end they increasingly became an end in themselves, the possession of the scholars who constituted them. To a greater or lesser degree, academics sought some distance from civics. The increasingly professionalized disciplines were embarrassed by moralism and sentiment; they were openly or implicitly drawn to the model of [a secularized] science as a vision of professional maturity.[6]

Bender might have added that the detachment of the disciplines from civic disputation was also a matter of political prudence, a way of preserving the research academy from external attack and politically motivated assaults on both funding sources and scholarly work.

The academy did not entirely abandon civic responsibility, of course. Following models established at Columbia, Stanford, and the University of

Chicago, and consonant with the recommendations of the so-called Harvard "Red Book" on *General Education in a Free Society* (1946), hundreds of campuses developed Western Civilization courses expressly intended to introduce students to a conception of their inheritance and responsibilities as leaders and citizens in democratic societies. The civic intentions and function of these courses were plainly articulated, at least in the period of their initial establishment.[7] While this clarity of purpose tended to erode over time, both for students and faculty members, the civic purposes originally attached to Western Civilization courses were freshly illuminated in the 1980s by those who fought for their continuation in the curricular struggles dubbed the "culture wars."

Notably, the civic values explored through twentieth-century Western Civilization courses were themselves defined in terms of the very ideals now espoused as universal in the secularized post-World War II conceptions of the university. The value and development of human reason, the worth of the individual, the rule of law, the complementarity of Western, democratic, and scientific values and institutions—in short, the substantive themes of an enlightenment universalism—these were the organizing topics mapped into these general education courses on Western Civilization and thereby imparted to undergraduates as the distinctive legacy of Western culture.[8]

Education for citizenship was no longer equated with moral development. Education for citizenship had rather become education in responsibility for the heritage of Western Civilization. This heritage was itself defined as a universal inheritance, what Irving Howe terms a "precious legacy," achieved initially through Western insights, developments, and victories but now a resource for the entire world.[9]

Tellingly, however, Western Civilization courses were typically taught outside the boundaries of the departmental disciplines, in the context of a general education widely viewed both by faculty and students as at best preparatory and at worst peripheral to the "real" work of college learning. In a universe where disciplines and departments reigned supreme, and where practical subjects such as business and education themselves aspired to standing as scientific "disciplines," the study of Western Civilization was indisputably "other." While the historians of ideas can readily discern clear connections between the themes addressed in these Western Civilization courses and the animating values of the newly dominant academic disciplines studied in the departments, it would have been the rare undergraduate who could even have discerned, much less critically assessed, any connections between Western Civilization courses and what they were studying in their major fields.

In this context, there emerged across the academy two fundamental disconnections between the undergraduate curriculum and concepts of citizen engagement and responsibility. The first disconnect was that between the departmental programs—usually the site of a student's primary educational allegiances—and the marginalized "civic" content of the general education curriculum. When students studied Western values and institutions, they did so outside the realm of and with no direct connections to their chosen fields. Conversely, when students studied in their majors, they were rarely confronted with topics or issues related to their responsibilities as citizens (the field of education is usually an exception to this generalization).

Ernest Boyer, speaking for many educators, vigorously decried this decoupling of academic fields and programs from a larger societal perspective in his 1987 report, *College:* "[I]n many fields, skills have become ends. Scholars are busy sorting, counting, and decoding. We are turning out technicians. But the crisis of our time relates not to technical competence, but to a loss of social and historical perspective, to the disastrous divorce of competence from conscience. . . ."[10]

The second disconnect was that between the actual content of Western Civilization courses and the students' self-identification as American citizens responsible for the policies and practices of a particular set of communities. Characteristically, Western Civilization courses covered ancient Israel, Greece, the Roman Empire, the rise of Christianity, and medieval and modern Europe. At best they included only a unit or two and frequently no unit at all on American society. The archetypal Western Civilization courses at Stanford and Chicago, for example, did not touch on American society. Thus, in these courses most directly tied to issues of civic values and participation, courses whose fundamental *raison d'être* was knowledge of the sources of democratic values and institutions, instructors left it to the students' own determination how the study of Western Civilization related to either the immediate problems or the constitutive practices of American democracy.

Let us bracket for the moment the complaints of contemporary critics that these Western Civilization courses simply dismissed huge portions of the wider world. The perhaps surprising reality is that they also gave short shrift to the complexity of even the American cultural and political landscapes.

HIGHER EDUCATION AND DEMOCRACY'S DISCONTENTS

Given these curricular patternings, few would have claimed by the second half of the twentieth century that course-taking was the primary way that postwar colleges and universities prepared undergraduates for their roles as American citizens. Rather, the university's primary self-understanding about education and citizenship came to rest on its claims of cultivating in students generalized capacities for leadership, especially intellectual discipline, critical thinking, and higher order analytical reasoning.

In a complex world, the academy prepared citizens, not by teaching them about any particular set of issues, but rather by developing minds that would become, as an outcome of higher learning, capable of engaging many issues. This is what you can expect to gain at the university, scholars told entering students. Whatever field you choose, you will learn there is a disciplined way of organizing questions and systemically exploring answers. This is the primary outcome of your liberal education: a capacity for disciplined inquiry which will be useful in any and every endeavor you choose.[11]

To what civic endeavors might students apply their newly honed analytical capacities? This was not judged an appropriate concern of the academic community.

Thus, even that small part of the curriculum engaged with issues of democratic institutions and values assumed a stance that was simultaneously universalizing—providing an education in the "most important" questions and traditions—and disinterested. Students were taught about the roots of the Western heritage and they were encouraged to develop their analytical intelligence. The choice of how, or even whether, to employ knowledge and intellectual skills in the service of democratic society was left entirely to each individual's independent judgement and decision.

HIGHER EDUCATION AND THE PROCEDURAL REPUBLIC

In the longer perspective of time, we can see a clear parallel between the academy's postwar emphasis on developing analytical capacities as its primary contribution to civil society and evolving understandings of liberal democracy in the political sphere. Political theorists have described the emergence in the twentieth century of what Michael Sandel termed the "procedural" republic, a republic which views democratic processes as a set of rules by which public decisions are negotiated, without regard to the relative merits of competing values and world views that undergird alternative courses of action. This procedural definition of the liberal state contrasts strongly, Sandel argued, with earlier eighteenth- and nineteenth-century public philosophies which placed strong emphasis on connections between the cultivation of personal virtues and the capacity for self-governance.

The procedural republic, as Sandel observed critically, does not involve itself with issues of civil values or virtues. Nor does it seek to espouse one version or another of a "good society." The liberal state, conscious of its responsibilities to a plural citizenry, is neutral on questions of value.[12]

Rather, the state guarantees the right of each individual to choose freely, without constraint, among competing conceptions of the good. Securing for each person the right to select ends for him or herself is the goal of the liberal state and the ultimate expression of political liberty. In contemporary liberal society

> statecraft no longer needs soulcraft, except in a limited domain. Tying freedom to respect for the rights of freely choosing selves . . . [dampen(s)] old disputes about how to form the habits of self-rule . . . [or] about the nature of the good life. . . . "[T]he problem of setting up a state can be solved even by a nation of devils," in Kant's memorable words. "For such a task does not involve the moral improvement of man."[13]

Instead, the procedural republic interferes in political society only to assure that individuals have fair access to a political and economic sphere, with each envisioned as open markets of freely competing individuals. The state guarantees a sphere of political liberty and action, and within this sphere, individual citizens independently examine alternatives, make choices, and take actions.

In the liberal academy, analogously, the point of the educational process is to foster procedural capacities for independent thinking and judging. The academy, like the procedural republic, does not presume to provide judgments on fundamental questions of public values—whether of the good society or the good life. The reigning twentieth-century American academic ethos has been so avowedly apolitical, in both the particular and the larger senses of political life, that the charge of "politicizing" a subject is a very grave critique indeed.

As we have seen, this education in intellectual skills and higher order capabilities is intended to prepare the individual to analyze issues and make judgments—in whatever sphere judgments need to be made. But the course of study leaves each learner free to explore on his or her own the applications of analytical intelligence to particular issues, or whether to pursue involvement in social issues and political activity at all.

DEMOCRACY'S DISCONTENTS

Holding until the next section of this chapter the vigorous critique of this Ivory Tower ethos which also flourishes in the contemporary academy, let us take the above summary as a broadly accurate description of the dominant contemporary relationship between academic training and preparation for citizenship. The obvious question to ask is: How well has it worked?

One way to address this question is to ask what the public itself expects of higher education. Does the public perceive a connection between the higher learning in the American academy and preparation for citizenship? Here the evidence is very plain. Study after study shows that broad samples of respondents value higher education almost exclusively for its capacity to provide education for employment and the economic sector. As James Harvey and James Imerwahr explain in a 1996 analysis of national polls and focus groups prepared for the American Council on Education, the public's support for higher education is a mile wide, but only an inch deep. The public (which the authors distinguish from policy elites) esteems education. But the public is essentially unaware of the academy's claim to foster preparation for citizenship. It is not that the public absolutely rejects these claims. It simply does not think about them.[14]

Even as students of all ages flock to the academy, they are not looking for, and do not necessarily place high value on the civic commitments still espoused in typical campus mission statements. Alexander Astin's research makes this point very clear. In annual reports issued since the 1960s, he and his analysts have reported a steady decline in first year college students' interest both in political issues and in developing a personal philosophy of life, a value that correlates with actual involvement in political activities. Astin is not shy about holding the academy complicit in failing to offer an education that actively challenges these trends by involving students with societal issues. "Most institutions," he concludes incisively, "have simply not put their 'citizenship' and 'service' commitments into practice."[15]

If we move beyond studies of public opinion and student values to the actual state of our civic life, the picture is mixed. Research plainly suggests that higher levels of education correlate with higher levels of civic involvement. But the increasing participation in postsecondary education has not led to a commensurate increase in civic activity. Moreover, micro studies show that college-educated people are currently more likely to give time to voluntary associations than to the political activities that are fundamental to democratic self-government.

Across the entire population, college educated and not, confidence in public institutions is in perceptible decline. So too is participation. Robert Putnam reports, "Surveys show sharp declines in many measures of collective political participation, including attending a rally or speech (off 36 percent between 1973 and 1993), attending a meeting on town or school affairs (off 39 percent), or working for a political party (off 56 percent)." Even voting, that most minimal index of involvement, has been on a steady downward trend for years. "[T]he weight of available evidence," Putnam contends, "confirms that Americans today are significantly less engaged with their communities than was true a generation ago."[16]

Beyond these indices of individual involvement, American society is replete with festering social problems that neither government nor citizens seem prepared to fully address. The list of democracy's discontents grows lengthier with each passing year: tense intergroup relationships, growing divides between rich and poor, large percentages of our children growing up in poverty, decaying inner cities, a school system that systemically fails millions of less well-off students, the persistence of high levels of social violence, the inequalities structured into our system of medical coverage and access to care, the tabloidization and sensationalization of political bibliographies, and the perceptible fear that privacy is under assault. Leon Botstein, a historian and president of Bard College in New York, offers a sour but incisive long-term perspective on our present political culture:

> There is a certain irony about the quality of the political debate in the United States today. It has reached its lowest point when the people going to the polls have had the most education; there is an inverse relation between the quality of political discourse and the number of degrees and years of college credit held by Americans. The political debate was better when fewer people had access to school. . . . We would have assumed that with the broadening of education the quality of political debate would improve. Today, the name-calling, inarticulate ugliness, and hypercritical obsession with private lives are incongruous with the efforts of education.[17]

Arguably, if we juxtapose our nation's distinctive achievement in producing more college graduates and matriculants than any nation in history with the manifest discontents that pervade American democracy, we must conclude that something is deeply insufficient in the way the academy both conceptualizes and advances its mission of educating students for their responsibilities as citizens.

Cultivating analytical abilities in citizens is certainly important to the health of a political democracy as it is to the modern economy. But it is not, I believe the evidence persuades us, sufficient to the vitality of a healthy and self-correcting civic society.

ALTERNATIVE COURSES: TOWARD THE ENGAGED ACADEMY

It is of course an overstatement in the service of emphasis to suggest that the regime of analytical capacities totally governs the academy's approach to fostering civic capacity and intelligence. At best, the concepts of value-free and objective inquiry fostered in the disciplines had a very short run before they began to generate vigorous critique and creative opposition. Over time, that opposition has generated not only alternative conceptions of the relations between intellectual culture and the civic sphere but thousands of new initiatives that instantiate strong and potentially productive new connections between learning and democratic engagement.

Scholarship for a New Academy

Writing for a panel of scholars advising the Association of American Colleges and Universities on the connections between diversity and democracy, philosopher Elizabeth Minnich observes that a "new academy" is growing up around the edges—and increasingly within the departments—of the twentieth-century university. The new academy was begotten to analyze and address pressing societal needs and issues; its scholars therefore welcome rather than avoid constructive engagement with wider communities and social action. Given this ethos, the new academy endorses and produces scholarship that seeks not just to describe the world but to make a better world.

"Imagine," Minnich invites us, as she turns a flashlight on the manifestations of this new academy breaking forth from the more established boundaries of disciplines and disciplinary culture.

> *Imagine a campus, unlike yours, perhaps, but familiar.* At the center are buildings that house administrative and professionalized disciplines' departmental offices, classrooms, spaces for lectures, plays, dances, and concerts. Many of these are ivy-covered. Near to these are the dormitories, and dotted around them are striking, sparkling new buildings that house programs well supported by the private sector. . . .
>
> On the periphery, there are slightly shabby houses now owned by the university. These are often hard to distinguish from the community that has relinquished them, except for discreet . . . signs in the front yard: Women's Studies, African-American Studies, Center for Collaborative Learning, Swedish-American Studies, Environmental Studies, Native-American Studies, Gay and Lesbian Studies, Peace Studies, Deaf Studies, Multicultural Studies, Hispanic Studies, Ethnic Studies, Labor Studies, Interdisciplinary Studies, Science and the Humanities programs, Asian-American Studies, Holocaust Studies, Institute for Technology and Values, Cultural Studies, Center for Research on Teaching and Learning, Continuing Education Center. . . .
>
> The "proper" campus paths do not reach to these buildings. To gain them, one must cross busy streets [leading to the larger community,] and those who work in these programs do so regularly.
>
> Today, many campuses look like that, although some have very few of the newer programs, or do offer them but keep them institutionally very marginal. Others, however, have already reached across their inherited boundaries so well that they have created a tensely exciting, creative mix of people, communities, and programs that led someone to call such campuses "cauldrons of democracy."[18]

In the scholarly fields Minnich identifies with the new academy, active engagement with social issues and challenges is not an awkward addition to the house of knowledge, rather it is foundational to the very mission of these fields and programs. Like the social sciences at the turn of the last century, these new "special studies" have sprung to life specifically to address actively debated questions about human society and the natural world, questions whose resolution will make a significant difference to the quality of both particular communities and our shared democracy.

None of these fields was born in response to generalized calls for civic action and the renewal of the public sphere. But separately and together, I suggest, the scholarly questions and approaches developed by these new fields, and others such as urban studies that Minnich might plausibly have added, make them natural educational sites and exemplars for just that renewed engagement with the quality of our public life that leaders on all fronts are urgently advocating.

Collectively, these programs are actively involved with such issues as social recognition, power and voice; with implicit and often explicit questions about equity and justice-seeking; with social responsibility and accountability for the physical environment and the role of technologies in a rapidly reconfiguring world; with issues of public policy and the difficult tradeoffs between competing goods in both the social and the natural environment. Students involved in these new programs, virtually by definition, probe central issues that confront us all as citizens in a self-determining democracy and in the global community as well. The questions about human society and the natural world that infuse these fields and animate their work are in fact concrete instances of the kinds of problems with which citizens need to be actively engaged.

The same argument could be made, it might be suggested, about virtually any scholarly field, whether "new academy" as Minnich describes it or "established disciplines" as most universities recognize them. The difference is a matter of histories and societal postures. In the established disciplines, as Bender observed,[19] scholarly methods have evolved from a means to an end to an end in themselves, with the production of knowledge the ultimate goal. The newer fields are no less concerned with knowledge, but they place far more emphasis on using knowledge to advance what they perceive as needed changes in the wider society. The implications for democratic citizenship and activism are powerful.

Learning Communities

These new scholarly fields are only a part of what I identify here as the emergence of an "engaged academy." These rapidly multiplying new fields and programs share considerable common ground with yet another educational movement that also holds potential significance for new conceptions of the relationship between education and civil society. Hundreds of campuses and thousands of faculty members are now experimenting with the development of academic learning communities: topically linked courses which students take as a set with the explicit intention of addressing major themes across the entire course cluster, from different disciplinary perspectives. In my own work with hundreds of campuses, I perceive the current interest in developing learning communities to be one of the most visible and significant national trends.

The idea for this innovation emerged 20 years ago through the efforts of Patrick Hill, then a professor of philosophy at the State University of New York at Stony Brook and now a faculty member at Evergreen State College. The movement took on major steam through the efforts of Barbara Leigh Smith and Jean MacGregor, who for more than a decade led the Washington Center for Excellence in Undergraduate Education, which made the promulgation of learning communities one of its central priorities. While learning communities are multiplying on every kind of campus and in every part of the country, they are especially predominant in Washington State, thanks to the statewide influence of the Washington Center. Evergreen State College itself has organized its entire curriculum on a learning community model.

The primary impetus for learning communities is integrative learning, an attempt to overcome the fragmentation of learning in the twentieth-century university. Patrick Hill has frequently observed that a further goal of clustered courses is to overcome the "will to totality" that thrives in every disciplinary community.[20]

Yet, the themes faculty groups select in developing linked courses frequently have manifest connections to the same ethos of societal analysis and change that animates the new academy. Learning communities explore such topics as "global hunger," "social movements," "American pluralism and the pursuits of justice," "economy and equity," "sustainable change," and "heterogeneity and interdependency." When students take a set of courses explicitly organized around such themes, the result is a miniature version of a program in one of the new societally oriented interdisciplinary studies. Here again students find themselves engaged with fundamental issues of civic aspiration and experience, issues deliberately chosen because they are important both to polity and policy. The potential implications for an informed and engaged citizenry are notable.

Hands-on Pedagogies

The civic potential of these new fields and programs extends well beyond their subject matter. Befitting their bridging role between the realms of scholarship and action, curricula in virtually all these new fields and programs routinely foster forms of learning that are engaged, action-oriented, and "hands-on." The most popular pedagogical strategies include:

1. **Collaborative Inquiry.** Students undertake their learning and problem-solving in group settings, both direct and online. They may work as a team, both in the classroom and outside it, with the instructor acting as coach as the group takes collective responsibility for defining and addressing a challenging question, problem, or task.

2. **Experiential Learning.** Students learn through direct experience in field settings, with open-ended problems, projects, and challenges. The instructor helps the students, either individually or as a group, learn to process their experience, put it in a context of general principle—practical, intellectual and ethical—and rethink their content learning in light of the field experience. The boundaries between theory and practice are blurred, with practice accepted as a legitimate source both of knowledge and challenge to reigning theories.

3. **Service-Learning.** Students become directly involved with societal issues and with groups seeking to solve problems and improve the quality of life for themselves and others. Again, the instructor's role is to provide social, moral, and technical context to help students generalize from the particular, connect scholarship with practice, and articulate grounds for commitment and action. Students establish new and reciprocal relationships with community leaders, and they come to recognize the legitimacy of experiences and perspectives very different from their own.

4. **Project-Based Learning.** Students organize and deal with unstructured problems, sometimes in concert with other students, and frequently in contact with off-campus groups, organizations, and issues. Often making use of educational technologies, students experience the excitement and the usefulness of creating new approaches and solutions, of bridging theory and practice, and of putting knowledge to work in applied situations.

5. **Integrative Learning.** Students are expected to generate links among previously unconnected issues, approaches, sources of knowledge, and/or contexts for practice. Such learning is frequently issue-oriented and multidisciplinary. Frequently it challenges the student to both critique and connect the disparate assumptions and mental models of multiple constituencies and communities, inside and outside the academy.

These hands-on pedagogies are scarcely exclusive to the new scholarly fields and programs, and faculty members who use them can now be found in virtually any field. Moreover, the common practice of double appointments in both established departments and new programs or fields is quite literally building two-way streets between the activist ethos of the new scholarly fields and the more detached ways of knowing established in older disciplines.

Nonetheless, it is fair to say that these hands-on pedagogies are more frequently and consistently emphasized in the disciplines and programs I am labeling the "engaged academy." In older fields and programs, the new pedagogies may be used, but they remain elective. Conversely, in new fields and programs, the hands-on pedagogies are likely to be part of required courses. Analysis of one's lived and prior experiences is, for example, a common requirement in women's studies, ethnic studies, and in programs oriented toward returning adults. Frequently these expectations are built into the introductory course or orientation. Again, many of the new fields make it a degree requirement for students to take part in an internship, course-based service learning, or other forms of direct experience with the subject matter. Hands-on forms of learning tend to be foregrounded simply because they are central to these fields' fundamental missions of fostering strong and generative connections between scholarly and applied knowledge. As one syllabus for a community-oriented course advises students, "We ask you to reaffirm one central precept, namely, that learning requires a serious commitment to both the subject at hand, and the voices and experiences of those engaged in the course and the community."[21]

Relational Learning

As the pedagogical list just cited suggests, a further characteristic of the new fields and programs that has important potential significance for civic engagement is the intrinsically sociable or communal character of their conception of learning. These collaborative models bring to higher education a new kind of dialogue between faculty and student. The goal of the teaching and learning process is not to turn the student into a disciple of the teacher but rather to involve both learners and teachers in the collaborative creation of insights, understandings, and capacities for action that no one of them could have achieved independently.

Drawing on the dialogue and insights of a national panel of scholars guiding AAC&U's American Commitments initiative, developmental psychologist Lee Knefelkamp and I have termed this approach "relational learning."[22] We depict this model for relational or collaborative learning in Figure 2, which weaves together concepts from the work of psychologist David Kolb and of the African-American feminist scholar, Patricia Hill Collins. To emphasize what is most distinctive about this model, we contrast it with David Kolb's own much-praised model for what he calls "experiential learning," given here in Figure 1. The core difference between these two models is that Figure 1 implicitly presumes an autonomous learner proceeding independently, while Figure 2 explicitly presumes that members of a group are learning from and working with one another.

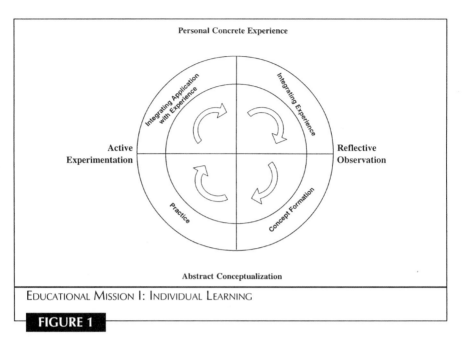

EDUCATIONAL MISSION I: INDIVIDUAL LEARNING

FIGURE 1

Source: Adapted from David Kolb, *Experiential Learning: Experience as the Source of Learning and Development* (Englewood Cliffs, NJ: Prentice Hall, 1984).

EDUCATIONAL MISSION II: RELATIONAL LEARNING

FIGURE 2

Source: Adapted from Patricia Hill Collins, *Black Feminist Thought: Knowledge, Consciousness, and the Politics of Empowerment* (New York: Routledge, 1990); Kolb, *Experiential Learning.*

As Figure 2 suggests, a relational approach sees learning as grounded, not in one individual's experience of understanding alone, but rather in the joining of multiple and disparate experiences and in collaborative dialogue about the meanings of those experiences. New concepts, frameworks, and actions emerge from a serious engagement with the views, experiences, and inclinations of others. Concepts are generated, not by one person alone, but by a group of people working through issues together. Because both concepts and applications are socially debated and negotiated, context and consequence are woven into their very fabric. The final test of theory becomes its usefulness in the intrinsically social contexts of actual practice.

In this relational model, the goal of collaboration is not only the refinement of analysis and theory but also the production of purposeful action in all its forms: judgment, decision-making, experimentation, and social effort. Crucially, in this model for learning, no student is left on his or her own to consider whether and how to apply knowledge to contexts of practice and problem solving. Insights, concepts, and plans are tested against the demanding standard of their actual utility in winning the assent of multiple stakeholders, in solving problems and in producing demonstrable improvement in social practices.

The implications of a relational approach for educating citizens are subtle but significant. Where in the traditional model, the academy works to develop an individual's analytical intelligence, this newer model develops collaborative capacities—for analysis, for action, and for learning from the consequences of actions. Students who have significant opportunities to learn in this mode internalize crucial skills of citizenship. Specifically, the ability and willingness to work with a group to analyze a problem, plan and implement a strategy, and work with others to evaluate the results.

Education for Pluralism

A relational approach to learning is also, by definition, a design for learning across human difference. Even in what may initially seem a homogeneous learning community, the challenge to solve problems collaboratively inevitably plunges the student into the challenges of negotiating diverse perspectives and aspirations. A group that seemed superficially similar will almost inevitably prove to have its own internal complexities.

However, more and more campuses and classrooms are manifestly heterogeneous—in race, ethnicity, sexual orientation, class, religion, ability, and age. And increasingly, faculty members who teach in collaborative, action-oriented programs are deliberately taking heterogeneity into account in designing their strategies for relational learning.

In designs for learning that consciously take diversity as an educational resource, each participant may encounter not only diverse and competing concepts but also the frequently passionate convictions of people who care about particular ideas and about the actual uses to which ideas will be put. Such encounters are anything but easy. But they are also essential in an adequate education for life and work in complex and intercultural communities. They teach what is arguably the fundamental learning for social responsibility in our time: the capacity to engage, respect, and negotiate the claims of multiple and disparate communities and voices.

A common beginning in such relational pedagogies is exploration of the learner's own sources of ideas, values, and commitments. The idea is that the learner needs to bring heightened awareness of his or her own predispositions to purposeful work with those of different orientation. Rather than assume that everyone does or should approach issues in the same way, the student is taught to recognize and respect others' perspectives and to take them into account in the learning experience. Education for pluralism does not begin with a sense of presumed commonality. Rather, it assumes diverse viewpoints and works toward the communality that can emerge from mutual respect and engagement.

Reports from campuses show that students involved in such learning experiences begin to make fundamental shifts not only in their sense of respect for and collegiality with classmates different from themselves, but even more crucially, in their fundamental sense of a need for one another's contributions. AAC&U's *Diversity Digest* reported recently on one such example.

> At Queens College in New York, eight students worked on a research project that examined relations among African-American and Asian-American residents in Brooklyn directly following a headline-making boycott of a Korean grocery store by African-American residents. Students, many of whom were Asian American or African American and from the local community, conducted interviews and found that there was less animosity between the two groups than many assumed after learning about the boycott from the media.
>
> One African-American student in the project, Sharon Bradley, expressed her surprise "at how many people thought that the boycott incidents were blown out of proportion." Another African-American student, Mica McCarthy, reported talking to more people who felt the boycotts were justified because of a pattern of "lack of respect for black customers." She believes that the project gave all of the students deeper insights into multiple perspectives on racial questions. "We met and freely discussed the survey results. We argued back and forth. I learned from the Korean students that Korean merchants are not getting rich off these small stores. It helps me to understand that they are being exploited as well."[23]

A white student taking part in the project went straight to the civic implications of this kind of learning experience. "We discussed everything with the black and Korean students," he noted. These conversations "gave us all broader perspectives on the questions we needed to ask."

Susan Steiner, director of Research and Sponsored Programs at California State University, Los Angeles, runs similarly diverse and community-based research projects there. She reports that these projects have helped to forge more productive bonds between the university and its neighboring communities. It is not a stretch to suggest that such efforts also forge new capacities for pluralist democracy among those who take part in them.[24]

GENERAL EDUCATION, PLURALISM, AND SOCIAL RESPONSIBILITY

Tellingly, these same orientations toward pluralism, relational learning, and activist pedagogies are beginning to make notable inroads into general education programs. In a 1997 study, AAC&U's Debra Humphreys reviewed recently revised general education programs at nearly 100 two- and four-year colleges and universities, representing the full spectrum of institutional diversity in American higher education.[25]

All the institutions studied were expressly committed to educating students for pluralism and diversity. Humphreys found this commitment reflected in newly structured degree requirements and general education courses that help students explore disparate cultures both in the United States and in the global community.

Humphrey's analysis suggests that college students in the United States are beginning to study a new set of general education topics and issues. These revised general education courses, she observed, confront students with issues of multiple and intersecting cultures, identity and community, equity and marginalization, power and social stratification, and with collective struggles both to reduce bias and to expand opportunity and social justice.

In these new general education courses, many taught by the same faculty who constitute the programs and departments of the new academy, students are reading works from and about diverse traditions, considering difficult social issues, examining the sources and histories of prejudicial exclusions and probing competing visions of human community. They are both studying and participating in community-based initiatives. In a number of the courses Humphreys reviewed, the syllabi include pivotal Supreme Court cases that reveal this nation's historic struggles with the meaning and application of our constitutional principles.

These new themes both respond to and provide resources for the rapidly increasing heterogeneity of American society and American college campuses. On many campuses, the typical general education classroom includes immigrant and international students; students who know racism at first hand; and students struggling with the prejudice that still nakedly confronts gays and lesbians. Participants come from several or even dozens of different ethnic groups and religious communities—some are handicapped, and some may represent in the classroom the fast increasing poles of income inequalities that mark this era in American and world history. At many campuses, the majority of the students taking these courses are older, female, and employed.

The civic significance of these new courses is both explicit and powerful. Quite intentionally, these courses seek to help students discover and own both roles and responsibilities in the creation of generative intersections among many social traditions, in the nurture of more just and productive social practices, and in the making of healthy, participatory, self-governing communities.[26]

This is, in short, a new approach to general education: intercultural, dialogical, participatory, and relational. Where older Western Civilization courses assumed and prepared students for a unitary world, these new courses presume and prepare students for multiplicity, heterogeneity, and complexity.

A small but rapidly growing body of research suggests that these new courses are already having a positive effect on students' civic attitudes. A large national study, for example, found that taking courses on ethnic studies had a positive effect on students' attitudes toward racial understanding and tolerance. Individual campus studies offer additional evidence that taking courses on topics such as race, ethnicity, culture, and bias positively influence both students' cognitive development and their interest in advancing intergroup understanding. Reviewing the emerging research, University of Michigan psychologist Patricia Gurin concluded: "There is a striking and consistent pattern of positive relationships between democracy outcomes and both classroom diversity and informal interactional diversity. . . ." Still preliminary, these findings certainly suggest that curricula which include active and experiential involvement with social issues hold real promise for democratic participation.[27]

UNFINISHED DESIGNS

Where does this analysis take us? In the argument thus far, we have seen the inherent limitations of the dominant twentieth-century approach to higher education for citizenship, and considered the proposal that something more is needed. We have also reviewed a broad array of creative innovations that hold promise for the renewal of civic engagement, from new scholarly fields to new curricular structures to hands-on and relational pedagogies. We have seen preliminary evidence that what I am calling engaged academy innovations result in increased commitment to an array of values and activities most would consider important in a pluralist democracy: tolerance, commitment to equity, civic attentiveness, and involvement.

However, something is missing in all this as well. Or, to put it another way, something important to this entire discussion remains so tacit, so subtly implicit in even these positive movements toward an engaged academy that we are in danger of missing it altogether—and therefore, I sometimes fear, of losing it. That something is a direct and explicit engagement with the challenges, responsibilities, dangers, and internal contradictions of democratic principles and commitments in and of themselves.

Many of the promising innovations we have reviewed—the new scholarly fields and curricular structures, service-learning and other activist pedagogies—are driven by a passion to help advance the aspirations to justice, equity, and democratic accountability that are both central to American history and yet still only partially achieved. Yet these democratic aspirations and principles are typically addressed in all these initiatives only by indirection, through attention to offenses against them rather than to the aspirations themselves.

Many new general education courses, for example, deal explicitly with issues of bias and discrimination, while a growing number of general education requirements literally mandate attention to the connections between difference and inequality. Yet only a handful of the new general education programs directly examine the value of equality itself, even though that is presumably both a core democratic principle and a difficult challenge both for American society and for nations around the world. Or, while a general concern with the increase of social justice is often given as a rationale for the kinds of scholarship, it is still extremely unusual to find either programs or courses that directly study our own and other societies' conceptions of justice. Justice is espoused as a value in the engaged academy; its complexities are not explored, either as premise or as practice.

If justice itself is more invoked than examined, the study of other core democratic principles and premises is simply absent from most students' college-level learning. We have, it seems, left democracy as a topic to specialists in political science and political philosophy. Or, equally troubling, we are assuming that the civics and government courses given to high school sophomores are the only formal preparation Americans need for the long-term nurture of democracy.

Surely these are troubling omissions. The issues facing American democracy are enormously complex and increasingly urgent. Globally, many nations are convulsed by political struggles whose outcome will increase or reduce the prospects for democratic self-governance and human dignity. Yet Americans remain stunningly detached from concern with democracy's world prospects.

Do we believe that American exceptionalism will protect our democracy even as others flounder or are suppressed?

Within our own borders, we also face fundamental challenges to inherited assumptions about the practice of democracy. The United States is, for example, in the midst of a major demographic transformation that will make issues of "group representation" a contested issue, in Congress and in the courts, for decades to come. Who among us is well prepared to deal with these issues?

The United States has been rethinking the balance in its federal system for several years, with polls showing an increasing popular favor bestowed upon state governments at the expense of the national government. Who among us is studying the tradeoffs at stake?

Technology is making the prospect of the instant referendum increasingly realistic. Have we considered the implications of this for what is supposed to be a *deliberative* democracy?

Popular discourse reveals a continuing tension between a privatized view of liberty and the expectation that citizens have responsibilities to and for one another. This tension governs many of our most heated debates, such as our system of taxation, Social Security, affirmative action, or the future funding of our schools. Where in the college curriculum are the values and principles at stake in all these debates either addressed or explored?

If we put all this together, it appears that, even as parts of the academy move toward a new engagement with societal issues, most students will not study in any formal way the complexities and challenges that are inherent in democratic values, aspirations, and practices, in and of themselves.

I write this after spending five years directing a national initiative explicitly concerned with developing connections between diversity and democratic aspirations in the context of general education requirements and courses. Based on our studies of new general education programs intended to explore American pluralism, and on five years' worth of active discussions on dozens of campuses as well, I have been persuaded that there is not just a neglect of but a resistance to college-level study of United States democratic principles, practices, and contestations. We are more eager to talk in our classrooms about world citizenship than we are about the responsibilities of United States citizenship.

Some of this resistance comes from a principled conviction that democracy ought to be studied in the schools, which everyone attends, rather than in college, which is not a universal experience. Some is residue from the 1960s, when many of today's faculty members were rightly troubled by calls to judgment-free patriotism in the context of the Vietnam War. Some is the legacy of the academic revolution with its emphasis on the separation of scholarship from practice.

This neglect of fundamental democratic principles and values is something the academy needs to rethink—collectively. With the great majority of recent high school graduates and ever-larger numbers of adults now enrolling in postsecondary studies, Americans have an extraordinary opportunity—and responsibility—to involve ever-larger numbers of students in systematic reflection on the founding premises, enduring challenges, and contested practices of a democratic community. Equally important, we have both the opportunity and the responsibility to help all our students discover meaningful connections between the knowledge, values, and skills they develop through their formal studies—both in general education and in their majors—and the democratic capacity, humanity, and sustainability of our shared world.

We cannot meet this responsibility in our current state of muted attention to the connections between college learning and the vitality of the public sphere. Nor can we meet this responsibility by enlisting a small part of the academic choir to take on yet additional roles as good citizens.

The Association of American Colleges and Universities has already made a set of recommendations about curricular commitments that can prepare all students for their roles in a diverse democracy.[28] The most important of these recommendations is that education for a diverse democracy should not be viewed as a topic for one or two discrete—and therefore marginalized—courses intended to replace the old Western Civilization sequence. Rather, it should be addressed recursively, across the curriculum, through a combination of courses taken in general education, topical issues explored in the context of one's major, and experiential learning expressly designed to develop dialogical capacities and collaborative problem solving.

Education for democratic involvement and social responsibility will mean different things in different fields of study. Future history teachers need one kind of preparation; future scientists another. But such preparation ought to be addressed conscientiously in every field and program in the higher education curriculum.

What is needed now is a far-reaching conversation about education for citizenship as an actively owned commitment of the American academy. These AAC&U recommendations provide a starting point for such a conversation. But the dialogue needs to begin.

NOTES

1. B. Barber, *Jihad vs. McWorld* (New York: Random House, 1995), 281–87.
2. C. West, "Learning to Talk of Race," in *Reading Rodney King/Reading Urban Uprising,* ed. R. Gooding-Williams (New York: Routledge, 1993), 257–60.

3. See, for example, Gerald Graff's description of "The Classical College," in *Professing Literature: An Institutional History* (Chicago: University of Chicago Press, 1987), 19–35. For a longer perspective and informed doubt that studying the classics reliably resulted in the education of "virtuous men," see A. Grafton and L. Jardine, *From Humanism to the Humanities: Education and the Liberal Arts in Fifteenth- and Sixteenth-Century Europe* (Cambridge, MA: Harvard University Press, 1986).

4. "Proceedings of the First Annual Meeting of the Association of American Colleges," *Bulletin, 1,* no. 1 (January 1915): 35.

5. T. Bender, "Politics, Intellect, and the American University," *Daedalus* (Winter 1997): 1–38.

6. Ibid., 6.

7. Committee on the Objectives of a General Education in a Free Society, *General Education in a Free Society* (Cambridge, MA: Harvard University, 1946). See also G. Allardyce, "The Rise and Fall of the Western Civilization Course," *American Historical Review, 87* (June 1982): 695–725; W.B. Carnochan, *The Battleground of the Curriculum: Liberal Education and American Experience* (Stanford, CA: Stanford University Press, 1993).

8. C. Schneider and members of the National Panel on American Commitments: Diversity, Democracy and Liberal Learning, *American Pluralism and the College Curriculum* (Washington, DC: Association of American Colleges and Universities, 1995): 15–16.

9. I. Howe, "The Value of the Canon," *Liberal Education, 77,* no. 3 (May/June 1991): 8–9. Excerpted from *The New Republic* (18 February 1991): 42–44.

10. E. Boyer, *College: The Undergraduate Experience in America. A Report from the Carnegie Foundation for the Advancement of Teaching* (New York: Harper & Row, 1987), 110–11.

11. The widely cited report *Integrity in the College Curriculum: A Report to the Academic Community* (Washington, DC: Association of American Colleges, 1985) provides a classic statement of the view that the college curriculum should foster "methods and processes, modes of access to understanding and judgment, that should inform all study." Such an education will prepare graduates, not only as human beings, but "for their obligations as democratic citizens." See especially pp. 15–26.

12. M. Sandel, *Democracy's Discontent: America in Search of a Public Philosophy* (Cambridge, MA: Harvard University Press, 1996).

13. Ibid., 321–22, citing "Perpetual Peach" (1795) in *Kant's Political Writings,* ed. Hans Reiss (Cambridge, MA: Cambridge University Press, 1970), 112–13.

14. J. Harvey and J. Imerwahr, *Good Will and Growing Worry: Public Perceptions of Higher Education* (Washington, DC: American Council on Education, 1996). Interestingly, a recent poll of 600 registered voters in Florida presented a somewhat more complex picture of these same priorities. Conducted by DYG Inc. in February and March 1998 to learn about public attitudes toward diversity in higher education, the poll found that 56 percent of the respondents considered it "very important" to prepare people for effective civic participation and leadership. This positive response compares, however, with 87 percent who considered it very important to provide basic skills; 76 percent espousing preparing for a career, 69 percent for preparing people to function in a more diverse work force, and 67 percent for "creating a better quality of life in Florida."

15. A.W. Astin, "Liberal Education and Democracy: The Case for Pragmatism," in *Education and Democracy: Re-imagining Liberal Learning in America,* ed. R. Orrill (New York: College Board, 1997), 211.

16. R. Putnam, "The Strange Disappearance of Civic America," *The American Prospect* (Winter 1996): 35–36.

17. L. Botstein, "What Role for the Arts?" in *A Light in Dark Times: Maxine Greene and the Unfinished Conversation*, ed. W. Ayers and J.L. Miller (New York: Teachers College Press, 1998), 63.

18. E. Minnich, *Liberal Learning and Arts of Connection for a New Academy* (Washington, DC: Association of American Colleges and Universities, 1996), 2–3. Minnich crafted this report on behalf of the National Panel for AAC&U's initiative, American Commitments: Diversity, Democracy and Liberal Learning.

19. Bender, "Politics, Intellect, and the American University," 6.

20. R.S. Matthew, B.L. Smith, J. MacGregor, and F. Gabelnick, "Creating Learning Communities," in *Handbook of the Undergraduate Curriculum*, ed. J.G. Gaff, J.L. Ratcliff, and Associates (San Francisco: Jossey-Bass, 1997), 457–75. Hill's analysis of the disciplines was a personal communication.

21. The syllabus is reproduced in D. Humphreys, *General Education and American Commitments* (Washington, DC: Association of American Colleges and Universities, 1997), 82.

22. L. Knefelkamp and C.G. Schneider, "Education for a World Lived in Common with Others," in *Education and Democracy: Re-imagining Liberal Learning in America*, ed. R. Orrill (New York: College Board, 1997), 327–44. See also P.H. Collins, *Black Feminist Thought: Knowledge, Consciousness, and the Politics of Experience* (New York: Routledge, 1990).

23. D. Humphreys, "Student Research Projects Strengthen Community Ties," *Diversity Digest*, 1, no. 3 (Spring 1997): 4–5.

24. Ibid.

25. Humphreys, *General Education*, 3–17; Humphreys, "Student Research."

26. Humphreys, *General Education*, 82.

27. Humphreys has summarized several studies of the impact of diversity course-taking on student learning in a 1998 briefing paper by the Ford Foundation's Campus Diversity Initiative, "The Impact of Diversity on College Students." The report can be found at <www.inform.umd.edu/diversityweb>. P. Gurin has compiled a more comprehensive study of recent research on diversity studies and student learning in an unpublished "expert report" prepared as part of the University of Michigan's response to *Gratz v. Bollinger*, a legal challenge to the university's use of affirmative action in its admissions practices. See also D. Smith, *Diversity Works: The Emerging Picture of How Students Benefit* (Washington, DC: Association of American Colleges and Universities, 1997).

28. Schneider et al., *American Pluralism*.

CHAPTER 6

The Civic Challenge of Educating the Underprepared Student

Alexander W. Astin

It goes without saying that higher education plays a major part in shaping civic life in modern American society. Our colleges and universities not only educate each new generation of leaders in government, business, science, law, medicine, the clergy, and other advanced professions, but are also responsible for setting the standards and training the personnel who will educate the entire citizenry at the pre-collegiate level. Higher education institutions can also exert important societal influences through the scientific, technological, and cultural knowledge produced by their faculties.

Even though the United States is generally regarded as having the finest post secondary education system in the world, there is mounting evidence that the quality of civic life and engagement in this country has been eroding in recent years. The list of problems is a long one: shaky race relations, growing economic disparities and inequities, excessive materialism, decaying inner cities, a deteriorating infrastructure, a weakening public school system, an irresponsible mass media, declining civic engagement, and the increasing ineffectiveness of government, to name just a few. In a democracy, of course, citizen disengagement from politics and governmental ineffectiveness not only go hand in hand, but also cripple our capacity to deal constructively with most of the other problems.

If higher education is indeed such a central player in the shaping of civic life in America, then one might reasonably ask, where have we gone wrong? That our system has the capacity, not to mention the responsibility, to begin focusing more of its energy and resources on such problems is reflected in a number of recent developments, including the rapid growth of the Campus Compact (which now numbers more than 500 member institutions that have pledged themselves to promote engagement in public and community service), the involvement of the American Association for Higher Education in a major effort to encourage service learning across the disciplines, and the recent commitment by the American Council on Education to undertake a "national initiative on higher education and civic responsibility."

Civic responsibility, however, is not something that higher education simply defines for itself and then attempts to meet through appropriate programs and policies. On the contrary, what constitutes our civic responsibility is something that is constantly being defined and redefined jointly by our institutions and the larger society. Sometimes the impetus for redefinition comes from the federal government, as was the case with the Land Grant Acts of 1862 and 1890, the G. I. Bill that came on the heels of World War II, and the various student financial aid programs initiated in the 1960s and 1970s. At other times the impetus comes from the states, as, for example, when they undertook a massive expansion of public higher education beginning in the late 1950s and initiated their own student aid programs in the 1960s. At other times the institutions themselves redefine their mission, as was the case when most colleges and universities abandoned their *in loco parentis* responsibilities during the 1960s and early 1970s.

This growing interest in service and civic engagement within the higher education community is also being encouraged and supported by public and private agencies outside of academe. An increasing number of philanthropic foundations, for example, together with the Corporation for National Service, are currently supporting a variety of institutional efforts to promote service-learning and to stimulate greater institutional engagement in public and community service. At the same time, several states are currently considering legislation designed to accomplish similar objectives.

Despite these promising developments both inside and outside of academe, the American system of higher education still has a very long way to go before it can claim to be genuinely committed to the task of renewing and revitalizing civic engagement and democracy in the United States. In the classroom, faculty continue to emphasize the acquisition of knowledge in the traditional disciplinary fields and the development of writing, quantitative and critical thinking skills, giving relatively little attention to the development of those personal qualities that are crucial to civic life and effective democratic self-government: self-understanding, listening skills, leadership, empathy, honesty, generosity, and the ability to work collaboratively. Most of these qualities exemplify aspects of what Daniel Goleman[1] would call "emotional intelligence." One seldom hears mention of these qualities or of "civic responsibility" or "citizenship" in faculty discussions of curricular reform, even though such concepts are frequently found in the catalogues and mission statements of colleges and universities. And while there have been some very promising developments in the curricular area—an increased emphasis on issues such as multiculturalism and the environment, for example—the general education programs in most institutions are still notably lacking in requirements that focus directly on issues of contemporary American civic life and democracy: the central role of information and the mass media, the possible causes of declining civic engagement and declining trust in government, the escalating role of money in politics, and the growing corporate influence. Despite the mounting evidence that student engagement in community service substantially enhances the undergraduate experience,[2] service-learning remains mostly a marginal activity on most campuses. Perhaps the best measure of how far we still have to go in the area of service-learning is the fact that we continue to regard institutions like Portland State University and Hampshire College as unusual and unique because they have been able to institutionalize the ethic and practice of service. Finally, in our hiring, tenuring, and other personnel practices, colleagueship and service to the institution and to the community continue to receive little, if any, weight.

What I am really suggesting here is that a genuine commitment on the part of our higher education system to renewing civic life and civic engagement in American society will require that we be willing to embrace significant changes in our curricula, teaching practices, reward system, and community relations, and, most importantly, in our institutional values and beliefs.

THE CENTRAL ROLE OF VALUES AND BELIEFS

I would argue that the essence of any organization or community of individuals is the *shared beliefs* of its members. This is true not only of colleges and universities, but also of churches, political parties, social clubs, unions, professional societies, and community organizations of all kinds. Even with organizations that are ostensibly based on physical or geographic factors such as race, gender, or national origin, shared beliefs are the "glue" that holds such organizations together and gives them meaning.

What shared beliefs and values would we be likely to find if we were able to look inside the heads of faculty colleagues in any academic department of a typical college or university? What are the purposes or aims about which they would be most likely to agree and which would therefore shape their day-to-day behavior and collective departmental decision making? While there would certainly be many areas where faculty colleagues differ in their beliefs, there are certain beliefs about which we would find a great deal of consensus. Consider the following faculty belief statements, prefacing each with "We agree that we should"

- garner more FTEs (faculty positions) from the administration
- get the administration to give us as much money as possible in our annual budget
- minimize teaching "loads" (without jeopardizing funding from the administration)
- maintain as much autonomy as possible in the conduct of departmental affairs
- enhance our department's/institution's reputation in the community/nationally
- recruit the best possible students ("best" meaning those with the highest GPAs, the highest test scores, and the strongest recommendations)

This last value would be hard to implement in most community colleges and other nonselective institutions, although there is good reason to believe that most faculty in such institutions wish they could implement it. A recent national survey of teaching faculty conducted by the Higher Education Research Institute[3] reveals that only 35.5 percent of community college faculty nationwide are satisfied with the "quality" of their students. This rate is lower than that found in any other type of institution. If our hypothetical faculty colleagues were working in a research university, we could add the following values to the list:

- recruit the best possible faculty colleagues ("best" meaning those with the most outstanding scholarly records and reputations)
- raise as much research and graduate fellowship money as possible
- publish as much as possible
- enhance the department's/institution's reputation as reflected in national rankings (faculty recruitment, publishing, and fund raising being the primary means)

There are, of course, many other beliefs and values that would be shared by at least some faculty in all types of institutions—being an effective teacher and mentor for students, serving the institution, being a good colleague, and serving the community—but the six values in the first list would be shared by most departmental colleagues in most types of colleges and universities. Indeed, to question any of these beliefs in the presence of departmental colleagues would be considered odd, if not a sign of derangement. And while the four beliefs in the second list would be most characteristic of faculty in research universities, many faculty in the larger state colleges and in many selective private colleges would share them as well.

The point to keep in mind is this: *these beliefs exert tremendous influence in higher education because they (1) are shared by most faculty; (2) are easy to articulate; and (3) translate readily into practice.* There are, to be sure, certain other beliefs—intellectual honesty and academic freedom, for example—to which most faculty also subscribe, but these beliefs are more abstract and have little effect on day-to-day educational practice and decision making. Perhaps most importantly, *they are not usually seen as competing with the values in the two lists.* And while it is true that values such as good teaching and good colleagueship frequently come into conflict with some of the beliefs in the two lists above, these other values tend to lose out because they are not embraced by all faculty and not so easily translated into practice. What is "good" teaching, anyway? And what is "good" colleagueship?

If we were to ask faculty to justify or rationalize the beliefs in the lists above, we would be likely to get two kinds of answers, which I like to characterize as the "excellence" and the "survival" arguments, respectively. The excellence argument states that the academic excellence of our department and of our college or university depends on having lots of resources and the autonomy to deploy these resources as we see fit. The necessary resources include bright students, lots of money, and—in the research-oriented institutions—exceptional faculty who are at the cutting edge of their fields. This "resource" argument would seem to account for most of the beliefs in both lists except the ones having to do with reputation, but such beliefs really have to do with the importance of having our "excellence" validated by the outside community. Excellence, in other words, is manifest in two ways: the *resources* that we acquire and the *reputation* that we enjoy in the eyes of others.

The "survival" argument is based on the realization that most other departments in our own institution, and most departments in competing institutions, are operating according to the same set of beliefs. Since there is a finite pool of resources in our institution, finite pools of outside public and private funding for higher education, and a finite pool of well-prepared students, and since everybody else is competing with our department and our institution for the largest possible share of these resources, we also have to compete to "survive." It's a dog-eat-dog world, and only the fittest—meaning those who can be truest to these beliefs—will be able to survive. In the research-oriented institutions, this competitive zero-sum game is further intensified by the competition for top scholars and research dollars. Interestingly enough, the reputational ratings game is also seen in the same zero-sum way: If competing departments or institutions are able to move up in the rankings, then someone else (us?) must be displaced. In other words, the competitive juices that get mobilized by these beliefs are focused both on resource acquisition and reputational enhancement.

An obvious problem with believing that "excellence" is defined primarily by an institution's resources and reputation is that such a definition fails to address directly our basic societal purposes of teaching and public service. We focus more on enrolling top students than on educating them well. Even in the open-door institutions, we tend to look at the student—any student—primarily as a means of resource enhancement. We focus more on enhancing our reputation in the eyes of the community than on serving that community. Not that we don't need reputations or resources to teach and serve, but rather that a unidimensional focus on resource acquisition and reputation building as ends in themselves can ultimately cause us to neglect our basic educational and service missions.[4] (Paradoxically, it can also cause those of us who work in research-oriented institutions to neglect our research mission, because we become focused more on acquiring top scholars and researchers than on developing the scholarly talents of the incumbent faculty.) In other words, if our primary business is, as we claim in our catalogues and mission statements, to develop talent, why shouldn't we also judge our excellence in talent development terms?

The roots of many of our seemingly most intractable problems can be found in this preoccupation with resource acquisition and reputational enhancement: the valuing of research over teaching, the struggle between equity and excellence, and the lack of community that we find on many campuses. We value research more than teaching because we believe that outstanding scientists and scholars will add more to our reputation and resources than will outstanding teachers or mentors. And when we define our excellence in terms of the test scores of our entering freshmen—the high-scoring student being viewed here as a "resource" that enhances our reputation—we set our sense of excellence in direct conflict with our desire to promote educational opportunities for those groups in our society whose test scores put them at a competitive disadvantage. Finally, when institutions focus on teaching loads and faculty FTEs, or when they place the highest value on the individual scholarly accomplishments and national reputations of the faculty, they reinforce the faculty's competitive and individualistic tendencies, making it very difficult for individual faculty to develop those qualities that help to promote a sense of community on the campus: good colleagueship, collaboration, sharing, community service, citizenship, and social responsibility. These latter qualities, of course, are the same ones that are needed to make any democracy work. Clearly, we can't expect our students to develop the personal qualities required for effective citizenship if we don't model some of those same qualities in our own professional conduct. Our students are going to be influenced at least as much by what we academics *do* as by what we *say* in our mission statements and classroom lectures.

EDUCATING THE UNDERPREPARED STUDENT

As I consider all of the ways in which our traditional beliefs about excellence and survival interfere with our ability to improve and strengthen civic life in

American society, no problem strikes me as being more important than the education of the so-called underprepared or "remedial" student. By examining this issue in some depth, we can begin to see how it might be possible for higher education institutions to become more effective agents of positive social change.

I want to emphasize that my principal interest here is higher education's larger responsibility to serve and strengthen democracy and civic life in America, and that there are many other issues that I could focus on: equity and affirmative action, the need to expand service learning, multiculturalism and diversity, strengthening and improving relationships with the local community, the absence of any real emphasis on citizenship in the curriculum, the lack of community on the campus, the need to reform teacher training and to develop better connections with the K-12 level. Rather than treating each of these other problems in a superficial way, I have chosen instead to examine one problem in some depth. In this way, I think we can gain a better understanding of the deeper value issues and institutional dynamics that need to be addressed before we can deal more effectively with any of these civic responsibility issues.

Let me begin by asserting what may seem like a radical proposition: The education of the so-called "remedial" student is the most important educational problem in America today. This is more important than educational funding, affirmative action, vouchers, merit pay, teacher education, financial aid, curriculum reform, and the rest. I would also like to propose that providing effective "remedial" education would do more to alleviate our most serious social and economic problems than almost any other action we could take. Finally, I would argue that we academics will not be able to make much progress in our efforts to achieve greater educational equity unless we are also willing to reexamine our traditional beliefs about excellence and survival.

The first two propositions are based on the realization that, if we fail to develop more effective means for educating "remedial" students, we will find it difficult to make much headway in resolving some of our most pressing social and economic problems: unemployment, crime, welfare, health care, racial tensions, the maldistribution of wealth, and citizen disengagement from the political process. I say this in part because (1) underprepared students have historically been the ones most likely to drop out at any level of education; and (2) persons with relatively low levels of educational attainment account for a disproportionately high number of welfare recipients, prison inmates, poor people, the unemployed, and people who don't vote. Beyond this, the issues of race relations and affirmative action are intimately connected to the issue of underpreparation, since we have created a competitive, hierarchical, higher education system which dispenses privilege on the basis of measures—the GPA and standardized test scores—that put our two largest racial minority groups at a competitive disadvantage. If our educational system allocated its resources more equitably across different socioeconomic and racial groups, there would be little need for affirmative action in admissions.

WHY DO WE SHUN REMEDIAL EDUCATION?

The underprepared student is a kind of pariah in American higher education, and some of the reasons are obvious. Since most of us believe that the excellence of our departments and of our institutions depends on enrolling the very best-prepared students that we can, to admit underprepared students would pose a real threat to our excellence. Why would any sane institution have any interest in admitting such students? But here we encounter a dilemma for those of us who work in the public institutions: since the law in many states requires that at least some underprepared students be given the opportunity to pursue postsecondary education, how can this be done so as not to put our sense of excellence at risk? The answer, of course, is that we have created hierarchical public systems of institutions where the least-well-prepared students are consigned either to community colleges or to relatively nonselective public colleges. And when we find ourselves forced to admit a few underprepared students—for example, to remain competitive in intercollegiate athletics, or simply to maintain enrollments—we likewise avoid having much contact with them by hiring part-time instructors from the outside to do the work.

These "tracking" practices exert a subtle but powerful influence on the attitudes and beliefs of our students and of the larger society, who are probably going to be influenced much less by what we *say* about such things as "equality of opportunity" or "educational equity" than by what we academics actually *do* about an issue like remediation. So when we hire cheap labor from the outside to do the remediation or try to avoid it altogether through selective admissions, we are sending an important value message—"we don't value the education of these students"—and we send this message not only to our own students, but also to the remedial students, to those who must teach them, and to the larger society. No wonder teaching underprepared students is viewed as unglamorous, unimportant, and—in many institutions—demeaning.

WHAT IS A "REMEDIAL" STUDENT?

Before proceeding any further in this discussion, I would like to add a word of clarification about terminology. The "remedial student" and "remedial education" are basically social constructions that have strong negative connotations. Just as in medicine one gives a "remedy" to cure an illness, so in education there must be something "wrong" with the student who needs to be "remedied." But there are at least three other aspects of the "remedial" concept that are misleading, if not downright erroneous. First is the use of categorical terminology to describe a phenomenon that is relativistic and arbitrary. Most remedial students turn out to be simply those who have the lowest scores on some sort of normative measurement—standardized tests, school grades, and the like. But where we draw the line is completely arbitrary: lowest quarter, lowest fifth, lowest 5 percent, or what? Nobody knows. Second, the "norms" that define a "low" score are highly variable from one setting to another. Let me quote one academic administrator's comments about his less-well-prepared students: "Some [students] . . . arrive seriously underprepared in English, foreign languages, history, or mathematics, and not infrequently in all those subjects . . . [resulting in a] diversion of effort into essentially remedial learning."[5] This happens to be a former dean of the Faculty of Arts and Sciences at Harvard, and he is speaking here, of course, about Harvard undergraduates. Finally, and perhaps most importantly, the problem with the concept of the remedial student is that there is little, if any, evidence to support the argument that these students are somehow "incapable" of learning, that they have markedly different "learning styles" from other students, that they require some radically different type of pedagogy, or that they need to be segregated from other students to learn. Indeed, there is a growing body of evidence suggesting that the lowest-performing students perform less well if they are segregated from other students in separate classes and separate schools.[6]

THE INDIVIDUAL AND THE INSTITUTION

One of the ideas that has intrigued me over the years is the frequent parallel that I find between what happens on the individual level and what we do at the institutional level. Just as individual citizens have responsibilities as well as rights, so do academic institutions. And just as excessive materialism and narcissism can interfere with the individual's ability to be a good citizen, so can an academic institution's preoccupation with acquisitiveness and self-aggrandizement interfere with its ability to be a "good citizen" in the community of institutions and in the larger society.

No problem in higher education, it seems to me, provides a better metaphor for understanding what ails our academic institutions and, indeed, our society, than does the underprepared student. Just as our preoccupation with materialism, individualism, and competitiveness makes it difficult for us to be responsible citizens who work cooperatively for the collective good of all citizens (especially the least advantaged ones), so does higher education's preoccupation at the institutional level with resource acquisition and reputational enhancement make it difficult to appreciate the critical importance of effectively educating all students, and especially those who are underprepared.

Let's examine this individual-institutional analogy in more depth. Just as most individuals will behave civilly and humanely toward those poorer or less well-educated people they happen to encounter in their daily lives, so are most colleges and universities willing to provide at least some special help for those few underprepared students they happen to admit. The problem is simply this: being "nice" to that handful of less advantaged fellow citizens who happen to cross our paths doesn't begin to solve the larger social and human problems of poverty, welfare, desperation, and lack of hope, for two very basic reasons. First, these people may well need much more than a friendly smile or a handout—a job (or a better job), for example, or more education, a better place to live, a sense of purpose, and some optimism about their futures. And second, since most of us have managed to isolate ourselves physically from our less advantaged fellow citizens, most of them have little or no contact with us. Similarly, in higher education we manage to avoid contact with most underprepared students through selective admissions, by tracking them into community colleges, by hiring outsiders to teach them, and by continuing to support grading and norm-based testing practices in the lower schools that almost guarantee that large proportions of them will be discouraged from even considering further education beyond high school. And recent studies[7] suggest that being successful even with those few underprepared students who have managed to gain admission to our more selective institutions may require a substantially greater investment of energy and resources than we are currently prepared to provide.

BEING "SMART"

Why do underprepared students make us so uncomfortable? Is it just that they are more difficult to teach and that their presence on campus threatens our sense of excellence, or are there deeper reasons? While our beliefs about the importance of resource acquisition and reputational enhancement are consciously acknowledged by most academics, there are other, closely related beliefs that are more "hidden," even though they can have profound effects on how we view underprepared students and the issue of remediation. One such belief, which is virtually never acknowledged, much less examined critically within academe, is what I like to call "the importance of being smart." We could use many other terms—brilliance, creativity, intelligence, and so on— but for the purposes of this discussion I will use the term "smartness." My many years as a scholar of higher education and as an employee of a research university convinces me that much of our fear of remedial students and much of our unwillingness to get involved in educating them can be traced to our uncritical acceptance of this belief and to the fact that most of us are not even consciously aware of the power and scope of its influence.[8]

I believe that our uncritical and largely unconscious adherence to being smart and to being seen by others as smart distorts academic life, corrupts the academic review process, and stifles innovation in higher education. But let us first consider how it influences the way we approach the underprepared student.

Most of us clearly favor our brightest students, not only in admissions and the award of financial aid, but also in the classroom. If bright students enroll at our institution and if they take our classes, then this reflects well on our own brightness: surely we must be smart if our students are so smart! But if our students are not so smart, then this reflects poorly on us. This may help to explain why so many academics keep such a close eye on the average test scores of their entering freshmen: if our students are getting smarter, then we are reassured about our own smartness; but if they are getting dumber, our sense of our own smartness is threatened. No wonder we hire others to teach such students or simply avoid them altogether through the use of selective admissions.

The first problem here is that we value *being* smart much more than we do *developing* smartness. In our relentless and largely unconscious preoccupation with being smart, we forget that our institutions' primary mission is to develop students' personal capacities, not merely to select and certify those students whose intellectual talents are already well developed by the time they reach us. This preoccupation with being smart is also part of the reason why we continue to support a grading system and a standardized testing industry that are geared to ranking and rating students rather than to reflecting how much they are actually learning. These assessment devices may be useful in identifying the "smartest" and "dumbest" students, but they imply a very narrow standard of "smartness" and are of little value either in helping students to learn or in helping us to evaluate the success of our pedagogical efforts. We have inflicted this same "normative" system of testing on the lower schools, such that politicians and the public now assess the "quality" of schools simply on the basis of which ones have the "smartest" students, rather than in terms of which ones are the most effective educationally. The truly insidious feature of normative assessment at the precollegiate level is that it sends powerful negative messages to the (relatively) lower-performing student: you're dumb, you're lazy, you're not "college material," you're a loser. No wonder so many young people lose interest in education before they ever reach college age.

A second problem has to do with our preferred ways of defining "smartness." The GPA and the SAT do indeed reflect some important intellectual qualities, but these rather narrow measures do a poor job of capturing some of the most important human qualities that should be central to our educational mission: creativity, leadership, moral character, the ability to work with others, civic mindedness, and social responsibility. Many of these same qualities, of course, are critical to the health of any democratic society.

Our belief in the importance of being smart also has many other subtle and distorting influences on our collegial relationships. Like any other professionals, we academics identify with and seek approval from our peers, and the manner in which we go about obtaining this approval is heavily influenced by the shared values that help to define our academic culture. We thus want to appear smart to our academic colleagues, and we have devised a variety of strategies for doing this. The surest way to gain peer recognition of our intellectual capabilities, of course, is through published research and scholarship, which no doubt helps to explain the inordinate weight we give to publishing, not only in the academic personnel process but also in graduate training.

In our more personal relationships with colleagues we employ a variety of strategies to make ourselves appear "smart." Some of us seize on every opportunity to demonstrate our intelligence or brilliance in the presence of peers, and very often this strategy manifests itself in committee, departmental, or academic senate meetings. Indeed, one could argue that such faculty assemblages provide a kind of theater where our more assertive faculty can demonstrate their critical thinking skills in the presence of colleagues. Such faculty, and the various performance venues that we provide for them, can pose serious obstacles to educational reform efforts. Thus, if someone were to present a well-thought-out plan at UCLA for, say, expanding service-learning, we can be sure one or more colleagues will rise to expound at length on all of its "defects." Let's look at these faculty dynamics in a little greater depth.

Criticism, of course, is central to problem solving and other forms of intellectual work, but in the hands of a sufficiently articulate faculty critic it becomes an end in itself—the virtuoso performance—thereby precluding any deep engagement with the problem at hand. Such faculty are especially skilled at exploiting their more passive colleagues' insecurities about being smart, for example, by suggesting that any change in policy or practice will compromise "academic standards."

Our preoccupation with being smart also corrupts the peer review process. If critical colleagues think a candidate is not smart enough, or are simply out to "get" someone they happen not to like, their verbal and written critiques can be absolutely devastating to the candidate's chances (not to mention self-esteem and morale). Academic research and scholarship, especially in the humanities and social sciences, is highly vulnerable to attack from a sufficiently determined critic, regardless of the quality of the work.

But knowing that colleagues attach so much importance to being smart can also cause us to err in the other direction. When we "like" a colleague who is up for review, we are inclined to pull our punches in criticizing that colleague's work, lest our criticism be interpreted by others as evidence that the colleague is not "smart enough." Even when we react to a colleague's work outside of the formal review process, we often temper our criticism so as to avoid "hurting" the colleague's feelings. In short, the enormous value we assign to being smart breeds a great deal of inauthenticity in the peer review process, whereby some colleagues are subjected to undeserved and humiliating attacks, while others are deprived of needed critical feedback that could ultimately improve their scholarship.

Institutional selectivity, of course, is intimately tied into our obsession of being, and being seen by others, as smart. Research universities, and selective institutions in particular, are very much like private clubs, where instead of money, power, or social status, intelligence and intellectual achievement—"smartness"—become the yardstick by which prospective members are judged. In the culture of academia, simply being admitted to or employed by a selective institution is a mark of individual smartness. If you have any doubts about this, consider that your institutional pedigree follows you around for the rest of your life. In much the same way that people living under a monarchy routinely judge each other's quality in terms of their bloodlines, so are educated people in the United States inclined to judge the quality of others on the basis of where they attended college. Even senior academics with long records of professional accomplishments are typically introduced to audiences by first reciting their academic pedigrees.

This discussion should not be construed as suggesting that intellectual prowess and critical thought are not important to academic work. There are, rather, two major problems that are created by our largely unconscious preoccupation with being smart. First, by overemphasizing the mere demonstration of intellect, we neglect its cultivation (which is, after all, what our educational mission is all about). Second, when we use simplistic yardsticks like an SAT or ACT score or the selectivity of one's institution as the principal indicator of that person's ability or smartness, we not only distort and misrepresent the wonderful diversity of abilities and talents of our students and ourselves, but also implicitly diminish the great social and cultural importance of "citizenship" talents such as empathy, self-understanding, honesty, responsibility, and the ability to work collaboratively. I might add here that this narrow approach to defining and assessing "talent" or "merit" has been turned against us, with considerable success, by the opponents of affirmative action.

What I am suggesting, in short, is that we need to (1) broaden substantially our conception of "talent" and "intelligence" to give much greater weight to civic and other "emotional" talents (e.g., Goleman, 1995);[9] and (2) move away from our preoccupation with competitive, one-shot normative assessment of talent (Who's on top? Who's average? Who's below average?) and begin instead to embrace more of a "value-added" approach which will focus on what our students are actually learning and how they are changing and developing over time. However, it is unlikely that we will be able to embrace either of these alternatives unless and until we first come to terms with the notion of "being smart," with what it means to us, and with the role it plays in our academic lives and our institutional culture.

CREATING A REAL HIGHER EDUCATION COMMUNITY

While American colleges and universities can be justifiably proud of their diversity and autonomy, a collection of 3,400 institutions simply "doing their individual things" does not make for a coherent or effective system. The same goes for any state system of higher education. The problem is not that we are all so wonderfully individual and diverse, but rather that the sum total of our individual uncoordinated efforts doesn't always add up to a meaningful whole. We each have become so preoccupied with our individual "excellence"—competing with others for the "best" students and faculty we can get—that we tend to lose sight of the fact that we are really part of a larger community of institutions that is collectively supposed to serve a very basic and critical public purpose: to educate the citizenry of the state. Unless we can sit down together and collectively begin to discuss our "systems" responsibilities to the larger society, our efforts to become "excellent" as individual institutions will continue to thwart our efforts to achieve real educational "excellence" as a system.

Nowhere is this tension between individual and community needs better illustrated than in the case of the lower-performing or remedial student. Among institutions that have more applicants than available places—and this includes most of the baccalaureate-granting colleges—nobody really wants these students. Since each institution aspires to greater excellence by recruiting the best-prepared students that it can, the underprepared students become pariahs to be avoided and shunned, not only because their presence on the campus detracts from our personal and institutional sense of "excellence," but also because they are regarded as difficult and expensive to teach. Such a policy might make sense from the myopic perspective of an individual institution that is striving for "excellence" in conventional terms, but it makes no sense from the perspective of a state system that is trying to educate the entire citizenry. If underprepared students are shunned by most four-year institutions because they threaten each institution's sense of academic excellence, how can we ever hope to give any real priority to educating such students?

In short, we need to realize that the significance of the underpreparation problem for each state's higher education system—not to mention its national economic and social significance—can hardly be overestimated. And, as I have already suggested, how effectively we deal with underpreparation has obvious relevance not only to retention and program completion, but also to enrollments, to transfer, to the status of underrepresented minorities, to the inner cities and the poor, to race relations, to crime and welfare, to economic development, and to the overall condition of our community and our democracy. Rather than seeing the underprepared student as a burden or as a threat to our sense of individual excellence, we need to understand that each of us, not to mention the communities we serve and the larger society, has an enormous stake in what happens to these students. In other words, the presence of the underprepared students in our institutions represents a tremendous opportunity for each of us to make a contribution to the welfare of the society and the quality of civic life. If nothing else, an extended interinstitutional conversation about this issue at the system level would make it clear that all of us in higher education—not to mention the rest of the society— have a heavy stake in finding and implementing the most effective ways of educating the underprepared student. And it will not be enough simply to talk about this issue. We also need to take action.

THE SYSTEMS APPROACH

Again, the only way to deal effectively with this or any other "systems" issue is to start acting like we are indeed a system. At the state and local level, we must sit down together—all types of institutions—and begin a serious discussion of our mutual ambivalence about remediation. These interinstitutional conversations could also cover a number of other related issues—coordination and expansion of community service and service-learning programs, community needs, local environmental problems, diversity and multiculturalism, sharing of resources, admissions, transfer of credits, etc.—but the one that cries out most urgently for attention is the underprepared or remedial student.

If we see fit to initiate "systems level" discussions of underpreparation at the state and national levels, it will soon become obvious that all types of institutions must share some of the responsibility for meeting this challenge, much like the agreement that insurance companies in most states have reached to share part of the responsibility for insuring "high-risk" drivers. It will also become obvious that the secondary school people should be invited to join in the conversation, and that we higher education folk must eventually form much closer partnerships with the lower schools in the interests of enhancing the quality of precollegiate education. But what about the poorly prepared students we now admit? While there are no doubt many excellent remedial or "developmental" programs already in place in institutions of all types, the hard data on results remain discouraging. Overall dropout rates, especially in the community colleges and state colleges, are still unacceptably high if not scandalous, and research shows that poor preparation—and all that goes with it—is one of the prime identifiable causes of the problem. For example, among full-time freshmen entering baccalaureate institutions, the six-year degree completion rate for the least-well-prepared students (those with C averages from high school and SATs below 850) is only 20 percent, compared to better than 80 percent among the best-prepared students (those with A averages and SATs above 1,300). It is thus not surprising to find that the low six-year degree completion rates for African Americans (31 percent) and Latinos (38 percent) are entirely attributable to their relatively poor academic preparation.[10] Are such results acceptable? Isn't it about time for the community of higher education to begin to take collective action to change these figures?

WHY "GOING IT ALONE" IS SO DIFFICULT

The necessity for us to move away from our purely individualistic mindset—what's best for my college or university?—and to adopt more of a collaborative or consortial approach to the underpreparation problem becomes clearer when we consider what might happen if an institution were to try to "go it alone." As long as the different colleges and universities in each state continue to operate independently and to persist in their traditional beliefs about excellence, any institution automatically puts its "excellence" at risk if it unilaterally chooses either to admit substantially greater numbers of underprepared students or to invest substantially more resources in educating such students. One possible consequence of trying to go it alone would be that the institution's main constituencies—its alumni, donors, and prospective students, together with their parents, teachers, and counselors—will begin to believe that the institution is "slipping" or "in decline" because it is "lowering its standards." These constituents, after all, subscribe to the same traditional beliefs about excellence. And as the word about the changed admission policies begins to spread across the state, the institution could start to experience a decline in applications. This is a real problem that cannot be easily dismissed, and it underscores, once again, the need for institutions to address the underpreparation problem collaboratively.

DEFENDING SELECTIVE ADMISSIONS AND TRACKING

If we could be successful in stimulating the kinds of "systems" discussions that I am envisioning, the conversation would soon begin to focus on the various arguments that we traditionally use to defend selective admissions. For example, a frequently used defense is the "prediction" argument: We select those students with the highest grades and test scores because these measures "predict" performance in college. While such an argument would make sense in employment—we hire "the best" to exploit their talents for the benefit of our company—it makes little sense in education. Even if students learned absolutely nothing in college, prior grades and admissions test scores would still "predict performance" in college (in fact, they would probably predict even better). I sometimes like to say that selective admissions is, in certain respects, the process where we admit only those students who already know what we're supposed to teach them. This would be the equivalent of saying that a hospital or a clinic should refuse to admit or treat the sickest patients because their condition "predicts" a poorer outcome than would be the case with patients with less serious illnesses. Just as medical treatment should strive to change an otherwise negative outcome through effective care and treatment, so should colleges and universities strive to change the "prognosis" for the underprepared student through effective educational programs.

Selectivity in admissions is also frequently rationalized on educational grounds. The brightest students, according to this argument, need to be around other bright students to realize their maximum potential. This is, in effect, the "center of excellence" argument, where the best students and the best faculty and the greatest resources are concentrated in one place. A closely related argument is to use selective admissions to insure academic standards. The rationale here seems to be that we guarantee high standards at the exit point by having high standards at the entry point. While there is no necessary reason why admissions standards should dictate graduation standards,[11] it is true that, if the institution utterly fails in its educational efforts with students, graduation standards will indeed be determined by admissions standards!

While there may be something to be said for the center of excellence concept at the level of an individual institution, this concept poses serious problems when it is viewed from a systems perspective. What civic interest is served by concentrating the least well-prepared students and the least resources in a separate set of institutions? How can such an arrangement be rationalized in terms of the larger interest of the community and the society? The fact of the matter is that it can't. To see why this is so, we can again use an analogy from medicine. For example, in trying to design a total health care system for our community, how much sense does it make to (1) refuse to treat the sickest patients; (2) establish a large number of underequipped and underfunded facilities for moderately ill patients; and (3) create a much smaller number of elite facilities with the finest and most advanced equipment and best-trained and highest-paid staff which would admit only people with common colds?

A KEY ROLE FOR STUDENTS

In taking more of a "systems" approach to the problem of underpreparation, it is important to keep in mind that our greatest untapped resource may be the students themselves. There is probably no other group better suited to tutoring underprepared students than their better-prepared peers. If such peer tutoring could be built into the curriculum in a systematic fashion, everyone would benefit: more pedagogical resources would be created to deal with underpreparation, the better-prepared students would have an opportunity to master course material in greater depth by teaching it to others, and the overall sense of a collaborative, caring, democratic community within the institution would be greatly strengthened. If such a mentoring and tutoring program were expanded to include a variety of service-learning opportunities for student tutors to work with underprepared students in the public schools, the bonds between the higher education institutions and the local community would also be strengthened.

OTHER BENEFITS OF COLLABORATION

The state-level "systems" conversations being advocated here would hopefully help to dispel some of the myths about underpreparation: for example, that such students are simply incapable of learning, or that underpreparation is a problem only for certain types of institutions (a high percentage of freshman at the University of Calfornia, for example, are required to take remedial English). It would also address some of the core issues that individual institutions will not, or simply cannot, address on their own, such as how are different types of institutions with a state system going to divide up the responsibility for teaching underprepared students? Is it educationally sound—in terms of the larger systems interest of effectively educating underprepared students—simply to track most of them into community colleges, which have the most limited educational resources? Have not the public universities already developed some expertise in this area, for example, through their special programs for athletes? Are there structural changes—such as making each community college a part of a university—that would help to bring more educational resources to bear on this problem? What can university research tell us about innovative approaches—such as cooperative learning and peer tutoring—that might be especially effective with underprepared students? Can some of the university's educational and social science research capability be focused more directly on assessing the impact of various approaches to remediation? Institutions of all types have already experimented with literally dozens of different types of programs, and it is a shame that so little systematic evaluation has been done so that all institutions could begin using the most effective approaches.

A major unanswered question that still needs much more study and analysis is the efficacy of various approaches to educating underprepared students. What works best, with which type of student, and under what conditions? It may well turn out that the most effective approaches are quite expensive, but this should not deter us from seeking the relevant knowledge. My own sense about the cost issue is that public resistance to increased educational spending is often based on these very same concerns about efficacy: Will our tax dollars really buy anything? Will the money really produce any results? If we could produce solid evidence documenting the efficacy of certain approaches to educating underprepared students, public resistance to greater spending would almost certainly diminish, especially in light of the enormous social and economic costs that would be associated with *not* doing an effective job with these students.

Here again we can see the potential power of interinstitutional collaboration, especially at the state level. Consider for a moment the opportunities for comprehensive research and analysis that could grow from an extended collaborative discussion involving institutions and systems of institutions at all levels. When one realizes that there are literally hundreds of "developmental" programs of all types and perhaps hundreds of individual courses being offered in our larger states, the possibilities for collaborative research are remarkable. Rather than isolated, one-shot studies where one course or one approach is studied in isolation, the large number and great diversity of programs would allow us to examine simultaneously the effects of many different approaches. Even if only a fraction of the institutions and programs in a state were to be studied simultaneously, the large numbers would still make it possible to design very sophisticated and comprehensive studies. This interinstitutional collaboration would also facilitate the development of excellent training programs for those who teach underprepared students.

What I am suggesting here is that research on programs for underprepared students and preparation of faculty to teach such students should be a collaborative effort carried out at the state level. Different states, in turn, can exchange intelligence gained from these studies with each other. In this way, the different approaches taken in different institutions and states can be viewed as a grand "natural experiment," where evaluators in the various institutional settings work together to identify the most effective educational strategies.

In short, these interinstitutional conversations would hopefully be successful in leading the participants to agree on the following:

1. Developing effective programs for lower-performing students at all levels of education is of vital importance not only to our educational system, but also to the state and the society at large.
2. Finding and implementing more effective programs for underprepared students is a "systems" challenge that must be accepted and shared by all institutions at all levels of education. In particular, the more selective or elite institutions need to assume a greater share of the responsibility for strengthening the education of such students.
3. Giving greater priority to the preparation of faculty and staff who work with underprepared students. Such preparation would be enhanced if it were done on an interinstitutional or systems basis.
4. Investing substantially more resources in collaborative efforts to experiment with alternative approaches to remediation and to implement large-scale collaborative studies of different approaches.

POSSIBILITIES FOR ACTION

The real question, I suppose, is *how* to effect this change from an individualistic/competitive to a community/collaborative or systems mentality. I'm not sure that any of us really knows. I sometimes have fantasies that UC Berkeley will someday soon call together all of the postsecondary institutions in the Bay area and just say, "let's do it." The fantasy continues: UCLA, not to be outdone, calls all the other southern California campuses together and says, "let's do it." And the other prestigious flagship universities—Michigan, Virginia, Wisconsin, Texas, Washington, and the rest—follow suit. And in the areas like Boston, where the prestigious institutions are mostly private, the initiative might need to come from places like Harvard. Fantasy or not, one thing seems certain: if a leading institution in any state were to propose something like this, the idea would quickly "trickle down" and be seriously considered by the rest of the public and private institutions in that state. And if the movement were to be started instead by a major state university system like the University of California, flagship universities in other states would be much more likely to consider it. In other words, if institutions at the top of the pecking order see fit to deviate from the sacred cow of selectivity, this in effect "gives permission" to the rest of us to do it.

It is always possible, of course, that the institutions that currently enroll most of the underprepared students will come to realize that they don't really need permission from the more elite institutions to give greater priority to educating the underprepared student. Current political trends, however, seem to be headed in the opposite direction. Major public college systems such as the City University of New York and California State University are talking about "phasing out" remedial education. One major problem is that many of the faculty in these institutions support these initiatives because they see the mere presence of underprepared students as thwarting their ambitions to attain greater "academic excellence." If the more elite public and private institutions continue to stand passively on the sidelines, these wrong-headed, antidemocratic, and self-destructive efforts to dump the underprepared completely out of the public college system may well succeed.

Another possible scenario would involve an initiative from state government. What if the legislature of a large state like New York, California, or Texas were to establish an incentive funding program which would, in effect, put a bounty on each underprepared student who successfully completes a postsecondary education program? Such an initiative would almost certainly change the institutional perception of the underprepared student from a "liability" to an "asset." It would also tend to encourage much greater interinstitutional collaboration, especially if the different public and private institutions within particular geographic regions were allowed to share the bounties.

Still another possibility would be grassroots efforts, possibly encouraged or sponsored regional consortia or by national associations like the American Council on Education or the Association of American Universities, where groups of similar institutions would jointly agree to substantially expand and upgrade their programs for underprepared students.

CONCLUDING THOUGHTS

The problem that plagues our contemporary democracy is in many respects the same problem that Alexis de Tocqueville [12] identified more than 150 years ago: the tension between individualism and community. This tension is exacerbated by the mistaken belief that we are independent of and separate from each other. Even our most recent research on students highlights the importance of community: The single most important source of influence on the individual student turns out to be the peer group. [13] We associate freedom with individualism, and democracy with community, but the two are really inseparable: we *create* our own democracy and our government through our individual beliefs and actions, while at the same time the condition and quality of our community and democracy define what kind of individual freedoms and what kind of life we enjoy. The real question is what kind of community and democracy we want to have.

In certain respects our preoccupation with enhancing resources and reputations and being smart is simply a reflection of our changing society, which during the past few decades has increasingly come to celebrate the values of materialism, competitiveness, and individualism. While it goes without saying that social institutions often mirror the values of the larger society, higher education's continuing adherence to these values represents a major obstacle in its efforts not only to deal with the problem of underpreparation, but also to enhance civic engagement and civic life and to promote the cause of educational and social equity in the larger society.

In short, the civic responsibility of higher education is really a matter of values and beliefs. The initial challenge for academia at this point is not so much to change our traditional beliefs, but simply to become more conscious of these beliefs and of the role they play in our professional lives. It is one thing to embrace beliefs that do no serve us well, but quite another to be largely unaware of these beliefs or of the extent to which they affect our policies and actions. I believe that an open inquiry into our most deeply felt beliefs will show, for example, that our preoccupation with acquiring resources, enhancing institutional reputations, being smart and being seen by others as smart has affected practically everything we do, and that many of these effects are contrary not only to our own best interests as academics, but also to the educational mission of our institutions. My use of the term "contrary" is by no means meant to suggest that intelligence and intellectual skills should not be central to the values that govern academic life. Rather, what we need to begin is a serious discussion of the extent to which we have come to worship merely *being* smart, as opposed to the value of *developing* smartness. Since this latter value is what excellent teaching and excellent education are all about, this discussion will almost certainly serve us well, not only in our efforts to effect meaningful reforms in our approach to educating underprepared students and fostering civic responsibility in all of our students, but also in our desire to lead more authentic and productive lives as academics.

NOTES

1. D. Goleman, *Emotional Intelligence* (New York: Bantam, 1995).
2. A.W. Astin and L.J. Sax, "How Undergraduates Are Affected by Service Participation," *Journal of College Student Development*, 39, no. 3 (1998): 251–63; A.W. Astin, L. J. Sax, and J. Avalos, "Long-term Effects of Volunteerism During the Undergraduate Years," *The Review of Higher Education*, 22, no. 2 (1999): 187–202; J. Eyler, D.E. Giles, Jr., and J. Braxton, "The Impact of Service-Learning on College Students," *Michigan Journal of Community Service-Learning*, 4 (1997): 4, 5–15; S. Myers-Lipton, "Effect of a Comprehensive Service-Learning Program on College Students' Level of Modern Racism," *Michigan Journal of Community Service-Learning*, 3 (1996): 44–54.
3. L.J. Sax, A.W. Astin, M. Arrendondo, and W.S. Korn, *The American College Teacher: National Norms for the 1995–96 HERI Faculty Survey* (Los Angeles: University of California, Higher Education Research Institute, 1996).
4. A.W. Astin, *Achieving Educational Excellence: A Critical Assessment of Priorities and Practices in Higher Education* (San Francisco: Jossey-Bass, 1985).
5. F.L. Ford, "Today's Undergraduates: Are They Human?" *Harvard Magazine*, 86, no. 4 (1984): 29–32.

6. J. Oakes and K.H. Quartz, *Creating New Educational Communities: Yearbook of the National Society for the Study of Education*, 94th vol., *Part 1* (Chicago: University of Chicago, 1995); J.E. Rossmann, H.S. Astin, A.W. Astin, and E. El-Khawas, *Open Admissions at CUNY: An Analysis of the First Year* (Englewood Cliffs, NJ: Prentice-Hall, 1975).

7. A.W. Astin, L. Tsui, and J. Avalos, *Degree Attainment Rates at American Colleges and Universities: Effects of Race, Gender, and Institutional Type* (Los Angeles: University of California, Higher Education Research Institute, 1996).

8. A.W. Astin, "Our Obsession with Being 'Smart' Is Distorting Intellectual Life," *Chronicle of Higher Education* (26 September 1997): A60.

9. Goleman, *Emotional Intelligence*.

10. Astin, Tsui, and Avalos, *Degree Attainment Rates*.

11. A.W. Astin, *Assessment for Excellence: The Philosophy and Practice of Assessment and Evaluation in Higher Education* (New York: American Council on Education and Macmillan Publishing, 1991).

12. A. de Tocqueville, *Democracy in America* (New York: Vintage Books, 1945).

13. A.W. Astin, *Assessment for Excellence: The Philosophy and Practice of Assessment and Evaluation in Higher Education* (Phoenix, AZ: Oryx Press, 1993).

PART 3

. . . .

Interactions with Other Sectors of Society

CHAPTER 7

How Concepts of Politics Control Concepts of Civic Responsibility

David Mathews

This volume is largely about civic responsibility, which often refers to what individuals owe each other—the duty to be at least respectful, tolerant, and civil, and hopefully reciprocal, caring, and benevolent. For my part, I would like to offer a somewhat different, though not incompatible, reading of civic responsibility, one that grows out of a concept of democratic politics which has fallen out of favor in the twentieth century.

All essays are journeys and this one is no exception. A brief word about where I am going may be helpful. After giving another view of civic responsibility and explaining the sources of this concept, I want to describe how and why it fell victim to frustrations with and eventually cynicism about our current political system. Because I don't want to give the impression that the prevailing outlook is permanent, I introduce some history to show how notions of politics, and particularly ideas about the role of the public, have changed over time and how they have influenced colleges and universities. Several pages are devoted to describing the way the current understanding of politics came to dominate academic culture by the middle of the twentieth century. This concept of politics leads to the interpretation of civic responsibility as primarily acts of individual altruism. Citizenship then tends to become disconnected from politics—particularly in the eyes of students. That is very troubling.

What can colleges and universities do about the atrophy of a central premise of our democracy—which is that "we the people" are the sovereign authority and are responsible for our collective well-being? Does the current distress of democracy really affect the self-interests of academe? I try to do more than say "I hope so." I make the case that our institutions need to reposition themselves in the public world to respond to a pressing question brought on by institutions like the University of Phoenix: What is unique about what we do? And doing that makes common cause with a citizenry that is also turning to the public realm to regain some of its sovereignty. The confluence of these forces can give academics a different experience with the public and that will broaden and enrich the concept of civic responsibility.

RESPONSIBILITY FOR OUR SHARED LIFE

So to begin: What if we thought of "civic responsibility" as responsibility *for* the civic realm, responsibility not just to other people but for what we and others share—for the goods we have in common, for the quality of our life together, for the creation of a just social order? While that wouldn't invalidate individualistic views of civic responsibility, such a frame of reference might expand our understanding of higher education's obligations and opportunities. It might raise useful questions about the responsibility colleges and universities have, not only for the civic education of students, but for the civic realm.

Because terms like "civic realm" and "shared life" may seem vague, let me use an example to clarify what I mean. A few years ago, our neighborhood formed a voluntary association to protect and maintain a narrow, winding, tree-lined lane that we use to get to our homes. It also gives the area where we live a distinctive character. Our shared life is a life of deciding on needed repairs, gathering to remove trees brought down by winter storms, and celebrating holidays together. Our relationship is a common good, as is the road. We are responsible for both; we are the ones who determine what happens to both.

A shared life that goes beyond a neighborhood could be called a public life, even a political life. The "political" can mean—and has meant—the field of associations, or that part of our life with others, in which we attend to our common business. One of the principal reasons for constructing such a realm is an interest in a just social order, a society where authority is exercised fairly. People create a public life when they join to decide which actions best promote their collective well-being. While these decisions may be as commonplace as how to protect a road, they are ultimately about how to achieve the highest goods obtainable through human action. Even in deciding what might appear to be purely practical matters—like how to reduce neighborhood crime—we are really determining what is most valuable to us. Are we willing to become a walled enclave in order to be safe? What kind of neighborhood, community, or country do we want? In other words, public life is an arena in which we define the ultimate ends and means of life together. Institutions derive their missions from these definitions. They continuously refine their purposes in ongoing exchanges with citizens in order to make them relevant to the public's agenda. When this interaction slows down or stops, governments, schools, civic organizations, and other instrumentalities begin to lose legitimacy. Although institutions may operate with internally generated objectives, they will have increasing difficulty finding their unique fit in society if they are out of touch with public life. I will return to this point later.

As you can see, I think of public life as more than the operation of governments or even the elections that constitute governments. Public life is political, but it includes all that has to be done in a polis, or body politic. I have this broader definition in mind when I ask you to consider the proposition that concepts of politics influence our understanding of the civic or public realm.

Because of the importance of all that happens in the public realm, it has a value in its own right. And, given this value, it deserves to be enriched and maintained. Who is responsible for this? Just as in the case of the lane where I live, citizens are. They are responsible for both the character and the viability of their shared life with others because they determine both. In this sense, citizens are genuine majesties: they have the power to make collective decisions that have significant consequences, provided they exercise it.

CITIZENS WITH THE OBLIGATIONS OF SOVEREIGNS

Although the notion that citizens are sovereign may seem far-fetched in an age when people feel politically powerless, the idea itself generates power. Americans seem to have had the strongest sense of responsibility for the public realm and the goods they share in common when they have had the strongest sense of their sovereignty.

I recall one citizen's account of what participation in the American Revolution had meant to him. He said it had given him a sense of being part of the "sovereignty of his country." That implied more than an obligation to other people, it implied responsibility for what he and other citizens were together—a sovereign entity.

Being part of the ruling authority of a new nation gave this eighteenth-century American a new personal identity, one that was public and quintessentially political. Although he was likely to have been an active member of a congregation, a person in touch with his roots, and a bearer of the interests of his occupation, he was not defined merely by his religion, ancestry, and economic situation. He was that and more. And his political identity prescribed his obligations: as a sovereign, he was accountable for the well-being of the whole of a new country and for the country as a whole.

STUDENTS AND THE SOVEREIGNTY OF THE COUNTRY

What has happened to this sense of being a public person, with the obligations of a sovereign? A few years ago, the Kettering Foundation asked that question of citizens in general and students in particular.[1] Neither had any great sense of sovereignty. The public realm, in their eyes, had been reduced to a system for electing representatives to govern, which had become corrupted by monied interests and powerful elites. Consequently, the product of that system, the government, was of questionable legitimacy. Even worse, young and old alike felt powerless to do anything about the situation. Most students wanted nothing to do with the political system. As I have reported elsewhere, the students we talked with were particularly turned off by the tone of politics and the negative tenor of what appears to be a grossly adversarial system, with no regard for fair play. That is why they said the political system is "a system I'd never want to be a part of."

This is not to say that these students didn't care about the issues confronting the country—about poverty, injustice, and threats to the environment. Despite charges that young people are totally preoccupied with personal self-interests, our study found that the younger generation is no more uncaring than the older generation is apathetic. The good news is that students care a great deal. The bad news is that they don't think the political system can solve the problems that worry them. The younger generation can be even more cynical than others about the way the political system operates, and far more pessimistic about their ability to change it for the better.

Students talked to the researchers more about their rights and about what government should do for them than they did about their obligations. Most saw political responsibility as a deferred duty, at best, something to take on after graduation. Their concept of citizenship is particularly interesting. They believed that "*politics doesn't have anything to do with being a citizen*" (emphasis added). In other words, their sense of citizenship is apolitical; it is largely social. "Politics," they said, "has nothing to do with my life." For students, citizenship often seems to be disconnected from politics; a good citizen is simply a good person, an individual living a responsible private life. That's very different from the way Americans who lived through the Revolution understood citizenship.

Even if students did imagine any political activity, it was confined largely to what they might do as individuals. As one confessed, we "still tend to do things that are more individualistic." They certainly didn't see themselves as part of a sovereignty or acting as a public. The perception that they were lone individuals up against an impregnable megalith, surely contributed to their sense of powerlessness.

Prior generations of students must have learned these lessons about politics well: most adults now have the same inability to imagine how citizens can change the political system. They increasingly reject the argument that their votes count because they see the enormous influence of powerful interests. In a study of the results from National Issues Forums on *Governing America*, we found that although people are convinced that citizenship must be reinvented in order for government and partisan politics to change, they have great difficulty imagining how citizens can reclaim their sovereignty. I cannot think of an outlook more debilitating in a country that wants to be democratic. It makes a desert of public life.

HIGHER EDUCATION'S ROLE

What about higher education's responsibility for students' understanding of politics and for the attitudes they develop? While most institutions are pledged to produce a new generation of citizens and leaders, many academics doubt that politics and political leadership can or should be taught in college (apart from teaching politics as a subject). Preparation for politics comes as preparation for life generally, so their argument goes, through the liberal arts, professional studies, and extracurricular community service.

Official proclamations and actual campus practice can be at odds, and yet attempts to reconcile the two are often unsuccessful. At one public university, a faculty member kept pointing out that, even though the catalogue proclaimed a commitment to a civic education, the faculty seemed unable to say how the curriculum met that pledge. Eventually, his colleagues solved the problem: They eliminated the statement about civic education.

While the curriculum-as-usual may be the best prescription for a political education, students in our study didn't think so. They questioned the liberal arts argument not because they dislike the subjects, but because they don't think political education comes primarily from "knowledge about things," which is the way they interpret the liberal arts. Some even questioned the political relevance of community service, not because it isn't appealing, but because it seems to be done more for personal satisfaction. It is more about helping others than finding political solutions to problems.

CONCEPTS OF THE PUBLIC

Intentionally or not, institutions of higher education teach politics, and the politics they teach carries with it a very definite notion of what the public is and what it can do. It also leads to the prevailing understanding of civic responsibility. In most cases, political life is portrayed on campus as it is in society generally—as a life of voting, obeying laws, paying taxes, and receiving government benefits. After graduation, most students plan to do all those things, but their sense of political duty ends there. They also expect to be socially responsible individuals and to perform their share of individual service. Yet, as I said earlier and as they make plain, these have nothing to do with politics. The politics they are "taught" defines citizens by their relationship to government rather than to one another and to what they share in common. The result is the apolitical concept of citizenship we uncovered in the research. Given this concept of politics, it is no wonder that students find it difficult to imagine what they can do publicly by forming relationships with one another—except, of course, through forming relationships in special interest groups and mass protests.

Institutional views of politics and the public don't come from classes or extracurricular projects but from the academic culture. They are embedded in the disciplines and professions, and implied in what institutions do when they reach out to those off campus with research and service. Higher education is, in fact, one wellspring of the conventional understanding of politics, one that doesn't have a role for sovereign citizens or a place for a vibrant public life that is more than social.

Take the case of public service. How is the "public" understood? As a body of sovereigns? All too often service to others, though done with the best of intentions to empower, nonetheless gives the impression that the "public" is the same as the "served." The concept of university service follows from academe's concept of knowledge. It is a particular kind of knowledge—scientific, expert, and professional. And we are all much the better for it; just consider the advances in medicine. Providing such professional knowledge implies, however, that the public is deficient in information or that what people do know is of a lesser order—a product of custom more than experimentation, an expression of opinion more than fact, a result of emotion more than reason; if citizens know anything, it is confined to the local and the immediate. Bound by their parochialism, they can't comprehend the larger world and its order. That can be done only by professionals armed with expert knowledge. Later, I will elaborate on why this happens even when institutions don't intend it, but for now, I want to emphasize the political consequences. This message is that citizens can never be more than amateurs, and amateurs certainly can't be sovereigns.

It is worth noting that, even though scientific knowledge dominates academe and is the model for understanding the social as well as the physical world, it is only one kind of knowledge. There is also a rich tradition of knowledge constructed by integrating human experience. This socially constructed knowledge is the source of what the Greeks called "practical wisdom," which tells us how we should act when there is no authoritative voice to guide us. Practical wisdom helps us with questions that have more than one answer. Yet such ways of knowing are not in vogue on most campuses.

The prevailing concept of what it means to "know" is certainly a powerful influence in academe. But I am not suggesting that the diminishing sense of a sovereign public comes solely or even primarily from the conventional episte-mology. I think that the current epistemology simply reinforces the prevailing concept of politics.

CHANGING CONCEPTS

Today's notion of the public is but one of many that have shaped and reshaped the work of colleges and universities over time. How these institutions have understood the public at different points in history is very telling.

The colonial colleges' concept of the public was as a congregation. Initially, that meant a single denomination (congregational in the case of Yale, for instance) and later several denominations (Princeton is usually credited with leading the way). We should be careful not to think of these congregations as purely religious bodies—their Protestantism was heavily political. Still, this definition of the public in a theocratic polity led colleges to develop a curricula best suited for training leadership for congregants and producing an informed laity. The sacred texts were the Protestant Bible and the classics (Greek and Latin literature).

By the end of the first quarter of the eighteenth century, the definition of the public moved beyond that provided by the church. The effect on academic institutions is well documented in the changing subjects of student debates. Abstractions of theology, ethics, metaphysics, and logic (for example, whether ideas are innate or whether cognition is more than sensory) gave way to issues of freedom and self-government. In 1725, students at Harvard University debated whether the legitimacy of government is based on the consent of the governed. The shift to the concerns of the public was particularly dramatic during Ezra Stiles's tenure at Yale College from 1778 to 1795.

Stiles sensed students' lack of enthusiasm for the internally generated topics dear to the theologians and metaphysicists on the faculty. While he kept these in order to sharpen students' skill in syllogistic debate, he added a wholly new agenda. In *Connecticut's Seminary of Sedition: Yale College*, Louis Leonard Tucker exemplified the new topics: "whether the present war be lawful on the side of America"; "whether Vermont is, and of right ought to be a separate and independent state"; "whether a standing army would be dangerous in America"; "which is preferable: the Polity of the American Republic, or that of the British Monarchy at its best Estate?" [2] Edmund Morgan wrote in his biography of Stiles, "he set the students to arguing questions that brought the Yale curricu-lum almost painfully up to date." [3]

The redefined public that pushed its way into the consciousness of higher education was a citizenry that held opinions on the subject of independence—and was willing to act on them. Civic responsibility in the revolutionary era took the form of public speeches in favor of liberty and symbolic acts showing opposition to the Crown. Tucker tells of Yale seniors who, on the advice of their tutors, joined the nonimportation movement by a collective pledge to abstain from "foreign spirituous Liquors." One student wrote home, advising his parents of his decision in this rueful note: "Shall not want that Sherry you Reserved for me before vacancy, as all the Scholars have unanimously agreed not to Drink any foreign spirituous Liquors any more, a Scheme proposed by Mr. Woodhull and seconded by the other Tutors and the scholars in succession; there was no Compulsion, but all a voluntary Act." [4]

Interestingly, when students argued for independence they addressed their fellow citizens, not just their classmates, as in this advertisement patriotic Yale students placed in the New Haven newspaper in 1769:

> The Senior Class in Yale College have unanimously agreed to make their Appearance at the next public Commencement, when they are to take their first Degree, wholly dressed in the Manufactures of our own Country: And desire this public Notice may be given of their Resolution, that so their Parents and Friends may have sufficient Time to be providing Homespun Cloths for them, that none of them may be obliged to the hard Necessity of unfashionable Singularity, by wearing imported Cloth. [5]

College curricula changed as a result of the new concept of the public. Students continued to read the classics but according to Lawrence Cremin, their interpretations were different:

> Eighteenth-century students read the Greek and Latin authors, as had students for generations, and they no doubt parsed and scanned and construed the texts. But they read the classics in their own ways and could be forgiven, perhaps, if they tended to learn from Aristotle the dangers of violating the immutable laws of God and nature, from Plutarch the glory of opposing tyranny even unto the death, from Cato the power of a virtuous republicanism rooted in the soil, from Cicero the excellence of reasonable laws and the hazards of arbitrary government, and from Tacitus the decadence of the later Roman (read English) empire. Somewhat in the fashion of the Renaissance students who entered school already familiar with the liturgy and only then learned to read it, the provincial student entered his academy or college filled with the political commonplaces of the day and only then learned their sources. [6]

In the postcolonial era, "completing the great work of the Revolution" is an apt description of the agenda that further transformed American higher education. While the public continued to be understood in political terms, its work broadened from a struggle for independence to the building of a nation. New institutions were established to take on the new mandate. Revolutionaries became a public of artisans, farmers, and teachers. Immensely proud of the liberty won on the battlefield, they recognized that continued freedom required self-determination and that the dream of self-government could not be realized by an ignorant citizenry. Higher education was to inform the public's judgment.

Even this brief account demonstrates how views of politics and the public have influenced the way colleges and universities go about learning, teaching, and serving. If I were to write more on the subject, I would follow up on the observation made by William Sullivan, one of the authors in this book, who has pointed out that in the early twentieth century the public domain was increasingly understood as a realm of "panhumanistic" ideals rooted in reform-minded Protestantism. That understanding encouraged higher education to think of itself as a movement devoted to the advancement of public ideals. This is particularly interesting because higher education today is more likely to be considered a managed enterprise than a moral crusade.

ORIGINS OF THE CURRENT VIEW OF THE PUBLIC

How did higher education get from its earlier notions of the public to the current understanding of citizens as voters, consumers, and clients? The change, brought about by a number of forces, was evident before the mid-twentieth century. Shaken by World War I and then a worldwide depression, followed by the rise of fascism, many elites were convinced that an increasingly technological world of global forces make a sovereign citizenry obsolete. Walter Lippmann made that case better than anyone else when he argued that citizens are like theatergoers who arrive in the middle of the third act and leave before the final curtain. They have neither the capacity nor the interest to direct public affairs responsibly. [7] The best citizens can do is to choose their leaders.

The devaluation of the public also came at the time that a new philosophy, supposedly nonpolitical, which I would call "professionalism," was taking hold. It accompanied the professionalization of most vocations and institutions. In higher education, it not only gave rise to professional schools but also to the professionalization of disciplines within the liberal arts. A new generation of academics began talking more to each other than to their fellow citizens, who could not understand their expert language. Tom Bender, a historian at New York University, noted that speaking in public to the public eventually became suspect. [8] As most educational institutions began to see their new mission as the preparation of "scientifically" trained professionals, academics intentionally developed a language that would be unintelligible to citizens.

I want to make a clear distinction between the philosophy of "professionalism" and professionals themselves because not all professionals are advocates of professionalism. I also want to acknowledge again that professional expertise has been responsible for many of the triumphs of this century. We all rely on professionals who excel in their work. No one wants a dentist who pulls the wrong tooth. [9]

Americans usually like the teachers they know and the doctors who treat them. What they don't like about professionalism are its patronizing assumptions about the public. Professionalism reduces a sovereign public to a collection of patients. Americans' perception that professionalism has little use for them can be traced to the early twentieth century, when this philosophy developed in response to what leaders saw as not only an obsolete but often dangerous citizenry. To put it bluntly, the popular unrest during depressions scared the devil out of the establishment. Spokesmen for angry farmers like Ben "Pitchfork" Tillman threatened the Democratic and Republican parties alike, drawing such stalwarts as William Jennings Bryan into the new People's, or Populist, Party. [10] The threat of popular, working-class discontent was still strong during the Great Depression of the 1930s when Father Coughlin infused old Populist themes with appeals to racial and religious prejudices and rallied a substantial national radio following.

These popular movements developed in an atmosphere of widespread political corruption. Votes were bought, ballot boxes stuffed, unfavorable returns thrown out. "We had to do it," one of the established leaders later confessed. "Those d___ Populists would have ruined the country!" [11] This corruption was among the issues that brought a new class of leaders to power. And these sons of established families and well-to-do businessmen became the dominant force in shaping the mind of modern America. Because they all sought "progress" of some kind, they are usually called Progressives. [12]

The new leaders wrote a new compact for America. They said, in effect, that they would take care of the public's problems—but in their own way. And the public by and large deferred to the rising class of professional leaders. Citizens bought what the professionals were selling—expertise. When Walter Lippmann argued that the public is a myth, a phantom, the charge stuck. New leadership set out deliberately and systematically to ensure that the citizenry was perceived as morally and intellectually incapable of governing itself. [13] Today we would say that was their "spin" on the public. They believed American democracy had to have guardians who will safeguard the true public interest from the masses.

The development of professionalism, and an accompanying romance with scientific objectivity, accelerated the displacement of the public and eventually—absent a meaningful concept of sovereign citizens—led to the redefinition of politics. Professionalism affected nearly every field—education, philanthropy, medicine, social work, and even journalism. At the same time professional city managers and civil service bureaucrats were replacing elected mayors and their cronies, professional caseworkers were replacing the "friendly visitors" of Jane Addams' settlement houses. These new caseworkers were "scientifically" trained in psychology and sociology; the citizens they ministered to became their "clients." [14]

The new professionals were not unsympathetic to those they served. On the contrary, their relationships with their clients were shaped by their professional concerns, which grew out of a conviction that the public is deficient and what it lacks can be supplied only by their expertise. The operative assumption is that the public is "sick" and cannot possibly get well without professional help, which is based on what science gives professionals—objective truth, expressed as facts. This change in the meaning of service has a great deal to do with the message about the public that I mentioned earlier.

The most powerful feature of professionalism is that its paradigm precludes any understandings of the public other than as a passive mass without the capacity to know its best interests. There can be no competing ideas. Citizens can't be seen as anything other than various kinds of clients—patients, consumers, readers. The idea that the public is a diverse body of citizens who claim responsibility for and act on their problems almost died in the late twentieth century. The term "public" has lost so much of its original meaning that it now suggests little more than an adjective for rest rooms that anybody can use.

This weakened concept of the public contributed to a growing conviction among professionals that citizens are apathetic. If people have little to do except vote every so often, it shouldn't be surprising that they are seen as being in a deep civic sleep most of the time. Their apathy was considered a blessing, since an active citizenry would inevitably interfere with the work of professionals. Once people have selected professionals, the code of professionalism calls for the public to leave them alone to do their jobs. It is impossible to conceive of the public helping professionals because, by definition, citizens have only marginal competencies.

Obviously such a public has neither the authority nor the power to be sovereign. At times, citizens might have to be consulted or grant permission, but it need not be taken more seriously than that. If the public is of little importance, then the public realm isn't really important either. Nothing significant happens there. The protection of common goods is delegated to governments and other professional institutions.

At this point, you may wonder whether my argument is overstated. Even if the lines are drawn too sharply, it is difficult to deny that the current ideas about politics lead to a weakened notion of the public and that leads to a weakened notion of political citizenship. If there is little that my fellow citizens and I can do as amateurs in a professional world, then all that is left for us is striving to be the best possible individuals. By alleviating the symptoms of problems that the political system can't solve, we can at least help one another. We can hope our example of good character and personal responsibility will influence others. Such altruism is certainly a necessary condition for democracy, though hardly a sufficient one.

HIGHER EDUCATION'S STAKE IN THE PUBLIC REALM'S VITALITY

Supposing my arguments have some merit, what can institutions of higher education contribute? What can they offer Americans who believe that nothing short of citizen action can stem the degradation of the political system but who can't imagine how individuals can create an effective public? Is it even realistic for educators to respond? Some will point out what is undoubtedly true: The current view of politics doesn't originate only in academic culture; it is based on what people see happening in legislative chambers, campaign headquarters, and newsrooms. Others might say, perhaps in private, that academe's self-interest isn't served by worrying about these kind of problems. After all, higher education enjoys immense prestige, has powerful patrons in business and government, and receives a steady stream of students who know that degrees are crucial to their financial futures. While academics may share the deep frustrations of students and other citizens regarding the political system, it is not clear what the institutions themselves have to contribute beyond their current efforts. In the current climate, not even Ezra Stiles would be able to put the public and its concerns on institutional agendas already burdened with issues like efficient management. And boards of trustees, though they are composed of citizens, may not see the strengthening of democracy as an institutional imperative, given all of the other matters they are obliged to consider.

Still, there are some interests in higher education which, although different from those of citizens, might help to revive the public realm. William Sullivan mentions one of these interests—the need for colleges and universities to recover a sense of purpose and integrity, to be able to define what is unique about what they do. Identifying that uniqueness will become increasingly important as society finds new and more efficient ways to produce knowledge, provide instruction, and deliver service. Traditional college campuses whose overhead includes the costs of permanent buildings, a resident faculty, and a rich extracurricular life, will be at a competitive disadvantage if efficiency is their primary objective.

Is there something really distinctive that traditional institutions have to offer? Answers can be found only in the public realm, where citizens decide what is truly valuable. And, that being the case, there is reason for institutions to reconsider their position in public life. Rather than engaging the public in public relations campaigns, they must be reengaged *by* a public, whose agenda is no longer what it was a half-century ago.

Based on some recent conversations with faculty senates, I have begun to think that faculty members may be the first to sense a vacuum around matters of purpose, the first to be concerned with identifying the uniqueness of what they do. Most didn't enter academic life in order to enhance people's marketability. They also may be more sensitive than administrators to students' frustrations with the political system and the need to find effective ways to respond to them. And certain groups in the faculty may be the first to become restive as expertise becomes less socially relevant. They may feel the absence of public happiness or fulfillment in their professional lives.

A DIFFERENT EXPERIENCE WITH THE PUBLIC

In these observations about faculty, I am not suggesting that change can come exclusively from within institutions. It seldom has. Usually there is a confluence of external and internal forces—for instance, a contrary-minded president like Stiles and a student body captured by the prospect of independence. Institutions of higher education are not likely to change their understanding of civic responsibility as individual responsibility, nor are they likely to instill a sense of obligation for what happens in the public realm, until they expand the prevailing conception of the political and the public. And that is not likely to happen until colleges and universities reposition themselves in the public realm so they can experience the citizenry in more ways than traditional teaching, research, and service now permit.

Happily, there are already some efforts at doing this. I have reported elsewhere on twenty-odd Public Policy Institutes (PPIs), which emphasize the "public" more than policy. They are providing space on campuses for citizens to develop the habit of deciding important issues together, and in doing so, begin to reclaim some of their role as sovereigns. This campus space is linked to space for public deliberation in communities. When these institutes bring faculty members and students into these settings, they provide them with a different way to experience the public.

The National Collegiate Honors Council is doing much of the same thing. Students are directly learning deliberative democracy by making decisions together on issues like the future of the Social Security system, affirmative action, and the type of postsecondary education needed for the twenty-first century. Like the students of Yale College, they are addressing their fellow citizens, not just their fellow students. The forums with students, faculty, and citizens on postsecondary education are an excellent example of academics repositioning themselves in the public world. They are providing a service, but not in the tradition of dispensing expert knowledge. By interacting with the public, they are constructing practical wisdom about the kind of education that will be needed in the future. The forums help to answer the question of what is uniquely valuable about colleges and universities.

One of the boldest experiments in repositioning higher education in the public world has been taking place at a private institution. The faculty of the College of St. Catherine's in St. Paul, Minnesota, has been challenging itself with the question of how it would go about its research, teaching, and service if these activities were considered "public work." [15] Some questions that arose from this self-examination are: Does our work have a public purpose? Can it be done in an open, public setting? Is it done by or with a public? Does it result in a public outcome or product? Using these questions to reimagine academic work has already led to new ways of teaching and to several new forms of community involvement.

All of these experiments are worth watching. They are based on distinctive ideas: The public is an important actor with crucial work to do. Citizenship is not divorced from politics. If higher education is a part of public life and if its reasons for being are to be found there, then these efforts serve the deeper interests of academe. Not only do they bring the experience of public-making to campus, they bring to life a richer concept of democratic politics, which will generate an expanded notion of civic responsibility.

NOTES

1. The Harwood Group, *College Students Talk Politics* (Dayton, OH: Kettering Foundation, 1993); The Harwood Group, *Citizens and Politics: A View from Main Street America* (Dayton, OH: Kettering Foundation, 1991).

2. L.L. Tucker, *Connecticut's Seminary of Sedition: Yale College* (Chester, CT: Pequot Press, 1974), 27.

3. E.S. Morgan, *The Gentle Puritan: A Life of Ezra Stiles, 1727–1795* (New Haven, CT: Yale University Press, 1962), 395.

4. *Connecticut Courant* (3 December 1764); F.B. Dexter, *Biographical Sketches of the Graduates of Yale College with Annals of the College History*, 6 vols. (New York: n.p., 1885–1912), 3:94.

5. *Connecticut Journal and New Haven Post-Boy* (6 January 1769).

6. L. Cremin, *American Education: The Colonial Experience, 1607–1783* (New York: Harper & Row, 1970), 459–60.

7. C. Rossiter and J. Lare, eds., *The Essential Lippmann: A Political Philosophy for Liberal Democracy* (Cambridge, MA: Harvard University Press, 1963), 108.

8. T. Bender, "The Cultures of Intellectual Life: The City and the Professions," *Intellect and Public Life: Essays on the Social History of Academic Intellectuals in the United States* (Baltimore, MD: Johns Hopkins University Press, 1993): 3–15.

9. D. Mathews, "The Public's Disenchantment with Professionalism: Reasons for Rethinking Academe's Service to the Country," *Journal of Public Service and Outreach, 1* (Spring 1996): 21–28.

10. J.D. Hicks, *The Populist Revolt* (Lincoln: University of Nebraska Press, 1961).

11. Ibid., 334.

12. R. Hofstadter, *The Progressive Movement, 1900–1915* (Englewood Cliffs, NJ: Prentice Hall, 1963).

13. W. Lippmann, *The Phantom Public* (New York: Macmillan, 1930).

14. E.C. Lagemann, ed., *Jane Addams on Education* (New York: Teachers College Press, 1985).

15. Public work is a concept developed by Harry Boyte of the Humphrey Institute at the University of Minnesota and Nancy Kari of St. Catherine's. See H.C. Boyte and N.N. Kari, *Building America: The Democratic Promise of Public Work* (Philadelphia: Temple University Press, 1996).

CHAPTER 8

How Far In? How Far Out?
Civic Responsibility and
the Journalism Educator

Jay Rosen

Among the major themes in modern social thought is the struggle to define a proper place for ideas and those who specialize in them. A struggle, I say, because there are two opposing viewpoints of learning that are always present.

One is the traditional claim for detachment from learning. It says that to know deeply about the world and keep humane learning alive, we need to step back. Distance is a virtue: By achieving the right distance, we inaugurate the quest to know. Learning requires contemplation. Knowledge demands patient study. Authority is won in a contest with others who have advanced the subject. The educated mind frees itself from passing trends and passions of the moment. The proper place for thought is outside the turbulence of modern life, at a quiet remove. The university, a protected institution, provides this sanctuary.

The opposing view stresses that there is no remove. To know deeply about the world is to find yourself immersed in it. Distance is a hazard: It can lead to cloistered learning, irrelevant abstraction, and a piling up of data in super-specialized domains. Or it pulls the community of inquirers away from humane and purposeful ends. Knowledge ultimately answers to a social need; authority for the learned is earned there. The place of thought is alongside and with the inhabitants of a civil society. At too great a remove, the educated mind suffers. The university, a grounded institution, acknowledges this perspective.

CIVIC DUTY AND PROFESSIONAL EDUCATION

We cannot quiet our minds by resolving this argument, but we can improve our minds by resuming it. We'll need to resume, if we're to travel anywhere on this book's theme of civic responsibility in higher education.

"Too far in? Too far out?" asked the philosopher Richard Rorty in a 1991 essay. He was writing about the proper role of intellectuals and academic experts within a troubled democracy.[1] Confronted with some of the more dismal facts about politics and public culture, should we take them in or take them on? I teach journalism at a research university in the media capital of the world, New York City. When I try to think about a scholarly duty that is specifically "civic," Rorty's question keeps coming to mind. How far into "journalism" should a university education go? How far outward should academic inquiry range? What's the proper distance between the two? Where's the vital connection? And what about that sprawling complex called the media? Do we teach about it, or teach against it?

In sifting through my choices, it matters whether I worry first about the distance or first about the connections. "Well, it's both," one can always say; and one would always be right. But this doesn't help in fixing a sense of civic duty. I need to know where I should start. The word "civic" suggests a world where there are others outside the university who have important claims upon this issue. To ask about them is to ask about your connection to them. But to ask about connection is also to inquire into the right degree of distance.

For example, the professional schools—law, medicine, business, social work, journalism, and education—acknowledge a special claim on them coming from the professions they serve. A law school that offered nothing of value to the legal profession would quickly cease to exist. But the lawyer's claim on the school of law is partial, in two senses. It is partial because it is not the only claim. The university makes demands on the law school, and so too can a society that needs more public-spirited lawyers. The profession's claim is partial in another way: it is bound to be self-interested, even parochial in outlook. Ask newspaper editors what they want in a journalism school graduate and they are likely to reveal a narrow view. "Someone who can go to work for me tomorrow" is a common reply. "Someone who can challenge me to rethink what I'm doing" is rare. A professional school that wants only to satisfy future employers is doing a disservice of some kind. But if its graduates cannot pass the bar exam or get a teaching license, then the school is failing at a different test.

How far in? How far out? When the university says it will educate young doctors, lawyers, teachers, managers, or journalists, it is implicitly saying it can find an answer to that question. In the end, though, the finding is left to faculty, students, parents, and deans. We who populate the academy must

continually assess our choices and the civic character they lend to learning.
For me, that means making certain distinctions.

JOURNALISM VS. THE MEDIA

"The media" as an object of public discourse came into common usage in the
1960s. It meant, initially, the news media, as referred to in Vice President
Spiro Agnew's famous speeches from 1969 to 1971 denouncing the "men of
the media" for their hostility toward Richard Nixon.[2] Agnew was talking then
about a limited group: the commentators at the major networks, the writers for
Time and *Newsweek*, and the editors of the *New York Times* and *Washington
Post*. Though he used the term "media," Agnew paid the practice of journalism
a high compliment, since he understood the media primarily as a producer of
news and commentary on national affairs. That is why the media mattered, he
said. That is why it must be denounced.

Journalism, at the time Agnew spoke, was still in control of the definition of
a much larger social complex, then emerging under the new heading "the
media." Today, the media includes not just the producers of news, but all the
purveyors of information, entertainment, and other programming forms that
have little or nothing to do with journalism. The media has expanded like the
television dial has expanded. The news has grown with it, spreading to 24-
hour networks, all-news radio, and countless sites on the World Wide Web.
But the growth has not necessarily been a triumph for journalism, which finds
itself under market pressure on a scale not seen before. We have more news
than ever, but a shrinking space for serious journalism, especially in proportion
to the total media product.

As a professor with a dual title, "journalism and mass communications," I
have to take these developments seriously. The best way to do that, I believe,
is to distinguish journalism from the media, while keeping a watchful eye on
both. Journalism, to me, is not an industry but a social practice or, as some call
it, a craft. We care about this craft, and give it a place in the university,
because it is connected to certain ideals—most obviously, our participation as
free-thinking citizens in the public life of our time. Journalism matters because
democracy matters. To study journalism is to ask what it can do for American
democracy, understood as an entire way of life, not only a system of government.

Our participation as citizens in the public life of our time requires much
more than information about, say, elections, parties, and political programs.
We need to know about each other, as well as our government. We need to
feel connected to public events, while staying informed about them. We need
to believe that there's a point to the exercise, that politics and citizenship are
not a waste of time. Journalism, from this perspective, is one of the cultivating

arts of democracy. Done well, it helps us make our way in the public world, as people who have a live stake in what happens there.

The media, by contrast, is a commercial empire that houses any number of practices, from book publishing to comedy writing to movie-making. It specializes in the production of audiences and the conversion of communication technology to commercial use. There is plenty of art and a good deal of craft in the media; and as everyone knows there is money to be made. The media matters in American democracy; indeed, it matters more and more, for the simple reason that much of what we have in common comes to us through that route. But does democracy matter to the media? The answer is yes and no. "Yes" because the empire is built on the blessings of freedom: open markets, free speech and press, the right to say what you want, live as you like, read what you choose. "No" because the media has no particular investment in the quality of our public culture, in the conduct of politics and civic affairs, in our choice to be active citizens instead of passive consumers, in whether democracy works for the many or only for the few.

To borrow the terms of political theorist Benjamin Barber, there's a "thin" notion of democracy embedded in the media, but a "strong" notion is inherent in journalism.[3] It cannot be a matter of indifference to journalists if politics becomes the playground of a privileged class. But for the media, there are always other playgrounds: sports, entertainment, consumer news—a limitless diet of services, products, and sites, all vying for our eyes and ears. Of course, there's a complication here. Journalism is one entry in that competition. The social practice stands (for the most part) within an industry's borders and it answers in certain ways to the media's demands. But if journalism becomes a mere reflection of those demands, if journalists themselves become media people, then democracy will suffer a loss—a prospect that worries many people in the craft these days.

What does all this have to do with civic responsibility in the university? As a professor in a journalism program, I feel a commitment to the "strong" notion of democracy embedded in the practice of journalism. I believe I should strengthen the practice where I can: in my teaching, writing, and research. That can mean defending journalism against the media and its thin commitment to democracy and public culture. The fortunes of a commercial empire are not my concern, although I try to monitor what happens in and around it. But the fortunes of journalism as a democratic art are very much my concern.

And yet here I confront Richard Rorty's question: How far in? How far out? Defending journalism as a social practice is tricky at those moments when journalists are themselves defensive about their work, parochial in their perspective, or hostile to questions coming from beyond their peers. For example, it is common for working journalists to say that it's not their job to worry about the consequences of what they report. As soon as we do that, they argue, we'll be on the road to self-censorship. This attitude can quickly cleanse the craft of any duty to reflect on harmful or insidious practices. I do a disservice to journalism if I accept such a prickly feature of its culture and pass that attitude along to my students. But I do a disservice to myself (and students) if I sever the connection to daily practice and become an alienated or exclusively academic critic, pronouncing upon the sins of journalism from a safe haven in the university.

My solution to this dilemma is to ask how journalism can deepen its sense of civic responsibility. If journalism is, in fact, a social practice of critical importance to a healthy democracy, as I believe, then wouldn't I also believe that it can be made stronger, just as democracy can always be made stronger? And if I do conclude that a better journalism lies within reach, then what is the reach of my own work in bringing that better work about? What should I do in my role as a professor?

THE CAMPAIGN FOR PUBLIC JOURNALISM

Since 1989, I have been trying to find an answer to that question. The work has engaged me with others in a campaign of sorts, designed to free mainstream journalism from the crippling illusion that it can prosper if politics, civic life, and public participation decay. The campaign has more than one name. I call it public journalism. Some prefer civic journalism or community journalism, or even "community-assisted reporting." The names don't matter as much as the aim: to restyle the work of the press, and its sense of public mission, so that both support a more active citizenry, a more vital public life.

There are several hundred journalists around the United States who have taken this message to heart; and they have begun to change their work and their philosophy to accommodate some rather unfamiliar ideas: that journalism can remain valuable only if public life remains viable, that getting people engaged in the world is the prelude to keeping them informed about it, that help in problem-solving is as vital as news of problems, and that improving public discourse is as worthy a contribution as passing along the discourse of the day.[4]

There are practical experiments that correspond to these ideas, most of them conducted by daily newspapers around the United States. For example, since 1990 papers like the *Wichita Eagle* and the *Charlotte Observer* have sought to uncover a "citizen's agenda" that can drive their election coverage. "What's on the public's priority list," discerned through the paper's reporting and research, replaces the usual focus on who's doing what to whom in order to win. Politics, in this approach, is defined as public discussion of public concerns. Campaign news can expect the candidates to serve that end. Having civic expectations ("here are the issues, lets talk about them") at the outset lends a different tone to political journalism, in that it invites citizens to a discussion involving the candidates. The newspaper tries to keep the dialogue focused on broad public concerns originating with citizens. Journalism emerges as a tool for better dialogue. The journalists who have experimented with the citizen's agenda don't mind saying that "democracy without deliberation" is something they're against.

Other news outlets, like the *Dayton Daily News*, have chosen the route of civic imagination when confronted with an urgent issue. The closing of a large military plant and the loss of thousands of job presented the Dayton paper with a choice in 1994: It could report on the situation as it stood, while urging action through its editorial pages; or it could go beyond that and help the community imagine what might be done. This paper chose the second course. It conducted a study of the plant and how it might be converted to civilian use. The paper then hired an architect to complete a rendering of four possible retoolings, each a way of imagining how the plant might regain a productive life in an era of peace. Other reports laid out the challenge facing public officials, civic leaders, business executives, and labor unions. Would they seize the moment and do something together? Or would civic imagination fail its test?

The *Daily News* didn't want Dayton to fail. And it tried to do journalism that would help the community act, without forcing the action or favoring the paper's pet plan. This is journalism in a more civic key. For it holds out the hope that politics can still be about problem solving, if people can overcome their divisions, sift among their choices, and deliberate together. Showing how such a thing is possible is what the journalists in Dayton decided to offer the community. When they made that decision, they were performing public journalism.

THE UNIVERSITY BEYOND THE CAMPUS

In deciphering the university's role regarding public journalism, I reasoned that I'm a professor, not a journalist, so what can I do? The answer, I discovered, was "a lot," even though public journalism appealed to a small minority in the mainstream press. Among that minority, there was a general sense that the craft was mired in some bad habits, or misfiring in its attempt to engage citizens. There was a desire to experiment with different practices, those that might contribute in some way to a stronger democracy. And there was an eagerness to learn from what others were doing. The more journalists I met who fit this description, the more I saw that they were moving toward the university—but not out of a desire to take classes and earn a degree.

Rather, they had uncovered problems that were stubbornly philosophical, as well as immediate and practical. They had set out on an experimental course that required them to be good learners, while remaining good journalists. They were confronting deep questions of civic purpose and professional commitment, concerns they could not address within the workaday vocabulary of the newsroom. They needed alternative languages, other frames for thought, varied definitions of their task—a whole range of intellectual tools to help them get where they wanted to go. All of which is the business of the university, and of faculty who teach there.

My role, then, was to think with and alongside these journalists, in a kind of floating seminar space that originated in the profession, rather than the academy. Public journalism was thus a name for a broad pattern of inquiry, which drew together practitioners and academics, newsroom life and intellectual life, civic purpose and professional ideals, democracy and the press. Throughout the 1990s, this inquiry came alive among journalists in local communities, deciding what to do about political news, crime reporting, or coverage of the local schools. It was there at "think–tank" sessions and professional conferences where public journalists gathered to learn from each other, or explain and defend their approach. It was seen in the pages of trade journals and press reviews, where the change in direction was hotly debated. It extended to professional educators and their students, as journalism schools caught wind of what was happening and incorporated it into the curriculum.

In all this I participated as a writer and speaker, along with thousands of others who wanted to join in—some by doing public journalism, others by studying and critiquing the results, and others only by arguing about it. My sympathies were clearly on one side: with the journalists who were struggling toward a more civic understanding of their work. For me, they represented a kind of college within the craft, a learning community trying to relearn the language of democracy, while simultaneously putting the newspaper out. I tried to strike up a collegial relationship with these enterprising journalists. They became, in a way, my discipline, for the ideas that mattered were the ones I could share with them. The research I did was an inquiry into what these journalists were doing. The scholarship I practiced was designed to aid in their practice, an ongoing experiment with the power of the press.[5]

A number of people in the medical field undertook a similar project about 15 years ago. Sometime in the late 1970s, they began to ask themselves whether they had defined their mission in the wrong way. What if, they said, a doctor's job (or a nurse's job) is not to cure disease, or treat the sick, or heal the injured, but rather to keep people healthy? Maybe a focus on injury and illness—what we might call a disease model of medicine—was too narrow. Maybe this narrow focus—the tendency to see people as patients, as bundles of problems—caused everyone to worry too little about preventive care.

For those in the medical field who started to think this way, a new term was needed to counterpose to the dominant framework, the disease model. Of course, simply recognizing the existence of the disease model was a kind of progress in itself, for when things are named they become thinkable, and so do their alternatives. In this case, the alternative that eventually emerged was called "holistic medicine."

Holistic medicine, when it started, was more of a premise, a possibility. The premise went like this: If curing disease and treating illness and injury was one way of doing medicine, then maybe keeping people healthy, or helping people maintain their own health, was a different way of doing medicine. Those who began this way didn't know exactly what they were about to accomplish. However—and this is the key point—they grasped that, in order to discover what holistic medicine was, they would have to begin talking and acting as if this thing called holistic medicine already existed.

The result? Today, holistic medicine means some very important things: a careful attention to nutrition and diet, an emphasis on exercise and stress reduction, preventive care during critical periods like pregnancy, and a general quest for healthier ways to live. The idea of an HMO—a health maintenance organization—owes something to the holistic approach. And it is not only the champions of holistic medicine, the believers, who support this approach. Almost everyone in America who pays attention to public discourse—everyone who reads the living section of the newspaper—realizes the importance of healthier living, including doctors who would never call their own approach "holistic." In a sense, holistic medicine has succeeded by losing its name, by becoming just good medicine, and part of sound practice in the field.

Of course, the disease model of medicine has not gone away. Where would heart surgeons be without the disease model? But there's now a challenge in the field, a different way of thinking about medicine that started as a premise and evolved into a practice—a practice that helped change American medical practice. Like holistic medicine, public journalism wants to begin in a different place. Rather than starting with the ruptures and breakdowns that make for news, it asks about the conditions that allow for a healthy public life. Public journalism rejects as too limiting a disease model of community life, in which things become interesting only when they begin to break down.

But just as an initial focus on health rather than disease didn't mean that doctors could stop treating the sick and injured, neither does an emphasis on the political health of the community mean that journalists can ignore the conflicts and ailments that inevitably occur in public life. By beginning in a different place, public journalists end up with a wider view of their responsibilities.

None of this requires a radical departure from traditional First Amendment notions. As a journalist from the Norfolk *Virginian-Pilot* said about the idea of listening carefully to citizens, "This is not exactly an epiphany." True enough.

But neither was good nutrition. There was nothing "new" about the notion that diet shapes health. But emphasizing diet was a departure from what medicine had become under the influence of the disease model. At the time, there weren't even nutrition courses in most medical schools, just as there are no journalism courses now in how public life works.

Just as the "new" approach to medicine could easily be seen as a return to traditional notions of care—indeed, to ancient wisdom about the body—so can public journalism be seen as a return to traditions in journalism that stress public service and a vital connection to the community.

CONCLUDING THOUGHTS

How far in? How far out? The answers I have come to are these: higher education can find a proper relationship to working professionals by aiding in their search for a deeper civic identity. In my field, this means distinguishing between journalism, a public practice, and the media, a private industry. Toward the media I recognize the importance of the scholar's traditional claim for detachment. Toward journalism, which is currently under threat by the media, I recognize a duty to connect with those who are trying to refashion the work of the press, so that it supports a healthier democracy. By attaching myself to their quest, I discovered that the borders of the university stretch beyond the gates of the campus. Professionals moving toward a stronger sense of civic duty cannot get there without improving their habits of reflection and inquiry—and that is the business of higher education. It may, in fact, be a duty.

For me, however, involvement in civic responsibility has been something of a relief. In the campaign for public journalism I found an antidote for my own sense of defeatism and despair as a scholar looking ruefully upon the media. Given what some in the press were doing and saying, there was reason to hope. There were people to root for. There was practical work to be done, which was also intellectual work. Perhaps this is the original civic duty we owe ourselves and our students: to avoid becoming cynical while still striving hard for truth.

NOTES

1. R. Rorty, "Intellectuals in Politics: Too Far In? Too Far Out?" *Dissent* (Fall 1991): 483–90.
2. See S. Agnew, "Speeches on the Media," in *Killing the Messenger,* ed. T. Goldstein (New York: Columbia University Press, 1989), 64–85.
3. B.R. Barber, *Strong Democracy* (Berkeley: University of California Press, 1984), 4, 131–32.
4. On public journalism, see J. Rosen, *Getting the Connections Right* (New York: Twentieth Century Fund, 1996). For a range of views among scholars, see J. Black, ed., *Mixed News: The Public/Civic/Communitarian Journalism Debate* (Mahwah, NJ: Lawrence

Erlbaum, 1997). For a first-person account from a journalist who helped give shape to public journalism, see D. "Buzz" Merritt, *Public Journalism and Public Life* (Mahwah, NJ: Lawrence Erlbaum, 1995). For a sympathetic view from a Washington journalist, see J. Fallows, *Breaking the News* (New York: Pantheon, 1996), chapter 6. For a highly skeptical treatment from a member of the National Press Corp, see M. Kelly, "Media Culpa," *New Yorker* (4 November 1996): 45–46, 48–49. A textbook that tries to explain public journalism for students and educators is A. Charity, *Doing Public Journalism* (New York: Guilford, 1995).

5. For reflections on the scholar's role in public journalism, see J. Rosen, "Public Journalism: A Case for Public Scholarship," *Change* (May/June 1995): 34–38.

CHAPTER 9

Integrating the American System of Higher, Secondary, and Primary Education to Develop Civic Responsibility

Lee Benson and Ira Harkavy

> It is not possible to run a course aright when the goal itself is not rightly placed.
>
> Francis Bacon, *Novum Organum* (1620)

> The school system has always been a function of the prevailing type of organization of social life.
>
> John Dewey, *Pedagogy as a University Discipline* (1896)

I believe that the community's duty to education is, therefore, its paramount moral duty. . . . I believe it is the business of every one interested in education to insist upon the school as the primary and most effective interest of social progress and reform in order that society may be awakened to realize what the school stands for, and aroused to the necessity of endowing the educator with sufficient equipment properly to perform his task.

I believe that education thus conceived marks the most perfect and intimate union of science and art conceivable in human experience. I believe that . . . the teacher is always the prophet of the true God and the usherer in of the true kingdom of God.

> John Dewey, *My Pedagogic Creed* (1897)

> Democracy has been given a mission to the world, and it is of no uncertain character. I wish to show that the university is the prophet of this democracy, as well as its priest and its philosopher; that in other words, the university is the Messiah of the democracy, its to-be-expected deliverer.
>
> William Rainey Harper, *The University and Democracy* (1899)

Democracy is the soul of America—its charter myth, its ultimate end-in-view (Dewey). Democracy, therefore, should be the soul of the American schooling system, particularly its most strategic component, the research university. Is it? Has it been? Rhetorically to some extent, practically no. Until now, we believe (and hope).

Following Donald Kennedy's provocative lead in a recent book, *Academic Duty*, we view American higher education as now in the early stages of its third revolution.[1] The first revolution, of course, occurred in the late nineteenth century. Beginning at Johns Hopkins in 1876, the accelerating adoption and uniquely American adaptation of the German model revolutionized American higher education. By the turn of the century, the uniquely American research university had essentially been created. The second revolution began in 1945 with Vannevar Bush's "endless [research] frontier" manifesto and rapidly produced the big science, cold war, entrepreneurial university.[2] The third revolution, we believe, began in 1989. The fall of the Berlin Wall and the end of the cold war provided the necessary condition for the "revolutionary" emergence of the cosmopolitan civic university—a new type of university engaged in the advancement of democratic schooling and practical realization of the democratic promise of America for all Americans.

How can the emergence of the cosmopolitan civic university be credibly explained? Largely (though oversimply), as a defensive response to the increasingly obvious, increasingly embarrassing, and increasingly immoral contradiction between the increasing status, wealth, and power of American higher education—particularly its elite research university component—and the increasingly pathological state of American cities.

To paraphrase Oliver Goldsmith's late eighteenth century lament for *The Deserted Village*, while American research universities flourished in the late twentieth century as never before, "ill fared the American city, to hastening ills a prey." If American research universities really were so great, why were American cities so pathological? After the cold war ended, the contradiction became increasingly obvious, troubling, indefensible, and immoral.

Put another way, the manifest contradiction between the *power* and the *performance* of American higher education sparked the emergence of the cosmopolitan civic university. Accelerating external and internal pressures forced research universities to recognize (very, very reluctantly) that they must—and could—function as institutions simultaneously engaged in advancing universal knowledge and improving the well-being of their local geographic communities, i.e., the local ecological system which symbiotically affects their "health" and functioning. Put another way, after 1989, the combination of external pressure and enlightened self-interest spurred American research universities to recognize that they could, indeed must, function simultaneously as universal and as local institutions of higher education—cosmopolitan civic institutions not only *in* but *of* their local communities.

To reduce (if not avoid) misunderstanding, we emphasize that we view the "third revolution" as still in its early stages. As the old academic joke has it, universities tend to move with all the speed of a runaway glacier. But things are changing, in the right direction. One indicator of positive change is the accelerating number and variety of "higher eds"—a less cumbersome term than "higher educational institutions"—which now publicly proclaim their desire to collaborate actively with their neighboring public schools and local communities. Predictably, public proclamations of collaboration, to date, far surpass tangible, interactive, mutually respectful and beneficial, collaboration. Nevertheless, progress is being made.

To help accelerate progress to the point where major changes become firmly institutionalized and produce significant results, we call for action-oriented acceptance of this radical proposition: All higher eds should explicitly make solving the problem of the American schooling system their highest institutional priority. Actively helping to develop an effective, integrated, genuinely democratic, pre-K through higher ed schooling system, we contend, should become the collaborative primary mission of American universities and colleges.

Primary mission doesn't mean sole mission. Obviously, American higher eds now have—and will continue to have—important missions other than collaboratively helping to solve the problem of the American schooling system. If space permitted, we would try to show in detail how those other missions would benefit greatly from successful collaborative work on the schooling problem. Here we restrict ourselves to a barebones statement of two corollary propositions: (1) Solving the overall problem of the schooling system must begin with changes at the higher ed level; and (2) Solving the overall schooling system problem would, in the long run, directly and indirectly give higher eds much greater resources than they now have to carry out all their important missions.

In the short run, we concede, our proposed mission change would require higher eds to experience the trauma entailed by any attempt to change academic priorities and cultures radically. In effect, we are calling on higher eds to reallocate the largest share of their intellectual (and other) resources to the immediate improvement of their neighboring public schools and communities. Given their present ferociously competitive, "pure research" orientation (fixation?), how in the world can we possibly expect higher eds to answer our call positively rather than derisively, dismissively, and contemptuously? Is our proposal to change academic priorities so lacking in good sense, so "revolutionary," that readers will angrily reject it as irresponsible, self-defeating, delusionary utopianism? To pun a phrase: Are we nuts?

We can pose the question less colloquially, more academically: Why should self-congratulatory, increasingly rich, prestigious, powerful, "successful," American universities undertake the terribly hard job of trying to transform themselves into civic institutions which actively, wholeheartedly, accept reciprocal and mutually-respectful collaboration with their local schools and communities as their categorical imperative for the new millenium? They should try to do that, we contend, for good institutional reasons: If they succeed, they will be much better able than they are now to achieve their self-professed, loudly-trumpeted, missions; namely to advance, preserve, and transmit the knowledge, as well as help produce the well-educated, cultured, truly moral citizens, necessary to develop and maintain a genuinely democratic society. [3]

We think it axiomatic that universities—particularly elite research universities with highly selective arts and sciences colleges—function as the primary shapers of the overall American schooling system. We think it equally axiomatic that the schooling system increasingly functions as the core subsystem—the strategic subsystem—of modern information societies. Contrary to orthodox Marxist ideologists, more than any other subsystem, it now influences the functioning of the societal system as a whole. Viewed systemically, on balance, it has the greatest "multiplier" effects, direct and indirect, short and long-term.

To understate the case extravagantly, to fully develop the cosmopolitan civic university dedicated to, actively engaged in, and pragmatically capable of solving the problem of the American schooling system will be extraordinarily hard. There is a great deal to think about, figure out, and do. Among many other things, to fully develop that new type of American university will require countering the dominant big science, cold war university strategy with a more compelling, more inspiring, more intelligent strategy. Fortunately, we do not have to invent an entirely new counterstrategy. Instead, we can (partially) go back to the future.

At the turn of the twentieth century, William Rainey Harper, the first president of the University of Chicago, and John Dewey, that university's most prominent scholar, eloquently and passionately placed schooling and education at the center of the American intellectual and institution-building agendas. We can follow their lead, stand on their shoulders, and work to realize their vision.

THE HARPER-DEWEY VISION: SCHOOLING AND PEDAGOGY AS THE ENDLESS AMERICAN FRONTIER

In 1904, Dewey quarreled with Harper and left Chicago for Columbia. His angry departure subsequently tended to mask the striking similarities in their overall vision and educational ideas. To quote intellectual historian George Marsden's highly insightful observation:

> At the University of Chicago Dewey was the head both of the Department of Philosophy and of the new Department of Pedagogy (later Education) in which he established his experimental school, where he tested his progressive theories of education. *Both in developing what became his instrumentalist philosophy and in his accompanying action-oriented educational theory, Dewey proved himself a kindred spirit to Harper. Dewey and Harper both believed in the redemptive functions of education. Dewey viewed the public schools as virtually the new established church, teaching the values of American democracy* [emphasis added]. Though Dewey had worked out the theory further than Harper, each believed that science was the key to finding unifying communitarian values, because only through science could one eliminate superstitions and sectarian differences and thus build an inclusivist "community of truth." Dewey's talk, presented to the students at Michigan, "Christianity and Democracy," and Harper's "Democracy and the University," despite some obvious differences, were two of a kind.[4]

Even more than Dewey, Harper made a critically important intellectual contribution when he identified the university as the strategic institution capable of creating a genuinely democratic society. For Harper, the American university had a singular purpose: its "holy" purpose was to be the "prophet of democracy." Indeed, no other "captain of erudition"—that remarkable set of religiously inspired, turn-of-the-century, university presidents who (contrary to the myopic village cynic, Thorstein Veblen) transformed the American university into a major national progressive institution—so passionately, so farsightedly, envisioned the university's democratic potential and purpose.[5] Profoundly religious, deeply dedicated to the progressive Social Gospel, Harper conceptualized the university as the holy place designed to fulfill democracy's creed: "the brotherhood, and consequently the equality of man." The university would fulfill that creed through "service for mankind, wherever mankind is, whether within scholastic walls, or without these walls and in the world at large."[6]

In his 1899 essay "The University and Democracy," Harper presented his radically anti-elitist, uniquely American, idea of the university in powerful, moving language:

> *The university, I contend, is this prophet of democracy—the agency estab-
> lished by heaven itself to proclaim the principles of democracy* [emphasis
> added]. It is in the university that the best opportunity is afforded to
> investigate the movements of the past and to present the facts and
> principles involved before the public. It is the university that, as the
> center of thought, is to maintain for democracy the unity so essential
> for its success. *The university is the prophetic school out of which come the
> teachers who are to lead democracy in the true path* [emphasis added]. It is
> the university that must guide democracy into the new fields of arts
> and literature and science. *It is the university that fights the battles of
> democracy, its war-cry being: "Come, let us reason together." It is the
> university that, in these latter days, goes forth with buoyant spirit to comfort
> and give help to those who are downcast, taking up its dwelling in the very
> midst of squalor and distress* [emphasis added]. It is the university that,
> with impartial judgment, condemns in democracy the spirit of corrup-
> tion which now and again lifts up its head, and brings scandal upon
> democracy's fair name. . . .
>
> *The university, I maintain, is the prophetic interpreter of democracy; the
> prophet of her past, in all its vicissitudes; the prophet of her present, in all its
> complexity; the prophet of her future, in all its possibilities* [emphasis
> added].[7]

For Harper, the new urban university in particular would be the strategic
agent (i.e., agency) to help America realize and fulfill its democratic promise.
Other presidents (e.g., Daniel Coit Gilman of Johns Hopkins, Seth Low of
Columbia), enthusiastically seized the opportunity to build their institutions
by working to improve the quality of life in American cities experiencing the
traumatic effects of industrialization, immigration, large-scale urbanization,
and the unprecedented emergence of an international economy.[8] But Harper
saw much further, went much further, than his presidential colleagues, when
he predicted that an institutional transformation—a positive mutation—
would result if universities engaged in planned interactions with their urban
environments. In 1902, speaking at Nicholas Murray Butler's inauguration as
president of Columbia University, Harper prophetically hailed the extraordinary intellectual and institutional advances which would come about when
that occurred.[9]

> A university which will adapt itself to urban influence, *which will
> undertake to serve as an expression of urban civilization, and which is
> compelled to meet the demands of an urban environment, will in the end
> become something essentially different from a university located in a village
> or small city* [emphasis added]. Such an institution will in time differen-
> tiate itself from other institutions. *It will gradually take on new character-
> istics both outward and inward, and it will ultimately form a new type of
> university* [emphasis added].

In that same address, in effect, Harper invoked Dewey's fundamentally pragmatic proposition that major advances in knowledge tend to occur when human beings consciously work to solve the central problems confronting their society. "The urban universities found today in . . . [the] largest cities in this country . . . and in [Europe] . . . ," Harper declaimed, "form a class by themselves, in as much as they are compelled to deal with problems which are not involved in the work of universities located in smaller cities . . . . [J]ust as the great cities of the country represent the national life in its fulness and variety, so the urban universities are in the truest sense . . . national universities." To conclude his address, he proclaimed that of all the great institutions in New York City, Columbia University was "the greatest." In Chicago, Harper certainly believed, his university held that preeminent position.[10]

Inexplicably to us, throughout his long career, Dewey gave little attention to the powerful role that universities could actively play in fulfilling America's democratic promise. He and Harper strongly agreed, however, that higher education's primary focus should be on schooling, education, and pedagogy. Given their basic conviction that democratic schools constituted the essential institutions for a democratic society, it isn't surprising that schooling took central stage for them. According to Dewey, universities should see "education . . . not merely as a *fitting topic for serious and prolonged study, but the most important of subjects for such study*" [emphasis added]. Like Harper, Dewey emphasized the great intellectual benefits which would accrue to the university if it focused on education and schooling. Rich and complex, the problem of improving education involved study of "civic . . . state [and federal] administration," "sociology of the child," history, psychology, philosophy, and "problems [that] are political, as well as economic." For its own sake and for society's sake, therefore, "the scientific study of education," according to Dewey, "should represent the finest self-consciousness of the university of its own work and destiny—of its mission for itself and for society of which it is both minister and organ."[11]

Unfortunately, after leaving Chicago for Columbia, Dewey essentially concentrated on the "reconstruction of philosophy" and did little to directly and practically connect universities to primary and secondary schools. For example, he failed to take advantage of the extraordinary resources that a teachers college could potentially mobilize to help shape democratic community schools in New York City and thereby advance education as a discipline in concrete real-world practice rather than in scholastic abstract theory. Unlike Dewey, Harper, until his untimely death in 1906, practically involved himself with public education. While president of the University of Chicago and terribly overcommitted in the heroic efforts which resulted in his premature death, he actively served on the Chicago Board of Education. Before Dewey arrived at Chicago in 1894, Harper had advocated and worked hard to construct an integrated educational system from preschool through the university. In Harper's grand vision, the University of Chicago functioned as the active central hub of a highly integrated network of schools, academies, and colleges. For him, "the sympathies of the true university will be so broad as to bring it into touch with educational problems of every kind."[12]

To realize in practice the promise of American democracy, Harper worked tirelessly to develop pedagogy as a university discipline of distinction and to make teaching at all levels a profession "equal" to any other. In 1896, the year Dewey began the Laboratory School, Harper enthusiastically proclaimed his "desire to do for the Department of Pedagogy *what has not been undertaken in any other institution*" [emphasis added]. Even more emphatically, Harper declared to a university trustee who implied that it was below the university's dignity to sponsor a journal focused on precollegiate schools: "As a university we are interested *above all else* in pedagogy" [emphasis added].[13] Harper's devotion to pedagogy logically derived from two propositions central to his vision for the University of Chicago in particular and for American universities in general:

1. "Education is the basis of all democratic progress. The problems of education are, therefore, the problems of democracy."[14]
2. *More than any other institution*, the university determines the character of the schooling system. To quote him: "Through the school system, the character of which, in spite of itself, the university determines and in a larger measure controls . . . through the school system every family in this entire broad land of ours is brought into touch with the university; for from it proceeds the teachers or the teachers' teachers."[15]

In our judgment, the Harper-Dewey "university-school partnership platform," is, to mix metaphors shamelessly, the appropriate launching pad to create the "new American cosmopolitan civic university." The task confronting American academics, we contend, is to realize in the twenty-first century the unrealized Harper-Dewey vision. For many reasons, among them the central place education now occupies in public concern and debate, the conditions are now much more favorable than ever before to create the schooling/education/pedagogy-centered university they envisioned.[16] Moreover, a variety of nationally significant, on-the-ground, university-school partnerships, including one which engages our own institution, the University of Pennsylvania, now provide the local bases to develop in practice the "new type of university" prophetically foreseen by Harper—the new type of university in which schooling and pedagogy function as the endless frontier for institutional and societal improvement.

PENN'S ENGAGEMENT WITH LOCAL PUBLIC SCHOOLS AS A PRACTICAL EXAMPLE OF "DEMOCRATIC DEVOLUTION REVOLUTION"

Since 1985, Penn has increasingly engaged itself with its local public schools in a comprehensive school-community-university partnership, the West Philadelphia Improvement Corps (WEPIC). In its 15 years of operation, the project has, of course, evolved significantly. Moreover, it has helped spawn a variety of related projects which also engage Penn with public schools in its local community, West Philadelphia. From its inception, we conceptualized Penn's work with WEPIC as designed to forge mutually beneficial and respectful, university-school-community partnerships. In recent years, we have begun to conceptualize that work in much broader terms namely, as part of a (literally) radical attempt to advance a "democratic devolution revolution."[17] It is from that "lofty perch," we believe, that an overview of Penn's work (and the work of many other higher educational institutions engaged with their local public schools) is best comprehended.

John Gardner, arguably the leading spokesperson for the "new American cosmopolitan civic university" (our term for it), has been thinking and writing about organizational devolution and the university's potential role for nearly a generation. For him, the effective functioning of organizations requires the planned and deliberate rather than haphazard devolution of functions:

> We have in recent decades discovered some important characteristics of the large-scale organized systems—government, private sector, whatever—under which so much of contemporary life is organized. One such characteristic—perhaps the most important—is that the tendency of such systems to centralize must be countered by deliberate dispersion of initiative downward and outward through the system. The corporations have been trying to deal with this reality for almost 25 years and government is now pursuing it. . . .
>
> What it means for government is a substantially greater role for the states and cities. And none of them are entirely ready for that role. . . . [L]ocal government must enter into collaborative relations with nongovernmental elements . . . .
>
> So how can colleges and universities be of help?[18]

In effect, Gardner powerfully extended the Harper-Dewey vision by proposing a multisided involvement in "contemporary life" for higher eds, including building community, convening public discussions, educating public-spirited leaders, offering continuing civic and leadership seminars, and providing a wide range of technical assistance (broadly conceived). An effective, compassionate, democratic devolution revolution, he emphasized, requires much more than practicing new forms of interaction among federal, state, and local governments and among agencies at each level of government. For Gardner, government integration by itself does not meaningful change make. New forms of interaction among the public, for-profit and nonprofit sectors are also mandatory. Government must function as a collaborating partner, effectively facilitating cooperation among all sectors of society, including higher educational institutions, to support and strengthen individuals, families, and communities.[19]

To extend Gardner's observations about universities (and similar observations by such highly influential thinkers as Ernest Boyer, Derek Bok, Lee Shulman, and Alexander Astin), we propose a democratic devolution revolution.[20] In our proposed "revolution," government serves as a powerful catalyst and largely provides the funds needed to create stable, ongoing, effective partnerships. But government would function only as a second-tier deliverer of services, with universities, community-based organizations, unions, churches, other voluntary associations, school children and their parents, and other community members, functioning as the first-tier operational partners. That is, various levels and departments of government would guarantee aid and significantly finance welfare services. Local, personalized, and caring services, however, would actually be delivered by the third (private, nonprofit, voluntary associations) and fourth (personal, i.e., family, kin, neighbors, friends) sectors of society. Put another way, government would not be primarily responsible for the delivery of services; it primarily would have macro fiscal responsibilities, including fully adequate provision of funds.

The strategy we propose requires creatively and intelligently adapting the work of local institutions (universities, hospitals, faith-based organizations) to the particular needs and resources of local communities. It assumes that colleges and universities, which simultaneously constitute preeminent international, national, and local institutions, potentially constitute particularly powerful partners, "anchors," and creative catalysts for change and improvement in the quality of life in American cities and communities.

For colleges and universities to fulfill their potential and really contribute to a democratic devolution revolution, however, will require them to do things very differently than they do now. To begin with, changes in "doing" will require recognition by higher eds that, as they now function, are a major part of the problem, not a significant part of the solution. To become part of the solution, higher eds must give full-hearted, full-minded devotion to the hard task of transforming themselves, to becoming socially responsible, civic universities. To do that well, they will have to change their institutional cultures and develop a comprehensive, realistic strategy.

One component of the strategy now being developed by Penn, as well as by an increasing number of other urban higher eds, focuses on developing university-assisted community schools designed to help educate, engage, activate, and serve all members of the community in which the school is located. The strategy assumes that community schools can function as focal points to help create healthy urban environments and that universities function best in such environments. Somewhat more specifically, the strategy assumes that, like higher eds, public schools can function as environment-changing institutions and become the strategic centers of broad-based partnerships which genuinely engage a wide variety of community organizations and institutions. Public schools "belong" to all members of the community. They are particularly well-suited therefore, to function as neighborhood "hubs" or "nodes" around which local partnerships can be generated and formed. When they play that role, schools function as community institutions *par excellence* . . . they then provide a decentralized, democratic, community-based response to significant community problems.

The university-assisted community school reinvents and updates an old and uniquely American idea, namely that the neighborhood school can effectively serve as the core neighborhood institution—the core institution which provides comprehensive services and galvanizes other community institutions and groups. That idea inspired the early settlement house workers; they recognized the centrality of the neighborhood school in community life and hailed its potential as the strategic site for community stabilization and improvement. At the turn of the twentieth century, it is worth noting, deeply motivated, socially concerned, brilliantly creative, settlement house workers such as Jane Addams and Lillian Wald pioneered the transfer of social, health, and recreational services to the public schools of major American cities. In effect, settlement leaders recognized that though there were very few settlement houses, there were very many public schools. Not surprisingly, Dewey's ideas about "the school as a social Centre" (1902) had been strongly, directly shaped by his enlightening experiences and discussions with Jane Addams (and others) at Hull House. In that highly influential address, Dewey explicitly paid homage to them:

> I suppose, whenever we are framing our ideals of the school as a social Centre, what we think of is particularly the better class of social settlement. What we want is to see the school, every public school, doing something of the same sort of work that is now done by a settlement or two scattered at wide distances through the city.[21]

Dewey failed to note, however, two critically important functions that the community schools could perform: (1) the school as a community institution actively engaged in the solution of basic community problems; and (2) the school as a community institution which educated young children, both intellectually and morally, by engaging them in real-world, community problem solving. He did recognize that if the neighborhood school were to function as a genuine community center, it needed additional human resources and support. But to our knowledge, Dewey never identified universities as *the* (or even *a*) key source of broadly based, sustained, comprehensive support for community schools.

To suggest the contributions which university-assisted community schools can make to an effective, compassionate, democratic devolution revolution capable of achieving Dewey's utopian goal of cosmopolitan democratic communities,[22] we summarily cite some results of the "community school-creating" efforts presently being undertaken by higher eds across the country: Undergraduates, as well as dental, medical, social work, education, and nursing students, are learning as they serve; public school students are also connecting their education to real-world problem solving and providing service to other students and community members; adults are participating in locally based job training, skill enhancement, and ongoing education; effective integration (as distinct from co-location) of services for school children and their families is now significantly under way in many communities.

It is critical to emphasize, however, that the university-assisted community schools now being developed have a long way to go before they can effectively mobilize the potentially powerful, untapped resources of their communities and thereby enable individuals and families to function both as deliverers and as recipients of caring, compassionate, local services. To make that point, we briefly recite the "narrative history" of our experience at Penn; it suggests both how far we have come and how far we have to go.

PENN AND WEST PHILADELPHIA PUBLIC SCHOOLS: LEARNING BY REFLECTIVE DOING

Following the brilliant leads provided by Harper, Dewey, and Gardner, we believe that, as is true of all American universities, Penn's highest, most basic, and most enduring responsibility is to help America realize the egalitarian promise of the Declaration of Independence in practice; to become a fully democratic society, the pathbreaking democratic society in an increasingly interdependent world, the exemplary democratic "city on the hill." Granted that proposition, how can Penn best fulfill its democratic responsibility? For reasons sketched below, we believe it can best do that by effectively integrating and radically improving the entire West Philadelphia schooling system, beginning with Penn but comprehending all schools within its local geographic community, West Philadelphia.

The history of Penn's work with West Philadelphia public schools has been a process of painful organizational learning; we cannot overemphasize that our understanding and activities have continually changed over time.[23] For example, as discussed below, Penn has recently embarked on two new, highly ambitious, ventures: (1) leading a coalition of higher eds, medical and other nonprofit institutions, for-profit firms, and community groups, to improve 26 West Philadelphia public schools; and (2) developing a university-assisted public school adjacent to campus, in partnership with the School District of Philadelphia and the Philadelphia Federation of Teachers.

Reaching this level of activity has been neither easy nor a straight path. Moreover, Penn is only now beginning to tap its extraordinary resources in ways which eventually will mutually benefit Penn and its neighbors and result in substantial school, community, and university change. Significantly, we have come to see our work as a concrete example of a general theory of action-oriented, real-world, problem-based learning. Our real-world strategic problem, we have come to see, has been, and continues to be, radically improving the quality of the entire West Philadelphia schooling system, beginning with Penn. Coming to see our work in terms of what we now conceive as the strategic schooling component of a complex urban ecological system, we are convinced, constituted a major conceptual and theoretical advance for us.

Ironically, and instructively, when we first began work on university-community relationships in 1985, we did not envision it in terms of schools, problem-based learning, or universities as highly strategic components of urban ecological systems. What immediately concerned us was that West Philadelphia was rapidly and visibly deteriorating, with devastating consequences for Penn. What should the university do? Committed to undergraduate teaching, we designed an honors seminar which aimed to stimulate undergraduates to think critically about what Penn could do to remedy its "environmental situation." For a variety of reasons, the president of the university, Sheldon Hackney, himself a former professor of history, agreed to join us in giving that seminar in the spring 1985 semester. The seminar's title suggests its general concerns: "Urban University-Community Relationships: Penn-West Philadelphia, Past, Present, and Future, As a Case Study."

When the seminar began, we didn't know anything about Dewey's community school ideas. We literally knew nothing about the history of community school experiments and had not given any thought to Penn working with public schools in West Philadelphia. For present purposes, we need not recite the complex, painful processes of trial, error, and failure which led us—and our students—to see that Penn's best strategy to remedy its rapidly-deteriorating "environmental situation" was to use its enormous internal and external resources to help radically improve West Philadelphia public schools and the neighborhoods in which they are located. Most unwittingly, during the course of the seminar's work, we reinvented the community school idea.

Public schools, we came to realize (more or less accidentally), could effectively function as genuine community centers for the organization, education, and transformation of entire neighborhoods. They could do that by functioning as neighborhood sites for a West Philadelphia Improvement Corps (WEPIC) consisting of school personnel and neighborhood residents who would receive strategic assistance from Penn students, faculty, and staff. Put another way, the seminar helped invent WEPIC to help transform the traditional West Philadelphia public school system into a "revolutionary" new system of university-assisted, community-centered, community problem-solving schools.

TRANSLATING THE UNIVERSITY-ASSISTED COMMUNITY SCHOOL IDEA INTO PRACTICAL ACTION

Given Penn's long, deep-rooted, institutional resistance to serious involvement with West Philadelphia's problems, the limited resources available to us, and the intrinsic difficulty of transforming conventional, inner-city public schools into community schools, we decided that our best strategy was to try to achieve a visible, dramatic success in one school rather than marginal, incremental changes in a number of schools. While continuing the WEPIC program at other schools, we decided to concentrate initially on the John P. Turner Middle School, largely because of the interest and leadership of its principal.

Previous experiments in community schools and community education throughout the country had depended primarily on a single university unit, namely, the School of Education, one major reason for the failure, or at best limited success, of those experiments. The WEPIC concept of university assistance was far more comprehensive. From the start of the Turner experiment, we understood the concept to mean both assistance from, and mutually beneficial collaboration with, the entire range of Penn's schools, departments, and administrative offices. For a variety of reasons, however, it soon became apparent that the best way to develop and sustain the Turner project would be to initiate a school-based community health program.

Given the development of a community health program at Turner in the summer of 1990, Professor Francis Johnston, chair of the Anthropology Department and a world leader in nutritional anthropology, decided to participate in the project. To do that effectively, for the fall 1990 semester, he revised Anthropology 210 to make it what we have come to call a strategic, academically based, community service seminar. Anthropology 210 has a long history at Penn and focuses on the relationship between anthropology and biomedical science. An undergraduate course, it was developed to link pre-medical training at Penn with the Department of Anthropology's major program in medical anthropology. Pre-med students are highly important in Penn undergraduate education and the department's program in medical anthropology is world renowned. Professor Johnston's decision to convert Anthropology 210 into a strategic, academically based, community service seminar constituted a major milestone in the development of the Turner community school project, in Penn's relation to the Turner School, and in our overall work with West Philadelphia public schools.

Since 1990, students in Anthropology 210 have carried out a variety of activities at Turner focused on the interactive relationships among diet, nutrition, growth, and health. The seminar is explicitly, and increasingly, organized around strategic academically based community service. After Professor Johnston increasingly began to focus his own research and publications on his work with Turner students and community residents, he increasingly came to function as a noteworthy example for other anthropology professors and graduate students; they are now integrating their teaching and research with the Turner program, or with other WEPIC programs in West Philadelphia public schools. Even more significantly, Anthropology 210 not only affected the anthropology department (which has recently developed an academic track in Public Interest Anthropology), its success has radiated out to other departments and schools. Undoubtedly, the program and Professor Johnston have played major roles in the increasingly successful campaign to expand strategic, academically based, community service at Penn.[24]

At present, approximately 80 such courses have been organized and are "on the books" at Penn, with 42 being offered during the 1998–99 academic year. Morever, an increasing number of faculty members, from wide range of Penn departments and schools, are now seriously considering how they might revise existing courses, or develop new courses, which would permit their students to benefit from innovative curricular opportunities to become active learners and creative real-world problem solvers.

THE CENTER FOR COMMUNITY PARTNERSHIPS AND PRESIDENTIAL AND FACULTY LEADERSHIP

Encouraged by the success of the university's increasing engagement with West Philadelphia, in July 1992, President Hackney created the Center for Community Partnerships. To highlight the importance he attached to the center, he located it in the Office of the President and appointed one of us (Ira Harkavy) to be its director (while continuing to serve as director of the Penn Program for Public Service created in 1988).

Symbolically and practically, creation of the center constituted a major change in Penn's relationship to West Philadelphia/Philadelphia. The university as a corporate entity now formally, organizationally committed itself to finding ways to use its truly enormous resources (broadly conceived) to improve the quality of life in its local community—not only in respect to public schools but to economic and community development in general.

The emphasis on partnerships in the center's name was deliberate; it acknowledged, in effect, that Penn could not try to go it alone, as it had long been accustomed to do. The creation of the center was also significantly internally. It meant that, at least in principle, the president of the university would now strongly encourage all components of the university to seriously consider the roles they could appropriately play in Penn's efforts to improve the quality of its off campus environment. Implementation of that strategy accelerated after Judith Rodin became president of Penn in 1994. A native West Philadelphian and Penn graduate, Rodin was appointed in part because of her intense commitment to improving Penn's local environment and to transforming Penn into a leading American urban university.

Rodin made radical reform of undergraduate education her first priority. To achieve that far-reaching goal, she established the Provost's Council on Undergraduate Education and charged it with designing a model for Penn's undergraduate experience in the twenty-first century. Following the lead of Penn's patron saint, Ben Franklin, the Provost's Council emphasized the action-oriented union of theory and practice and "engagement with the material, ethical, and moral concerns of society and community defined broadly, globally, and also locally within Philadelphia." The Provost's Council defined the twenty-first century undergraduate experience as

> . . . provid[ing] opportunities for students to understand what it means to be active learners and active citizens. It will be an experience of learning, knowing, and doing that will lead to the active involvement of students in the process of their education.[25]

To apply this Franklinian-inspired approach in practice, the Provost's Council designated academically based community service as a core component of Penn undergraduate education during the next century.

Building upon themes identified by the Provost's Council, Penn's 1994–95 annual report was entitled "The Unity of Theory and Practice: Penn's Distinctive Character." Describing the university's efforts to connect theory and practice, President Rodin observed that

> . . . there are ways in which the complex interrelationships between theory and practice transcend any effort at neat conceptualization. One of those is the application of theory in service to our community and the use of community service as an academic research activity for students. *Nowhere else is the interactive dimension of theory and practice so clearly captured* [emphasis added].

>   For more than 250 years, Philadelphia has rooted Penn in a sense of
>   the "practical," reminded us that service to humanity, to our commu-
>   nity is, as [Benjamin] Franklin put it,"the great aim and end of all
>   learning." Today, thousands of Penn faculty and students realize the
>   unity of theory and practice by engaging West Philadelphia elementary
>   and secondary school students as part of their own academic course
>   work in disciplines as diverse as history, anthropology, classical studies,
>   education, and mathematics.
>
>   For example, anthropology professor Frank Johnston and his under-
>   graduate students educate students at West Philadelphia's Turner
>   Middle School about nutrition. Classical studies professor Ralph Rosen
>   uses modern Philadelphia and fifth century Athens to explore the
>   interrelations between community, neighborhood, and family. And
>   history professor Michael Zuckerman's students engage West Philadel-
>   phia elementary and secondary school students to help them under-
>   stand together the nature—and discontinuities—of American na-
>   tional identity and national character.[26]

The 1994–95 annual report illustrated and advanced a fundamental, far-
reaching cultural shift that had begun to take place across the university. By
the end of her first year in office, Penn's president had significantly increased
the prominence of undergraduate education, defined the linkage of theory and
practice (including theory and practice derived from and applied within the
local community) as the hallmark of Ben Franklin's university, and identified
academically based community service focused on West Philadelphia and its
public schools as a powerfully integrative strategy to advance university-wide
research, teaching, and service.

Presidents can provide leadership, but it is faculty members who develop
and sustain the courses and research projects which durably link a university
to its local schools and community. More specifically, it is through faculty
teaching and research that the connection to local schools is ultimately and
durably made. We gave high priority, therefore, to increasing the number and
variety of academically based community service courses. Thanks in large
measure to President Rodin's strong support, the number of academically
based community service courses has grown exponentially; from 11 when the
center was founded in 1992 to 80 in the spring of 1999. As a result of the
highly positive reaction to those courses, the long term process of radically
changing Penn's undergraduate curriculum has gained accelerating momentum. In addition to the development of the Public Interest Anthropology track
previously cited, after years of complex negotiations, a new interdisciplinary
minor in Urban Education has recently been created and hailed by undergraduates. A joint program of the School of Arts and Science (SAS) and the
Graduate School of Education (GSE), the new minor includes faculty advisors

from anthropology, classical studies, earth and environmental science, education, English, history, linguistics, mathematics, sociology, and urban studies. Appropriately enough, in the fall 1998 issue of the School of Arts and Sciences alumni publication which focused on the urban crisis, Dean Samuel Preston voiced his strong support for the urban ed minor, as well as for increasing the number of academically based community service courses:

> Together with the Graduate School of Education, SAS is offering a new interdisciplinary minor in Urban Education. The minor explores the crisis in public education in course work, in field research, and in hands-on study that uses the network of neighborhood schools the University has developed. SAS has been closely involved with the West Philadelphia community through Penn's Center for Community Partnerships. A number of our faculty focus their research on Philadelphia communities and regularly teach courses that put our students in touch with students at local schools. Penn students join with the students from surrounding neighborhoods to gather data, conduct interviews, and explore community problems such as inadequate nutrition or the presence of lead and other toxins in homes. These service learning courses are one way that Penn mobilizes its academic resources in mutually beneficial partnerships with its neighbors. *Surveys have shown that students are enthusiastic about how community service experiences enrich their Penn undergraduate education. Arts and Sciences aims to develop more of these service learning approaches to education because of their value to students and their benefits to the community* [emphasis added].[27]

Dean Preston's support is enthusiastically echoed by the dean of the college, Richard Beeman. Until recently, Beeman, an early American historian and a long time friend and colleague of ours, had been openly skeptical of the value of academically based community service at a major research university. But in a spring 1998 speech to faculty and students, "Academically-Based Community Service: From Skeptic to Convert," he publicly "confessed" (sic) that he had undergone something like a mind-and-spirit "conversion" experience. Translating his "personal conversion" into "institutional action," Dean Beeman is now leading the development of an experimental college within the College of Arts and Sciences in which problem-based learning and academically based community service will function as central components. To quote his statement in the SAS alumni publication cited above:

> I really cannot tell you how much I believe in the value of what is being done in those courses. They give our students a problem-oriented experience in learning, and all the research literature shows that the best learning takes place, not in studying theories and abstract forms, but in solving concrete problems. *I am committed to getting first rate*

*faculty involved in that effort as an important definition of their contribution
to undergraduate education at Penn* [emphasis added].[28]

The School of Arts and Sciences is one of several Penn schools which, in recent years, has strengthened its connection with West Philadelphia public schools. Penn's institutional commitment has also dramatically increased. Increasingly, President Rodin has made the Urban Agenda a centerpiece of her administration and emphasized five major areas of activity for Penn's work in West Philadelphia: clean, safe, culturally diverse, and exciting neighborhoods; retail improvement; improved housing; enhanced economic development; and, most centrally, excellent public schools.

Practicing what she preached, in June 1998, President Rodin announced that Penn would accept the leadership of two cluster resource boards which serve the public schools in West Philadelphia and also entered into an innovative partnership with the school district of Philadelphia and the Philadelphia Federation of Teachers to establish a new pre–K-8, university-assisted, public school in West Philadelphia. Leadership of the cluster resource boards involves Penn working closely with the school district, nonprofit institutions, for-profit firms, and community groups to coordinate, leverage, and advocate for needed services and supports for children and their families from 26 West Philadelphia public schools. Each cluster includes one comprehensive high school and its "feeder" elementary and middle schools.

Construction and development of a university-assisted public school designed to serve as a demonstration school for other public schools in West Philadelphia, and throughout the city, undoubtedly constitutes the most significant and innovative component of President Rodin's expanded commitment to school improvement. Located near the Penn campus, the school will be built on land Penn has contributed for that purpose. Serving approximately 700 children, it will receive an annual operating subsidy of $1,000 per child from Penn. In effect, in describing this initiative, President Rodin echoed and extended the visionary program William Rainey Harper outlined more than a century ago for a school/education/pedagogy-centered urban university:

> Good schools for area children are also a must if our community is to thrive. For a number of years, Penn students have participated in extremely effective service-learning projects coordinated by Penn's Center for Community Partnerships at local public schools. Penn students, faculty, and staff will continue to student-teach, serve as mentors, and provide other assistance at these and other neighborhood schools. Now, in addition, the University may well take this commitment one step further and work with others to establish Penn-assisted K-8 school in University City [the neighborhood immediately adjacent to Penn's campus]. Planning is in the early stages, but we believe this could be a significant and cooperative approach that would

create greater educational opportunities for area youth, enhance our local fabric, and strengthen relationships between the community, our Graduate School of Education, and other schools at Penn.[29]

It cannot be overemphasized that the accelerating changes in Penn's relationship to its local schools are not atypical, not unique to Penn. More or less, similar changes throughout the country testify to the growth of a "university civic responsibility movement"—a national movement designed to construct a genuinely democratic schooling system and advance American democracy. Regrettably, space constraints prevent us from developing that point in detail and permit us only to briefly quote the Chancellor of the University System of Maryland, Donald N. Langenberg. Referring to the collaborative enterprise undertaken by the University of Texas at El Paso and local public schools as exemplifying a national movement, he noted that their successful collaboration had taught university observers a powerful lesson:

> We have come to believe strongly, and elementary and secondary schools have come to believe, that they cannot reform without us . . .
> *This is not telling them how to do it, but both of us working together to fix what's wrong with our education systems* [emphasis added]. . . . We prepare teachers for the public schools, and we admit their students. *So its our problem just as much as theirs* [emphasis added].[30]

SUMMING UP AND LOOKING FORWARD

Chancellor Langenberg's observation neatly returns us to the central component of the Dewey-Harper-Gardner vision: To educate young people so that they function as active, informed, intelligent, moral citizens in a fully democratic society, requires a highly interactive and collaborative, effectively integrated, genuinely democratic schooling system, from preschool through the university and beyond. Alas, American society is a long way from having realized the radically improved schooling system which Harper, Dewey, Addams, Gardner, Boyer, Bok, Kennedy, Shulman, Astin, and others envisioned and, in different ways, worked to achieve. Times are changing, however; signs of progress can be found across the educational landscape. Among other reasons for the change, we suggest, the emerging revolution in American higher education and society is transforming the big science, cold war university into the cosmopolitan civic university—a uniquely American "new type" of institution dedicated to the construction of a genuinely democratic schooling system and the development of a fully democratic society.[31]

To succeed, revolutions require agents dedicated enough, wise enough, and powerful enough, to implement radical plans for action. Inspired by Harper and Gardner, we have proposed that American universities play that role. Our "revolutionary" proposal is quintessentially American. It calls on research universities to take the lead in revolutionizing the overall American schooling system. Somewhat more specifically, our proposed "schooling revolution, American style" calls on each higher ed to make its highest priority the radical integration and improvement of the overall schooling system in its "home community," i.e., the community in which it is located, the schooling system and community ecological system which it can most directly, most powerfully, affect and which can directly, powerfully, affect its own "health" and functioning.

To conclude, we summarily restate our thesis. Neither Frederick Jackson Turner's Western pioneering frontier nor Vannevar Bush's big science, pure research frontier constitutes the truly American "endless frontier." The truly American endless frontier is the democratic schooling frontier. "Conquering" that frontier would dynamically help America fulfill its democratic promise, honor its charter myth, and achieve its ultimate end-in-view. It is time to realize in practice the Harper-Dewey vision of the uniquely American schooling/education/pedagogy-centered university. Realizing their vision, we believe, would constitute the third—the most progressive, most far-reaching, most authentically American—revolution in the history of American higher education.

NOTES

1. D. Kennedy, *Academic Duty* (Cambridge, MA: Harvard University Press, 1997), 265–88, 299.

2. For a highly perceptive, devastatingly critical analysis of V. Bush's report, *Science and the Endless Frontier*, see D.E. Stokes, *Pasteur's Quadrant: Basic Science and Technological Innovation* (Washington, DC: The Brookings Institution Press, 1997).

3. For an illuminating discussion of the American university's democratic mission, see C.W. Anderson, *Prescribing the Life of the Mind* (Madison: University of Wisconsin Press, 1993); I. Harkavy, "School-Community-University Partnerships: Effectively Integrating Community Building and Education Reform," *Universities and Community Schools*, 6, no. 1–2 (1999): 7–24.

4. G.M. Marsden, *The Soul of the American University: From Protestant Establishment to Established Nonbelief* (New York: Oxford University Press, 1994), 250–51; A.W. Wirth, *John Dewey as Educator: His Design for Work in Education (1894–1904)* (New York: Wiley and Sons, 1964), 35–52.

5. For a stimulating discussion of Harper and the concept of captains of erudition, see S.J. Diner, *A City and Its Universities: Public Policy in Chicago, 1892–1919* (Chapel Hill: University of North Carolina Press, 1980).

6. Quotations are from William Rainey Harper's 1899 Charter Day address at the University of California, "The University and Democracy," reprinted in Harper, *The Trend in Higher Education* (Chicago: University of Chicago Press, 1905), 21, 28–29.

7. Ibid., 19–20.

8. For a discussion of Gilman and Low and their efforts to build and strengthen Hopkins and Columbia through a connection to the city and its problems, see Harkavy, "School-Community-University Partnerships," 10–14; J. Elfenbein, "To 'Fit Them for Their Fight with the World': The Baltimore YMCA and the Making of a Modern City, 1852–1932" (Ph.D. diss., University of Delaware, 1996); T. Bender, *The New York Intellect: A History of Intellectual Life in New York City, from 1750 to the Beginnings of Our Time* (Baltimore, MD: Johns Hopkins Press, 1987), 279–84.

9. Harper, "The Urban University," reprinted in Harper, *Trend in Higher Education*, 158.

10. Ibid., 158–60.

11. From John Dewey's 1907 essay, "Education as a University Study," as reprinted in *John Dewey: The Middle Works, 1899–1924*, vol. 4, 1907–1909, ed. J.A. Boydston (Carbondale: Southern Illinois University Press, 1976), 158–64.

12. University of Chicago, *The University and the City: A Centennial View of the University of Chicago* (Chicago: University of Chicago Library, 1992), ix–x; Wirth, *John Dewey as Educator*, 46–48. The quoted phrase can be found in Harper, "The University and Democracy," 6–7.

13. As quoted in Wirth, *John Dewey as Educator*, 47–48. For Harper's brilliantly prophetic argument that realization of America's democratic promise required raising the status of teaching at all levels to at least equal that of any other profession, see his *Trend in Higher Education*, 186–94.

14. Harper, "The University and Democracy," 32.

15. Ibid., 25.

16. Among other "influentials" strongly supporting the idea of a pedagogy-centered university effectively integrated with secondary and primary education, L. Shulman has been one of the most persuasive; see his "Professing the Liberal Arts," in *Education and Democracy: Re-imagining Liberal Learning in America,* ed. R. Orrill (New York: College Entrance Examination Board, 1997), 151–73.

17. Discussion of the concept of a democratic devolution revolution is found in testimony by I. Harkavy before the Subcommittee on Housing and Community Opportunity of the Committee on Banking and Financial Services of the House of Representatives, 105 Cong. 1 sess. (Washington, DC: U.S. Government Printing Office, 1997).

18. J.W. Gardner, "Remarks to the Campus Compact Strategic Planning Committee," San Francisco (10 February 1998).

19. Ibid.

20. See E.L. Boyer, "Creating the New American College," *Chronicle of Higher Education,* 9 (March 1994): A48; D.C. Bok, *Universities and the Future of America* (Durham, NC: Duke University Press, 1990); Schulman, "Professing the Liberal Arts"; A.W. Astin, "Liberal Education and Democracy: The Case for Pragmatism," in *Education and Democracy,* 207–23.

21. From John Dewey's 1902 essay, "The School as Social Centre," as reprinted in *John Dewey: The Middle Works, 1899-1924,* vol. 2, 1902–1903, ed. J.A. Boydston (Carbondale: Southern Illinois University, 1976), 90–91.

22. For a fuller discussion of Dewey's utopian goal of cosmopolitan democratic communities and of university-assisted community schools, see L. Benson and I. Harkavy, "Progressing Beyond the Welfare State," *Universities and Community Schools, 2,* no. 1-2 (1991): 2–28; L. Benson and I. Harkavy, "School and Community in the Global Society," *Universities and Community Schools, 5,* no. 1-2 (1997): 16–71. We created *Universities and Community Schools* in 1989 as a means to advance mutually beneficial,

innovative partnerships between universities and local schools in general, and university-assisted community schools in particular.

23. For an illuminating discussion of the concept of organizational learning, see W.F. Whyte, ed., *Participatory Action Research* (Newbury Park, CA: Sage Publications, 1991), 237–41.

24. For more complete accounts of Professor Johnston's work, see L. Benson and I. Harkavy, "Anthropology 210, Academically Based Community Service and the Advancement of Knowledge, Teaching, and Learning: An Experiment in Progress," *Universities and Community Schools, 2,* no. 1-2 (1994): 66–69; I. Harkavy, F.E. Johnston, and J.L. Puckett, "The University of Pennsylvania's Center for Community Partnerships as an Organizational Innovation for Advancing Action Research," *Concepts and Transformations, 1,* no. 1 (1996): 15–29.

25. Provost's Council on Undergraduate Education, "The 21st Century Penn Undergraduate Experience: Phase I," *University of Pennsylvania Almanac* (May 1995): S-1.

26. University of Pennsylvania, *Annual Report, 1994-1995* (President's Report), Philadelphia, 1996.

27. S.H. Preston, "Dean's Column," *Penn Arts and Sciences,* Philadelphia (Fall 1998): 2.

28. Preston, "Dean's Column," 9.

29. J. Rodin, "Penn and West Philadelphia: A New Model for Progress in the Community," *The Pennsylvania Gazette* (November 1997): 10.

30. *The Chronicle of Higher Education* (20 November 1998): A20.

31. For a very recent, robust, and stimulating discussion of America's democratic promise, see H.C. Boyte, "Off the Playground of Civil Society: Freeing Democracy's Powers for the 21st Century," (Paper presented at Duke University, 23 October 1998). Given space constraints, we have not been able to spell out in detail our conception of a "genuinely democratic schooling system" and a "fully democratic society." We do that in our forthcoming book, *Progressing Beyond John Dewey: Radically Reconstructing American Universities to Construct a More Democratic Society* (co-authored with our colleague, John Puckett). Strong support for our argument that universities will be handsomely rewarded (in various ways) if they really make solving the schooling problem their highest priority is found in an enthusiastic article in the *New York Times* (1 March 1999) pp. B1, 5. The headline reads, "Large Gift to Education School Raises Hopes a Trend Is Starting: $21 Million Is Dedicated in Record U. Conn Donation." The article notes, "It is the biggest donation ever made to a school of education," cites other recent very large gifts to schools of education, and quotes the perceptive observation of S.H. Fuhrman, Dean of Penn's Graduate School of Education: "These [large] donations may be presaging a new era . . . [since] donors are making the statement that improving education ranks up there with eradicating a dreaded disease."

CHAPTER 10

Supporting Community Involvement in the Digital Age

Penelope Eckert and Peter Henschel

I n our rapid-paced and increasingly digitized lives, it is easy to come under the impression that values are changing—that something is being lost. It is almost routine for every generation to see changes in the next generation as constituting a loss of traditional values, skills, and knowledge. But usually there are new values, skills, and knowledge that supplant some of the old, and that are eventually integrated into traditional ways of doing things. The exercise of civic responsibility—the recognition that one has an obligation to engage with others in the service of one's community—appears to be one area that is undergoing significant changes in current decades. We argue that these changes do not constitute loss, but important new beginnings.

The current belief that today's young adults are less engaged in community activity may have some basis in the statistics. Today's young adults are less engaged in the political process than their parents. Less than 20 percent of 18- to 20-year-olds voted in 1998, and just 16 percent report volunteering in a political campaign.[1] There is some evidence as well that these young adults place little priority on being a "... good American who cares about the good of the country,"[2] and that they place less value on their identities as Americans.[3] The reports of these findings tend to be worded negatively—there is something that the older generations valued that the younger generations value less. But before we conclude that this difference signals a loss in civic respon-

The authors express their gratitude for all the work and insights of the Institute for Research on Learning (IRL) and its people that informed the perspective in this essay. Particular thanks go to Susan Allen, Dr. Mimi Ito, and Teri Whitehair, who shared their intellectual and editorial wisdom.

sibility, we need to consider the positive. What does this generation value that the older generation does not? Before we can conclude that young people do not have a sense of community obligation, we need to ask how they view service, and how they define community. How do they see themselves in relation to nations, local communities, and other social structures? It may well be that what is changing is not the degree of commitment but forms and interpretations of commitment and responsibility.

CIVIC RESPONSIBILITY AS WE KNOW IT

Our understanding of civic responsibility is based in a tradition of locally organized engagement. In the mid-to-late eighties, one of us (Henschel) served as deputy mayor for Management and Programs for the City and County of San Francisco. During that time, he observed firsthand what concerted, tenacious effort from a focused band of citizens could accomplish. From a wide array of examples, we highlight the following: Creating a broad constituency for affordable housing; motivating voter registration; driving the collective will to reform crucial day-to-day city hall operations; reforming the city charter; creating the constituency for a new main library; building the war chest to restore the cable car system; and building an extraordinary grassroots fabric of commitment to fight AIDS and support AIDS patients. In all of these cases, ordinary citizens acted in extraordinary ways to make great things happen, and they were all done within local organized groups of activists. This kind of engagement—what we have traditionally thought of as the prototypical exercise of "civic responsibility"—is located directly in the geographic communities that people live and work in. It provides opportunities for people to work with their neighbors, and to gain control over conditions in their community—to make a mark.

Young people are less engaged in this kind of civic participation. But does it mean that they are not committed to being positively engaged in their community? A 1999 study by the National Association of Secretaries of State (NASS) indicates that although interest and participation in the political process is declining, young people's volunteerism is very much on the rise. Rather than making their mark through the political process, or through civic organizations, young adults seek a personal connection, engaging directly with those in need of their services, rather than in projects with others like themselves. One is more likely to find them in homeless shelters, soup kitchens, hospitals, and schools than in meetings of community and civic organizations. And if they are uninterested in abstract national loyalties, they associate good citizenship with direct responsibility for others. According to the NASS report, 94 percent of the 18- to 20-year-olds surveyed agreed that "the most important thing I can do as a citizen is to help others." It is clear, then, that people are still deeply committed to public service, but the forms and terms of this service are changing. There is a very strong sense of responsibility to others, but a personal one-on-one responsibility. Does this represent a loss of community engagement? Is there a rise in individualism as people are inclined to say?

If young people are not doing what we think they ought to be doing in the realm of civic responsibility, we might ask what they are doing and why. Before we invest any more effort trying to figure out how to engage young people more effectively in our traditional forms of community service, we should try to recognize and understand the nature of the service in which they are engaged. In particular, what is the significance of the one-on-one emphasis in service?

We find it suggestive that the same generation that is engaging in direct local volunteerism is also engaged in cyberspace. The stereotypic view of young people's involvement in cyberspace is that their activity is depersonalized and depersonalizing. People who spend hours on the computer are viewed as antisocial; as running away from community engagement. It is commonly said that young people are being entertained by computers, and that their computer activity shows a loss of the ability to engage with others and to entertain themselves. We note that a certain amount of this concern comes from a generation that grew up watching lots of television, and whose elders were concerned with their passive engagement with that medium. While computer games may be played alone, the player's role is not passive. But this is not all there is to it. Those who engage in computer games often develop considerable skill, not the least of which is basic computer skill. Many members of the younger generation have grown up with a kind of familiarity and ease with computers that most of their elders will never know. The "digital age" is overwhelming to most and immensely disorienting to many. But for a significant portion of the young people entering college today, the digital world is home. The forms of engagement afforded by the digital world may well have had a profound effect on the ways in which these people pursue a variety of activities, including the ways in which they engage in their social and political environment.

Many of us view digital technology as a support for the pursuit of traditional activities, and certainly this function has been very important. The Internet has many implications for the enhancement of traditional forms of political participation. For geographically based groups, online community networks can enhance the possibilities for local participation and civic life. With the communicative capabilities of the World Wide Web, it is no longer necessary to organize large numbers of people to get political processes moving. Citizens in all parts of the country are mobilizing in vast numbers via email and the Web to lobby their representatives in localities, state capitals, and in Washington. All indicators point to an explosion in the sheer volume of such transactions, forcing even the most "cyberphobic" public official to pay attention and provide online access. To some extent this amounts to a transfer of activity to a new medium, speeding up and intensifying traditional activity, but it produces no serious qualitative change in how the political process is pursued. However, cyberspace now provides the potential for a single individual or a small number of individuals to initiate a political or social process or movement in new, startling ways. This reality is becoming part of a redefinition of the relation between the individual and society.

The new technologies and networks also have the power to engage like-minded individuals in new kinds of informal communities that are independent of local and face-to-face contact. At the same time, it is not unusual for relationships and communities that are forged online to come together in the face-to-face world as well. But most crucial, community is being redefined through new communications technology. People are no longer dependent on local networks to find others who share their interests or convictions. All kinds of groups form online, based entirely on shared interest and activity, and spanning geographic areas. This also changes the situation of hitherto marginalized groups such as children, the elderly, and minority groups of all sorts. Online groups such as "SeniorNet Online," "Net Noir," and "Planet Out" provide opportunities for people to form new kinds of affiliations that are not limited to specific geographic localities. And kids these days can organize fan clubs, online discussion groups that are meaningful to them. In these communities, people who have felt excluded in the past find power and voice, and the possibility of engagement without dependence on existing institutional power structures. The web provides the potential to pull away from the local—to engage in global communities based on shared interests and concerns. If it is luring people away from geographically local engagement, it is bringing them into close contact with distant people they may share something with. And if it deemphasizes a variety of kinds of local (and national) loyalties, it is making them citizens of the world.

The Web also provides new ways of interacting with information—supporting more collaborative ways of constructing knowledge. People are not simply gleaning hard facts from the Web; they are engaging with others who share their interests, exchanging information, and helping each other probe the meaning and use of that information. The very generation that is disengaged from the political process is deeply engaged in forcing the democratization of information—pulling the control of knowledge and information from those with enormous resources and opening it up to anyone who can get online. Online groups are opening up knowledge and discussion of hitherto mystified areas such as health and financial investments, and the free software movement is eroding the control over operating systems and software development that has been in the hands of a few powerful corporations.

These activities are anything but politically disengaged, but they are radically different from the activities we are used to. The younger generation has its own platform to work from. Rather than trying to participate in the lower rungs of established social and political organizations, or trying to create such organizations in the traditional sense, they are using the Internet to create opportunities for relatively egalitarian many-to-many participation. If they are not joining our generation's organizations, they are finding meaningful forms of participation in communities that are supported by, or initially created in, cyberspace. These communities are not geographically confined, and are based more often on issues, causes, or themes that transcend place.

Our challenge is to find and support the connections between the "older," more traditional forms of engagement and the "newer," emerging forms. Building bridges between the two requires that we find ways to learn from each other. Just as the older generation may feel stymied by the apparently structureless social space of the Web, there may be barriers to young people's access to locally based communities. Our ideas of what constitutes effective civic participation need to change to reflect new realities. We have to recognize that there are multiple ways of being involved and of being effective. But in all cases, the key is access to participation. People seek the opportunity to contribute meaningfully to the communities that are most meaningful to them. To the older generation, these communities may be local; to the younger generation, they may be increasingly virtual. The older generation may underappreciate the potential of participation in virtual communities because they cannot visualize their place in them. By the same token, the younger generation may have difficulty finding ways to bring their egalitarian forms of participation into sync with the forms of local engagement that are currently legitimized as community participation. In both cases, the challenge is to learn new forms of participation, and such learning requires access.

ACCESS TO PARTICIPATION AS THE KEY TO LEARNING

Access has been a central theme in the theories of learning that we have been developing at the Institute for Research on Learning (IRL). In our work, we seek to understand how and what people learn in their everyday lives. We study learning as it happens informally in everyday life, as people learn what they want and need to know in order to pursue activities that are important and meaningful to them. We study how learning is organized in communities—how it serves the social life of communities and the people that make up the communities.

The seminal work of Jean Lave and Etienne Wenger at IRL led to a social theory of learning based in community participation. Thinking about how people learn in apprenticeship situations, Lave and Wenger developed the concept "community of practice,"[4] which brings together knowledge, learning, and social practice. A community of practice is an aggregate of people who come together around some enterprise. That enterprise could be anything—playing music, selling drugs, inventing a widget, learning math, or even being a family. United by this common enterprise, people come to develop and share ways of doing things, ways of talking, beliefs, values—in short, practices—as a function of their joint engagement in activity. Simultaneously, social relations form around activities, and activities form around relationships. Particular kinds of knowledge, expertise, and forms of participation become part of individuals' identities and places in the community. People do not learn isolated facts or skills, but learn practices—ways of participating. Lave and Wenger [5] emphasized the relation between learning and community participation, noting that learning is accomplished through participation in community practice, and that one's life in such a community involves ever-changing forms of participation. A newcomer may learn by observing and working at peripheral tasks, then gradually moving closer to the center of the practice. One's identity, one's forms of participation in the community will change as one's knowledge changes; and the desire to participate will serve as powerful motivation to learn. At IRL, our pursuit of learning has led us to study communities of practice of all sorts, from preadolescent children engaging in informal play to claim processors in a major insurance company. Everywhere we have gone, we've witnessed people learning not just *through* participation, but *for* participation. Learning is not simply a matter of an individual accumulating knowledge, but of engagement with others in meaningful activity.

Thus learning is powerfully linked not just to motivation but also to one's identity. Learning is driven by who we are and who we wish to become. This insight seems to be true whether we are talking about apprentices, gangs, college sports teams, or teams of seasoned software engineers. There is an intimate relation between who we are and what we know, and between who we want to be and what we learn. Thus access to learning opportunities is not simply the availability of instruction, but the availability of meaningful forms of participation. In order to learn, people need access to the forms of community activity that provide exposure and experience, and that promise to reward learning with enhanced possibilities for participation. Learning is a process of social transformation, changing the learner's sense of his or her own meaning in the world, and of his or her potential to contribute to the community.

This perspective has led IRL to develop seven basic principles of learning:

1. **Learning Is Fundamentally Social.** Schools and workplaces commonly require participants to choose between learning and social fulfillment. This is a choice that should never arise. An important part of what makes people successful and productive is their ability to integrate their work with their social lives. They forge their identities and connections

around their work, their knowledge, and their contributions to the communities in which they participate. Yet most students and workers in our society are currently expected to live differently—to maintain a distance between learning, work, and social activity.

2. **Knowledge Is Integrated in the Life of Communities.** Knowledge, activity, and social relations are closely intertwined, whether in families, scientific communities, jump rope groups, jazz bands, or design teams. United by a common enterprise, people come to develop and share ways of doing things, ways of talking, beliefs, values—in short, practices—as a function of their joint involvement in mutual activity. These informal groups are called "communities of practice" because they are defined not only by their membership, but by shared ways of doing things. Every individual belongs to, and seeks membership in, many communities of practice. In communities of practice, social relations form around activities, activities take shape through relationships, and particular kinds of knowledge and expertise become part of individuals' identities and places in the community. Because shared knowledge underlies this activity, learning is the means by which people gain membership, and participate in community activity.

3. **Learning Is an Act of Membership.** The motivation to learn is the desire to participate in a community of practice. Learning is not just the activity of a sole individual, but the primary vehicle for engagement with others. It is what enables people to enter and participate in new communities of practice, and it is what enables them to continually modify their places in and contribution to the community. Every act of learning brings a change in one's relation to the community—a change in one's identity. The key to enhancement and motivation in learning lies in the intimate connection between the desire for participation and the role of new knowledge in enabling that participation.

4. **Knowing Is Engagement in Practice.** Learning is a continual transformation of our knowledge and understanding. In our day-to-day lives, we are continually expanding our knowledge, as we engage with others in a range of endeavors. We glean knowledge from observations of, and participation in, myriad situations and activities. Sometimes we are consciously trying to learn something; most of the time we do not even notice that we are learning. Only in the classroom is knowledge presented in the abstract, and only in the classroom are people expected to demonstrate knowledge through abstract performances. Informal kinds of learning seem easier than classroom learning—not necessarily because what we are learning is simpler, but because it is embedded in activity that makes it familiar, and that enables us to make sense of new information.

Those who can adapt and learn swiftly in new situations are people who can figure out what the characteristics of the situation are, what its relation is to situations that they already know, what there is to learn, and what new knowledge they need in order to be able to participate productively in the situation. This kind of activity requires confidence in one's ability and right to participate.

5. **Engagement Is Inseparable from Empowerment.** Individuals perceive their identities in terms of their ability to contribute—and in terms of their contributions—to a community. Meaningful participation in a community involves the power to affect the life of that community. Settings and situations that provide the greatest potential for learning, therefore, will be those in which participants have meaningful and active roles—in which they are engaged in real action that has consequences not only for them but for their community as a whole.

6. **"Failure" to Learn Is a Common Result of Exclusion from Participation.** Learning requires access and the opportunity to contribute. People have difficulty learning when they are only accorded marginal or tentative membership. Limited privileges of participation do not entail rights to contribute and make meaning, hence do not provide opportunities for engaged learning. This deeper perspective requires a more textured understanding of the means and implications of discrimination and exclusion.

7. **We Already Have a Society of Lifelong Learners.** Learning is a natural part of being human. We all learn what enables us to participate in the communities that matter to us. People are learning all the time, but what they are learning is not necessarily in their best interests or in the best interests of society. People learn what enables them to participate in communities of practice—not just any communities of practice, but those that appear to them to be real, to be available, and to hold possibility for meaningful participation. Depending on availability and opportunities for meaningful participation, people may seek their potential in all kinds of communities. It is this need for meaningful participation that motivates the gang member and the honor student, the scientist and the huckster, the public servant and the drug dealer.

THE GENERATION DIVIDE

Learning is not simply an acquisition of knowledge, but a change in identity: We are what we know and we learn in order to become. As we learn, our possibilities, our perspective, and our place in the world all change, however minutely. As we examine higher education to find how to enhance students' opportunities to incorporate public service into their lives, we need to consider the relation between learning, participation, and identity. In higher education, attention to learning is focused on academic subject matter. But many other kinds of learning are taking place as well, in informal activity as well as in the classroom, the library, and the lab. How students integrate all of this learning is what will determine the kind of people they will become and how they will live in the world after graduation. And their commitment to public service may well depend on the extent to which they are able to integrate service into all of this learning.

We might examine the nature of the communities of practice that form in our colleges and universities—what opportunities students have to integrate their broader social concerns, and their community service in their day-to-day activities, and what opportunities they have to develop enduring communities of practice around these concerns. Students' identities undergo an enormous transformation in the course of their undergraduate years. They develop new networks, new ways of life. They come to participate in a wide variety of communities of practice as they move onto campus or as they balance their lives at home with their lives in college. They participate in communities of practice built on friendship, cohabitation, eating, social activities, classes, study groups, teams, musical groups, political organizations, sororities, fraternities, and online chat groups. They explore the academic terrain, eventually choosing majors. In doing so they may become part of a department, or of a cohort of majors. They find ways to balance all of these forms of participation, and their ability to thrive depends on the freedom and care with which they come to form and participate in these communities of practice, on their ability to develop strong and meaningful forms of participation in them, and on their ability to integrate them.

Students' ability to thrive and succeed in community service depends on their ability to integrate this activity into their other interests, and their lives on campus. It is all too easy for colleges and universities to support students' expansion of networks in such a way that they become increasingly homogeneous and elite. The challenge is to enable students to participate in enduring communities of practice that transcend the campus, that enable them to engage in an ongoing basis with people of other ages and from other backgrounds. This engagement cannot be an individual foray away from the secure environment of school. It must provide students with access to meaningful forms of participation—with a sense of agency and direct connection to the communities of practice that they hope to serve. And this engagement must be sufficiently long to provide the sense of continuity that makes experience real. What kind of continuity can students have beyond the individual course, the quarter, semester, or academic year?

The challenge for our schools, colleges, universities, and communities is to support students' engagement in service, and to support their incorporation of that engagement in their sense of themselves. This means that we need to pay attention to the opportunities we provide for meaningful forms of participation in communities of practice based in community service. We also need to recognize the communities of practice and the forms of participation that they have developed for themselves. If we take into consideration what appears to be this generation's preference for direct one-on-one engagement, we need to examine the structures within which this engagement can unfold. And given the current generation's access to online action, we need to examine the ways in which online practices might change and enhance our own vision of community service. Their desires may have more to do with providing access to others—to sharing their voice, and sharing their sources of information. Are we recognizing the value of this kind of concern and this kind of action? Are we supporting it and finding connections to other forms of service?

Students' engagement in the world online has brought about subtle differences in their forms of participation, and in their sense of themselves in relation to the rest of society. As we consider what it will take to engage youth in our projects and dreams, we need to share in theirs. We need to recognize the changes in forms of public participation that the digital age has brought about, and the interests and needs that have given rise to those changes. Youth have not simply jumped online to become slaves to what the Internet has to offer. They have used the opportunities offered by the Internet to transform public participation to fit their ideals of direct access, free information, and democracy.

The older generation invented information technology, but it is the younger generation that has figured out how to live with this branch of knowledge. As we confront what appears to be a continuing decline in young people's interest in the activities that we have traditionally considered key to civic involvement and civic responsibility, we should recognize that young people's civic responsibility is far from being absent, but that we have not yet recognized it. We have simply failed to see new forms of engagement that the younger generation has developed both online and offline, and we have failed to recognize the desire for voice and new kinds of democratic values that have given rise to those new forms. If we look below the surface, we may see how the basic word "community" is being redefined and recast. In the transition into the digital age, we are witnessing drastically changing possibilities for community formation, dynamics, and purpose. If we cannot make sense of these communities, we are missing the opportunity to recognize civic engagement and to appreciate its transformation. If we cannot make sense of the nature of the knowledge and identities that are being forged in these communities, we cannot hope to engage them in the service of projects that we believe to be important. And if we cannot make sense of the projects that the younger generation believes to be important, our own are likely to become stale.

NOTES

1. National Association of Secretaries of State, "New Millennium Project. Part I. American Youth Attitudes on Politics, Citizenship, Government, and Voting" (Lexington, KY: Author, 1999), 15. National Association of Secretaries of State, 501 Darby Creek Road, Lexington, KY 40509.
2. Ibid., 16.
3. W. Rahn, "Generations and American National Identity" (Paper presented at the Communication in the Future of Democracy Workshop, Annenberg Center, Washington, DC, May 1998), 8–9.
4. J. Lave and E. Wenger, *Situated Learning: Legitimate Peripheral Participation* (Cambridge: Cambridge University Press, 1991); E. Wenger, *Communities of Practice: Learning, Meaning and Identity* (Cambridge: Cambridge University Press, 1998).
5. Lave and Wenger, *Situated Learning*.

PART 4

• • • • • • • • • • • •

Perspectives from Different
Sectors of Higher Education

CHAPTER 11

A Community College Perspective

Paul A. Elsner

T he Maricopa Community College District's journey into service-learning and the promotion of social responsibility has been a long and worrisome one. This journey has been a long one for several reasons. At Maricopa, we began introducing the idea of social responsibility into our dialogues at the earliest inception of the Campus Compact initiative. I represented the community college sector on the original Executive Committee of Campus Compact when it met at Georgetown University in the late 1980s. At the time, I was an active participant in the Business-Higher Education Forum and some of its members, most notably Donald Kennedy at Stanford University, the late Father Timothy Healy from Georgetown, the late Howard Swearer from Brown University, and Frank Newman at the Education Commission of the States, had entered into discussion about the disinclination of students in American higher education to commit to public service.

Tom Wolfe was writing *Bonfire of the Vanities* at that time, and the junk bond scandals dominated the news. A few higher education leaders—Frank Newman and Donald Kennedy—began to raise the question as to whether our "best and brightest" could be persuaded to choose public service such as teaching, social work, and reworking our social agenda so that the best of innovation and the best of creativity would be brought to bear on our growing and evident social problems. I remember sitting at a table at the Business-Higher Education Forum and listening to the above-mentioned leaders at a meeting in Phoenix, Arizona.

Alexander "Sandy" Astin of UCLA continued to report the results of his longitudinal studies on freshman attitudes. These studies, at that time, began to show the drop-off of student expression of personal goals that would incorporate public service. Moreover, students in these studies—who in the early 1950s and 1960s had expressed the desire to find a meaningful philosophy—had now subverted such personal convictions and values to getting "ahead" in life, which to most meant getting a good job. The "me too" generation was, for the most part, seeking professional degrees and vocational prosperity—in short, "getting a good job and making money" was the predominant issue. Goals that would assist them in finding "themselves" (values) hardly seemed to enter their thoughts.

A joke circulated around higher education folks at the time. It was said that a higher education policy analyst, having read Astin's studies, indicated that he was shocked that the goal of almost 80 percent of the students was to make money. The story goes that a second analyst entered the conversation saying, "It's not true that 80 percent want to make money, only 60 percent want to make money, the other 20 percent want to make a hell of a lot of money!"

The general climate was that higher education—while delivering up specialization, strong professional careers, and good placement in the job market—also came with a value system that included a great lifestyle. Therefore, in the early 1980s higher education's song began to be lamenting the loss of a sense of social responsibility among our students.

This loss of social responsibility did not strike community colleges as a big problem. This seemed to be a problem from which we were nicely protected. We believed that this might have been an issue among students who were largely residential and more financially well-off than community college students—most likely committed to a "yuppie" or "boomer" life.

Therefore, our earliest challenge at Maricopa was to try to translate what Campus Compact meant for the community college movement. Susan Stroud, who at that time was the executive director of the Campus Compact offices at Brown University, came to the Maricopa Community Colleges. We held open dialogues with our college presidents, faculty, and students about the values of volunteerism and the commitment to social responsibility. One might say that we "stumped" this issue like an organized political campaign. People in the Maricopa Community Colleges did not jump out of their chairs on hearing the message about the values of volunteerism and commitment to social responsibility. In fact, the general reaction was, "What is the chancellor talking about and why is he talking about it?" Luckily, we hit a vein of strong interest in the student activities and students services people at the colleges.

The Maricopa Community Colleges' philosophy of student government has been to teach leadership and leadership skills—part of the enduring purpose of student government. In addition, the colleges' various clubs, councils, and student networks had been tied to student government processes—particularly their budget allocation systems—that often allowed small amounts of money to trickle down to student clubs and activities.

The most congenial place for the early marriage of volunteerism and student activities was at Maricopa's GateWay Community College, where there had been a long tradition of advisors linking their club activities to volunteer programs through the various departments, particularly the allied health departments. One of the first meetings that I attended when I arrived at the Maricopa Community Colleges was a meeting of club presidents who reported on their duties and responsibilities over the year. Almost all of these reports involved activities like teaching oral hygiene to elementary and preschool youth in day care centers. Often the capacities that students had acquired in their training programs were turned to volunteer service in the community. One striking example of service-learning today at GateWay Community College is their heating, ventilation, and air conditioning program. Technicians from that program go out into the community to help older people prepare their evaporative coolers for the summer heat.

So there was a small tradition of service-learning and the promotion of volunteerism in the Maricopa Community Colleges, but there had been no strategic emphasis on setting up programs to promote social responsibility.

The formation of Campus Compact and the "racheting-up" of the national dialogue by Frank Newman and others helped us think through a broader strategy for service-learning in the Maricopa Community Colleges. Early on, we brought Frank Newman to Maricopa to address our Leadership Breakfast assembly—a group of some 300 managers, executives, and faculty. This meeting took place at Scottsdale Community College. On the very day that Newman came to address Maricopa's leadership community, he was called out of our meetings by two or three members of the national press to comment on the central value of a Campus Compact initiative that had begun forming.

In his address, Newman underscored the need for us to look to innovations beyond technology and the management and administration of programs. He asked us to really engage in finding uncommon solutions to common problems like the school drop-out crisis, the breakdown of the family unit, the examination of neighborhoods and community building. What Newman asked us to do was to consider being innovative social engineers and entrepreneurs as well as entrepreneurs in the training and outreach programs to which community colleges were already so well committed.

In the months following Newman's visit, we circulated Robert Bellah's book, *Habits of the Heart*. I believe I sent out about 200 copies to various leaders in the Maricopa Community Colleges. In one of the early advisory committee meetings of our National Center for Campus Compact for Community Colleges, we invited Dr. Bellah to address our internal community and our advisory committee. We held various conversations around Bellah's book and attempted to think about how his book reflected our own professional community. We were saddened to learn that at Maricopa the philosophical and ideological platform had not been more strongly built around the Campus Compact initiative. We were looking for philosophical underpinnings; and while Bellah's book helped us think through the larger social dilemma of disconnection, isolation, and the lack of personal fulfillment—even in very successful lives such as our own—we did not see our way to build the kind of tight philosophical framework that would have allowed us to export the Campus Compact movement more broadly among community college leaders in the national community. Campus Compact remained a "hard sell."

The community colleges, however, did take a very pragmatic and simple approach to incorporating much of the interest of student volunteerism to the more traditional extension of the college's capacity—that is, the student activities approach by which student clubs would volunteer their services in helping out in the community. Our early vision at Maricopa began by trying to think about how the community college could develop a center for public policy and social service. Several of us here at Maricopa had dreamed that if we could have students volunteer in a homeless shelter, food kitchen, or crisis nursery center, that we could move them into a more reflective stage where they would begin to ask questions about why we have crisis nursery centers in our society or in our community. We hoped that this reflection would reach a maturity where students would be taught to do analytical and fundamental research about the community and—in the case of crisis nursery centers for example—a student might ask himself/herself questions: What is child policy in Arizona? What does it look like? Where do we stand compared to other states? What is involved in a comprehensive, coherent children's policy for a city, region, state, or even for that matter, for a nation?

We hoped that these volunteer activities and the following reflective and analytical work would mature into a major research effort. We hoped it might turn into something like a capstone paper at the end of sophomore year. Or that a student might decide to intern on a legislative committee that dealt with such issues as children's policy, literacy, or adult and juvenile incarceration. We hoped that these students would come to understand the dynamics of taking testimony, of immersing themselves in hearings, legislative processes, and the writing of ideal statutory language, and so on.

At about the same time that this vision was being discussed, we were awarded the responsibility and charter for forming the National Center for Campus Compact for Community Colleges. The staff at Brown University gave some small financial support for organizing a center that would work with community colleges by providing a clearinghouse for best practices in setting up programs that promoted civic responsibility and volunteerism. The Maricopa

Center for Campus Compact assumed the responsibility for providing informational workshops and orientations for setting up programs of social responsibility and for setting forth a consistent vocabulary and conceptual framework for such programs.

A national search was conducted for an executive director. Lyvier Conss, a very able and expansive leader, was brought to Maricopa to give shape to the center. She proceeded to visit several states and developed special-segment interest groups. Lyvier began to cultivate communications with the broader community of community college faculty and staff who were committed and were already beginning to develop volunteer programs and service-learning activities on their campuses. She also established relationships with several state Campus Compacts that were an important segue into reaching and promoting structures in states for community colleges to get quality information and good data about the best practices.

In addition, the National Center for Campus Compact for Community Colleges held an annual conference that still takes place in Scottsdale, Arizona, bringing in approximately 300 to 400 national Campus Compact leaders. These leaders come together to discuss programs, issues, and practical matters of service-learning. Numerous speakers and scholars attend this annual conference to help shape visionary models in service-learning. Conss continues to manage a vast communications network and a recognition system that promotes Campus Compact agendas in hundreds of community colleges throughout the United States. She has also tied her programs to other Maricopa networks including the National Institute for Leadership Development, an institute that promotes women in management and for CEO positions in community colleges. She has worked with Maricopa's National Academy for Division Chairs and mid-level academic administrators. She has held forums in almost every national higher education association and, of course, conducted several forums at the American Association of Community Colleges (AACC). Conss is the principal spokesperson for social responsibility-based programs for the American Association of Community Colleges and works with staff at AACC. Conss has sponsored or conducted forums at the American Association for Higher Education (AAHE), the American Council on Education (ACE), the Association of Community College Trustees (ACCT), and many other groups. These presentations have provided her an audience to translate this important agenda that is now well ensconced in the philosophies of community colleges all over the nation.

In attempting to describe Maricopa's commitment to social responsibility, I would describe three to four areas where community colleges are heavily involved in the promotion of social and civic responsibility. Sue McAleavey and Terry Pickeral of Mesa Community College have developed a schema that outlines the motivations for service-learning and volunteerism. They say that

motivations can be generated through humanitarianism, spiritual commitment, religious conviction, or other motivations in our notion of volunteerism
and social responsibility. I mentioned that the early formation of Campus
Compact did not lay out a fundamental supporting premise for why students
would want to volunteer or give of themselves to their communities. Maricopa
struggled with this in its early stages. If I recall correctly, there was even an
absence of this kind of discussion at the Executive Committee meeting of
Campus Compact. In fact, one of the early inquiries that Bellah and his team
made at Berkeley that formed the basis for *Habits of the Heart*[1] was the central
question, "Why do people volunteer?" Bellah's research team saw this imbedded in Rotary clubs and church and volunteer organizations, but raised the
larger question as to whether a society would gravitate toward these commitments if there was a shift in the younger generation's attitudes about their
sense of involvement or ownership of community problems. One could argue
that we have not seen promising change in the demeanor of even policy
makers who are elected to public office, who often are motivated by single
issues and are more likely than ever to support more laissez-faire market forces
as the basic solution for most of society's problems. The notion that all boats
will rise in a favorable economic tide suggests more than just a trickle down
philosophy. This is an inherent premise among conservatives and there seem
to be more conservatives than ever in policy shaping roles.

McAleavey and Pickeral[2] classify the motivations for service-learning and
volunteerism in the following categories:

1. **Charity**—something given to help the needy; an act of benevolence,
   e.g., donating money, clothing. Tends to give immediate (if short-term)
   assistance, such as volunteering in a crisis nursery center.
2. **Philanthropy**—works to increase the well-being of humanity, e.g., en-
   dowments, charitable aid, civic organization involvement, fund raising.
   Tends to be longer term than charity and geared toward sustained
   efforts.
3. **Social Justice**—advocacy for principles of moral rightness; the quality of
   being fair or impartial, e.g., calling elected officials, writing letters,
   lobbying, initiating special interest groups, civic involvement, etc. Tends
   to aim at changes in social institutions in examining barriers to access
   resources.
4. **Social Transformation**—a commitment to a different social order based
   on equality, justice, and freedom from oppression. Focuses on empowerment of those declared "needy" via neighborhood development. A
   process whereby "clients" are turned into service providers, as opposed
   to "agency" involvement which is sometimes perceived as part of the

problem, e.g., community mobilization, folk schools, cooperatives, food drives, etc.

From the beginning, Maricopa tried to build volunteer service and civic responsibility as not just an episodic experience for students, but as a long-term behavioral construct. Sue McAleavey's examinations and motivations are an important premise on how one looks at why students participate in community work. We had little to go on in the Maricopa Community Colleges in that the models most often cited in our Campus Compact network with the four-year universities were models which mobilized residential students to reach out into poorer communities for tutoring, counseling support, role modeling as big brothers or sisters, and support for recreational and after school activities. We generally saw these to be more short term and, while very valuable, still largely charitable. If our students volunteered in a soup kitchen, we eventually wanted them to ask why we have soup kitchens. We hoped that students would see a larger role and the developing of their own capacity to change the order of things they saw in the community.

However, they had to have outlets as well as tools and skill sets to move to these less episodic and more long-term involvements. It was Father Malloy, at Notre Dame, who advised the Campus Compact Executive Committee to think about the kind of theory of human development we are interested in as a segue into "Why Campus Compact?" Father Malloy had indicated that his internship in Latin America when he was a young man had been a defining experience for him. We saw this occur with a student in one of Marybeth Mason's classes. Mason, a faculty member who at the time was teaching at Chandler-Gilbert Community College, described for us a student whose general demeanor was "gloom and doom." The student arrived in Mason's composition class wearing black clothes, black eye shadow, and black fingernail polish—in general, her entire outlook was black. As a result of working with deprived children at a nursery in the community, this student began to expand her outlook and gradually redefine her persona. The volunteer student became so engaged in working with children that she soon altered her appearance to brighter clothes, a brighter disposition, and began to think of working with children as a life career. I know that one cannot generalize about the developmental stages this particular student experienced as a result of her volunteer assignment, but there are Chandler-Gilbert faculty who feel that the volunteer component required and suggested in many courses at Chandler-Gilbert Community College (with 87 different agencies aligned to take students on carefully appointed assignments) is the basis for helping, particularly younger students, chart their developmental stages on a much more positive, personal, and constructive basis.

Mason has been one of the outstanding leaders in the Maricopa Community Colleges in developing pedagogies around service-learning and volunteerism. She took responsibility for integrating service-learning into certain English department offerings while she was an activist faculty member for service-learning at Chandler-Gilbert Community College's main campus. She sees, at the risk of over simplifying her philosophy, "the community as larger world space for students." If volunteer experience can be a defining moment for students, Mason explains how personal self-concept, life space, and larger possibilities open up for students who have had even limited volunteer experience.

To some faculty, volunteering in a socially responsible way means expansion of life space, revision of self-concept, and general personal growth. Other faculty have remarked to me that even postadolescents are tentative about their self-worth, their place in society, and their feelings of the elusiveness of meaning in their lives. We know that adolescents, through normal development, are very inner-directed and often riddled with doubt—"I'm too fat, I'm not very smart, I'm too tall, I'm not capable, I'm not popular." This self-doubt can carry over into younger college students and may even be symptomatic of some of our older students—especially doubtful returning students whose lives have been shattered by layoffs, divorce, and other life dislocations.

The Maricopa Community Colleges were satisfied and thrilled with Chandler-Gilbert Community College's virtually wall-to-wall promotion of volunteerism among its students. However, in the early stages we did not look to the more profound developmental aspects that were planned for students by Mason and some of her followers.

Chandler-Gilbert Community College, one of the newest colleges in the Maricopa system, built a framework for social responsibility very early. Rather than creating a marginalized structure for achieving this goal, they incorporated the whole panoply of student services, activities, functions, and structures. They hooked up student life with student responsibility. This was not just a lumping together of programs; the entire student activities program moved toward the support of faculty in making carefully assessed appointments and assignments so that students landed in the right volunteer arrangement, one that is consistent with their interests and their developmental stages.

This was no small undertaking in that the deployment and logistics of running volunteerism in 87 different agencies called for the complete alteration of the traditional student activities and student services apparatus at Chandler-Gilbert Community College.

Maricopa recently created the Williams Campus, an interesting extension of Chandler-Gilbert Community College. The Williams Campus is an air base formerly called Williams Air Base. This reuse has created the opportunity to design an academic village and an innovative learning environment—one which Mason describes as follows:

> Our learning community integrates first year composition, film, literature, and computer technology . . . designed to encourage students to either research, read, write, or review and discuss topics of interest . . . focused around the theme of "creating community in a changing world." This integrated series of courseware attempts to have students experience the creating of community in a changing world.

Basically, students are encouraged to move around the world studying everything from Brazilian films to Southwestern Hispanic literature. It is important for students, according to Mason, to understand resolving conflict in building family and community, and how communities differ in their respective cultures and geographical settings, and how community is redefined from one another depending on the location, country, values, and culture of a region.

Netscape and Microsoft protocols are a requirement of the course. Students are required to attend off-campus cultural events like art exhibits, multicultural festivals, and musical performances—all relevant to their reading. A service-learning component is set forth to require students to process values, seek clarification of attitudes and social mores, and to look at different views of personal development and civic responsibility outside the walls of the classroom by performing community service. According to Mason's course descriptions, everything that is learned in the classroom must be extended to a meaningful context in the real world.

Students are assigned to volunteer in such places as the House of Refuge East, a transitional housing project for formerly homeless families. They can select a Head Start pre-school program located within the academic village we call Williams. Students attend community events. They listen to various speakers. They carry out community-based organizational projects. Mason has students read works like *The House on Mango Street*, by Sandra Cisneros, to look into how family and community bond in Hispanic culture. Students watch films like *Boys in the Hood*, *El Norte*, *Philadelphia*, *The Long Walk Home*, and *The Grapes of Wrath*.[3] She asks her students to think about the concept of community. The concept of "community" in a neighborhood like Watts compared to the concept of "community" from a migrating Central American family's vision or dream of "community" is very different. She asks them to think about the kind of bonded community constructed around, for example, being gay and being drawn together as a community as a result of their experiences with HIV.

When students complete Mason's sequence of literature, film, writing, and the uses of technology, it is hoped that they will have a deeper and more profound sense of community. They immerse themselves into diverse communities as volunteers, aides, and interns, and it is believed that the students' profound sense of community will make them more effective facilitators, leaders, and shapers of community destiny.

Marybeth Mason has idealized for us all what we dreamed about in the early days of Campus Compact. She not only has an academic village into which she can reach for living examples of displaced and separated students, but she can give the students a reflective academic context in which they can fully develop their largest capacities as future citizens and leaders.

There are too many features of the work Mason and her colleagues have done with this academic village to list them all here and still do them justice. However, it is hoped that these brief illustrations indicate the lengths to which she has gone to build a sense of a larger human community to which we all belong.

Another across the board, almost wall-to-wall commitment to service-learning occurs at GateWay Community College—another college in the Maricopa Community College system. Earlier I mentioned that GWCC had entered into volunteerism and social responsibility through its club councils and student activities agendas. Since GWCC has among its curriculum many technical and occupational programs—ranging from nursing, medical radiography, and respiratory care, to court reporting—the college puts out a general prospectus for all faculty and leadership to support service-learning enterprises. Below is an example of the kinds of service-learning projects that GWCC students conduct.[4]

Nursing. Students conduct health screenings and provide preventative health care information (hygiene) to students at local elementary schools. They also participate in community health fairs, flu shot clinics, The Race for the Cure, and the Maricopa County Community Health Immunization Program, and conduct universal precautions workshops for GWCC automotive and liberal arts students.

Medical Radiography. Students gather and develop materials and conduct informational presentations and demonstrations for Breast Cancer Awareness and Early Detection booths at health fairs held at a local mall. In conjunction with Save the Family, students conduct basic health care and hygiene information sessions for children and their guardians.

Surgical Technology/Perioperative Nursing. Students engage in various community service activities, including local health fairs and The Race for the Cure. Surgical technology students practice their skills as they are mentored by registered nurse first assistant students who are performing porcine surgeries.

Health Unit Coordinating. Students participate in several projects including "Beautiful Alternatives," a local program that works to rebuild self-image for women with cancer. Students also assist with information booths and first aid stations for The Race for the Cure and assist with health screenings at local elementary schools.

Respiratory Care. Students design and present "The Hazards of Smoking" and "The Hazards of Inhalants" programs to middle school students at local elementary schools. Students also plan and conduct on-campus activities for the Great American Smoke Out, participate in health screening for local elementary schools, and assist with information booths at The Race for the Cure.

Physical Therapist Assisting. Students conduct scoliosis screenings on children at local middle schools and teach body mechanics workshops to GWCC nursing students.

General Business and Computer Information Systems. Students participate in career fairs at local elementary and high schools.

Court Reporting. Students conduct demonstrations at local high schools and serve as notetakers for hearing-impaired students on the GWCC campus.

Automotive Technology. Students, in conjunction with the Arizona Automotive Service Association, conduct car care clinics for a local senior citizen community and the GWCC neighborhood and participate in career fairs and career awareness panels at local elementary and high schools.

Heating, Ventilation, and Air Conditioning. HVAC students service and repair evaporative coolers for low-income, elderly metro-Phoenix residents who are identified by the AZ Foundation for Senior Living.

Honors. Students incorporate service-learning experiences to support their research for completion of their honors projects. Also, students assume leadership roles in related service-learning projects as part of their honors requirements. Students, identified by faculty from each division, participate in a leadership course and a curriculum specific service-learning project.

Spanish. Students prepare and read stories (in Spanish) to young children at local elementary schools.

English. Students engage in language arts/writing lab projects and tutoring activities with students at local elementary schools. Students serve as judges for creative writing contests conducted with local middle schools during Creative Writing Month in April.

Psychology. Developmental and abnormal psychology students provide services in a variety of agencies including Head Start, Boys and Girls Clubs, and homeless shelters.

Reading. Students participate in reading/tutoring programs at local elementary schools and in a family literacy project at a local shelter.

Social Sciences. Students provide service in projects at local human service agencies and schools. Service includes feeding the homeless, assisting with recreation activities at a senior home and a teen runaway program, supporting classroom teachers at local schools, and participating in holiday food/toy collection and distribution.

Math. Students tutor children at local elementary and middle schools.

Communications. Students assist children at a local elementary school in writing letters to Santa Claus as part of the Van Buren Association's Christmas Wish project and participate in a lunch hour reading/tutoring program at a local elementary school. Students also assist with registering over 3,000 participants for The Race for the Cure.

At GWCC, stand-alone volunteerism is seen as too episodic. Like Chandler-Gilbert Community College and Mesa Community College, the staff at GWCC assist the faculty in using reflection about their volunteer service as a means of discussion in the classroom as well as the reinforcement and reflective aspects of carrying out social responsibility. At GWCC, they believe that to process a service-learning experience, a student should be asked to move through a "what?" "so what?" "now what?" continuous reflective inquiry.

In response to "what?" students are asked to answer "What happened at the service site? What service did you perform? What people did you interact with? What were your roles? What career opportunities did you observe?" They are then asked to describe their experiences in written form.

The question "so what?" asks "What was the significance of the service? What did it mean to you personally? What are your negative and positive feelings about the service site, the people, and the experience? What did you learn that enhances your classroom instruction? What did you learn about the people at your service site and what are their similarities and differences to you? What skills and knowledge learned in the classroom did you use/apply? What skills or knowledge did you lack? How can you get these needed skills?" They are then asked to examine these questions.

The "now what?" question raises such issues as "What impact might your service have on your lifelong learning process? What impact did your experience have on your every day life? What insights did you gain that might assist you in your career or in selecting a career? What is the connection of this experience to your future? What did the experience teach you about community involvement, citizenship, and your civic responsibility? What is the relationship of your service experience to the "big picture," such as major societal changes, global change in the community, paradigm shifts, the social contract, etc.?"

LESSONS LEARNED AT MARICOPA

There are several factors of success or failure with regard to service-learning on which Maricopa's program directors would agree. We offer the following lessons learned:

The CEO Must Take the Lead

It is even more important that the CEO go beyond his or her rhetoric—they should "walk the talk." Dr. John Cordova, president of South Mountain Community College, one of the smaller Maricopa Community Colleges, sets such an example. Although busy running his college, this president finds time to volunteer to read to preschool children in the college's daycare center. He also works with community groups on leadership training and conveys principles of personal growth. Cordova is active in advising troubled youth in the community, attempting to get them on the right track.

Building a Sense of Social Responsibility Requires Broad-Based Support across the College

Launching volunteer programs from one section of the college can work—student clubs, for example—but it is preferable to build a college-wide strategy.

Volunteer programs can easily become marginalized. It is important to avoid being regarded as "that volunteer project over there." Programs of the kind I have described here should find themselves in every facet of the curriculum—in student services, athletic programs, the president's office, and even the custodial and operational areas. Service-learning should be a pervasive program for which everyone claims ownership.

While the CEO's Commitment Is Important, Programs Should Not Be Top Down

Programs for service and volunteerism should have self-organizing characteristics. They should hold opportunities for discovery and creativity. They should be constantly "thought up" and brought into action. Multiple, self-organizing efforts and new innovations should grow out of an open structure.

An Enabling Infrastructure Should Be in Place

Some point of intelligent coordination should exist. Placement of students and staff in various agencies needs to be coordinated. Assessment of matching volunteers to receiving agencies must be provided.

Promotion and budgetary studies have to be maintained. An advisory role for evaluation and strategic alignment with other college goals should be considered and assured. Dissemination of good information and the providing of training for volunteers are both necessary—they can make or break a program. Solid responsibility does not occur in a vacuum, unsupported, and standing alone. The best programs require integration into many college mainstreams.

Both the Leadership at the Maricopa Community Colleges and National Policy Planners May Have Underestimated the Interest and Zeal for Volunteer Experiences

It is easy to typecast segments of higher education. Some of us felt that in community colleges like Maricopa, where 50 percent of the students work full-time and 80 percent work full- or part-time, there would be little interest in service-learning.

It is easy to overgeneralize student characteristics. In reality, community college students have strong inclinations toward service-learning. Many have "bumped around" in life, some are raising children, and numerous bring special knowledge and resources. Many of our older students have already had exemplary volunteer service experiences before they come to us.

Sue McAleavey from Mesa Community College and Martha Bergin from GateWay Community College, both service-learning leaders and policy thinkers at Maricopa advise that we not underestimate service-learning as a powerful pedagogical leverage. Both McAleavey and Bergin see subject disciplines come alive under service-learning. Bergin writes:

> There are more modalities for teaching . . . Involvement physically, intellectually, morally, and emotionally helps to support holistic learning processes. By this, I mean that it is tougher to stay detached. I would say that service-related learning experiences involve or touch core value systems and this invokes, for me, the theoretical explanations about emotional intelligence, which is where I would look to explain these learning processes, and to explain what I mean by "holistic" learning.[5]

Service-Learning Is a Slow Evolutionary Process

Service-learning should be thought of as a decade process at the minimum. Michelle Bush, Lyvier Conss, Sue McAleavey, Martha Bergin, and Marybeth Mason—all would agree that we should expect to be in service-learning for the long haul, probably because of its vastly integrative character with learning organizational support and infrastructure. Service-learning is not a "quick fix" or a passing vogue. It requires persistence and staying power. The Maricopa Community Colleges' staff and faculty have been at this for a very long time. They have regrouped, revised, and perfected their strategies. They are still discovering the power of service-learning.

Space does not permit me to include the kind of testimony and review offered by many Maricopa leaders that I would like to in this chapter. The editors of this book have asked that I comment on Maricopa's interpretation of social responsibility and service-learning, therefore I have confined my remarks to Maricopa's experiences. Many other community colleges in our

Campus Compact Center also stand out as leaders in this area. I have not mentioned the many national leaders, such as Broward Community College, or the Community College of Denver, and so many others who have led the battle for service-learning and who have integrated service-learning into their college's mission and vision.

It is our hope at Maricopa, a hope we wish for many of our national colleagues, that service-learning will work itself fully into the personal ideology of every community college leader and be a pervasive part of this important segment of higher education—the great community college movement.

In closing I offer a final comment from Marybeth Mason who says so much about lessons learned in such a powerful way:

> The second way in which service-learning has impacted me is on a very personal level. When I began requiring my students to serve, I became a much more committed server myself, and with that new commitment came a heightened sense of understanding about the needs of my community. I have worked with abused and neglected children, homeless families living in both emergency and transitional housing facilities, women fleeing abuse seeking shelter in a place where they cannot be found, and many lonely elderly. I have seen firsthand the effects of poverty and discrimination, the lack of affordable health care, insurance, and child care, the lack of education, the prevalence of drug and alcohol abuse, the trap of credit card addiction, the lack of availability of birth control and sex education programs, and the lack of familial support. But I have also seen the strength and resilience of children, the tenacity and determination of mothers and fathers, the joy of telling and listening to stories from generations past, and the satisfaction on the faces of my students that comes with giving. I have been exhilarated by the new friendships I have developed with those who work in nonprofit agencies. I have watched and learned from their commitment, resourcefulness, and professionalism as they work day after day to do so much with so little. My family has joined me in service and together we have been reminded so many times of how fortunate we are for all we have. It's not an unfamiliar refrain; I hear it from my students all the time and must agree, "When I serve, I give a little but receive so much more in return.[6]

NOTES

1. R. Bellah, R. Madsen, W. Sullivan, A. Swidler, and S. Tipton, *Habits of the Heart: Individualism and Commitment in American Life* (New York: Harper & Row, 1985).
2. S. McAleavey and T. Pickeral, "Motivations for Service-Learning/Volunteerism," unpublished document for the Maricopa Community Colleges (1998).
3. M. Mason, excerpt from the syllabus for the Williams Campus, "Creating Community in a Changing World" (1998).

4. M. Bush, Director, Community Partnership Programs, GateWay Community College, personal communication, November 5, 1998.

5. M. Bergin, in-house memo, January 27, 1999.

6. M. Mason, in-house memo, January 29, 1999.

CHAPTER 12

The Perspective of a Comprehensive University

Judith A. Ramaley

WHAT IS A CIVIL SOCIETY?

When the *Kettering Review* published some articles reflecting on the concept of a civil society[1] more than a decade ago, a civil society was described as "that great web of associations, organizations, and institutions in which citizens gathered by habit and inclination, according to their particular interests. Educational, religious, and commercial, these civil entities represented the human life of the civilized world." Through the social capital that was built up,[2] this web of relationships generated the wherewithal to bridge the gap between individual interests and the workings of government, somewhere in that process producing the political capital to make this mediation possible.

The problem with civil society conceived of in this way is that the associations that make up such a fabric are often in the hands of the elite, and therefore, only the elite are likely to have a voice. Michael Schudson[3] has made the case that the "good citizen" in eighteenth-century American politics was a gentleman. "The nineteenth century brought rule by numbers, majorities of associated men organized in parties; and twentieth century American politics is rule by everyone, and no one, at once."[4]

David Mathews suggests that in a world where everyone, and no one, has a voice, civic groups, including educational institutions, can substitute for the

---

Note: Comprehensive universities are those that offer baccalaureate programs and graduate education through the masters degree.

public and actually block broader participation in civic life.[5] Mathews lays out a picture of a true civic society for our era as follows: "Civil societies become democratic when there are opportunities for people to learn the importance of listening to all views, even those they dislike, of 'working through' conflicting approaches to solving a problem, and of building common ground for action." Let us take this definition of a civil society as our goal in discussing how a comprehensive university can play an active role in generating the capacity for a community to behave collectively in this manner.

Drawing from a large literature on the civil society going back to Aristotle's *Politiike Koinonia* and the later Roman *Societas Civilis*, Bruce Sievers captures the essential features of a civil society today.[6] They are: (1) the presence of a set of mediating institutions or NGOs [nongovernmental organizations], such as schools, churches and the press; (2) procedural rules and values required to sustain these mediating institutions by ensuring legitimacy and fairness in decision-making; (3) individual rights; and (4) a sense of common purpose and civic responsibility as a necessary complement to individual rights.

WHAT IS CIVIC VIRTUE?

Civic virtue has classically been defined as both knowledge of the public good and the sustained desire to achieve it.[7] Underlying this definition is the supposition that community leaders have "both the opportunity and incentives to acquire the necessary knowledge and the predisposition to act steadily on the basis of that knowledge."

Our current discussions about civic engagement are driven by two underlying fears.[8] They are: (1) We are losing confidence that we can, individually or collectively, control the forces that influence our lives; (2) From family to neighborhood to nation, we are afraid that the moral fiber of community is unraveling around us. "In traditional—both modern and classical—definitions of democracy, the prevailing subject is 'we,' but in a social world made up exclusively of sovereign, autonomous groups predicated on an exclusive disconnectedness, self-interest, and self-definition, 'we' is replaced by an objective, distant, unknown 'them.'"[9] In this unsettling environment, it is time to work toward a broader, more enriching sense of community and public purpose.

WHAT KIND OF DEMOCRACY SHALL WE WORK TOWARDS?

R. Guarasci and G.H. Cornwell call for a new working model of democracy that blends the traditions of both experiences of democracy, "a wholly different ideal of the democratic community in which both difference and connection can be held together yet understood to be at times necessarily separate, paradoxical and in contradiction to one another."[10] In this new democratic accommodation to our growing diversity and multiplicity, we will need to build a society in which any individual "may hold many sub-identities at once and in which power, prestige, and social standing are multiplicious and nonhierarchical." We must simultaneously be connected and distinct and singular. A college or university can model this broader and more inclusive concept of democracy and civic virtue. This is what we mean by calling colleges and universities to exercise their civic responsibilities.

What is ironic here is that the sheer complexity of public affairs today means that "experts" and "professionals," who, of course, abound in our higher education institutions, as well as in other civil associations, are generally no more competent than ordinary citizens to behave in ways that promote a renewal of democracy. If this is true, we must take some time to describe the kinds of competencies that we will all need in order to support genuine community engagement.

If a truly multicultural and open democratic way of life is our goal, we need to discover feasible ways to raise citizen competencies as well as our own competence, to live in this complex, interconnected, and distinct mode. We must, in fact, discover what multiculturalism really means and develop in our schools, on our campuses, and within our communities a genuine multicultural competency, as well as an ability to do public work together. This is true regardless of what our missions and scope of responsibilities are.

According to K. Manning and P. Coleman-Boatwright, a "multicultural organization is one which is genuinely committed to diverse representation of its membership; is sensitive to maintaining an open, supportive and responsive environment; is working toward and purposefully including elements of diverse cultures in its ongoing operations; and is . . . authentic in its responses to issues confronting it."[11] To accomplish this, a campus community must place a strong emphasis on a set of shared values, on effective and inclusive communication, and upon cultural knowledge. Institutions that do this can enrich the educational experience of their students, promote personal growth and a healthy society, and strengthen communities and the workplace through university-community relationships. In other words, the campus community can itself act as a working model of democracy, as "a way of living with others in a shared struggle to solve problems and not just a system of government."[12] A democracy, in simple terms, is not a system of government. It is a way of life. It is, to quote Dewey again, "a way of associated living, in which reciprocity and connectedness are essential."[13]

WHAT DOES IT MEAN FOR A UNIVERSITY TO EMBRACE ITS CIVIC RESPONSIBILITY?

A university that embraces its civic responsibilities sets itself the goal of playing a role in generating a renewal of democracy through the expectations we have of ourselves as scholars and administrators, our aspirations for our students, and the nature and intentions of our own institutional relationships with the broader society of which we are an integral part.

The most fundamental means by which any educational institution can enhance civic responsibility is: (1) to find a means to link learning and community life through the design of the curriculum; and (2) to serve as a center for community building. Beyond these fundamental means, an institution will use its distinctive strengths based on its traditions, institutional history, and resource base to contribute through scholarship and outreach or engagement to the strengthening of community life and community capacity to identify and solve problems. In all cases, what the institution is doing is helping its students, faculty, staff, and the citizens of the communities it serves learn how to make informed choices together, an essential skill of civic responsibility and a core competence of a civil society.[14]

Linking Learning to Community Life

There is no better source of a philosophy linking education and democracy, learning and life than the work of John Dewey.[15] For Dewey, education is not a preparation for some remote future. It is meaningful in its own right. As he wrote, "Education is not preparation for life. Education is life itself." Dewey argued that democracy, as well as education itself, must be a "way of life" built on the concepts of growth, individuality, and an ongoing experiment in associated living. Where better to conduct such an experiment than on our own campus? In our own era, there is no longer a clear boundary between education and life. If all of us must be lifelong learners, then responsible community life depends upon our ability to learn together and to apply what we learn with the goal of a greater good that we can discover together.

If we truly believe that "the path to a civil society goes through the University,"[16] then we must think of our academic community as a product of both head and heart. Damon suggests that young people require three attributes in order to participate meaningfully in civic life. These are "intellectual abilities such as reasoning skills, literacy and the knowledge of history and economy required for making informed judgments. Second, moral traits such as dedication to honesty, justice, social responsibility, and the tolerance that makes democratic discourse possible. And, finally, practical experience in community organizations, from which young people can learn how to work within groups, in structured settings."[17] Any institution, whatever its mission, can utilize the medium of the curriculum and its requirements for its students as a vehicle to exercise its civic responsibility.

A Center of Community Life

With respect to the institution as a center of community life, David Mathews argues that school reform must be recast as "community building."[18] He makes the case that the very mission of a school and, by extrapolation, a public university, should be derived from the purposes and shaped by the experiences of the community that the school or university serves. In the beginning, our schools were "chartered to do the important work of our country."[19] In a sense, either formally or informally, a regional comprehensive institution or a state university also is chartered to do this work. My own institution, the University of Vermont and State Agricultural College, a public research land-grant institution, is formally called an "instrumentality of the state" in our charter. Whether the charter is real or metaphorical, it is a significant factor to keep in mind in deciding how a particular institution will interpret its civic mission.

THE COMPREHENSIVE UNIVERSITY AND REGIONALISM

Comprehensive universities are institutions that have some research and graduate programming capacity and a strong affinity for a particular region. Usually, the mission of these institutions carries a special responsibility to serve the needs of a particular place and a particular population. For this reason, it is important to define what a region is and how this concept shapes the way in which a comprehensive university exercises its civic responsibilities.

It is especially easy to see the growth of regionalism in urban areas. To reflect this phenomenon, Neil Peirce has used the term "citistate" to describe the critical convergence of economic activity, governance, and social organization that has begun to replace the nation-state in the past decade as a center of political, social, and economic activity.[20] While this trend may not be fully appreciated, as political and geographic boundaries give way to the influences of a global age, the regional relationships of comprehensive universities are playing an ever-increasing role in providing a network of communication, collaboration, and partnership that strengthens the relationships which are contributing to the growing importance of these economic and social centers.

It is becoming clear that "knowledge, learning, research, information and skill are the raw materials of commerce,"[21] as well as the basic ingredients that can rebuild a sense of civil society. In its series of reports on the research university at century's end, the Kellogg Commission on the Future of State and Land-Grant Universities has elected to refer to this phenomenon as the emergence of the "learning society." In his book *Regional Excellence*, William R. Dodge talks about what it means to work together on a regional basis in order to compete globally and flourish locally.[22] Dodge lays out the challenges that a regional approach can address better than the traditional forms of government. They are: (1) complex problems with many dimensions; (2) the withdrawal of citizens from public discourse and public life; (3) the disconnect between political boundaries and the actual dimensions of regions; (4) the growing fiscal, economic, and racial gaps that divide communities, especially between central cities and surrounding suburban and exurban settings; and (5) the challenges of global competitiveness.

As a nation, we are organized to respond to challenges at municipal-county, state, and national levels. Meanwhile, our real problems play out at neighborhood, regional, and international levels. The problem-solving and service-delivery capacity of the governmental and civil organizations that we possess are being overwhelmed by the size and complexity of regional challenges. As Dodge points out, "most of these mechanisms lack timeliness, flexibility, inclusiveness, stability, or clout."[23] The only societal entity that can bridge these gaps physically, intellectually, and economically is the comprehensive or state university. In many cases, even the scope of a single institution is not enough if the region encompasses other states or more than one nation. In this case, a comprehensive institution can only play a truly regional role if it develops meaningful collaborations with other higher education institutions serving other parts of a region that cross state or international boundaries. To think and act regionally, we will have to reinvent government, create a different kind of accessible and responsive educational system, focus economic and community development strategies beyond the usual political jurisdictions, and face up to the complex social and environmental problems that cloud our efforts and place constraints on our options.[24] The only thread holding all of these elements together is the comprehensive or state university.

THE ATTRIBUTES OF REGIONAL CITIZENSHIP AND SENSE OF COMMUNITY

John Gardner[25] has described the qualities and attributes that define civic virtue and civic responsibility at a regional level. These attributes can be our guide in examining how a comprehensive university can contribute to the creation of a regional strategy and regional citizenship.[26] The checklist, adapted slightly from Gardner and Dodge, is as follows:

- wholeness and inclusiveness, incorporating diversity
- a reasonable base of shared values
- caring, trust, and teamwork
- effective internal communications
- affirmation, confidence in the importance of the community

- links beyond the community, especially between rich and poor, that maintain open, constructive and extensive relations with the world beyond its boundaries
- development of the imagination and civil responsibility of the region's young people
- a forward view and a willingness to examine and experiment with options
- a means to involve all interested parties

HOW COMPREHENSIVE UNIVERSITIES CAN EXERCISE CIVIC RESPONSIBILITY

As an institution of higher learning, a university has three avenues for building a civil society. These are research, teaching, and service. This repertoire can be expressed either traditionally or in innovative and blended formats. It can also be expressed locally, regionally, or on a larger scale, depending upon the mission and resource base of the institution. We will focus on the regional and local roles of comprehensive universities, arguing that despite the aspirations of many of these institutions to embrace the values, characteristics, and structure of a traditional research university, it is, in fact, time to move beyond this form of mimicry to consider a fresh and innovative interpretation of how to use the traditional activities of research, teaching, and service to embrace a regional and community agenda and to offer an exemplary educational experience to students and a rewarding and stimulating professional life for faculty and staff. In the discussions of the Kellogg Commission on the Future of State and Land-Grant Universities, we have found it helpful to replace the traditional terms research, teaching, and service with the richer and more multidimensional terms discovery, learning, and engagement. Each of these terms, by itself and in combination with the others offers a refreshing perspective on how a comprehensive university can use its intellectual resources and its relationships to promote civic virtue and a civil society.

Discovery

The origins of the shift in emphasis from research to discovery and from teaching to learning can be traced to Ernest Boyer. In 1990, Boyer opened up a new way of talking about scholarship when he published *Scholarship Reconsidered*.[27] By recasting the nature of intellectual work, Boyer started a conversation that has gradually led to a new way of thinking about how knowledge is created, interpreted, and shared. Without abandoning the traditional values of clarity of purpose, rigor, significance, and integrity that have always characterized the best scholarly work,[28] he suggested that discovery, sharing, and application can take place in many settings and can involve many different participants. Today we can find examples at most comprehensive universities of the entire spectrum of scholarly achievement—laboratory-based and community-based, individual and collaborative, disciplinary and interdisciplinary. In all of these cases, we can identify multiple participants and multiple settings and modes of inquiry. All of these forms of inquiry contribute to our ability to achieve our mission of creating, interpreting, and sharing knowledge and all are equally valid. They are not, however, equally accepted as scholarly work by many faculty.

By broadening the definition of legitimate scholarly work to include the concept that a scholarly agenda can be created in partnership with community participants, we have created the fundamental means by which faculty and students can begin to establish the kind of community-based inquiry that can promote enhanced community capacity for informed choices and shared decision-making. Many comprehensive institutions, still seeking to emulate the forms and values of the most distinguished research universities, may find this broader concept difficult to absorb. However, several institutions, including Portland State University and Oregon State University, have incorporated their own interpretation of Boyer's definitions of scholarly work into their promotion and tenure guidelines and have worked out ways to document and assess scholarly work conducted in a collaborative or community-based mode.

Learning

A second critical philosophical change that must be introduced in order to support a full acceptance of a civic mission and civil responsibilities is the shift from an emphasis on teaching and the role of faculty as chief interpreters and transmitters of knowledge to an emphasis on the centrality of learning and the role of students as participants in scholarly work. This shift opens up the possibility of utilizing settings other than the classroom as environments to promote learning and also opens up a richer repertoire of ways in which students can learn, while at the same time offering something of value to the community. In this way, students can both acquire the habits of civic virtue and assist the institution in exercising its collective civic responsibility.

Engagement

A truly entrepreneurial university must be able to adopt the qualities of flexibility and creativity, as well as the capacity to support and encourage imaginative action and the ability to identify and successfully manage risk, all of which characterize a successful entrepreneur. A university must also be able to create conditions that support entrepreneurial activity that will enhance the economic base and promote opportunities for the citizens of the region it serves and the state, if statewide issues are in its mission. This will be both our challenge and our opportunity as an engaged university for the twenty-first century.

Most comprehensive institutions must embrace some variation of the following major goals of engagement in the years ahead:

- to create a well-educated and skilled workforce
- to generate the foundation of knowledge and innovation that supports a high quality of life and economic development
- to support good schools and healthy, sustainable communities
- to generate the knowledge that will support effective natural resource management and sustain the quality of the environment; in rural areas, this includes attention to the working landscape and sustainable agriculture
- to partner with organizations and communities to ensure that every resident of the local and regional community has an opportunity to succeed

To accomplish this, an institution should consider adopting three related and mutually reinforcing strategies:

1. **Educational reform** that prepares students for a lifetime of learning and that emphasizes rigorous academics for every student, as well as educational planning, and school-to-career opportunities.
2. **Workforce development strategies** that focus on long-term workforce development, as well as on the immediate training needs of employers and employees. These approaches should emphasize a career orientation, rather than a job orientation, and promote the development of leadership at both the community and, where the population is large enough, neighborhood level.
3. **Economic strategies** effectively aligned with investments in education and research that link meaningfully with community development strategies that are designed to enhance the quality of life in a neighborhood, a community, or a region.

Traditionally, universities have used terms like outreach, professional service, or public service to describe the application of knowledge to contemporary problems such as workforce development and economic and community development. Increasingly, these concepts, all of which refer to valid parts of both a faculty role and a university mission, are being subsumed under a broader, more encompassing term, engagement.

What is engagement and how does it differ from the more customary terms outreach and service? Professional service or outreach is a process of knowledge and technology transfer that is primarily one-way, namely from the university to key constituencies. In contract, engagement refers to an initiative characterized by shared goals, a shared agenda, agreed upon definitions of success that are meaningful both to the university and to the community participants, and some pooling or leveraging of university and public and private funds provided by other participants. The resulting collaboration or partnership is mutually beneficial and is likely to build the capacity and competence of all parties.

Institutions are more likely to elect to use outreach for fairly straightforward questions and problems and will initiate engagement activities to address more complex issues that lack clarity (i.e. fuzzy problems when either the question or the solutions are unclear) or issues that must be explored with the use of leveraged funding from multiple parties. Engagement has a number of beneficial side effects. In addition to promoting the creation of greater community competence to identify and address important issues, engagement offers all of its participants an opportunity to discover, interpret, and share knowledge—in other words, to participate in lifelong learning.

In her text *Knowledge Without Boundaries*, Mary Walshok discusses what our nation's research universities can do to support economic and community development, contribute to the enhancement of professional practice and the workplace, and sustain civic life and democracy in this country.[29] These arguments also apply to comprehensive universities. As Walshok points out, all fields of knowledge—the arts, humanities, social sciences, as well as the biological and physical sciences and professional fields—have undergone significant transformation as a result of research findings and paradigm shifts. "Such developments in new knowledge continuously transform how we understand and how we shape our physical, economic, and social worlds."[30]

An increasing proportion of our population "must constantly integrate new knowledge into their everyday activities,"[31] and all of us will need a knowledgeable base from which we can make informed and considered judgments as professionals, as citizens, and as family members. It is our assumption that the nation's public research universities will play a primary role in enhancing our human capabilities throughout our lives by generating new knowledge, serving as a source of knowledge, and supporting community capacity to explore and work on the complex issues of society today. An institution that accepts this responsibility can be called "an engaged university."

Until recently, lifelong learning was thought of as individual professional and personal development. In a recent survey completed by the Eagleton Institute of Politics at Rutgers University, 91 percent of respondents agreed that "lifelong learning" is defined as "the process of intellectual and professional renewal that leads to both personal enrichment and occupational

growth." A minority of respondents, however, took exception to this definition for several reasons.

1. The term "renewal" fails to take into account the growing need for the
   continuous creation, acquisition, and application of knowledge and the
   patterns of learning associated with "reflective practitioners."
2. The term "personal enrichment" overlooks the importance of lifelong
   learning for fostering both effective citizenship and community development.
3. The definition focuses exclusively on individuals and fails to take into
   account the building of intellectual and problem-solving capacity of
   groups of people in neighborhoods, communities, and organizations.
4. The definition fails to address the importance of applying skills to solve
   new kinds of problems.

Most continuing education divisions will continue to offer valuable programming for professionals. However, it is now becoming clear that community-based lifelong learning is an essential condition for the sustaining of our
democratic way of life. We need to understand the importance of an enlightened and capable citizenry to the democratic way of life and contribute to the
maintenance of our sense of community through the generation of greater
social capital as well as human capital. The challenges of this kind of learning
must be accepted by the entire university community. They represent a critical
component of a fully developed approach to engagement, since the support of
individual and shared lifelong learning (a "learning society") will be essential
for the creation of the competencies of a civil society.

According to Robert Putnam, who has made a study of the revitalization of
democracy in this country, "by analogy with notions of physical capital and
human capital—tools and training that enhance individual productivity—
'social capital' refers to features of social organization such as networks, norms,
and social trust that facilitate coordination and cooperation for mutual benefit."[32] In his studies of the structure of Italian communities, Putnam found the
correlation between civic engagement and effective government was virtually
perfect.[33] In his view, to revitalize our democracy, we should "begin by
rebuilding social capital in our communities, by renewing our civic connections." In earlier generations, civic and service organizations and church
groups were the bonding agents for community life. Today, the mechanism for
building social capital may be the engagement of universities in community
and economic development and in shared learning experiences reinforced by
the inclusion of community-based learning opportunities in our curriculum.
Such experiences also prepare our students for successful leadership and
service after graduation.

THE CREATION OF LEARNING COMMUNITIES

What does it mean for a university to behave collectively as a responsible citizen? The rationale for the newer forms of public scholarship (discovery), community-based or service-learning (learning), and community-university alliances (engagement) is complex. These activities provide a response to

- the growing demands to prepare civic-minded students
- the need to prepare students to be successful in the workplace
- the desire to address the complex social, economic, and cultural needs of our communities
- the value of opening up the community as an extended classroom to encourage richer student learning
- the growing expectation that colleges and universities will be good citizens in their communities and assist with economic and community development and, in many instances, the revitalization of community and neighborhood life

Adoption of a commitment to civic responsibility and community involvement also provides an answer to a question raised by David Cooper at Michigan State, who reacted to the results of the most recent UCLA survey of college freshmen by suggesting that, "[t]he sad truth is that the UCLA survey reveals more about the adult world than about young persons poised on the thresholds of their own adult lives. What inner resources of moral and emotional intelligence, self-renewal, and social idealism have we equipped them with during their formative years?"[34]

There are many ways to accomplish all of these goals, but the way that is especially suited to the local and regional focus of a comprehensive university is the creation of learning communities that promote discovery and application using issues and problems identified by the community. A good definition of the qualities of such a model has been provided by Aaron Brower and Karen Dettinger,[35] based on the work of Faith Gabelnick and her colleagues.[36]

> Learning communities . . . must integrate academic subject matter and social interactions while providing a physical space or facility for an intellectually stimulating environment to emerge. Furthermore, learning communities must be designed to develop a triad of responsibilities within students—professional, ethical, and civic.

At Portland State University, an institution that has incorporated a community base called University Studies into its entire general education curriculum, the concept of a learning community has been broadened to include a dedicated space and a distinctive curricular design in the freshman, sophomore, and junior years and a capstone experience in the senior year that utilizes the community itself as the intellectually stimulating environment.[37] Although the Portland State example is particularly comprehensive, many institutions have begun to involve their students in community-based learning through a variety of forms including service-learning, internships, practica, and capstone experiences either in general education or in the major.[38] Sometimes, there is enough interaction between individual students and between the institution and community agencies, organizations, and associations that a special kind of learning community develops, sometimes sustained over time and sometimes flickering into and out of existence as relationships form and change.

In many cases, an institution will elect to establish a continuing learning environment in which undergraduate students, graduate students, practitioners, and faculty interact in a way that blends the activities of applied research, improvement of professional practice, and preparation for the profession into an integrated whole. When fully developed, these entities acquire a life of their own. This model is especially well developed in teacher education where professional development schools and school development institutes have been in place for a decade or more. Consider the example of the long-term partnership between the University of Vermont (UVM) and the Essex Junction Schools. In this case, UVM is playing a regional role similar to a comprehensive institution, due both to its state mission and as a function of the size and scale of the state of Vermont, which is smaller in population than most metropolitan regions. A problem-based school development process, according to education professor John Clarke and his colleagues,

> . . . gathers the energy and talent of a school faculty and focuses it on specific and immediate problems that come up during a school reform effort. Conducted over several years, simultaneous team investigations of problems in teaching and learning constitute a method for linking school development to professional development and creating a professional community capable of sustaining long-term educational reform.[39]

In this different kind of learning community, what appear to be small steps that adapt teaching gradually force the whole system to change. In turn, the schools in Essex Junction have become more meaningfully coupled to changes in their community, in the state, and in educational reform across the country. They are moving toward David Mathews' ideal of the community-based school. In this example, UVM plays the role of helping to bring people together and, through the research capacity of its faculty and teacher education students, helps to consolidate and interpret the work being done by the teachers. Through a several-year process, the interaction also raises the research competency of the school faculty and leaves them able to make informed choices based on a shared body of knowledge that they can generate together about complex problems that do not lend themselves to simple answers. In addition, UVM helps to satisfy the need for broader connections beyond the edges of Essex Junction that John Gardner identifies as essential to effective community building.

The UVM-Essex Junction relationship illustrates most of the basic philosophical conditions that must be met for a university to become fully engaged with the communities it serves. It also shows a particularly productive use of the concept of engagement to address complex and ill-defined problems. The traditional outreach and consultative mode would not work well on fuzzy problems of this kind. What is going on here is a form of scholarly inquiry conducted in a school setting with a mixed team of university faculty, students, and school faculty. For this to work, the faculty of the College of Education and Social Services at UVM had to embrace a broader definition of scholarship and take a different role than the traditional faculty role in promoting the formation of a genuine learning/scholarly community in the Essex Junction Schools. The process also changed the culture of inquiry in the schools. As Clarke and his colleagues report, "gathering new information about a problem from background and action research prevents a team from becoming just one more committee that sits together to hash out a recommendation based on what the members already happen to know."[40]

PARTNERSHIPS

As we approach a new century, we can discern the outlines of a new approach to regional development elicited by the increasingly multidimensional and interrelated challenges facing communities and regions. Collaborations and long-term partnerships are especially appropriate as a means for addressing the reform of large-scale systems, such as education, health care, public safety, economic development, and job creation, corrections and social services or workforce development that face communities today.[41] There are a number of lessons to be drawn from the partnerships that we have already seen put in place. I will draw heavily from Holland and Gelmon and Holland and Ramaley[42] to describe these lessons.

1. Each partnership has unique elements shaped by the history, capacity, cultures, missions, expectations, and challenges faced by each participating group or organization. What must remain as a constant, however, is that any partnership must be based on the academic strengths and philosophy of the university. The other constant feature must be the fact that the needs and capacities of the community must define the approach that the university should take to forming a partnership.

2. An ideal partnership matches up the academic strengths and goals of the university with the assets and interests of the community.

3. There is no such thing as a universal "community." It takes time to understand what elements make up a particular community and how people experience membership in the community. It is not easy to define who can speak for the community just as the university itself is not monolithic. Often, partnerships are fragmented by competing interests in the community itself.

4. Unless the institution as a whole embraces the value and validity of engagement as legitimate scholarly work and provides both moral support and concrete resources to sustain it, engagement will remain individually defined and sporadic. Such limited interventions cannot influence larger systems on a scale necessary to address community issues.

5. It is important to take time to think about what the university actually can bring to a partnership. Universities with limited research capacity and few graduate programs will find it difficult to provide the kinds of applied research and technical assistance that many communities need. Sometimes it is possible to make an alliance with a research university to broker and focus the research interests of faculty and graduate students on local problems. If sufficient research capability is not available, it is best to consider engagement as primarily a function of the curriculum.

6. A good collaboration will continue to evolve as a result of mutual learning. To be successful, collaboration should be built on new patterns of information gathering, communication, and reflection that allow all parties to participate in decision-making and learning. This requires time and face-to-face interactions.

7. Some communities are being partnered to the point of exhaustion. It is often necessary to identify ways to help community organizations and smaller agencies create the capacity to be an effective partner.

8. The early rush of enthusiasm can be replaced by fatigue and burn out, unless the collaboration begins early on to identify and recruit additional talent to the project or the collaboration. This is true both within the university community, where a few dedicated faculty cannot be expected to carry the entire engagement and civic responsibility agenda, and within the broader community, where a small number of community leaders and volunteers cannot be expected to handle a sustained effort over time. Both the university and its partners need to find ways to involve a truly representative cross-section of the talent in the community.

9. Like any other important effort, community partnerships must be accompanied by a strong commitment to a "culture of evidence." It is

important to keep a running assessment of how well the partnership is working from the point of view of all participants.

CREATING CONDITIONS THAT SUPPORT MEANINGFUL ENGAGEMENT

Universities and colleges can no longer be self-contained. Significant change to incorporate a strong community base for research and education, however, requires (1) the possibility of reward or benefit for faculty and staff; (2) individual influence and inspired leadership; (3) an institution that is structurally open to external influence; (4) educational planning and purposefulness that recognizes the value of active and responsible service-learning that has a real community impact; and (5) a willingness to adopt a shared agenda and a shared resource base over which the institution has only partial control.

Regardless of local circumstances and institutional traditions and history, there are a few conditions that must be in place for a community-based strategy to work. First, community-based work must be valued as a meaningful educational experience and a legitimate mode of scholarly work. Second, the evaluation of faculty and student work must include rigorous measures of the quality and impact of community-based scholarship, and professional service must be recognized as a component of staff work as well. Third, mediating structures must be provided to help faculty and students identify community-based learning and research opportunities, and technical support must be available to help faculty and students use these opportunities and assess the results of such programs, both from their own point-of-view and from the perspectives of the community and its priorities and experiences. Finally, opportunities must be provided for faculty, staff, and students to develop the skills to participate in research and curricular programs in a collaborative mode with partners from different academic disciplines and with significant community involvement.

It is unusual for an institution to undertake institution-wide transformational reform. However, it is sometimes necessary to think on this scale in order to open up the possibilities for an institution to incorporate civic responsibility into all of its educational and scholarly activities. Higher education is changing in subtle ways all the time, but these changes tend to be initiated randomly and do not usually spread beyond the point of origin. To move an institution intentionally in a desired direction, four conditions must exist, or be set in place, if they do not already exist. They will be summarized here, but those interested in exploring this issue further may wish to consult the case study of Portland State University which is one of the few institutions in recent years to undergo truly transformational change.[43]

1. A compelling case for systemic or transformational change must be made. Most people are unwilling to embark on major change without both a compelling reason and the confidence that their efforts will be supported and recognized.
2. There must be clarity of purpose. Even when the reasons are clear, the goals must also be clear. Otherwise, there will be no way to judge the value of the efforts made or to convince honest skeptics of the value and legitimacy of the work.
3. There must be significance of scale. Most change is too small and piecemeal to make a real difference in an organization. The choice of the first project is critical.
4. A conducive campus environment is essential. There are many barriers to change at most institutions. Some time must be spent identifying factors that will impede change.

There remains an argument among observers and practitioners of change whether large-scale change can occur in the absence of some serious and ongoing crisis. Given the traditional strengths of higher education and the slowly growing pressures on our enterprise, it behooves us to anticipate changing social and economic conditions in society and respond to them, before mandates are imposed upon us. In some cases, unfortunately, change has clearly been driven by external mandates, a serious fiscal crisis, or troubling internal problems.

Most of the change that has occurred in the United States, in both corporate settings and in higher education, has taken the form of restructuring, another name for downsizing, usually involving budget reductions that result in an institution doing less with less; or reengineering—the redesign of programs and services that allow an institution to do more or better with less.

Only in a few instances have either corporations or universities actually considered a regenerating strategy. By a regenerating strategy, G. Hamel and C.K. Prahalad mean that it is possible to regenerate purpose, meaning, and direction without a crisis.[44] Success in the future will be played out in a different context than today. In the future, there will be changes in what students learn, where and how they learn, and who facilitates that learning. In other words, we may see a change in the rules of engagement in an established industry; redrawn boundaries within the industry; and perhaps even an entirely new industry.[45] For higher education, this may translate into transformed institutions, new learning enterprises, and new collaborations and partnerships.

Here are the kinds of questions that an institution should ask itself in order to establish clarity of purpose as a starting point in instituting intentional or transformative change without a precipitating crisis to generate the need for change[46] (modeled on Hamel and Prahalad, 1994). They should be asked not just once, but continuously.

- What are our core values and what is our mission?
- What lessons can we draw from our own history and tradition?
- What new core competencies will we need in the future?
- What core competencies must we retain and enhance?
- What organizational values and principles will guide our decision-making?
- What new educational models must we build?
- What new alliances must we need to form?
- What promising programs must we nurture?
- What long-term regulatory initiatives must we pursue to reshape the marketplace in which we operate regionally, statewide, or nationally?
- What new learners must we serve?
- How will we generate the resources to invest in new competencies?

An important step in the process of change is to have a firm grasp on your actual condition before you begin. A useful way to assess the role of service or engagement in your institution environment is to use the matrix developed by Holland[47] who creates a scale of low, medium, high, and full integration of service into an institutional mission. The scan is comprehensive and includes the wording of the mission itself, promotion, tenure and hiring policies, organizational structure, student involvement, faculty involvement, community involvement and the content, perspective, and intended audiences of campus publications and communications.

If your institution already has a strong commitment to service or engagement, you may wish to undertake an evaluation of the effectiveness and impact of this effort using a model such as that developed by Gelmon, et al.[48] This approach provides a methodology that assesses community impact from the point of view of the faculty, student, and community participants and the organizations that are involved, including the campus community. If you are just thinking now about moving to a larger scale involvement, you may want to consider introducing the theme of data collection and quality assessment early in the process.

Once an institution has decided how it wishes to interact with its external environment, it is time to set a direction for change. There are many ways to describe the change process. The one I use, which is based on my experience at Portland State University, as well as my conversations with other institutions that are seeking to undertake genuinely transformational change, has four stages. This model is derived from concepts originally developed by Michael

Heifetz in *Leading Change, Overcoming Chaos*.[49] In a large organization, there can be many interlocking change cycles going on simultaneously.

The stages of intentional and large-scale change are:
1. Preparing a receptive environment
2. Choosing the first project
3. Making connections and sustaining change
4. Rebalancing the institution and building a constituency for sustainable change, using the same techniques as community organizers use at the grassroots level
5. Consolidating and learning from experience that sets the stage for the next cycle

Most campuses require several interventions, described below, to create a receptive environment for meaningful change.

1. A redefinition of faculty roles and rewards is often required, and a conscious linkage must be made between faculty work and the tasks required to achieve the institutional mission. This generally requires a reworking of the standards and components of promotion and tenure.
2. Most of the procedures and policies of an institution have accumulated over time and often are both overly complex and unintentionally fail to facilitate or reward the behaviors and working relationships that are needed to achieve the changes desirable for the future. In addition, the introduction of new technologies, as well as new working relationships with other organizations, changes the kind of support structure needed and the competencies of support staff. Old systems of work classification and traditional forms of employee development often cannot keep pace with these changes.
3. Many institutions fail to take into account the importance of students in shaping the institution, as student employees, as participants in outreach and public service, as participants in research activities, and as members of the community that the institution serves.
4. In many institutions, individual departments act as self-contained entities and reward department-centered activity but not participation in cross-disciplinary work or campus activities that benefit the institution but not the department directly.
5. One way to bring the work of departments into alignment with the needs of the institution as a whole is to create a direct relationship between the setting of goals and priorities at the department level and institutional goals and to link resource generation in part to contribution to campus goals.

For a strategic resource cycle to work and to be sustainable, an institution must have three elements in place: (1) clarity of vision and purpose translated into goals and objectives; (2) a clear understanding of how resources are generated and consumed by its activities; and (3) a culture of evidence that provides good measures of the results obtained by various programs and activities and a model whereby the future setting of goals and the distribution of resources is guided by outcomes.[50]

CONCLUSIONS

A university that embraces a strong civic mission can accomplish a number of goals at once. A civic mission represents a powerful response to the challenge posed by William Sullivan several years ago, when he asked "whether [higher education] has the ability and the will through leadership, institutional design, teaching and research, in creating a new form of intellectual life for the public good."[51] The rationale for the growing service-learning and engagement movement is complex. These models allow an institution to respond to the growing demand for civic-minded graduates who are also competitive in the workplace; to address the complex social, economic, and cultural needs of our communities; and to create, within neighborhoods, communities and regions, the capacity for the exercise of informed choices and a civil society. While expressing a deep commitment to civility, community, and engagement, universities can also strengthen their ability to accomplish their core mission of scholarship, leadership, and education.

NOTES

1. R.J. Kingston, "Editor's Letter," *Kettering Review* (Fall 1998): 5–7.
2. R.D. Putnam, "What Makes Democracy Work?" *National Civic Review, 243* (1993): 101–07.
3. M. Schudson, *The Good Citizen* (New York: Martin Kessler Books, 1998), 7.
4. Ibid.
5. D. Mathews, "Afterthoughts," *Kettering Review* (Fall 1998): 74–76.
6. B. Sievers, "Can Philanthropy Solve the Problems of Civil Society?" *Kettering Review* (December 1997): 62–70.
7. R. Dahl, "Participation and the Problem of Civic Understanding," in *Rights and the Common Good*, ed. A. Etzioni (New York: St. Martin's Press, 1995), 261–70.
8. M.J. Sandel, *Democracy's Discontent: America in Search of a Public Philosophy* (Cambridge, MA: Belknap Press of Harvard University, 1996).
9. R. Guarasci and G.H. Cornwell, *Democratic Education in an Age of Difference* (San Francisco: Jossey-Bass, 1997), 2–3.
10. Ibid.
11. K. Manning and P. Coleman-Boatwright, "Student Affairs Initiatives Toward a Multicultural University," *Journal of College Student Development, 32*, no. 4 (1991): 367–74.

12. Mathews, "Afterthoughts."

13. R.D. Boisvert, *John Dewey: Rethinking Our Time* (Albany: State University of New York Press, 1998), 105.

14. D. Mathews, *Is There a Public for Public Schools?* (Dayton, OH: Kettering Foundation, 1996); Kingston, "Editor's Letter," 7.

15. Boisvert, *John Dewey.*

16. W. Damon, "The Path to a Civil Society Goes Through the University," *The Chronicle of Higher Education* (16 October 1998): B4–5.

17. I would add that knowledge of *all* of the domains of the liberal arts is essential, including science and mathematics, the arts, and literature.

18. Mathews, *Is There a Public for Public Schools?*

19. Ibid.

20. N. Peirce, *Citistates. How Urban America Can Prosper in a Competitive World* (Washington, DC: Seven Locks Press, 1993), 12.

21. Ibid.

22. W. R. Dodge, *Regional Excellence. Governing Together to Compete Globally and Flourish Locally* (Washington, DC: National League of Cities, 1996), 20.

23. Ibid.

24. N. Peirce, "New Lessons in Regionalism," *Connection, XIII,* no. 2 (1998): 37–42.

25. Dodge, *Regional Excellence.*

26. J. Gardner, *Building Community* (Washington, DC: Independent Sector, 1991).

27. E. Boyer, *Scholarship Reconsidered: Priorities of the Professoriate* (Washington, DC: The Carnegie Foundation for the Advancement of Teaching, 1990).

28. C.E. Glassick, M.T. Huber, et al., *Scholarship Assesses Evaluation of the Professoriate* (San Francisco: Jossey-Bass, 1997).

29. M. Walshok, *Knowledge Without Boundaries* (San Francisco: Jossey-Bass, 1995), 97–102.

30. Ibid.

31. Ibid.

32. R.D. Putnam, "Bowling Alone: America's Declining Social Capital," *Journal of Democracy,* 6, no. 1 (1995).

33. Putnam, "What Makes Democracy Work?"

34. D. Cooper, "Running on Empty: Are College Freshmen Really So Stressed Out?" *The National Teaching and Learning Forum, 7,* no. 1 (1997): 6.

35. A.M. Brower and K.M. Dettinger, What IS a Learning Community?" *About Campus* (November/December 1998): 15–21.

36. F. Gabelnick, J. MacGregor, R.S. Matthews, and B.L. Smith, *"Learning Communities: Creating Connections Among Students, Faculty, and Disciplines." New Directions for Teaching and Learning* (San Francisco: Jossey-Bass, 1990): 23.

37. M.F. Reardon and J.A. Ramaley, "Building Academic Community While Containing Costs," in *Handbook of the Undergraduate Curriculum,* ed. J.G. Gaff and J.L. Ratcliff (San Francisco: Jossey-Bass, 1996), 513–32; C.R. White, "A Model for Comprehensive Reform in General Education: Portland State University," *Journal of General Education, 43,* no. 3 (1994): 168–229.

38. B.A. Holland and S. Gelmon, "The State of the 'Engaged Campus'," *AAHE Bulletin, 51,* no. 2 (1998): 3–6.

39. J.H. Clarke, S.D. Sanborn, et al., *Real Questions, Real Answers* (Alexandria, VA: Association for Supervision and Curriculum Development, 1998), vi, ix.

40. Ibid.
41. B.A. Holland and J.A. Ramaley, "What Partnership Models Work to Link Education and Community Building?" Report prepared for the Joint Forum of the U.S. Department of Education and U.S. Department of Housing and Urban Development, Portland, Oregon, 1998.
42. Holland and Gelmon, "The State of the 'Engaged Campus' "; Holland and Ramaley, "What Partnership Models Work to Link Education and Community Building?"
43. J.A. Ramaley, "Large-Scale Institutional Change to Implement an Urban University Mission: Portland State University," *Journal of Urban Affairs,* 18, no. 2 (1996): 139–51; J.A. Ramaley, "Shared Consequences: Recent Experiences with Outreach and Community-Based Learning," *Journal of Public Service and Outreach,* 2, no. 2 (1997): 19–25.
44. G. Hamel and C.K. Prahalad, *Competing for the Future* (Boston: Harvard Business School Press, 1994).
45. Ibid.
46. Ibid.
47. B. Holland, "Analyzing Institutional Commitment to Service," *Michigan Journal of Community Service Learning,* 4 (Fall 1997): 30–41.
48. S.B. Gelmon, B.A. Holland, et al., *Healthy Professions: Schools in Service to the Nation* (Portland, OR: Portland State University, 1997).
49. M.L. Heifetz, *Leading Change, Overcoming Chaos* (Berkeley, CA: Ten Speed Press, 1993).
50. J.A. Ramaley, "The Making of a Budget: Strategic Thinking at a Public Research University," *Vermont Connections,* 19 (1998): 8–15.
51. W.M. Sullivan, "The Public Intellectual as Transgressor," *Higher Education Exchange* (Dayton, OH: The Kettering Foundation, 1996): 17–22.

CHAPTER 13

A Liberal Arts College Perspective

Gregory S. Prince Jr.

Colleges and universities have an obligation to their students and to society to promote civic responsibility. This obligation requires colleges to model the behavior they seek to inspire in their students. Henry David Thoreau, defining responsible citizenship in "Civil Disobedience," said it best: "a corporation of conscientious men [and women] is a corporation *with* a conscience."[1]

CIVIC RESPONSIBILITY AND EDUCATIONAL DIVERSITY

Promoting democratic values, civic responsibility, and good citizenship has been a central function of higher education in the United States since the first colonies. The earliest colleges trained the clergy, often with the premise that graduates help maintain a well-ordered, healthy society—socially, morally, and economically. Dartmouth College, for example, was founded in 1769 to train ministers because ministers were needed for churches that would provide spiritual sustenance for towns that the founders hoped would be established on land they owned in the upper Connecticut River valley. Ministers and churches, in short, had economic as well as spiritual value.

Education was integral to creating society's infrastructure and to transmitting its values. Civic infrastructure was synonymous with civic responsibility, as were piety and commitment to the established Puritan and Congregational faiths. In the new world, civic responsibility was so central to the purposes of education that it did not exist as a distinct concept. It was the totality of collegiate education.

The evolution over three centuries of what civic responsibility encompassed, and how and in what manner educational institutions promoted it, became a particularly strong force for institutional differentiation, especially at the postsecondary level. The diversity represented by land-grant universities, technical universities, military academies, comprehensive research institutions, residential liberal arts colleges, and community colleges evolved from a common beginning, the need for new concepts of educating citizens for productive, responsible civic life. The range of higher education institutional diversity in the United States rests fundamentally on different visions of what civic responsibility involves and how it should be promoted or instilled in citizens. Central to the mission of land-grant universities was service to society through the generation of new knowledge and its application to specific problems. Technical universities, founded at the end of the nineteenth century at a time of great faith in technology and progress, extended that tradition, confident that the well-being of society would be ensured by citizens well trained in science and technology. Since the 1960s, community colleges have defined their mission as being a gateway to helping citizens enter society economically, politically, and socially. The country has benefited immensely from this diversity and its collective effect on promoting civic responsibility. Conversely, no single form of higher education should claim special privilege in this effort.

As the 1990s draw to a close, however, higher education is witnessing yet another transformation. "Just-in-time" education, exemplified by the Western Governor's University and the University of Phoenix, may offer a special challenge to the underlying commitment to civic responsibility embodied in the diversity of U.S. higher education. These institutions emphasize the economic benefits of higher education to the citizen and to society; perhaps for the first time economic productivity has become the full, rather than just a part, of the substance of civic responsibility. Citizen education has become subsumed in just-in-time inventory management. Today, any national discussion about educating for civic responsibility faces the challenge of the growing focus on simply turning out economically productive citizens as the core of higher education. Absent is any sense that responsible members of the civic polity must also possess the capacities for social criticism and activism.

LIBERAL ARTS EDUCATION AND THE LIBERAL ARTS COLLEGE

Liberal arts colleges remain among the most radical inventions and enduring social forces created in the "new world" colonies. These institutions, by blending utilitarian purpose with the assumption that knowledge is an interconnected whole, created a form that critiqued and changed, not simply transmitted, culture. The eighteenth-century minister did not just study theology, he studied the totality of knowledge as a manifestation of God's creation and God's order. Dichotomies did not exist in this integrated world. Knowledge was divided into its parts, but the parts were viewed as an inextricable whole.

The liberal arts education at the core of these institutions incorporated the totality of knowledge in preparing the individual for a productive and constructive role in society. Such education represented a conserving, integrating, and stabilizing force in society that, ironically, introduced a destabilizing, renewing, change-oriented approach never anticipated. Embracing the totality of knowledge as the basis for the best preparation for the minister made logical and full sense in the holistic, church-based communities founded in the early colonies. A familiarity with the totality of knowledge as the basis for the education for one profession came to be seen by many as the logical approach to education for all professions.

The Enlightenment, political revolutions in the United States and France, growth of democratic culture, emergence of the scientific method, and other profound and diverse cultural forces began to transform the universality of liberal arts education from a content base to a concept base, just as society as a whole began to emphasize the importance of procedural fairness and rights in its definitions of the good society. If ministers needed to study the totality of knowledge, then so too would others seeking to lead society benefit from the same breadth, as knowledge itself was a whole. And if all would benefit, then the benefit must be redefined from the specific knowledge that one acquires to the purposes for acquiring that knowledge. As more students and purposes were served, those purposes became more universally defined.

Liberal arts education grew to become an education in *how* to think, not an education in *what* to think. Content was a means to an end—the development of a capacity for critical thinking. Late eighteenth- and early nineteenth-century assumptions that this "means"—the content of a liberal arts education—was universal and could provide the standards for judgment, made it possible to embrace the critical, or questioning, dimension of a liberal arts education. The rise of the concept of an education to promote scientific reasoning and critical thinking, based on the integrated, universality of knowledge, had a profound impact on the concept of what educating for civic responsibility and educating responsibly in the civic polity was to mean.

The mid-nineteenth century emphasis on promoting critical thinking inevitably introduced into the concept of educating for civic responsibility the need to be constructively critical by measuring social norms, behavior, and values against the ideals implicit in the totality of the knowledge studied. This emphasis continued to be reinforced by the late nineteenth century and early twentieth century reform and progressive social movements. Civic responsibility remained central to the mission of liberal arts education, but grew to include a responsibility to promote reform and improvement. It encouraged social criticism and social change, not simply blind acceptance of the past and present. Even if the practice of critique and the voice for social change were often silent or muted, the standard was accepted rhetorically and, occasionally, had major effect. Liberal arts education both shaped and was shaped by periods of social change, from the abolitionists to the progressives to the New Dealers.

The voice for critical social thinking, muted by World War II, the Korean War, and McCarthyism, reemerged on U.S. campuses in the last half of the 1950s, stirred by revolutions and intense social protests abroad and by ferment at home. At Yale University, for example, refugees from the Hungarian Revolution and anti-Apartheid student refugees from South Africa helped stir critical questioning. Spread among many campuses, these "immigrant" students had exercised the critical capacities inherent in a liberal arts education, found their societies wanting, and acted to bring about change at great cost to themselves. Their actions and their presence had a profound effect on U.S. campuses and U.S. college and university students.

Between 1955 and 1957, the demography of undergraduate classes shifted dramatically. World War II and Korean War G.I. Bill students had passed through the system and were replaced by younger students who had few first-hand memories of World War II, and none of the Depression. The new students had not postponed their lives for years to fight wars. Instead, they had a new sense of fear about the atomic world, the cold war, and the possibility of global destruction.

The questioning and unrest that exploded in the 1960s in the civil rights and antiwar movements began after 1955, when at least some of these younger students, in the face of the complacency of the Eisenhower years, began to ask what their role should be in the society and why they were either not "active" in the way French, Hungarian, or South African students were, nor motivated as the older students were who had already experienced so much of life before they arrived in college. What justified their presence? What should their cause be? To veterans of World War II and Korea, education for civic responsibility seemed as obvious and simple as it had for the Puritans in 1655. To the 18-year-old entering college in the mid- to late 1950s, the meaning was far less clear, and, in a prosperous peacetime America, the generation had the luxury to contemplate and extend constructive critical thinking.

The response to the unease of students and their questions about their purpose came appropriately from students themselves. As if to underscore that, liberal arts education had become an attitude of mind as much as, if not more than, a body of knowledge. An example of this came from a group of students at North Carolina Agricultural and Technical State University in Greensboro, North Carolina. One Sunday evening this group of students asked why they should not be allowed to eat at the downtown drugstore, what they should do as responsible citizens about what they perceived as a major injustice, and what kind of meaning could their lives have if they were denied basic dignity.

The Greensboro sit-in that these students undertook two days later profoundly affected the civil rights movement. It also redefined what promoting civic responsibility meant. The students in North Carolina decided to act, not just know; they decided that civic responsibility was about promoting change, not just preserving order. They made a statement about civic responsibility, about civil rights, and about learning by doing. A conversation by a small group of students in a residential college dormitory on a Sunday evening led to a momentous act of U.S. social protest. A model, if not a pattern, emerged, consonant with the long tradition of a liberal arts education's encouraging difficult social discourse and a reflective examination of our society, the "critical" element in educating for civic responsibility and educating responsibly. That element is not always accepted in the society and is a contributor to deep underlying tensions in the society.

Questions and unease also were growing for the teachers of these students. In the second half of the 1950s, faculty from Amherst, Smith, and Mount Holyoke Colleges and the University of Massachusetts at Amherst concluded that liberal arts education needed radical change and developed a model for that change, *The New College Plan*, that influenced a range of new colleges and 12 years later led to the opening of Hampshire College, in Amherst, Massachusetts, dedicated to the proposition, as its motto *Non Satis Scire* proclaims, that "to know is not enough."

In 1960, many condemned the fruits of liberal arts education, and generational tensions were on the rise. The drive in the 1960s certainly was generational, but beneath these differences were profound questions that continue to divide society, all of which center on what civic responsibility means. Educating responsible citizens requires developing in them what former Connecticut Commissioner of Education Andrew G. DeRocco calls "skeptical reverence."

Today's culture wars about the relevance of non-Western values in examining the values and principles of the society illustrate the value of "skeptical reverence." Those who attack the "relativism" of multiculturalism ironically abandon a central principle of liberal arts education—the importance of including the totality of knowledge as the base for developing critical thinking. They attack multiculturalism as the source of a relativistic thinking in which all traditions are given equal value, when those promoting multiculturalism would argue that the responsibility in liberal arts education to make value judgments requires the inclusion of all knowledge.

These debates inevitably complicate the obligation to promote civic responsibility, since the definition of "civic" has been broadened to include global, not just local, communities. Civic responsibility is far more complicated when global diversity is valued and a desire exists to preserve the richness of cultural diversity rather than to submerge all into the one. We now recognize and celebrate that E Pluribus Unum has more than one meaning and that we can be one by deriving strength from richness and diversity, or we can become one by demanding conformity and similarity.

The concept of educating for civic responsibility becomes a touchstone for measuring and distinguishing most of the critical issues facing higher education because it is the locus of where educational institutions interact with the needs and expectations of society as a whole. Each institution will approach it differently, but each institution needs to understand explicitly, not just implicitly, its centrality if it is to develop an effective relationship with the larger community.

AMBIVALENCE ABOUT CIVIC RESPONSIBILITY

Ambivalence about educating for civic responsibility emerges from a failure to grasp how the meaning of that term lies at the heart of major political and social flash points in our society. A full examination of the sources of this ambivalence cannot be covered in a limited article, but two writers, Robert Bellah and Michael Sandel, offer important insights.[2] Bellah's Habits of the Heart: Individualism and Commitment in American Life and The Good Society and Sandel's Democracy's Discontent: America in Search of a Public Philosophy pursue a common theme about what has undercut the public philosophy of the United States. Bellah argues that the United States has overdeveloped its public philosophy about individualism and failed to develop a public philosophy that stresses community values. In The Good Society, Bellah expands the argument to note that, in stressing individual values, society inevitably weakens institutions and ignores the important role of institutions in making possible individualism and freedom.

Michael Sandel's Democracy's Discontent offers an insightful discussion of this challenge. Sandel argues that our society has been confronted since its founding by a tension between the values of what he calls the "procedural republic" and those of the "substantive republic." The former asserts that the central duty of government is to

> . . . provide a framework of rights that respects persons as free and independent selves capable of choosing their own values and ends. Since this liberalism asserts the priority of fair procedures over particular ends, the public life it informs might be called the procedural republic.[3]

In contrast, substantive republican theory assumes that liberty and freedom depend on "sharing in self-government," a concept that is more than just voting but involves discourse: "it means deliberating with fellow citizens about the common good and helping to shape the destiny of the political community." Sandel concludes that the triumph of the procedural republic in the United States over two centuries has created a discontent in our society because the public philosophy it espouses cannot "secure the liberty it promises, because it cannot inspire the sense of community and civic engagement that liberty requires."[4]

The central tenet of the procedural republic—that government should be "neutral on the question of the good life"—is contemporary in its origins.[5] Liberal arts education, by emphasizing the critical and analytical skills as its central tenet, independent of any body of knowledge, parallels the move toward the procedural republic. Determining education for civic responsibility represents not just a difficult question but rather the ultimate question. It requires nothing short of developing a new public philosophy for the country that will allow education to move beyond growing bifurcation between the procedural and the substantive republic.

Political debate in the United States today over welfare, affirmative action, foreign relations, reproductive health, social security, education, and even the impeachment of President Bill Clinton demonstrates the danger that occurs when the two concepts lose natural connections that used to bind them together. Fragmentation and narrowing foci have destroyed what used to be an integrated, if imperfect, whole. Questions about how to educate for civic responsibility cannot be answered until society answers the question of whether that whole can be reestablished, its flaws corrected.

Democracy's Discontent goes on to issue a blunter warning to advocates of the procedural republic. If the substantive republic disappears, and with it the debate about what characteristics should shape the good society, the resulting vacuum could be filled by those espousing simplistic, rigid, exclusive positions that deny the complexity of the good society, as evidenced by the rise of the Christian right as a force in U.S. politics. With some prescience, Sandel noted, almost as an aside in developing this theme, "absent a political agenda that addresses the moral dimension of public questions, attention becomes riveted on the vices of public officials."[6]

If higher education is going to succeed in educating for civic responsibility, it must be willing to engage in that discussion, and it must be willing to demonstrate how citizens can discuss the values and substance upon which a responsible and inclusive society should be formed. Although many intellectual trends from postmodernism to conflict resolution resist accepting this responsibility, avoiding such discussion imperils our democracy. To develop that public philosophy, society must deal openly and honestly with the failure of past and present public philosophies. It is not enough to condemn slavery. As a society we must discuss what would be appropriate restitution or reparation. We must examine a public philosophy that leads to an increasingly smaller percentage of individuals controlling a growing percentage of national wealth.

Our political discourse has suffered as well. While liberals have focused on procedural values and conservatives on substantive values, both have found their positions wanting. Affirmative action reveals this dilemma. In the debate over affirmative action, those normally advocating the need for a commitment to substantive values revert to the language of the procedural republic in arguing that no law should single out a group according to race or gender. Advocates of affirmative action argue that a substantive test must be applied with respect to the impact of discrimination. If inequality exists because of past discrimination, then society has an obligation to redress that past injustice, even if it means limiting the procedural rights of a generation that did not create that discrimination.

EDUCATION FOR CIVIC RESPONSIBILITY

As complicated as the questions about civic responsibility facing society may be, the pedagogical strategies that should be pursued to advance civic responsibility are relatively straightforward. An education for civic responsibility must begin with a broad national debate about the tension between the procedural and substantive republic and with the acceptance that a new public philosophy must emerge. Two visions of the republic must be integrated into a whole through public discourse. From time to time these issues are debated in public but usually without a broad effort to include all those who might be interested, especially young people. Including them in a national conversation about the nature of rights, freedom, and responsibilities to society would be the most effective education for civic responsibility.

We must first engage in a dialogue about civic responsibility to understand how we can educate for it. No successful approach to educating for civic responsibility can exist if the society does not first address the tensions Sandel and Bellah have highlighted. In a community dedicated to educating for civic responsibility, neutrality with respect to political and social issues, to international controversy, to personal values, and to standards is no longer possible. The desire for neutrality has as much to do with the disarray in the teaching of civic responsibility as any other single factor.

Educating for civic responsibility must embrace the following guidelines:

1. an integrated, holistic view of knowledge;

2. an inclusive view of the civic polity that celebrates its diversity;
3. a simultaneously global and local definition of responsibility;
4. an integrated view of the human and natural environment;
5. an education that emphasizes developing skeptical reverence;
6. an inquiry-based, active-learning model in which students work to solve real problems and in so doing combine action with reflection, analysis, and evaluation;
7. a commitment to promoting constructive social change—a commitment that requires constructive, open involvement with the community on the part of individuals and on the part of institutions, independent of individuals;
8. an understanding of the complexity of the concept of civic responsibility; and
9. a commitment to establishing fundamental principles, rejecting both extremes of moral neutrality and simplistic, exclusive moral judgments.

Educational institutions offer numerous areas in which to apply these guidelines and integrate them into a liberal arts education. Community service programs sponsored by student organizations or by the college, to be sure, can be a critical component, but achieve their impact when they take place in the context of reflection, analysis, and questioning about what kinds of social change are needed to mitigate the circumstances initially requiring that community service. An education for civic responsibility is about developing supportive behavior patterns towards others in the community. For example, on college campuses today, one of the most difficult issues flows around what is meant by free speech and how the college should respond to free speech issues. Emotions run the highest when free speech protects racist and sexist language, but it is just those kinds of situations which offer the best chance to educate for civic responsibility. They help students understand the complexity of these issues so that they can avoid simplistic, formulaic solutions. Abstract issues are made real because the institution must make judgments with respect to individual cases and to policy and must engage the community in some form in testing the judgments and the response.

As a personal example of the need to make judgments, when I first arrived as president of Hampshire College, I proposed that we should handle these difficult conversations and debates with what I call the "principles of discourse," principles essential to the well-being of higher education in the same way that free speech is essential to the society as a whole. The principles of discourse value truth and seeking truth, but require that individuals pursue truth using *all* available evidence and the rules of reason, logic, and relevance. The principles do not allow distortion of data, no matter how important the ends or the personalization of the disagreement. Institutions dedicated to questioning truth cannot survive, let alone thrive, if these principles do not apply.

In 10 years, the community has debated intensely the application of these principles in different contexts, but the community, to date, has never challenged their existence or utility as a tool to evaluate behavior and even, if need be, to discipline members of the community. The community has accepted that the neutrality of the free speech standard for the society as a whole cannot apply literally in an academic community. If it did, scientists, who clearly have the right to publish reports on their work, could not be disciplined for knowingly distorting data from experiments.[7]

CIVIC RESPONSIBILITY AND THE LIBERAL ARTS COLLEGE

Liberal arts colleges' distinctive position in promoting civic responsibility in U.S. education lies in their residential nature, not just in their commitment to liberal arts education. They challenge educators to move students beyond passive study of theory and issues relating to civic responsibility by providing "laboratories" for testing those theories. Over two centuries, liberal arts colleges have varied greatly in the intensity with which they have embraced this "laboratory" concept as an essential part of their educational mission. To the extent they do not embrace the opportunity, they diminish greatly the opportunity to promote civic responsibility. The combination of the principles of a liberal arts education presented within a living and acting residential community—the hallmark of most liberal arts colleges—is a powerful form of education, one that instills reflection and skeptical reverence even while requiring individuals to make judgments and live out the principles being studied or examined. Residential liberal arts colleges have an unequaled potential within higher education to integrate knowledge and action in a holistic educational community. Unfortunately, many of these colleges do not seize that opportunity. The efforts of larger universities to create liberal arts "honors" colleges within their midst, however, shows the value placed on this form of education.

As residential liberal arts colleges embrace responsibility for constructive criticism and the promotion of constructive social change, they also face a particular challenge rooted in their residential nature. Students in particular, but the community as a whole, have a special opportunity to fulfill the obligations of civic responsibility. The residential dimension of these colleges requires young people to put into practice values evolving from the attitude of skeptical reverence developed in a liberal education. The residential dimension creates a laboratory in which civic responsibility can be promoted, tested, acted upon, refined, and then periodically reviewed. Implicit in the residential liberal arts college is the assumption that knowing is not enough. Individuals must translate theory and principles into the action of daily civic life.

The commitment to maintain a residential environment that, in effect, is a laboratory for testing and promoting civic responsibility levies a special obligation on these institutions to help generate a new public philosophy that preserves and extends the values gained in the procedural republic but that reintroduces substantive communitarian values. By creating manageable, integrated living and learning communities they most fully embody the guidelines of educating for civic responsibility. The extent to which these communities also reflect the diversity of the national community enriches the "laboratory" experience.

Dormitory life, a social context in which students confront many of the issues of civic responsibility, provides the most obvious laboratory environment. Whether it be noise control, trash collection, or substance use, creating a chance for young people to work out social arrangements on their own can provide strong learning environments. All residential educational institutions offer this opportunity. The advantage that the residential liberal arts institution has is one of scale. More people will know each other, and the process of developing arrangements will involve less anonymity. In the end, however, the real issue is the extent to which an institution—college or university—is prepared to make civic responsibility an explicit, as opposed to an implicit, goal.

While the dormitory offers a valuable laboratory, on many campuses the most compelling "teachable moments" for civic responsibility are embedded in committee work, that butt of countless genteel academic gibes. Clearly, large state universities, community colleges, private universities, and residential liberal arts colleges offer countless venues for this much-maligned service, which nevertheless creates a "real world" educational experience about civic responsibility. The advantage the residential liberal arts college offers, however, is again one of scale and the ability to encompass the whole enterprise. Students can be involved realistically in academic issues, social issues, student life issues, and working condition issues. More to the point, they are in a physical place where it is possible to encourage involvement and to model the behavior of civic responsibility. The residential liberal arts college has an advantage because it can develop bodies and policies that allow individuals to look at the whole and to overcome fragmented views of special interests. But the process, whether in a university or in a residential liberal arts college, is never simple because of the different perspectives represented and because of issues of power.

On many campuses these compelling "teachable moments" for civic responsibility embedded in committee work are lost when debate, negotiation, and decision-making are reduced to power struggles. At such times, students lose their understanding of the distinctions between power and result or effect. I am constrained to add that faculty and administrators often fall victim to the same struggle, and tension emerges.

My own campus has numerous examples of such squabbling, as all campuses do. But by taking to heart the notion that educating for civic responsibility involves inquiry-based, active-learning in which students work to solve real problems with reflection, analysis, and evaluation, Hampshire has created a holistic environment for students to apply the knowledge as they acquire it. Hampshire College expects its students to exercise extraordinary decision-making power over their individual academic programs, which they must negotiate and contract for with faculty members. The same is true for community life, which is governed by a constitution drafted by faculty and students. Even in the most sensitive area of all—evaluation and reappointment of faculty—the college expects students to participate as full members of the community.

Hampshire, of course, is only one of many colleges that not only fosters but expects full student participation in the governance life and committee work of the college. Marlboro College (Vermont) and Pitzer College (one of the Claremont, California, colleges), to name just two, operate with an inclusive, town-meeting model of campus governance in which all members of the community are expected to participate. The system is effective, perhaps in part because of the scale of the community, but in large measure also because the community sees campus governance as a formal, integral, explicit part of the education provided to everyone in the community.

Connecticut College has developed an imaginative framework in which to carry on a dialogue that promotes an education for civic responsibility. In governing processes and governance and advisory committees, the college delineates which groups have a voice in developing policy, those that have a vote, and those that have a veto. Faculty, staff, and students learn how to use "voice, vote, and veto" to be effective within a policy-making governance system, and the clarification of roles helps reduce tension and shift the focus in community discussions from who has the power to how does one use the system to make one's position most effective in shaping policy. "Voice, vote, and veto" creates a strong laboratory environment in which participants can practice civic responsibility.

In one final area, scale works both for and against the residential liberal arts college. For an institution to establish the laboratory environment necessary for students to understand the complexity and excitement of working for civic improvement, the institution itself, independent of students and alumni, must address critical social and community issues, be they urban renewal, teacher improvement, or arms control. Smaller institutions may have an advantage in reaching a consensus about how to act as an institution, but they often, but certainly not always, may have fewer resources to effect real social change.

Many institutions reject this calling to effect social change on the grounds that they are educational, not service, organizations and therefore should not take stands. Such a limitation on the role of the institution in promoting civic responsibility has dire consequences. It encourages students to see institutions as neutral parties in public debate, divorced from solving social problems. Just as faculty and administrators model civic responsibility for students who serve on committees with them, the institution as a corporate entity must "act the talk" and set an example. Without this crucial step, we cannot expect to restore the lost faith in institutions; we cannot renew the "substantive republic."

Institutions must judge themselves first by the quality of education that they provide their students. At the same time, however, a secondary standard by which they judge themselves must be the difference that the institution, independent of its students and alumni/ae, makes as an institution. Smaller institutions will have more difficulty in making that difference but they can do so. Trinity College, in Hartford, Connecticut, has taken a major lead in promoting urban renewal around the campus and in supporting programs to support physical changes. Many academic institutions are playing that role, and such activities offer a superb opportunity to involve undergraduates in activities promoting civic responsibility.

Service-learning courses are proliferating throughout higher education, and these courses offer another opportunity to educate for civic responsibility when the service opportunities involve a critical approach to social conditions. Hampshire College has always had a community service requirement, but part of that requirement involves students reflecting on all aspects of the service they provided and on developing strategies or participating in activities that can lead to social change, not just service. Its core program is led by the Center of Public Service and Social Change. The two always must be linked together.

A CORPORATION WITH A CONSCIENCE

Liberal arts colleges, in educating for civic responsibility, ultimately must make the ethical questions of conscience Thoreau raises in "Civil Disobedience" real and meaningful to students. All educational institutions have that responsibility. Each must determine what special characteristics it has to lend leverage to the pursuit of that goal. For the residential liberal arts college, it is scale and its residential nature. For the land-grant university, it is the public mission and the platform it has that insures the society will pay attention even if it disagrees. No person, no institution, however, has the luxury of remaining neutral, separating, as Thoreau said, "action from principle—the perception and the performance of right" for to do so violates a principal goal of a liberal arts education: to prepare individuals to judge wisely and to act humanely and responsibly.

NOTES

1. H.D. Thoreau, *Walden and Civil Disobedience,* ed. O. Thomas (New York: W.W. Norton, 1966), 225. All further quotations from Thoreau are from this text.

2. R. Bellah, *The Good Society* (New York: Random House, 1996); R. Bellah et al., *Habits of the Heart: Individualism and Commitment in American Life* (Berkeley: University of California Press, 1996); M. Sandel, *Democracy's Discontent: America in Search of a Public Philosophy* (Cambridge, MA: The Belknap Press of Harvard University Press, 1996), 4. All further quotations from Sandel are from this text.

3. Sandel, *Democracy's Discontent.*

4. Ibid., 7.

5. Ibid.

6. Ibid., 323.

7. The principles of discourse Hampshire College uses are:

    1. Value truth and the process of seeking truth as ends in themselves;

    2. Accept responsibility to articulate a position as close to the truth as one can make it, using to the best of one's ability available evidence and the rules of reason, logic, and relevance;

    3. Listen openly, recognizing always that new information may alter one's position;

    4. Welcome evaluation and accept and even encourage disagreement and criticism even to the point of seeking out for ourselves that which will disempower our position;

    5. Refuse to reduce disagreement to personal attacks or attacks on groups or classes of individuals;

    6. Value civility, even in disagreement; and

    7. Reject the premise that the ends, no matter how worthy, can justify means which violate these principles.

CHAPTER 14

A Historically Black College Perspective

Gloria Dean Randle Scott

BACKGROUND

The exploration of the experiences of historically black colleges in preparing their students for civic engagement begins in the early days of the young American republic with its ambitious goal of a true democracy. When Alexis de Tocqueville made early observations on the American "experiment," he was most fascinated by the tendency of these Americans to join in with neighbors and be involved with the matters of (the) community. He further observed that this was probably the true strength of the democracy and noted that if ever the citizens ceased to be involved, the experiment in democracy would very easily go the way of older governments and ideologies and become anarchy or oligarchy. However, when Tocqueville was writing, his observations were primarily focused on white Americans, as black Americans had no status except as property. It was not until after the Civil War that black Americans began to have real opportunities for either education or civic engagement. Since that time historically black universities have played a special role in promoting civic engagement. Although the first opportunities for any form of formal education for slaves was in the Northeast, it was in the South that the majority of educational institutions for blacks were founded.

INTRODUCTION

The nation's historically black colleges and universities (HBCUs) were founded over a period of 110 years from 1837 (Cheney State University) to 1947 (Texas Southern University). Seventeen of the institutions are land-grant colleges and universities, created specifically (by the second Morrill Act) to serve African Americans in the 17 southern and border states, following the original public and charge to reach out to improve the life chances and the quality of life for rural America. The extension centers of the 17 land-grant institutions were in the vanguard of public higher education with regard to initiating and implementing programs of civic engagement for their students. The earliest institutions immediately formed programs of civic engagement after the Civil War; they were all tasked with the expectation that their students would embrace civic responsibility and that deliberate, intentional efforts would be a structured part of the institution's purpose and mission. In short, the institutions were expected to provide direction, training, and opportunities to practice civic engagement and community building, such as cooperative programs for building housing and shelter for families, similar to the Habitat for Humanity program.

These historically black colleges and universities are located in Ohio, Pennsylvania, Maryland, District of Columbia, Delaware, Virginia, West Virginia, North Carolina, Tennessee, South Carolina, Georgia, Florida, Alabama, Mississippi, Louisiana, Texas, Arkansas, Oklahoma, and Missouri. Many of the institutions are church related and were founded by religious denominations and the Freedman's Bureau. For 16 decades, they have had primary responsibility for the social, political, economic, personal, and educational development of the black communities. These institutions were immediately charged with developing a critical mass of blacks who could impart knowledge and become professionals, and with educating black workers who could challenge the continuous threats to the survival of the black community while working to achieve equality in the larger American society. This duality of function has defined the relationship and direction of historically black institutions with their students and their orientation to civic engagement during the 162 years of their existence.

When black colleges were first founded, the community involvement of their students was anchored in their communities of origin. Even when not geographically adjacent, the development of "the black community" was always considered the responsibility of all black citizens of the town, city, state, and ultimately, in the 1960s, the region and the nation. The experience of historically black colleges and universities in preparing students for civic engagement is inextricably bound to the missions of the institutions.

The two original medical colleges for educating African Americans—Howard University Medical School and Meharry Medical College—provide an example of community involvement. Both functioned as providers of medical care for indigent African Americans as well as those of other races. Students from Meharry Medical College made annual trips to HBCUs and African-American community centers to conduct physical examinations required of students attending those colleges and elementary schools as a part of their (service-learning) commitment to the communities.

The construct of civic development was the right auricle of the heart of HBCUs, joined by the left auricle of teaching and learning, and the left ventricle of creating new knowledge, all of which combined to make up the core of American higher education: teaching, research, and public service. Historically black institutions, however, always had, as the right ventricle, a fourth purpose—the pursuit of social justice, which is the core of civic engagement, and the strengthening of democracy. In many cases, the communities built themselves around these institutions. The church and the college were the only social institutions that "drew people together," acting as the centers for common interests and endeavors. The institutions of higher learning were the heart of development for African Americans.

During the 1960s, students from historically black colleges and universities exercised the highest and most intensive form of "civic engagement" when they led the movement to engage the entire country in the pursuit of social justice, the first such student engagement in the history of the republic. This action exemplifies the dual mission of HBCUs both to produce an educated populace and to prepare the students for civic engagement.

In 1970, the Ford Foundation funded a major conference exploring the future of the Negro college. Fifteen articles resulted from this conference and were published in the summer issue of *Daedalus*, "The Future of Black Colleges." Four of these articles provide background for this contemporary exploration of "The Experience of Historically Black Colleges and Universities in Preparing Students for Civic Engagement," and thus provide a catalyst for serious discussion of the long- and short-term goals of black people. Many of the institutions and their constituents internalize the expectation of specific responsibility for improving the conditions of black Americans as a primary way of creating civility in the larger society. At many HBCUs, credit for service emerged early in the form of internships, field placements, and special studies and as an integral part of traditional class assignments. Support of community organizations through volunteer assignments is well documented from the late 1880s to the present. The current expectation of involvement is through formalized service-learning programs and requirement of a certain number of volunteer hours as a part of the general education curriculum.

In 1971, Mack Jones defined the role of service at HBCUs as follows:

Since their inception Black colleges have had built-in anthitical goals and objectives. The White community, as is always the case with groups enjoying superordinate status in society, has sought to maintain its position of dominance at the expense of Blacks, while the latter have sought to achieve equal status, and both have sought to use the Black college as an instrument in their struggle. This assumption must be the focal point of any intelligent discussion of the success of the Black College in meeting responsibility to the larger Black community.[1]

Patricia Roberts Harris, former U.S. Secretary of Health, Education, and Welfare, U.S. Secretary of Housing and Urban Development, and Ambassador to Luxembourg, describes the black college as the major black community employer, and through its graduates, it is consistently adding to its constituency of intellectual blacks. "Through the production of this constituency, the Black college created a community, the middle-class Black community. The creation and replenishment of an entire community was the most significant role played by the Negro College."[2]

HBCUs have played a crucial role in creating an educated, middle-class constituency that views and understands civic engagement as primary for the survival of the Negro and for the survival of the democracy. Black communities held high expectations of the students who attended the black colleges and universities in their areas. The colleges developed seamless, continuous, programmatic involvement for their students. It was not uncommon in the late 1800s and early 1900s to have institutions close for a time to send the students into the immediate community, and also to far away communities to assist with house and neighborhood building, or the "raising of a church," or to teach simple reading and numbers.

The high expectations held by the institutions for their students in the area of civic engagement provided a foundation of information and behavior for the several closely knit relationships that formed. These relationships were fueled by the high expectations that constituents would learn and practice civility and engage in civic responsibilities while they were students. The colleges regularly involved students in civil explorations towards pushing back the race barrier. Under the assumption that students were being educated, and therefore would be involved in many forms of "activism," churches, political groups, black organizations, business, and civil rights organizations (such as the National Association for The Advancement of Colored People [NAACP] in the early days, and later the National Urban League [NUL], and the Student Nonviolent Coordinating Committee [SNCC]) all provided numerous opportunities for college students to be involved. The concept of "grass roots" involvement from the basic communities, with little to no financial participation, grew heavily among black college students. It was expected that they, the "talented tenth" as described by W.E.B DuBois, would "lead the race in civic endeavors." Presidents of colleges, in the daily and/or weekly chapel programs, vespers or convocations, regularly called attention to the citizenship responsibility of the college students because they were the recipients of college educations.

The institution sought to deliberately create "community," and a community of educated African Americans who could and would foster the political, social, and economic activities for the black community. It is no accident that the strongest student political group first formed in America was formed on the campus of Shaw University in Raleigh, North Carolina. The SNCC became a most formidable force in the pursuit of social justice for African Americans. Its origin preceded the "Weathermen," and its theme was nonviolence in contrast to the violence of the Weathermen. In fact, many persons credit the speech that was given in the chapel at Bennett College in 1958 by Rev. Martin Luther King Jr. with "igniting" the flame of interest and involvement among students from Bennett, Shaw, and North Carolina A & T State University. Within a year after SNCC was founded, these students participated in sit-ins and escalated to a new height the boycott that was so effectively used in Alabama. The boycott process was organized by, supported by, and made successful by students from historically black colleges and universities. The short chronicle that traces the civic engagement of the students in North Carolina is as follows:

- February 11, 1958, Dr. Martin Luther King Jr. spoke at Bennett College in Greensboro, North Carolina, when no other institution or church would allow him to speak for fear of retaliation of some kind (numerous students from area colleges were present);
- March, 1959, King spoke at Shaw University; the SNCC was founded at Shaw University in Raleigh, North Carolina;
- October, 1959, Bennett students planned a boycott of downtown Greensboro stores and postponed it until after the semester was over;
- February 1, 1960, four students from North Carolina A & T State University sat in at Woolworth's in Greensboro, North Carolina;
- students from A & T and Bennett College launched the highly viable and effective student immersion in the central civic engagement toward social justice and focused on racism as a major social policy issue to be dealt with by civic engagement.

These students completed college and became the core and fringes of the black middle class and the educated class, transferring the responsibilities of civic engagement to their adult lives in the communities and towns where they lived and worked. They moved it into the corporate boardrooms of America.

They moved it to challenge many social policy issues of the nation. The impact of early expectations and the mentoring during college years by administrators, faculty, and staff in the HBCUs was to produce not only the black middle class but the leaders for community and civic engagement.

Dr. Benjamin Mays, former president of Morehouse College in Atlanta, Georgia, through his weekly speeches on civic engagement, set his expectations that Morehouse students would learn about civility and would become engaged. One of his regular speeches, given at Morehouse, Bennett College, and other colleges, was entitled, "Creative Living for Youth in a Time of Crisis." The centerpiece of this speech was to motivate the students to live creatively in order to manage what he defined as a social revolution in America—the May 17, 1954, Supreme Court decision, *Brown v. Board of Education*, 347 U.S. 483 (1954). He indicated that this decision had unearthed a "crisis in human relations." He essentially told the students that the only way out was through civic engagement. He said, "It created a social revolution in America, particularly in the South, because we are not ready, we are not willing to implement democracy, and we are not ready, and we are not willing to implement Christianity. We live in a crisis . . . How can you live creatively in a time like this?"[3]

Dr. Willa Beatrice Player, president emerita of Bennett College, also regularly spoke to Bennett students and students at many other colleges and universities, including Ohio Wesleyan. She often utilized the paradigm of "Tumult and Challenge." In a speech given to the students in 1959 she said,

> "We are in the throes of utter despair in the area of human relations, because of the command of the Supreme Court of the United States to desegregate in housing, recreation, transportation and public education. Each new gain in civil rights reflects new bitterness in personal and interpersonal relationships, so that our era is too often subjected to violence and mob rule. We are living in a time of great turmoil when men refuse to accept the fundamental ideas which admit that all men are made in the image of God, and as such should have equal opportunity to increase in status."[4]

It is clear that the routine interactions of the several HBCU presidents with their students regularly motivated expectations that HBCU students should be involved in the highest forms of civic engagement. The nation and our democracy benefits tremendously from this active, core group of citizens bound for the middle class economically, with high expectations set from their college experience to adulthood for continually escalating civic engagement from being a good citizen to leading the way. This created a common thread of responsibility: "you are your brother's and your sister's keeper; you are in fact expected to be the guardian of civility in our democracy."

HBCUs have also provided the core leadership that changed the status of blacks in the United States. This core leadership among American blacks in contemporary times is nurtured by both historically white and historically black institutions. However, black institutions award a high percentage of the baccalaureate degrees for black people, though they enroll less than 20 percent of the total black student population. If one scans the black population for civic engagement and leadership in social, political, economic, and educational development, one finds a disproportionately high number of blacks from historically black colleges and universities. With the W.E.B. DuBois-Booker T. Washington debate, and the succession of black leaders coming primarily from Negro colleges, it is clear that one contribution of the Negro college was the creation of a core concept of civic engagement which transmits the training, expectation, and implementation to the next generation.

Many of the black colleges and universities were "dragged" to another level of consciousness, as their students played roles in ending segregation in the 1950s and 1960s through massive demonstrations, both on and off the college campus. The middle-class graduates of HBCUs continue to play an important role in supporting civil rights. If the black college did no more than increase the number of literate, competent black citizens who do vote, its contributions would be mammoth. Additional new members of the black educated class " . . . are needed to serve a community and fill a void not served by anyone else or not served well."[5]

Elias Blake Jr., educational researcher, defined and cataloged leadership roles for black colleges. He stated,

> . . . as these schools move into the second hundred years their role must be diversified. They will continue to be of critical importance to the future of Black Americans, but in a different way. They must develop some uniqueness in supporting a truly pluralistic society. Differences are not respected in America, despite its official rhetoric. . . . Colleges and universities should start now to consider their role in the reshaping of America as a civilization.[6]

St. Clair Drake, professor of anthropology and sociology, posits in his article, "The Black University in the American Social Order," that "It is possible to visualize a group of undergraduates studying diligently for their degrees but all devoting some of their time—not all of it—to community projects . . . or graduate and professional students maintaining liaison with the Black community as they develop their own skills."[7] He also proposes the use of "leadership potential and seriousness of purpose" as traits to be considered when admitting students to college in order to emphasize the serious need for graduates who will make civic engagement a central part of their college and/

or university experience. This emphasis will promote responsibility for the creation of a civil society within a democracy that practices genuine civility and implements equity.

The contemporary movement toward service, community service, service-learning, and/or civic engagement is, for these colleges and universities, simply an extension of commitments they have made since they were founded. The original founding of these institutions was inextricably bound to the communities from which they sprang and to the extreme need in which they were formed, and also to the expectation that they, along with the churches, would share the burden, the task, and the opportunity to provide for the full education and human development—of the individuals within the community and for the collective society. This clearly sets HBCUs apart from counterparts—traditionally white mainstream colleges and universities, most of which do not have a history of, or an early and vital mission to sponsor solutions to community problems or respond to human needs.

Several programs at HBCUs are "tutorial," meaning they present black history and promote recognition that blacks have made many contributions in the United States during the past three centuries. In addition to these educational programs, HBCUs often participate in community redevelopment and improvement in the physical structures of the communities near the colleges. These activities include organizing recreation and afterschool and Saturday programs for black youth; conflict resolution; preschool activities; and offering use of campus physical facilities. Through these activities, black colleges are engaged in the creation of community as well as in the service of a community.

CASE STUDIES

Case study is one method for understanding how HBCUs traditionally prepared and currently prepare their students for civic engagement. The following case studies demonstrate HBCU programs in civic engagement and service-learning that are similar to those at other institutions. One private and two public HBCUs are discussed: Bennett College in Greensboro, North Carolina; North Carolina Agricultural and Technical State University (NCATSU) in Greensboro, North Carolina; and Texas Southern University in Houston, Texas.

Bennett College is a small, residential, baccalaureate, all-female private college affiliated with the United Methodist Church, celebrating 125 years during the 1998–99 academic year. NCATSU is a medium-sized, public land-grant, state-supported, doctorate-granting, coeducational, 109-year-old institution. Texas Southern University is a medium-sized, public, state-supported, doctorate-granting university that is 52 years old.

These institutions all are known for the involvement of their students in service and civic engagement, though these programs are manifested through different approaches. Bennett College and NCATSU are well known for student leadership, organization, and management of the nonviolent pursuit of social justice as an act of civility and civic engagement. The case study data come from documents, reports of first-hand involvement, and observations in the institutions. In all three institutions, the mission and purpose include civic engagement in some form.

Bennett College

Founded in 1873 in the basement of a church, Bennett College has demonstrated the continuity of civic engagement by its students for more than 100 years. From the earliest days of Bennett Seminary, the focus included a deliberate goal of helping the citizens of the Warnersville area. Student interaction within the community, which helped to support the newly formed institution, was a mutual survival action. The biography of an early student, David Dewitt Turpeau, describes how the students often went into the community to assist and provide support for families. Teaching the adults in the community to read (early literacy classes) anchored the commitment for service.

The theological foundation provided the basis for the "service mission." There are numerous examples of such early involvement, including assistance with construction of houses (early Habitat for Humanity-style projects), cultivation of land for food supplies, and helping the community to improve its collective strength as well as helping individual citizens to improve their "lot." Bennett taught its students to participate and engage in, as well as take seriously, the mission to be engaged in civic responsibility and citizen development.

Bennett College earned its title as an "activist institution" early, and has maintained that status through contemporary expressions of activism, civic responsibility among students, and the "corporate collective" civic responsibility of the institution as a whole. It has taken seriously the public service and outreach mission of American higher education and manifested it through its ongoing expectation that its students, faculty, and staff would participate in civic engagement.

Bennett has promoted and motivated civic engagement through its fundamental pursuit of social justice. The college has been inextricably bound with its community of southeast Greensboro, the area of the city which has historically, and still has, the highest concentration of African Americans, as well as with the city as a whole.

During its first 53 years, Bennett College was a coeducational institution, and students were engaged in improving the community through various outreach institutes to assist with home management; early childhood education and day care; gardens to provide food; citizen participation (i.e., helping citizens to learn political structures, and when finally allowed, helping citizens to register to vote); participating in precinct activities; assisting with access to voting polls when voting was extended to African Americans; and volunteering to tutor children in the neighborhoods. The college consistently operated some form of outreach education to the children of the community. Faculty also volunteered for these improvement activities. Books and other literature that the college owned were accessible to community residents, especially the religious community. Cultural events were shared with and open to the community. The campus facilities were utilized as "community gathering places." The college housed the city library for Negroes—Carnegie Negro Library—for 44 years.

In 1926, and at the time Bennett reorganized to become Bennett College for Women, the service expectations for students were literally "built in" among the tenets for reorganization, i.e., for providing an education that would create strong, functional, and productive women. The social justice theme continued as a form of civic engagement. Civic participation was also seen as a way that students could prepare for jobs in public and governmental service. Students were taught through regular classes and special "workplanning" sessions on how to "listen to the communities that we serve."

The last six decades of civic engagement for Bennett women include major leadership roles in improving life for both adjacent and distant communities, for the wider African-American segment of society, and for women in particular. Involvement has included engaging in community discourses about the censorship of movies featuring African Americans; intensive voter registration and voting drives; restructuring physical buildings in the community; providing assistance classes and conflict resolution training for youth in the community; volunteer teaching and support for a summer opera camp for community youth; and interacting with Greensboro governmental leaders through organized discourses about the community. The women of Bennett College continue to meet and exceed the expectation that they will always be in the forefront of civic engagement.

In the research study *Taking Women Seriously*, "respondents talked about Bennett's commitment to community service. Currently students must log 40 hours of community service as a requirement for graduation. While this is a new requirement, students made it clear that community service and activism have always been an important part of Bennett."[8] Community involvement, or civic engagement, helps students succeed; helps with student's total development; provides role models for students; and facilitates acquisition of leadership skills. The college focuses on motivating, facilitating, and teaching civic engagement in order to produce women who as students and alumnae will take the initiative to do things on their own that benefit themselves and their communities.

Contemporary civic engagement manifests itself through the Americorps Service Learning Program; Project Safety Net; the Learn/Service Programs; the Adult Computer Literacy Program; and sponsorship of Girl Scout troops by the Bennett College Campus Girl Scouts. The college initiated the American Humanics Certificate Program for nonprofit, entry-level education, which directly merges civic engagement with local youth and economically disadvantaged families. The Bennett College Student Volunteer Corps represents the clear legacy of civic engagement.

North Carolina Agricultural and Technical State University (NCATSU)

In the historical and contemporary sense, NCATSU has a strong record of preparing students for civic engagement. NCATSU is a public, state-supported Morrill Act 1890 land-grant university. NCATSU prepares its students for civic engagement through four major thrusts. Student government leaders are encouraged, to learn the political framework of the university and the community in which it serves; to learn how to be interactive in helping to satisfy the human needs of young people and adults; to learn how to strengthen community organizations and participate as responsible and informed citizens; and also to learn how to provide tutorial programs in various academic disciplines. Students in engineering and planning interact with redevelopment programs that affect African-American communities in Greensboro.

Many other academic departments engage students, faculty, and staff in the process of civic responsibility and engagement. For example, the Social Work Department established an Urban Institute in the 1970s for research, training, and development on urban issues. Students were placed in agencies to learn to advocate community engagement in urban issues. In the past 25 years, this institute has grown to be a major training and educational source for students and the community to participate in decision-making affecting the Greensboro community.

Student volunteer groups provided alternative schools and curricula for young African-American children. Well-known graduates used their training to create their careers in civic engagement and to pursue social justice through sit-ins and boycotts of businesses that refused to serve African Americans. One such graduate, Reverend Nelson Johnson, founded Greensboro Association of Poor People (GAPP) and a faith community steeped in civic engagement. Another graduate, Reverend Jesse Jackson, founded People United to Save Humanity (PUSH). One of the byproducts of institutional involvement in preparing students for civic engagement is enjoying the future involvement of these students as active, productive, involved citizens.

North Carolina Agricultural and Technical State University is known worldwide for its student civic engagement as well as its pursuit of social policy revision and broader racial empowerment. The four students who led the Woolworth sit-ins, through their actions, demonstrated the implementation of their formal educational process together with the influences of informal educational processes, such as the speeches of national leaders who provoked thought about civic responsibility. The 1958 speech by Dr. Martin Luther King Jr. at Bennett College provided additional motivation for students at Bennett College and NCATSU, which culminated in organizing the entire city to address the issues of racial discrimination. The students at NCATSU have had direct and immediate exposure to civic engagement through various forms of practicum work and through new structures of "external schooling" and outreach efforts.

Texas Southern University

From its inception in 1947, Texas Southern University, formerly known as Texas State College for Negroes, was immersed in the task of educating its students and guiding their service-learning through civic engagement. A black man, Heman Sweat, applied for admission to the law school at the University of Texas. His application was denied because he was a Negro. He brought suit against the university for denied admission. The response from the state legislature of Texas was to form a law school at Texas State College for Negroes, so that blacks could attend law school. Much later, states in the South, through a regional compact, agreed to pay costs to attend Northern colleges and universities for those black people who wanted to attend the professional schools in the South, such as law, veterinary, medical, and dental school.

The first students at Texas Southern University were engaged in community outreach. They involved the black community in supporting better educational opportunities. The students in the evening school became involved with community citizenship development to assist in the "birth of the new institution that would bring a new educational access to southern blacks." The students organized communities in Houston and encouraged school children and adults to become involved in the development of Texas Southern University. School children contributed nickels, dimes, and pennies to a fund to buy bricks for the first building at Texas Southern. Through student involvement, the Third Ward community where Texas University would be located became integrally involved in the development of the university. The entire Third Ward community became stakeholders in Texas Southern University and various segments of the community brought diverse contributions to and expectations from the university for the Negro citizens of the Third Ward. The local high school in the Third Ward, Jack Yates High, was immediately involved in "precollegiate partnerships" with the university. The university students tutored academic subjects, taught drama and debate to Jack Yates students, and provided many performances of various musical forms from opera to light comedy. The art department engaged children at a very early age. Professor John Biggers, an artist, promoted art for the community through the art program at Texas Southern and through his students who formed art programs in the local parks and housing projects. The athletic programs at the university provided "heroes" for the community through its student athletes, who inspired young black boys in the Third Ward. At a time when Big Brothers and Big Sisters and Boys and Girls Clubs were closed to black youngsters, the Texas Southern gymnasium and outside athletic fields provided "big brother" interactions for youth in 1949 and 1950. The tradition has continued. It is a part of a two-way nature of civic engagement. This university, very much a part of the community, started and strengthened the civic relationship.

The university has continued to promote the high level of involvement of its students in service to the community, as well as development (intellectual, social, and economic) of the community adjacent to it in the Third Ward. It has extended its outreach to all areas of the city and to the surrounding rural areas where blacks live. The vehicles and processes through which students were prepared for civic engagement from 1947 to 1997 includes three categories: (1) academic service-learning activities based on subject knowledge, including internships, mentoring, and field practicum assignments under supervision; (2) leadership training for students; and (3) formation of community partnerships that improve neighborhoods physically and assist with the development of its inhabitants for economic and social growth (including formation of a Community Development Corporation that students from the former School of Public Affairs help to operate).

The university is actively involved in setting high expectations for student participation and engagement. Reorganized in the early 1970s as one of the first urban universities, Texas Southern internally developed many of the approaches and programs used in the formation of the Campus Compact a decade later in 1985. In the 1960s, students were fired upon by the Houston police as they demonstrated with the community for social justice for African Americans in Houston, and some were killed. A mural produced over four decades by art students depicts the range of civic engagement by Texas Southern students. This mural is on the walls of one of the first buildings on the Texas Southern University campus and is still a major outreach project for children of Houston and other artists as well as historians and political scientists who study and write about the modern civil rights movement.

Texas Southern has a commitment to promote and implement active involvement in: supporting community development which empowers people to be active members of communities and to participate in the workforce; changing American education from early childhood through adult education; encouraging economic empowerment through voluntary activities of the business majors; and facilitating civic and legal discourse and action through the voluntary activities of the law students. This commitment is demonstrated through two major initiatives: (1) Economic and Community Development—creation of Economic Empowerment Zones for nonprofit groups, businesses, and organizations with the Third Ward Row House Project in which undergraduate and graduate business students are involved; and (2) formation of partnerships—especially with the Houston Negro Chamber of Commerce—for further development of communities in which students participate.

CONCLUSION

There is ample evidence that black colleges and universities, from their inception to the present day, have embraced the philosophy that knowledge is the impetus for work and service toward the advancement of humankind. As we approach the threshold of the new millennium, educational, social, cultural, economic, business, political, and religious needs still require astute skills and talents to address those needs effectively.

In many ways, needs are more concentrated than before, currently ranging from social and racial discord, to the widening economic gap between the "haves" and "have nots," to the technology revolution. Filling these needs keeps historically black colleges and universities revising, updating and improving their teaching and learning environments in order to merge service, civic engagement, social responsibility, and the ultimate responsibility for the future with the education required to produce the leaders for the next century. History has left a great legacy and has anchored these institutions in place to meet the contemporary challenge.

Historically black colleges and universities will continue to make meaningful contributions and will be noted as champions of unique perspectives in learning and service. It is the responsibility of historically black colleges and universities to continue to build upon their legacy, and to ensure preparation of men and women for service and lifelong living and learning through active civic engagement and citizen responsibility.

NOTES

1. M.H. Jones, "The Responsibility of the Black College to the Black Community: Then and Now," *Daedelus, 100*, no. 3 (1971): 732–45.
2. P.R. Harris, "The Negro College and Its Community," *Daedelus, 100*, no. 3 (1971): 700–31.

3. B. Mays, "Creative Living for Youth in a Time of Crisis," Bennett College, Annie Merner Pfeiffer Chapel, Greensboro, NC (30 March 1958).
4. W.B. Player, "Over the Tumult—The Challenge," (Delaware, OH: Ohio Wesleyan University, 1959).
5. Harris, "The Negro College," 731.
6. E. Blake Jr., "Future Leadership Roles for Predominantly Black Colleges and Universities in Higher Education," *Daedelus*, 100, no. 3 (1971): 745.
7. S. Drake, "The Black University in the American Social Order," *Daedelus*, 100, no. 3 (1971): 890.
8. E.M. Tidball et al., *Taking Women Seriously: Lessons and Legacies for Educating the Majority*, American Council on Education Series on Higher Education (Phoenix: Oryx Press, 1998), 94.

FURTHER READING

Brawley, James P. *The Clark College Legacy: An Interpretive History of Relevant Education. 1862–1975.* Princeton, NJ: Princeton University Press, 1977.

Brimmer, Andrew F. "The Economic Outlook and the Future of Negro College." *Daedelus* vol. 100, no. 3 (1971): 539–72.

Brown, Millicent E., and Lea E. Williams, eds. *A Celebration of 60 Years of Student Activism in Pursuit of Social Justice at College 1937–1997.* The Bennett College Social Justice Lecture Series 1. Greensboro, NC: Bennett College Women's Leadership Institute, 1998.

Brubach, S. John and Willis Rudy. *Higher Education in Transition: An American History: 1956.* New York: Harpers and Brothers, 1958.

Bryant, Ira B. *Texas Southern University: Its Antecedents, Political Origin and Future.* Houston, TX: D. Armstrong Co., Inc., 1975.

Chafe, William H. *Civilities and Civil Rights: Greensboro, North Carolina and the Black Struggle for Freedom.* New York: Oxford University Press, 1980.

Davis, Ollye G. *Public Policy Studies in the South: A Selected Research Guide.* 3rd ed. Atlanta, GA: Southern Center for Studies in Public Policy, 1981.

Fact Book On Higher Education in the South 1970. Atlanta, GA: Southern Regional Education Board, 1970.

Freedman, Mervin B. *The College Experience.* San Francisco: Jossey-Bass, 1967.

Gibbs, Warmoth T. *History of The North Carolina Agricultural and Technical College, Greensboro, North Carolina.* Peosta, IA: William C. Brown Company, 1966.

Godwin, Winfred L. "Southern State Governments and Higher Education for Negroes." *Daedelus.* vol. 100, no. 3 (1971): 783–97.

Hogg Foundation for Mental Health. *Report of the First National Congress of Black Professional in Higher Education.* Austin, TX: University of Texas, 1972.

Johnson, Tobe. "The Black College System." *Daedelus* vol. 100, no. 3 (1971): 778–812.

Kennedy, Robert F., et al. *Civil Rights and the South: A Symposium.* New York: Da Capo Press, 1971.

O'Connell, Brian. *Effective Leadership in Voluntary Organization: How to Make the Great Use of Citizen Service and Influence.* New York: Walker and Company, 1976.

Rama, D.V. *Learning by Doing: Concepts and Models for Service Learning in Accounting.* AAHE Series on Service Learning in the Discipline. Washington, DC: AAHE, 1998.

Rothman, Michael. *Service Matters Engaging Higher Education in the Renewal America's Communities and American Democracy.*

Tolbert, Kenneth S. *Black Colleges as Instruments of Affirmative Action.* Washington, DC: Howard University Institute for the Study of Educational Policy, 1982.

United States. Cong. House. Congressional Black Caucus. *National Policy Conference on Education for Blacks Proceedings, March 29-April 1, 1972.* Washington, DC: GPO, 1972.

United States. Dept. of Health, Education and Welfare. Federal Interagency Committee on Education. *Federal Agencies and Black Colleges, Fiscal Year 1971.* Washington, DC: GPO, 1971.

West, Cornel. *Race Matters.* New York: Random House, 1964.

CHAPTER 15

A Religious-Based College and University Perspective

William J. Byron

Because words are important, it is necessary for me to begin my discussion of "religious-based" colleges and universities with an explanation of what I understand such institutions to be.

My experience in higher education—as student, professor, and administrator—has been, with the exception of doctoral studies at the University of Maryland and brief postgraduate work at Harvard, exclusively in Catholic colleges and universities. I belong to a religious order, the Society of Jesus (Jesuits), that has a special relationship with 28 colleges and universities in the United States and with many others around the world. In addition to service as dean, president, and faculty member in several Catholic universities, I have first-hand experience as consultant, visiting lecturer, or trustee with many of the 200-plus member institutions in the Association of Catholic Colleges and Universities here in the United States, and I've worked with Catholic universities in Italy, Taiwan, Chile, Ireland, and Indonesia. This chapter on civic responsibility and church-related higher education will reflect that experience.

Using the term "religious-based" is probably not the best way of expressing the relationship between the educational institution and its sponsoring religion. The choice of words in the following headline from the fall 1998 issue of *P/PV News* (a publication of Private/Public Ventures, a Philadelphia-based research and service-project evaluation center) is instructive: "Faith-Based Institutions As Anchors for Local Partnerships Serving High-Risk Youth." The use of "faith-based" says a lot. Researchers like the term because it helps them get at the rationale (the connection between faith, reason, and action) that underlies service-learning projects in the nonpublic sector of education. (Does religion make any difference?) Sponsors of what might otherwise be called "religious-based" or "church-related" higher education like it because they know that one religiously sectarian academic roof will almost always cover faculty and students of firm but differing faith commitments. In most church-related institutions of higher education, faith is presumed to be a value that will be respected by all members of the academic community even though not all will share the same faith. Indeed, the diversity of faith commitments in such institutions is taken to be an enriching element of the academic environment.

My personal preference is for the term "faith-related" to describe the institutions discussed in this chapter. They are not necessarily "owned and operated" by any church, even though there may be a special relationship to religious authorities that is not simply historical but a living reality expressed in respect and service. Typically, institutional autonomy and academic freedom will characterize these schools; civic authority will grant the charter, regional accrediting bodies will certify them, and governance will be entrusted to independent, self-perpetuating boards.

The modern Catholic college in the United States is chartered by the state and owned by a corporation that is often identical with the independent board of trustees. In some cases, a religious community like the Jesuits, Franciscans, Benedictines, Congregation of Holy Cross, Sisters of Mercy, Christian Brothers, or any one of dozens of others, will provide an identifiable tradition, a "spirit," and a core group of religious faculty and administrators that give the enterprise a distinctive character. Often, this special "spirit" is the key to understanding a given institutions's approach to preparing young men and women for civic engagement.

Such a spirit is not peculiarly Catholic. Brandeis or Yeshiva have a spirit, a characteristic approach to education and training; so do Pacific Lutheran, Southern Methodist, Baylor, Brigham Young, or any other religiously inspired, faith-committed, church-related, religiously based college or university that operates in the United States as institutional proof of our constitutionally protected guarantee of the free exercise of religious conviction.

WHY DOES A UNIVERSITY-RELATED CHURCH MAKE SENSE?

Before answering the question of how a faith-related college prepares students for civic and political life, and before addressing the parallel issue of such an institution's own proper role as responsible "citizen," I want to offer a view on why these institutions are in the business of higher education in the first place. Here I will have to speak from my Jesuit, Catholic experience and I will use, for purposes of illustration, Georgetown, the Jesuit and Catholic university where I now work, and Loyola College in Maryland, where I once taught and now serve on the board of trustees.

Central to any Jesuit work is the development of human potential. The positive side of human potential, in the Jesuit view, stretches into eternity, toward union with the Creator of that human potential. The negative side points to the possibility of eternal alienation, to permanent frustration of that potential.

Formal education's interests are coextensive with the entire range of positive possibilities for human development. Throughout their over 450-year history, Jesuits have recognized this and have, almost from the beginning, chosen formal education, beginning at what we would call the secondary level, as an extraordinarily valuable instrument for their work in the development of human potential.

Higher education touches that range of positive possibilities in a privileged way. Skills and maturity acquired in primary and secondary stages of educational growth make possible, at a later stage, the conscious pursuit of wisdom. Not information only, nor technique, nor accumulated experience, but wisdom is a real possibility at the stage of human development associated with higher education. At this level, educators have the privilege of grouping themselves into communities of inquiry that may become or beget wisdom communities. At the level of higher education, educators have a responsibility to work for the formation of wise and reflective human beings.

Let me quote from the "Complementary Norms," a work that the Jesuits' 34th General Congregation attached to our Constitutions. (A General Congregation is the highest legislative body in the Jesuit order; as the numerical designation of this one indicates, only 34 have occurred in the entire history of the Society of Jesus.) Our renewed Constitutions and their Complementary Norms were published in 1996. Here, as expressed in the first paragraph of No. 289 of the Complementary Norms, is the official Jesuit answer to the question, "Why we are in higher education?"

> Universities and institutions of higher learning play an increasingly important role in the formation of the whole human community, for in them our culture is shaped by debates about ethics, future directions for economics and politics, and the very meaning of human existence. Accordingly, we must see to it that the Society [of Jesus] is present in such institutions, whether directed by itself or by others, insofar as we are able to do so. It is crucial for the Church, therefore, that dedicated Jesuits continue to engage in University work.[1]

In the Jesuit view, higher education is a medium; it is not just a means. It has intrinsic value. Involving, as it does, the pursuit of wisdom, higher education is worth much in purely human terms and thus worthy of dedicated human effort. But the worth of higher education, as both means and medium, transcends the human and touches the divine. That is why, it seems to me, a completely secular university is not really a university. If closed to a faith dimension, to an exploration of the transcendent and an examination of revelation, a "university" is hardly universal in its interests and thus holds questionable claim on that name.

The Jesuit purpose in higher education is to move the minds and hearts of developing human persons. The direction of this movement, Jesuits believe, is Godward, which is why they believe theology is an essential part of a college education. The norm is truth (and that's why Jesuits believe philosophy belongs in the curriculum). The hoped-for outcome is wisdom, hence, the importance of the humanities in Jesuit education. And wisdom, in the Jesuit understanding, is a gift from God that enables the recipient to understand what is truly important and really significant in events past or present (the humanities help a student discover this). Although no one can predict the future, the wise man or woman, having experience in sorting out the truly significant in past and present events, is well positioned to make wise choices en route to an unknown future.

More concretely, now, what does this mean?

Loyola College in Maryland, founded by the Jesuits in 1852, put together in the fall of 1998 a "Middle States Working Group on Jesuit and Catholic Identity." Its membership was Jesuit and lay, male and female, and representative of the campus community. Its mission was to produce a document for review by the reaccreditation team scheduled to visit the college during the next academic year. This document highlights the Jesuit character of the college and reads in part as follows:

> In 1599, the Spanish Jesuit Diego Ledesma listed four reasons why the Society of Jesus involved itself in education: (1) to give students "advantages for practical living"; (2) to "contribute to the right government of public affairs"; (3) to "give ornament, splendor, and perfection to the rational nature" of humanity; (4) to be "a bulwark of religion and guide man most surely and easily to the achievement of his last end." Ledesma's definition focuses clearly on what Jesuit education hopes for in its students, and any mission statement faithful to the Jesuit spirit must keep students and our responsibility to them at its center. With a bit of "translation" into late twentieth-century American terms, Ledesma's words still point clearly to key distinguishing characteristics of a Jesuit education: (1) it is eminently practical, focused on providing students with the knowledge and skills to excel in whatever field they choose; (2) it is not merely practical, but concerns itself also with questions of values, with educating men and women to be good citizens and good leaders, concerned with the common good, and able to use

their education for the service of faith and promotion of justice; (3) it celebrates the full range of human intellectual power and achievement, confidently affirming reason, not as antithetical to faith, but as its necessary complement; (4) it places all that it does firmly within a Christian understanding of the human person as a creature of God whose ultimate destiny is beyond the human. To put these goals in the words of the Decrees of the 34th General Congregation, Jesuit education encourages students and their teachers alike not only to seek knowledge for its own sake, but also to ask continually the key question, "Knowledge for what?" It also insists that answers to that question be formed in the context of vigorous intellectual activity that excludes no evidence from the investigation, including the evidence of the deposit of Christian faith.[2]

Loyola, along with all the other Jesuit schools, colleges, and universities throughout the world, is working now to realize an ideal articulated by the Superior General of the Jesuit order, Pedro Arrupe, at the Tenth International Congress of Jesuit Alumni of Europe, in Valencia, Spain, on July 31, 1973. After noting that "education for justice has become in recent years one of the chief concerns of the Church," Father Arrupe said:

> Today our prime educational objective must be to form men-for-others; men who will live not for themselves but for God and his Christ—for the God-man who lived and died for all the world; men who cannot even conceive of love of God which does not include love for the least of their neighbors; men completely convinced that love of God which does not issue in justice for men is a farce.[3]

The entire address was controversial because it called for change and pointed the Society of Jesus clearly in the direction of the promotion of social justice. The men-for-others theme (later edited to read "men and women for others") soon spread all over the world and gained ever wider acceptance in Jesuit educational circles.

The right slogan or phrase can set the direction for an institution and even define the culture within which teachers and learners interact. "Men and women for others" sets a target for Jesuit educational effort, moves the educational process into community service, and helps educators foster a sense of civic responsibility in their students. Getting them down on paper and accepting them as official ensures that high ideals become grounded in decisions and behavior.

In a similar way, the idea of "the other fellow first" sets the tone and articulates the dominant value that pervades the experience young boys enjoy at Camp Dudley on Lake Champlain in Westport, New York. Dudley, originally sponsored by the Young Men's Christian Association (YMCA) and now a nondenominational camp fostering Christian values, is the oldest continuous summer camp for boys in the United States. I've served as a visiting chaplain there in the past as part of an ecumenical rotation of responsibility for the Sunday chapel service. When I once asked a chubby eight-year-old, first-time camper what he liked about Camp Dudley, his instant reply was, "No one here makes fun of you." A motto, slogan, or theme can help to shape a culture, form character, and guide behavior.

In August 1992, a discussion paper[4] drafted by a group of faculty and administrators at Georgetown, the oldest (founded in 1789) Jesuit university in the United States, was presented to the campus community as a baseline document for the development of a strategic plan for the entire university. This document reaffirmed "the Jesuit conception of education as pursuit of knowledge in service of the world." It spelled this notion out in words that I still find compelling and that I offer now as an example of a statement that could influence curriculum decisions and out-of-class service opportunities aimed at fostering in students a sense of civic responsibility.

> Georgetown seeks to be a place where understanding is joined to commitment; where the search for truth is informed by a sense of responsibility for the life of society; where academic excellence in teaching and research is joined with the cultivation of virtue; and where a community is formed which sustains men and women in their education and their conviction that life is only lived well when it is lived generously in the service of others.

Notice the four themes in the statement:

- Commitment
- Responsibility (for the life of society)
- Cultivation of virtue
- Conviction that life is lived well only when lived generously in the service of others

By reducing these four themes to four words—commitment, responsibility, virtue, and service—you have four pillars on which to place an undergraduate educational experience, which in turn will serve as a platform to support postgraduation participation in civic life. And consider the potential of words like "living generously in the service of others" for setting a given campus apart from others, indeed for creating a unique campus culture conducive to the cultivation of civic virtue.

PREPARING STUDENTS FOR CIVIC AND POLITICAL LIFE

The Council on Civil Society, a joint project of the Institute for American Values and the University of Chicago Divinity School, issued a report in 1998 calling for society-wide discussion of the connection between morality and the maintenance of a sound social and political order.[5] The report concludes with five "Summary Propositions."

- democracy depends upon moral truths
- most moral disagreement calls for civility, openness to other views, and reasonable argument in the service of truth
- democracy embodies the truth that all persons possess equal dignity
- civil society embodies the truth that we are intrinsically social beings, cooperating with one another in order to know who we are and how to live
- democratic civil society is a way of living that calls us fully to pursue, live out, and transmit moral truth[6]

These propositions would receive a warm welcome in any religious-based or faith-related educational institution. They will surely underlie what such institutions attempt to do by way of cultivating the civic mind in their students. However, the 24-member interdenominational group of scholars, pastors, and social commentators who issued the call wanted all to understand that "civil society" is, in their view, a "new term" in public debate.

> Fairly suddenly, the prosaic world of civic participation, family dinners, PTA meetings and youth soccer has acquired a profound public significance. Despite a partisan and often rancorous political climate, Democrats and Republicans alike now extol the concept of civil society. Indeed civil society is increasingly touted as a newfound wonder drug for curing any number of problems, from fragmenting families to the decline of voter participation. Yet at present, the term is a bit like a Rorschach test: it can mean whatever anyone wants it to mean.

> To us, civil society refers specifically to relationships and institutions that are neither created nor controlled by the state. The essential social task of civil society—families, neighborhood life, and the web of religious, economic, educational, and civic associations—is to foster competence and character in individuals, build social trust, and help children become good people and good citizens.

> Ultimately, civil society is a sphere of our communal life in which we answer together the most important questions: what is our purpose, what is the right way to act, and what is the common good. In short, it is the sphere of society that is concerned with moral formation and with ends, not simply administration or the maximizing of means.[7]

Church- or faith-related colleges and universities would all presumably affirm the importance of moral formation. They want, in the words of this call, "to foster competence and character in individuals" on their way to becoming

"good citizens." They would never want to separate, let alone place in opposition, the notions of "civil" and "civic" as informing their educational objectives. They teach (and expect) civility on campus and hope for civic responsibility in postgraduation years.

The civil and civic blend nicely in the important work of James Youniss and
Miranda Yates, whose research demonstrates that participation in community
service and civic activities has a positive influence on young people's political
understanding and future civic engagement.[8] In an article they authored with
Jeffrey A. McLellan,[9] Yates and Youniss bring a developmental perspective to
the question of how individuals become adults whose civic engagement will
help improve society. Civil society is constructed, in their view, "by individuals
who are constructing their civic identities."[10] These researchers focus on
psychological identity and its development in the context of service.

> Our thesis is that participation in organized groups during the adoles-
> cence-youth era has a lasting impact for two reasons. First, on a
> practical level, it introduces youth to the basic roles and processes (i.e.,
> organizational practices) required for adult civic engagement. Second,
> on a personal level, it helps youth incorporate civic involvement into
> their identity during an opportune moment in its formative stages.
> Participation promotes the inclusion of a civic character into the
> construction of identity that, in turn, persists and mediates civic
> engagement into adulthood. The formation of civic identity, then, is
> the hypothesized developmental link across time and the factor that
> differentiates adults in the degree of their civic engagement.[11]

How does this developmental dynamic work? According to Yates and
Youniss, if youth participate, they will come to see that actions that will sustain
civic society are interdependent; that a common purpose is served by group
discipline; that differences among participants can be worked out; and that
"multiple perspectives can be coordinated."[12]

By offering youth meaningful participatory experiences, educators, according to Yates and Youniss, "allow them to discover their potency, assess their
responsibility, acquire a sense of political processes, and commit to a moral-
ethical ideology.[13] To put the matter simply, action is essential for identity
development and no education, let alone education for civic responsibility, is
complete without it.

The Reverend James L. Heft, S.M. (Marianists), provost of the University
of Dayton, asks, "Can Character Be Taught?"[14] and asserts that character
education is "inescapably craftsmanlike."

> There is an ancient Chinese saying that goes "if I hear, I forget; if I see,
> I remember; if I do, I understand." It is a mistake, then, to separate
> intelligence from discipline, or discipline from virtue. This is why many

who support character education recommend strongly various forms of service for students, service that takes them outside of themselves and makes them aware of the needs of others.[15]

Loyola College in Maryland, a Jesuit institution that some 20 years ago absorbed Mount St. Agnes College, a liberal arts college for women founded by the Sisters of Mercy, has a Center for Values and Service. Its 72-page 1997–98 student handbook of "Community Service Opportunities" offers the following reply to the question, "Why Service?"

- To assist others in need and to learn from individuals different than you, whether by age, economic means, education, physical ability, background, culture, or ethnicity
- To develop and experience community with and among other student volunteers as well as with the people you serve
- To examine your own values, attitudes, and beliefs about the world
- To understand how the economic, political, and cultural structures of our society affect others
- To discover or affirm your faith relationship with God and to respond to that relationship through service
- To develop a lifelong habit of service, a concern for others, and an understanding for social justice in light of the Jesuit/Mercy traditions
- To see Baltimore [Catechism] as part of your classroom learning
- To develop leadership skills
- To gain experience in your academic or future career field while making a difference in your life and the lives of others[16]

Some form of voluntary community service is an important component of the education Loyola wants to provide; the college views service as a distinctive feature of its program that helps to set it apart from other colleges and universities. Acknowledging that there has been an "explosion in service-learning on campuses across the U.S.," Loyola's academic planners designed a "service leadership" program to meet the need "for students to develop leadership capabilities through service-learning. Our experience at Loyola College has led us to believe there is a need for a developmentally based program combining service learning and leadership."[17]

Educators have an understandable concern about assuring the firmness of the connection between service and learning. Conceivably, an undergraduate could have four years of service or one year's service four times. In other words, it is possible not to grow as a result of the experience. It can happen that in the mind of the developing student, no learning link is forged between the off-campus service experience and the on-campus classroom and library exposure to the theory and history that can, quite literally, make the service experience meaningful. Religious-based colleges and universities will, in many cases, have experience with confronting this problem. Seminaries associated with their religious denominations usually have mandatory field education programs intended to help young men and women, who are on their way to ordination, not simply experience forms of pastoral or social ministry but draw from that field experience a better understanding of their textbook theology.

Whether it is ordained ministry or secular engagement that lies ahead for the graduate of a religious-based higher education institution, that institution's sponsoring religious body hopes the learning years will produce an informed citizen of two worlds, whose lifelong commitment to service will advance the common good.

Although Youniss and Yates based the conclusions in their book, *Community Service and Social Responsibility in Youth* (1997) on empirical work with Catholic high school students, their study, which supplements their own empirical work with an exhaustive review of the empirical literature on service by adolescents, provides a remarkably useful theoretical foundation for colleges and universities interested in articulating the learning theory that underlies a solid service-learning program. Their work is helpful in enabling me to respond to the question of how a faith-related college or university can effectively prepare students for civic engagement.

Youniss and Yates offer 10 ideas that reflect their thesis that "service can provide concrete opportunities for youth to develop an increased understanding of their membership within a societal framework and their responsibility for society's future."[18] All 10 ideas touch upon the common themes of engaging youth in society and making service an integral part of personal identity. Service must not be presented to young persons as an isolated experience; it needs to become integrated into their lives. The process is developmental.

Readers can consult the Youniss and Yates book for a fuller explanation of each of the following points.[19]

1. **Meaningful Activity.** The quality rather than the quantity of service is the important point. A meaningful or quality experience, as opposed to a "make work" situation, should include responsibility for decision making; identification and reflection upon one's personal values; working closely with adults; facing new situations; and receiving blame or credit for one's work.

2. **Emphasis on Helping Others.** Care should be taken to avoid overemphasizing the benefit of the experience to the service provider. Put the emphasis on helping others to encourage caring attitudes and foster a commitment to social justice.

3. **Integrated Part of Articulated Ideology.** This means connecting service to the defining goal or mission statement of the school, or at least

explaining its consistency with a stated mission. This is usually easier to do in religiously based institutions.

4. **Group Rather Than Individual Action.** A sense of group awareness is important; collective action thrives on a clearly defined sense of the "we" who do the action.

5. **Reflective Opportunities with Peers.** Reflection on the experience is essential. Personal essays aid reflection; peer discussion groups are important complements to private reflection.

6. **Service Organizers as Models and Integrators.** Adults who organize the service opportunities and work along with the students provide admirable and imitable examples that the "message" can be lived.

7. **Site Supervisors as Models.** People who work full time at the service sites "can be models of moral commitment who offer their perspective on social problems and the dynamics of trying to alleviate these problems. While the ability of staff members to be educators may be limited by time and resources, this potential should not be overlooked when service organizers select sites and establish relationships with the staff at these sites."[20]

8. **Acknowledging Participants' Diversity.** Typically, the mix of participants, site supervisors, service organizers, and recipients of the service will be quite diverse. This can cause discomfort that should be acknowledged because diversity of race, class, and gender can affect the service experience; it is something that should be talked about as part of reflection on the experience.

9. **Sense of Being a Part of History.** This sense enables the service to have a powerful impact on identity development. "[Y]outh become invested in service when they believe that their actions are helping to make history. On the other hand, it is also easy to understand how youth can maintain the disengaged role of voyeur when service is treated as an isolated or decontextualized event."[21]

10. **Responsibility.** Service helps focus students on their responsibilities rather than on their rights and freedoms.

In listing "Responsibility" as their tenth "idea," Youniss and Yates put the spotlight on the person and convictions of the charismatic teacher in the school that sponsored the service experience they observed: "In the final analysis, *either we care about these problems or we do not.* If you do care, then you will want to know more, to be informed, to be able to think critically, and thus be prepared to make your response to this world." To underscore this point, the teacher quoted to his students an excerpt from Martin Luther King, Jr.'s final sermon: "For when people get caught up with that which is right, and they are willing to sacrifice for it, there is no stopping point short of victory."[22]

I would like to re-address the question that I left hanging earlier in the chapter: Is there any difference between service-learning in state-supported or public schools, and in educational institutions that are faith-related? I think there is. The difference relates to the faith commitment or faith relatedness of the educational institution. If a faith dimension is part of institutional purpose and identity, it will find expression in the institutional statement of mission. Because faith is personal, the value commitment of the institution can be more easily internalized and personalized. Doing this off-campus service, a student might explain, is part of being a Catholic, an observant Jew, a practicing Presbyterian. Moreover, if the school compels some form of service as a curricular requirement, it is more likely to pull this off if the requirement is backed by a religious principle. On the other hand, if the service is voluntary, motivation for voluntary action can be heightened by the same religious or moral principles of justice and love.

The difference will emerge in the rationale, in the articulation of the reason for service involvement. This is not to say that the service rendered is qualitatively better or discernibly different from service rendered for secular, civic, or patriotic motives. The difference will be hidden, so to speak, in the personal identity development of the service provider. Service originating in faith-related colleges and universities is less likely to blur the distinction between the political and the moral aspects of this educational activity. Youniss and Yates are helpful in raising this distinction.

Consider a concept such as social responsibility that could be interpreted in either a political or a moral sense. One could be responsible to the community by fulfilling civic duties such as voting in an informed manner. Or one could be responsible in a moral sense by putting the community's well-being before one's personal interests. We do not address which criteria to use in deciding between the political and moral and we recognize the power of ideology to make the politically preferred position appear as if it were a moral necessity.[23]

I think it is more likely that an appreciation of the principle of the common good, or, to put it as Yates and Youniss do, "putting the community's well-being before one's personal interests," will more readily emerge in a faith-related, religiously motivated, morally principled educational environment. Institutions rooted in religious conviction try to promote community and control, contain, or eliminate individualism. The graduates they hope to produce simply would not fit the following description:

> Individualists, as the name implies, are not trying to create a community but rather aiming to free themselves from the fetters of social restriction. They thrive in loose organizational structures, around which they can move freely without long-term commitment, able to negotiate their own dealings with other individuals. Well being for them means the freedom to pursue self-interested ends. It is the well-

being of the narrowly defined ego, the ideal of negative freedom from interference.[24]

Most faith-related colleges and universities would claim that they are educating men and women of conscience, competence, and commitment to the common good. They integrate service opportunities into the educational experience precisely to enhance the likelihood that they will achieve this goal.

Forgetting for a moment the mission-statement rhetoric or the expression of educational ideals by religiously based institutions, it is a demonstrated fact that school type, or school characteristics, affect participation rates of students in service opportunities. A 1997 national study of student participation in service activity concluded that:

> Students in private schools were more likely than those in public schools to report they participated in community service (66 percent versus 47 percent). This difference was most pronounced when comparing students in church-related schools to public schools (69 percent versus 47 percent). Students in church-related private schools also differed from the general pattern by being more likely to have participated regularly (40 percent) than to have participated once or twice (18 percent).[25]

These data do not, of course, show anything about the lasting impact on civic behavior, or the character-shaping contribution made by school-based service. This study presumes that the positive influence of the experience will last over time. The data simply show higher participation rates in what I would describe as faith-related schools.

A FAITH-RELATED COLLEGE OR UNIVERSITY AS RESPONSIBLE CITIZEN

I see a parallel between the social responsibility model[26] I use with students in my course "Social Responsibilities of Business," a required course for seniors in the School of Business at Georgetown, and a model of social responsibility applicable to any college or university, but, in the present instance, applied specifically to a faith-based college or university. A business organization, if it is to be socially responsible, should be economically healthy, law-abiding, ethical, and, philanthropic. Hence, a four-level frame of reference must be used in examining any private sector business corporation's social responsibility. These levels are (1) economic; (2) legal; (3) ethical; and (4) discretionary/ philanthropic. The fourth simply means being a good corporate citizen even when considerations of profit, law, and strict ethical obligation do not require it.

A university that is faith-related and aspires to responsible institutional citizenship should be (1) academically sound; (2) operating within all applicable legal, professional, and accreditation agency guidelines; (3) ethically consistent internally and externally; and (4) present to the off-campus community in a positive and meaningful fashion. In this case, the fourth level means using both institutional mind and "muscle" (i.e., the institution's prestige, contacts, influence, and ability to affect change) for a broader community good (the common good).

Peter Maurin, whom Dorothy Day credited as her mentor and motivator in founding the Catholic Worker movement, remarked that the trouble with the world was that the people who do all the thinking never act, and the people who do all the acting never think. As a good citizen, the institution of higher learning has to do both. It is chartered to think; it sometimes needs encouragement and prodding to act outside the groves of academe—to become an institutional actor or agent of change. Think, for example, of portfolio management, investment and purchasing policies, and public statements about, or advocacy for, change in public policies not directly related to education.

The faith-related institution often has difficulty in discovering for itself what might be called a "sense of the appropriate" when it comes to action that is not purely academic. All Catholics, for example, not just their colleges and universities, have been puzzling since 1967 over the meaning and implications of the following words that issued from an international synod of bishops in Rome (a synod is a gathering of representatives of national or regional episcopal conferences from around the world, together with *ex officio* participants and some appointed by the pope): "Action on behalf of justice and participation in the transformation of the world appear to us as a constitutive dimension of the preaching of the gospel, or, in other words, of the Church's mission for the redemption of the human race and its liberation from every oppressive situation."[27] If the institution's faith relationship is to the Roman Catholic Church, such a statement concerning the "constitutive" nature of action (not simply reflection) on behalf of justice—for example, constitutive to the gospel values that presumably have a lot to do with defining the mission, purpose, and identity of the institution—should command respect and some response. In fact, responsive citizenship will mean something special for a faith-related institution, even one that is scrupulous about avoiding a mixture of religion and politics, and sensitive to the separate realms of church and state. There is, however, as such institutions would insist, no constitutionally mandated separation of church and society. Conscious of their duties in both realms—civic responsibility and religious fidelity—faith-related colleges and universities will necessarily find themselves exercising what they judge to be appropriate measures of social responsibility in both the moral and political orders.

Inescapably, the faith-related college or university, as citizen-actor and as institutional educator of the young, lives in overlapping spheres of influence: academy and community, faith and reason, town and gown, mind and matter.

Ignatius of Loyola, founder of the Jesuit order, wanted his colleges to be located in areas where students could "listen to the conversation of the city." Jesuit colleges, like so many other faith-based institutions, want their students and their schools, for sound educational reasons, to participate in that conversation by word and action on their way to becoming and remaining responsible citizens.

NOTES

1. *The Constitutions of the Society of Jesus and Their Complementary Norms* (St. Louis, MO: The Institute of Jesuit Sources, 1996), 305.
2. Memorandum, Office of the Academic Vice President, Loyola College in Maryland (20 November 1998).
3. P. Arrupe, *Men for Others: Education for Social Justice and Social Action Today* (Washington, DC: Jesuit Secondary Education Association, 1974), 1–2.
4. Georgetown University, The President's Strategic Planning Task Force, Strategic Plan for Georgetown University. Discussion Draft of August 1992, Part II.
5. *A Call to Civil Society: Why Democracy Needs Moral Truths* (New York: Institute for American Values, 1998).
6. Ibid., 27.
7. Ibid., 6.
8. J. Youniss, of the Catholic University of America, and M. Yates, of Brown University, are co-authors of *Community Service and Social Responsibility in Youth* (Chicago: University of Chicago Press, 1997), and editors of *Roots of Civic Identity: International Perspectives on Community Service and Activism in Youth* (New York: Cambridge University Press, 1999).
9. J. Youniss, J.A. McClellan, and M. Yates, "What We Know About Engendering Civic Identity," *American Behavioral Scientist*, 40, no. 5 (March/April 1997): 620–31.
10. Ibid., 621.
11. Ibid., 623–24.
12. Ibid., 624.
13. Ibid., 629.
14. *Journal for a Just and Caring Education*, 1, no. 4 (October 1995): 389–402.
15. Ibid., 400.
16. Center for Values and Services, Loyola College in Maryland, 1997–98, *Community Service Opportunities*, 5.
17. Internal Working Paper, Office of the Academic Vice President, Loyola College in Maryland (undated; distributed to the Board of Trustees 19 November 1997).
18. Youniss and Yates, *Community Service*, 135.
19. Ibid., 136–52.
20. Ibid., 145.
21. Ibid., 149.

22. Ibid., 151 (emphasis in original).

23. Youniss and Yates, *Roots of Civic Identity,* 13.

24. M. Douglas and S. Ney, *Missing Persons: A Critique of Personhood in the Social Sciences* (Berkeley: University of California Press, 1998), 122.

25. U.S. Department of Education, Office of Educational Research and Improvement, National Center for Educational Statistics, *Student Participation in Community Service Activity* (April 1997), 13–14.

26. See A.B. Carroll, *Business and Society: Ethics and Stakeholder Management,* 3rd ed. (Cincinnati, OH: Southwestern College Publishing, 1996), 35–40.

27. "Justice in the World," a document produced by a synod of Roman Catholic bishops meeting in Rome, 30 September to 6 November 1971; reprinted in Michael Walsh and Brian Davies, eds., *Proclaiming Justice and Peace: Documents from John XXIII—John Paul II* (Mystic, CT: Twenty-Third Publications, 1984), 190.

CHAPTER 16

A Research University Perspective

Mary Lindenstein Walshok

T his chapter raises questions about what is needed to draw America's nationally distinguished colleges and research universities into the civic lives of their communities. The author suggests the answer lies in better connecting academic and civic knowledge, through collaborative agenda setting, research, and scholarly work.

INTRODUCTION

On many campuses today, particularly research universities and the nationally distinguished liberal arts college, there is much ambivalence about what, if any role, such campuses should play in the civic issues of their regions. These nationally distinguished campuses are characterized by an academic "culture" which draws a line between "reflection" and "engagement" and celebrates an academic "lifestyle" for the most part based on full-time residential students and full-time, lifelong scholarly careers for faculty. Such campuses typically value a certain "distance" from day-to-day concerns and problem solving. Quite often, their physical location is also isolated from everyday affairs in rural, suburban, or park-like settings or walled-in enclaves in more urban landscapes.

I am both a product of such institutions and an enthusiastic member of a distinguished research university community as a professional. As such I am deeply committed to their core missions and the ways in which they conduct their "business." Where I diverge from the prevailing views on campuses such as mine is in my understanding of the nature of the "new," "knowledge based" world in which we find ourselves and the implications this has for the core intellectual work of the academy. Its implications extend far beyond the outreach initiatives too often pursued out of political or financial necessity or the service-learning provisions, which enhance the student experience and increasingly new student recruitment efforts. It has fundamental implications for how we define what needs to be known, who is qualified as an expert, and how knowledge in the society and knowledge in the academy can or should be linked.

Campuses such as mine continue to define the knowledge work they do in terms of the three legged stool metaphor—research, teaching, and public service, each leg of which is separate and distinct. Campuses such as mine see no real "intellectual benefits" in service and while deeply committed to the teaching/learning engagements with full-time, for the most part younger students, have yet to grasp the extent of the knowledge needs and intellectual rewards of engagement with the growing world of "lifelong" learners. We continue to operate institutionally on a fragmented industrial model of knowledge work even though our basic research and scholarship provide the seed corn for most of the developments which are fundamentally transforming the traditional paradigm of how knowledge is developed and used in work, organizations, and community life.

This civic disconnect within the academy and how to address it is my central preoccupation as an educator. It is both my belief and my experience that those institutions whose primary identity is based on a culture of basic research and scholarship have as vital a civic role to play (albeit a distinct one) as do colleges and universities with an explicit urban mission or campuses with a strong commitment to pre-professional and professional education. I would argue further that not only do institutions such as mine have a vital role to play in communities, but that through the proper expression of that role, the core intellectual work of the institution will be enriched.

THE GROWING IMPORTANCE OF KNOWLEDGE TO CIVIC ISSUES

The custodial staff at the University of California is "online." Cleaning and maintenance assignments as well as inventories of supplies and materials are all computerized. Forty or more languages are spoken in most urban school districts while the costs and benefits of bilingual education are debated in every district across the land. Modern telecommunications, which has contributed so significantly to global prosperity and interconnectivity, has also given rise to 100 channel environments which fill the airwaves with contentious radio talk shows and trivia-laden news panels 24 hours a day. As 20 percent of the population gets more and more educated and "literate" in the technologies shaping the new economy, 50 percent of urban males of color are dropping out of school. Each of these issues is not well understood among academics or the general public. How academics research and elucidate these issues needs to be informed by actual experience, just as how citizens and communities make sense of these issues requires the intellectual resources of the academy.

Technology, demography, and the global economy are transforming the content of everyday life at the local level. As a consequence, macro trends and issues, which used to be the province of "intellectuals," national policy makers, and syndicated columnists, shape the discourse and decisions of local industry, governments, and civic associations in concrete and complex ways. Instantaneous communications and networked transportation systems combine with the mobility of capital and global manufacturing and distribution systems to make it possible for "local" innovations and "local" talent to play on a world stage without having to leave home. Bill Gates in Seattle, Michael Dell in Austin, Ben and Jerry in Vermont, and Eli Calloway in San Diego speak to the devolution of wealth, power, and influence from a few major centers to a network of regional centers of significant economic, social, cultural, and increasingly political momentum.

Life is more complex in such regions and more challenging in both practical and intellectual terms than in previous eras. In such environments, knowledge per se and the kinds of knowledge discovery, development, validation, and dissemination capacities inherent in mature colleges and universities, represents a significant regional asset. In such environments the content of everyday life also is of sufficient breadth and depth to engage serious scientific and scholarly inquiry. In past periods, one thought of places such as Venice, Paris, London, or New York as the primary cauldrons of intellectual and scholarly fermentation. In this new "knowledge age," many more locales hold this promise: Stockholm, Barcelona, and Glasgow in Europe; and Pittsburgh, Atlanta, Chattanooga, San Diego, and Portland in the United States. San Diego is located at one of the most densely populated and frequently crossed international borders in the world. Portland leads the nation in addressing the vexing challenges of sustaining a precious natural environment while building globally competitive industries. Pittsburgh and Chattanooga are global models of how to transform a decaying industrial urban core into a livable city. Atlanta exemplifies how national industries and high tech can transform a basically agricultural economy.

These examples are relevant because they speak to the complexities shaping civic life everywhere and the regional contexts, which are home to institutions of higher education across the land. Nonetheless, the disconnect between the central preoccupations of our nationally distinguished colleges and universities and the civic needs and concerns of regions continues.

THE DISCONNECT BETWEEN THE ACADEMY AND COMMUNITY

There is much talk nowadays about the whys and wherefores of the isolation of America's colleges and universities from the intellectual issues, social problems, and human concerns characterizing the regions in which they operate. It ranges from observations about the putative superior value of basic research and independent scholarship, to the need for "value free" analyses, to concerns about the competencies young people need to be effective citizens as well as workers, to a preoccupation with creating new "incentives and rewards" for faculty to engage in public service. None alone is sufficient to address the deep cultural and functional divide that continues to exist.

Dan Yankelovich, the distinguished market researcher, author, and president of the Public Agenda, suggests there are 10 campus characteristics which need to be addressed before specific strategies to overcome the disconnects can be developed. In a speech to a major gathering of the American Association for Higher Education (AAHE) in January 1999, Yankelovich shared his ideas about the culture and practices of academia, which reinforce the continuing lack of meaningful connections to community. Quoting his points, they include:

1. **Low Level of Interest.** Unlike most professionals, scholars have the privilege of focusing their interests and attention on issues of concern to them in their own work. In research universities, these interests rarely focus on the communities in which they reside.
2. **Specialization.** Rarely do the problems of the local community or region correspond to the ways in which academic knowledge is divided and subdivided.
3. **Lack of Incentives.** Scholars, especially younger faculty people, have little incentive, or even a disincentive, to involve themselves in local issues: it doesn't advance tenure or promotion, and it associates them with low status "applied knowledge."
4. **An Invalid Assumption.** Scholars tend to assume that the appropriate course of action follows from a correct definition of the problem, whereas more often than not this assumption fails to hold in the world of action.
5. **A Different Time Frame.** Scholars rarely share the same time frame and sense of urgency to solve problems as members of the community.
6. **Language.** Each field develops its own jargon and rhetoric that serves to block communication with the community.
7. **Nonrelevance of the Fact/Value Distinction.** Social scientists, in particular, are uncomfortable in settings where people co-mingle facts and values as a single indivisible whole.

8. **Difference in Subculture Values.** The values of the academic subculture are strikingly different from those of the larger community, creating a divide between them.

9. **Ill at Ease with Power.** Scholars are often uncomfortable in the world of power and consequently often fail to correctly assess the political cross-pressures operating in a community.

10. **Will/Skill Dilemmas.** The most intractable community problems involve will/skill dilemmas: problems where both the will to solve the problem and relevant skills are lacking. Most scholars are unfamiliar with knowledge strategies needed to deal with these kinds of issues. [1]

Yankelovich's key point is that the knowledge paradigm within which universities operate is at odds with that of communities because it assumes only one valid form of knowledge, knowledge associated with science. Communities draw upon many paradigms and it is essential for academics to understand and engage those as well as their own if genuine discourse is to happen.

Of most significance in all of this is that the challenge to civic engagement is an intellectual and cultural one as much as it is a problem of models, rewards, and incentives. It is also the case, as will be argued in the following section, how campuses determine to overcome the disconnect will vary enormously depending upon campus culture, history, and capacities as well as the particular needs and circumstances of the community.

At the same AAHE session at which Yankelovich spoke, Michael Schudson, a distinguished professor of communication and MacArthur Fellow suggested that strategies for addressing the barriers described by Yankelovich vary by institutional "type." Within research universities, how the disconnect is addressed is more likely to be linked to activities which resonate with their identities as centers of knowledge discovery and development than with the incorporation of a whole new set of "service" related incentives and activities.

At the same meeting of AAHE, Michael Schudson and the author, co-directors of the newly formed, PEW-funded, UCSD Civic Collaborative with Dan Yankelovich, described the goals and major activities of such a collaborative within the context of a major research university. Schudson pointed out that

> UCSD's identity and success lie with its record of research. The premise of the Collaborative is that research faculty who become more mindful of the life of their own community will become more alert, enterprising and informed scholars. This is especially true for faculty and graduate students in the social sciences, but it applies to those in the arts, humanities, medicine and natural sciences as well. [2]

I emphasized that a major objective of the Civic Collaborative is to connect academic knowledge of the kind that resides in a research university with civic knowledge of the kind to be found in the larger community to both enlarge the capacity of everyone to address community issues and the intellectual horizons of the humanities and social sciences faculties in particular. We hope to bridge the current gap between academic and civic knowledge at UCSD with the following sorts of activities:

1. Conduct dialogues, roundtables, and commissioned papers seeking a better understanding of the forms of both academic and civic knowledge.
2. Develop models of how a research university can learn from its community through such things as (a) designing mechanisms that draw civic knowledge into academic discourse; and (b) creating learning opportunities for faculty and students in the community, through mini research grants and activities which encourage thinking, writing, and research concerning San Diego.
3. Identify important databases and sources of civic knowledge about San Diego, and connect these to analogous sources of academic knowledge at UCSD.
4. Introduce the community to the resources and unique research capacities represented by a campus such as UCSD.
5. Sponsor conferences, collective research enterprises, journal issues, and edited books which describe what we are learning, both about the region and about our process of deliberately attempting to close the gap between academic and civic knowledge.

These detailed points developed by Schudson suggest a somewhat different way of thinking about civic engagement and contributions than is typically discussed in higher education forums. However, it is a way of defining the opportunity and challenges that both resonate with the culture of research universities and complement many of the more direct service, technical assistance, applied, and contract research activities being pursued in other campus settings. It opens the door to providing the critical convening, discussion, and analytic activities which can fill regional knowledge gaps, enhance public understanding of issues, and influence policy. Even to accomplish what Schudson proposes requires important attitude shifts, new functions, and supportive institutional mechanisms.

CLOSING THE GAP BETWEEN ACADEMIC AND CIVIC KNOWLEDGE

Colleges with scholarly depth and basic research universities represent unique resources in their communities. Their approaches to inquiry, and their traditions of openness and disinterestedness, and their orientation to learning (which is typically analytical, reflective, and critical), make them ideally suited to be conveners and facilitators of dialogues on controversial issues and contradictory positions—to serve as "honest brokers" in regions typically characterized by fragmented specialists and special interest politics. The infrastructure of support for research and scholarship such institutions possess, in the form of libraries, labs, archives, databases, and topical specialists, also equips them to develop new knowledge or search broadly for information and unique knowledge resources which can fill important regional "knowledge gaps." Finally, their participation in national and international networks of discourse and expertise allows them to connect regional concerns and competencies to global resources. If, however, they are to realize these capacities in civic contexts, they need to address three critical factors:

1. building a culture, which supports multidirectional dialogues and shared expertise;
2. integrating professionals committed to knowledge dissemination and integration into the academy; and
3. developing institutional mechanisms with the resources and programmatic capacities to support initiatives focussed on marrying academic and civic knowledge needs and interests.

The critical dimensions of the first characteristic are anchored in a perception of the university as one of many knowledge resources in the community rather than as the "only" or even the "premiere" knowledge center. It requires faculty who are ready to learn from the community as well as teach, whose orientation is one of genuine interest, curiosity, and ultimately respect. This in turn fosters exploration and discovery, as well as conversations and dialogue, which in turn begins to build mutual understanding and trust. With that, the opportunity to serve as a convener of larger groups around broader issues can occur in an atmosphere which encourages mutual learning and shared agenda setting.

The San Diego Dialogue, a university-based cross-border regional research policy analysis, and community dialogue initiative is a good example of this principle. It grew out of a series of initially fragmented conversations with a diverse range of thoughtful, but unconnected individuals, about the emergent forces shaping the San Diego region. Of particular concern to all of them was the absence of leadership capable of integrating the achievements of the past with the promise of the future. Drawing upon these early conversations, the Dialogue convened a small group of academics and community leaders who initially thought a community "visioning" process was needed, but they wanted first to learn more about the changing region. Facilitated by a thoughtful academic (now the Dialogue's director), topics of concern, about which more was needed to be known, were identified. This gave rise to a series of "conversations" with practitioners and academics from around the country with relevant knowledge or experience, as well as data gathering and some new research on regional topics about which little was known.

Within a year, the importance of San Diego's relationship to Tijuana emerged (to the surprise of most) as one of the critical factors shaping the region's future. Unbeknownst to traditional civic leaders, Tijuana was growing in as fast and economically complex ways as San Diego. Through the Dialogue process they discovered that Japan Airlines was flying daily nonstop flights into Rodriguez Field; there was rapid growth in Tijuana-based manufacturing facilities, such as the SONY plant, which was producing 50 percent of the televisions SONY sold in North America; offices of professional firms such as Price Waterhouse and Baker and McKinsey were opening in Tijuana; and demographic analysis revealed a significant increase in well-educated, affluent Mexicans in Tijuana. The Dialogue's reports and early networking activities with Mexican academics, industrialists, and professionals resulted in a completely changed sense of the region's capabilities and future opportunities. This shared understanding built a deep commitment to supporting the Dialogue as a regional "intelligence" resource. Over six years, what began as an exploratory process has grown into a multifaceted program of regional conversations, research projects, community forums, and leadership briefings supported by a quarterly journal, newsletters, and regular policy papers on regional issues.

The Dialogue is funded by more than one million dollars from private sources annually and has grown to 120 members, another 300 friends, and a staff of 12. It evolved out of an exploratory and dialogic process which built a broad base of stakeholders in the community and the academy. It is not a public service program in response to an RFP, which will end when the funds dry up. It is a university-sponsored, community-anchored institutional mechanism, which serves an important civic purpose with strength and integrity. It continuously serves as a convener of otherwise disconnected or contradictory interests which through discourse and knowledge development, elucidates important regional issues. As such it builds on the distinctive culture and capabilities of its research university home.

Equally important to building the civic connection is the integration of new kinds of intellectuals and knowledge professionals into the fabric of university life. At research institutions, faculties rely on research assistants and post-doctoral students, comprehensive libraries and well-equipped labs, release time to write books and pursue new research topics, and project grants and fellowships to focus energy. They also turn to substantively knowledgeable editors when they publish in journals or publish with university presses. Engaging civic agendas in an intellectually meaningful way requires similar teams of variously competent individuals.

The San Diego Dialogue once again is a case in point. It has a diverse staff of "enablers," people who are good at networking and facilitating conversation; people who are good at articulating issues and identifying expert resources; people who can manage research and policy analysis in a timely manner; people who can communicate with diverse constituencies and the media; and people who can fund raise and nurture members and supporters. All of these competencies "partner with" expert faculty to yield academically credible and civically valuable knowledge on such topics as cross-border health issues, regional infrastructure needs, closing the achievement gap in the public schools, or sustainable economic development. A core group of academically qualified professionals committed to realizing the civic benefits of knowledge bring unique skills and perspectives to the partnerships with faculty whose competency and expertise are in specialty fields. The combination is unbeatable.

A culture which assures dialogue and collaboration and a cadre of knowledge professionals who partner with expert faculty represent two of the essential ingredients linking academic and civic knowledge. The third is supportive institutional mechanisms. Institutional mechanisms are stable, funded activities, offices, programs, and products. These activities and programs represent the deliverables emerging from the partnerships between faculty, other knowledge professionals, and community resources. They are the "place" where the academic and the civic are connected. These enabling mechanisms require leadership support on campus and in the community; regular streams of funding and in kind contributions from both the campus and the community; shared governance and accountability in both the academic and civic spheres; a disciplined schedule of activities and products; and a commitment to broadly communicating with constituencies about concerns, results, and activities. These are not the sorts of things large numbers of faculty can easily integrate into existing research and teaching missions without skilled and knowledgeable partners. These are not the sorts of things traditional academic departments and schools, originally organized to educate the young and pursue scholarly work, are capable of managing. However, they represent the capabilities through which and resources upon which campus-wide academic knowledge can draw to build two-way bridges with community groups, civic knowledge resources, and timely regional trends and issues. Here again, the case of the San Diego Dialogue might be instructive.

In its start-up phase, the Dialogue was opportunistic in terms of issues and funders, building its credibility and support base through timely and useful events, studies, and reports. Through a slow process of institutionalization, the Dialogue has retained its capacity to be opportunistic and responsive while managing a coherent set of annual programs and products. These include four membership plenaries annually on issues of current interest coming out of staff-supported study groups; topical faculty and student-conducted research and policy papers stimulated by the plenaries and funded by a consortium of San Diego and Tijuana companies; publication of a quarterly journal; three to four leadership forums on cross-border issues presented by senior Mexican and United States officials; community forums on issues affecting the region; and periodic luncheon roundtables with elected officials. Special events for "friends and donors" have also become part of the annual schedule. In all of these events, activities, and research projects, the Dialogue facilitates collegial participation among diverse faculty and community members. All of these activities represent "institutional mechanisms" through which academic and civic purposes are married. They assure continuous dialogue and shared agenda setting and build a broadly networked "community of learning."

CONCLUSION

This chapter focussed initially on the unique characteristics of nationally distinguished colleges and universities, which, like all campuses, are facing new claims for civic engagement. It outlined some of the distinctive barriers to engagement as articulated by the thoughtful analyst and author Dan Yankelovich. It then suggested that research universities may have a unique contribution to make because of the intellectual traditions they represent and the knowledge development capacities they have. However, if universities are to fully realize those capacities and play their much-needed role as convenors of discourse groups, clarifiers of timely issues, and articulators of civic alternatives, they need to possess three essential characteristics. These three characteristics—a culture of dialogue and shared agenda setting, a willingness to partner with new kinds of knowledge professionals, and a commitment to well-funded and effectively managed institutional mechanisms—create an "enabling environment" for connecting academic and civic knowledge. Using the example of how the San Diego Dialogue was formed and developed as a university-based, community-anchored, cross-border forum, the chapter has provided readers with both ideas and practical examples of how it is possible to close the gap between academic and civic knowledge.

NOTES

1. D. Yankelovich, Panel Presentation Remarks presented at the American Association for Higher Education meeting, San Diego, CA, 23 January 1999.
2. M. Schudson, Panel Presentation Remarks presented at the American Association for Higher Education meeting, San Diego, CA, 23 January 1999.

FURTHER READING

Walshok, Mary Lindenstein, *Knowledge without Boundaries: What America's Research Universities Can Do for the Economy, the Workplace and the Community.* San Francisco: Jossey-Bass, 1995.

PART 5

· · · · · · · · · · · ·

Special Challenges

CHAPTER 17

Civic Engagement and the Academic Disciplines

Edward Zlotkowski

We do, however, take as axiomatic that current levels of political knowledge, political engagement, and political enthusiasm are so low as to threaten the vitality and stability of democratic politics in the United States. We believe political education is inadequate across the board.

> ASPA Task Force on Civic Education in the 21st Century,
> *PS: Political Science* (1989)

[U]sing education to change civic participation is more easily outlined than accomplished. . . . if you propose a curriculum that promotes active citizenship in a society where apathy reigns, the reforms implemented are likely to produce only diluted versions of the envisioned changes.

> Hindy Lauer Schachter, "Civic Education: Three Early American Political Science Association Committees and Their Relevence to Our Times,"
> *PS: Political Science* (1998)

[T]he action is all peripheral: it takes place at the level of departmental faculties. . . . Departments are the units in which the institution's strategy for academic development is formulated in practice.

> D. Kennedy, "Another Century's End, Another Revolution for Higher Education," *Change* (1995)

[F]aculty stressed that the rewards and recognition system in place in their disciplines influenced strongly how they allocated their time. For many faculty, it was the standards and expectations of the discipline and not the priorities of the institution that determined their priorities.

R.M. Diamond and B.E. Adam, *The Disciplines Speak: Rewarding the Scholarly, Professional, and Creative Work of Faculty* (1995)

DEFINING THE PROBLEM

The four statements cited at the start of this chapter may be said in their aggregate to define the problem of successfully formulating and implementing a strategy of civic engagement in and through higher education. The first and second statements suggest the sheer magnitude of the task: Currently "political education is inadequate *across the board*" [emphasis added] and, even were this deficiency remedied, we would still be faced with failure if our remedy were to be applied in the context of a politically "apathetic society." The third and fourth statements directly address the challenge of devising an educationally effective remedy; namely, that institutional mandates will, in most instances, flounder on the rocks of departmental autonomy, and institutional priorities may be less influential than disciplinary norms.

It was this set of considerations that originally precipitated and continues to guide the work that has come to be identified with the American Association for Higher Education's (AAHE) monograph series on service-learning in the academic disciplines. However, the beginnings of that work lie with another national organization: Campus Compact.

Founded in 1985 as an "organization of college and university presidents committed to helping students develop the values and skills of citizenship through participation in public and community service,"[1] the Compact quickly found that the task it had set itself was more difficult than it had anticipated. Hence, it commissioned Tim Stanton, then associate director of Stanford's Haas Center, to investigate how its effectiveness could be enhanced. In a 1990 report entitled "Integrating Public Service with Academic Study: The Faculty Role," Stanton suggested that although faculty buy-in was key to almost any kind of long-term institutional undertaking, ". . . with some exceptions, faculty have been noticeably absent from these [service] activities. Little attention has been given to the faculty role in supporting student service efforts and in setting an example of civic participation and leadership through their own efforts." From that point on, the Compact's civic engagement strategies—as well as those of its affiliate state compacts and other groups such as the Council of Independent Colleges—have had a significant faculty component.

One especially concrete outcome of this new interest in faculty participation was the creation, under the Compact's auspices, of a new national association. The "Invisible College," as this new association called itself, was initially conceived of as a

> faculty-based organization which would provide a free space for faculty to explore the difficult issues raised by service-learning. . . . This organization [would] create a national faculty voice that could speak alongside the COOL's [Campus Outreach Opportunity League] national student voice and the Compact's national college president voice.[2]

And it was within the context of this new association that the plan for a series of volumes on service-learning and the academic disciplines first took shape. In May 1994, my role as series editor became official.

Eventually, the home of this series migrated to AAHE which, thanks to the commitment of then vice president Lou Albert, was willing and able to provide the concrete resources needed to see the series through to publication. Currently nearing completion—after almost four years of work by more than 300 academic contributors—the monograph series has turned out to be far more than a peer-reviewed demonstration that civic engagement through community-based work is possible across the entire academic spectrum; it has also become an effective tool for continuing and deepening the conversation in disciplinary circles about what it means to do such work.

The importance of recognizing the disciplines as strategic leverage points would be hard to underestimate. Their influence—through their organization into academic departments—is, of course, the point of the third and fourth statements with which this chapter began. On the institutional level, it is the department rather than the administration that determines *how*, if not actually *what*, policy decisions are implemented; on the cultural level, the agenda of a faculty member's discipline often takes precedence over her/his commitment to institutional priorities. In other words, as important as presidential leadership and institutional mission are with regard to civic education and civic empowerment, they cannot achieve even modest goals without the *active* cooperation of an institution's faculty—organized into discipline-based departments. As Eastern Michigan's Deborah DeZure, director of the Faculty Center for Instructional Excellence, has noted in explaining her center's highly successful discipline-focused strategy:

> While useful in many ways . . . centralized services are often underused by faculty, rejected by many as too remote from their disciplinary teaching concerns. For many faculty, *teaching* means *teaching history* or *teaching music* or *teaching biology*. For them, instructional development should become more disciplinary, engaging these faculty by exploring

issues of teaching in the context of their departmental expectations and their disciplinary values and modes of discourse [original italics].[3]

Thus, the *institution-specific* efforts begun by the Compact early in the decade have found in AAHE's monograph series a critical *discipline-specific* complement. Even on the department level, specific strategies for and concrete models of academically rigorous "public work"[4] now lie close at hand. But equally important has been the role the series has played in helping extend and deepen the dialogue about what it means to do such work within specific disciplinary contexts. Despite much initial public skepticism, the national associations corresponding to the series' 18 disciplines/interdisciplinary areas have proven themselves to be invaluable allies in facilitating that dialogue and in putting community involvement/civic literacy on the national educational agenda. Indeed, if American higher education is to reposition itself to meet the citizenship needs of the twenty-first century, it will only be with their help.

DISCIPLINARY TRADITIONS

One could hardly blame anyone for seeing the disciplines as a primary obstacle instead of a possible ally in promoting greater civic engagement. A quick scan of documents such as those contained in Diamond and Adam's *The Disciplines Speak* (National Disciplinary Association descriptions of legitimate faculty work) or the Association of American Colleges and Universities' (AAC&U) *Reports from the Field* (National Disciplinary Association descriptions of goals for the undergraduate major) reveal, for the most part, little recognition of civic engagement as part of the disciplines' self-understanding of what they are about. This is not surprising since, in many instances, the governing boards of these national associations are in the hands of academics whose primary commitment is to specialized research. Indeed, many disciplines continue to experience a process of internal ramification whereby the distinctions between disciplinary subdivisions threaten to shatter the original discipline into a collection of so many new, ever more narrowly defined academic areas.

Nor is the problem "merely" one of functional organization. History, tradition, even intellectual momentum would seem to lie with those forces in the academy that favor academic insularity over civic engagement. Some, in fact, have proposed that our prevailing academic configuration, with its characteristic disciplinary fragmentation and specialization, represents a natural outcome not just of the modern university in its original, nineteenth-century conception but of even older, deeper assumptions that can be traced back to René Descartes and the seventeenth-century foundations of modern science. Thus, for example, Bruce Whilshire has argued that "[Descartes' philosophical thought] anticipates the contemporary research university and its master problem: despite its vast research capacities and its knowledge, it exists in strange detachment from crucial human realities. . . ."[5] Such detachment substitutes for direct engagement a realm of "objective" problem-solving in which the universal validity and applicability of the modern scientific method is assumed, and the only task is to parcel out problems among a variety of disciplinary researchers:

> The secular university—the knowledge factory—emerged within [a] modern myth [whereby] science is forever complete with respect to basic method and to mastery of all the basic physical laws [and] all that needs to be done to know and control the world is to locate each scientific specialty, await the results from each and then, if we wish, add them up.[6]

The consequences of this conceptual template have been far-reaching. They include, in addition to the elimination of all things subjective from the domain of valid knowledge, the development of a concept of academic "professionalization" that actually feeds upon its separation from nonexpert knowers. Whilshire describes how, in the late 1800s, an ideal of scientific expertise quickly came to prevail across the academic spectrum:

> The trend to greater specialization was not limited to the sciences. A secular ethos of proficiency and expertise created a tidal force that carried the humanities with it. In the 1870s and 80s two hundred learned societies were formed in addition to teacher's groups. Every university divided itself into departments according to the divisions of these academic professional associations. Authority was now vested with master knowers in specialized areas as these knowers were recognized within that sector nationwide. Professional groupings began to shoulder aside local communities. Individual advancement within professions tended to supplant civic duty.[7]

To be sure, many of the new specializations that emerged at this time (e.g., sociology and political science) had as their original goal social reform and service to society. Such a goal, however, had difficulty surviving the demise of the Progressive Era when conservative political forces and disillusionment following upon World War I combined to push academic research away from direct social applications.[8] With the advent of the cold war and its own brand of conservative reaction, direct social applications again came under direct attack from the right.[9]

However, even more potent than the threats of right-wing politicians was the attraction of government money. America's competition with the Soviet Union meant that technological expertise and specialization were now a matter of national importance, and once again, developments in more technical areas had a ripple effect across higher education. As Lewontin points out in his essay "The Cold War and the Transformation of the Academy":

> Although the power to command . . . favorable conditions of employ-ment [as a result of Government investment in research] accrues at first-hand to established academics in the natural and some of the social sciences, primarily at large research universities, it has changed the relationship between institutions and academics generally. . . . Lower teaching loads in science have meant lower teaching loads in the humanities. [10]

Furthermore, the availability of research money did more than tip the balance further towards specialized research. It also reinforced a trend evident from the earliest decades of the modern university: the tendency to substitute disciplinary stature for local engagement.[11] Thus, the disciplines became the conduits if not the cause of an ever greater distancing of the academy from concrete social problem-solving.

When one adds to all these factors the wedding of America's post-World War II hegemony to its championing of behaviorism as an especially American approach to knowing,[12] one can well understand why the cold war decades may have marked the high water mark of disciplinary withdrawal from civic engagement.

SIGNS OF CHANGE

In his often fiercely polemical review of contemporary higher education, *Killing the Spirit: Higher Education in America*, Page Smith opines that the allegedly scientific objectivity of the social sciences, their elevation of detachment over engagement "has run out its string."[13] Whether or not such a generalization is justified—especially in light of the powerful conceptual and organizational forces identified in the last section—it does seem clear that the end of the cold war both coincides with and contributes to the emergence of important new developments in the way in which at least some of the disciplines understand their purpose and their responsibilities to a larger civic whole.

Indeed, even in the case of the Diamond/Adam and AAC&U disciplinary statements previously referred to, one can find many sometimes subtle, some-times more explicit indications that America's national disciplinary associa-tions are hardly the socially impervious monoliths they are often made out to be. Thus, for example, the statement by the Association of American Geogra-phers (AAG) on faculty roles and rewards actually recognizes the discipline's closeness to real-world problem-solving as one of its important strengths.[14] The corresponding statement by the American Chemical Society contains the in some ways startling recognition that

> . . . the creation of new approaches to stimulating the interest of elementary school children in science and the communication of such insights through books, monographs, reports or publications represent *an important form of scholarship.* Interest in the area of *outreach as an area of vital importance to the discipline of chemistry* is relatively new and undeveloped [emphasis added].[15]

Or, to take an example from the AAC&U volume on student goals, we can find the following from a report sanctioned by the American Psychological Association:

> We recommend an additional component for all undergraduate majors in psychology. An interpersonal skills and group-process laboratory is included in all of our proposed models in order to develop students' abilities to work in groups. Whenever possible, we recommend that this laboratory (or the senior year applied project) be combined with a community-service component. . . . Supervised community service can instill a sense of responsibility that is critical for informed citizenship while addressing a broad range of human needs.[16]

Suggestions of a similar nature can be found in the disciplinary statements of several other disciplines in both volumes.

Sentiments such as those just cited clearly represent disparate expressions of civic consciousness in a culture that may at first seem uniformly hostile to change. I mentioned in the last section the grip that academics from research I institutions have had on the governing boards of many national disciplinary associations. One could easily make the case that it is their personal and professional influence rather than the appearance of random statements of civic obligation that continues to define the operative culture of the disciplines. However, even in this regard there have been some notable recent developments. For example, incoming presidents of both the Academy of Management and the National Communication Association have demonstrated a strong commitment to service and social engagement—a commitment that has already had a significant effect on their associations' national programming. In other disciplines (American Sociological Association and American Political Science Association), influential member researchers whose agenda includes non-elitist community engagement are making their voices heard more effectively than ever before.

Thus the question suggests itself: Do the phenomena just referred to point to any larger, deeper trends? Can we identify any more than purely local factors at work here?

In an extensively researched, multipart essay entitled "The Condition of American Liberal Education," Bruce Kimball suggests that there now exist across the American higher education landscape a set of "seven . . . recent developments in liberal education" that can be "collectively construed as 'pragmatic,' either in the sense of being conceptually rooted in pragmatism or in the sense of being rationalized, justified in principle, by pragmatic concepts."

> It might even be said that pragmatism is now infusing liberal education: that pragmatism is pouring over and through the academic dikes that long kept it outside of the liberal arts and that a broad consensus is therefore emerging around a view of liberal education that may be termed "pragmatic."[17]

These seven developments include: (1) multiculturalism; (2) values and service; (3) community and citizenship; (4) general education; (5) commonality and cooperation between college and other levels of the higher education system; (6) teaching as learning and inquiry; and (7) assessment.[18]

Whether or not one accepts Kimball's interpretation of these developments as collectively sharing a neo-pragmatist identity, it would seem hard to deny his more fundamental, descriptive claim that these developments are increasingly familiar, even ubiquitous features of our educational landscape. Take, for example, the statements by the American Chemical Society and the American Psychological Association that were cited earlier in this chapter. The first clearly reflects a concern with "cooperation between college and other levels of the higher education system" while the second explicitly points to the importance of "community and citizenship."

Pragmatism, of course, immediately conjures up the legacy of John Dewey with its emphasis on the educational power of reflective practice and democratic deliberation. Several influential educational thinkers have recently returned to these concepts, insisting that experientially based, constructivist approaches to education[19] and/or democratic practice inside and outside the classroom[20] must be part of higher education's future. It is interesting, in this regard, to note the many, varied ways in which these ideas have found their way into disciplinary thinking and area-specific concerns.

For example, several technically oriented disciplines (e.g., engineering, chemistry, and accounting) have lately published new guidelines on the competencies henceforth to be required of their students. These include, to cite the Accounting Education Change Commission's monograph *Intentional Learning: A Process for Learning to Learn in the Accounting Curriculum*, such nontechnical, citizenship-related items as "awareness of personal and social values"; "ability to interact with culturally and intellectually diverse people"; and "knowledge of the activities of business, government, and nonprofit organizations, and of the environments in which they operate."[21] In fact, the new competencies are more weighted toward general communication and social skills than they are toward any form of discipline-specific expertise.

Looking towards the opposite end of the academic cultural spectrum, we find new emphasis being placed on a distinction between "Orators and Philosophers."[22] This distinction—between the private sphere, which emphasizes reason and analysis, and the public sphere, which emphasizes language and action—has become a commonplace in disciplines such as English and communication studies. As the rhetorical tradition gains more and more adherents, it drives the focus of the discipline away from a search for rational certainties and logical distinctions to questions of policy and public effectiveness. Needless to say, this latter tradition accords well with the values that inform pragmatism.

One final example. At the beginning of this section I referred to the claim made by Page Smith, himself an eminent historian, that the social sciences had just about "run out [their] string," meaning that their claims to scientific objectivity had largely exhausted their usefulness, leaving in their place a need to reconsider the value of *engagement* as a vehicle of scholarship. In a recent essay, "Listening to the Evidence: Service Activity and Understanding Social Phenomena," the philosopher Hugh Lacey[23] directly challenges the value of the social science's traditional claim to be value-free:

> While sound understanding is opposed to both ideology and illusion, it is not uninformed by values. From values one cannot derive what is possible, but values can attune us to realms of possibilities that are worthy of investigation. Moreover, in human affairs certain possibilities can be realized only if there are people who hold certain values, who desire that those possibilities be realized, and who are motivated to act to bring them to realization.

In linking understanding, values, and engagement, Lacey's essay parallels the work of an ever growing number of social scientists for whom participatory action research—i.e., research *in* and *with* communities—has begun to replace an older model of merely applied research—i.e., research *on* communities.

Reconceptualizations of the health professions with a shift from corrective clinical practice to preventive community-based practice, management education's "diasporic shift"[24] to real-world learning, renewed interest in "public history," "public science," and "civic journalism"—taken together, all these and other largely unconnected phenomena suggest at least three things. First, the observation made by Kimball and others that some kind of shift is taking place and that much of that shift bears some kind of conceptual resemblance to the ideas and values of American pragmatism is probably accurate. Second, whatever is taking place represents an aggregate of "local" responses that leave intact the academic paradigm that has set the agenda during the cold war decades. What Gene Rice has said of changing faculty expectations in general can also be seen to apply, *mutatis mutandi*, here: While "one set of performance criteria coming out of an earlier era" continues to prevail," faculty are also beginning "to respond to the imperatives of a vigorous change agenda. . . ."[25] Third, the new developments coming to the forefront may very well make civic responsibility and citizenship skills less foreign to higher education's agenda but they do not by any means guarantee that change—even educationally progressive change—will lead to significant civic results.

THE TASK AHEAD

If the first and second sections of this chapter have any validity, our final task must be to suggest how, given the importance of the disciplines, the departments organized around them, and the national disciplinary associations that service them, the conceptual openings identified above can be strategically used to leverage a renewal of civic engagement. Any such strategic plan, it seems to me, must begin with one incontrovertible fact: disciplinary perspectives and disciplinary identities—no matter how misguided or even counter-productive—really do matter to the vast majority of faculty. Hence, no plan of action that hopes to be successful can afford to gloss over what the disciplines claim as their conceptual and cultural inheritance. The by and large very progressive statement by the Association of American Geographers referred to earlier makes this point explicitly clear. Having included in its statement a significant section on outreach and the many ways in which geographers can and should reach out to more than just their peers, the report warns:

> The fulfillment of *civic* responsibilities should not be confused with professional citizenship. However laudable, an activity that is not grounded in disciplinary knowledge, faculty role expertise, or both, has no place in faculty reward evaluations [original emphasis].[26]

The distinction the geographers make here between "civic responsibilities" in a broad sense and "professional citizenship" is of primary importance to almost all members of traditional disciplines. Nothing is more common, in my experience, than for someone trained in one discipline to recognize all kinds of civic opportunities in other disciplines while earnestly defending the limited opportunities open to his/her own. Unless faculty can be made to feel that what is being asked of them genuinely conforms to their professional image of themselves, they will not act.

From this it follows that our first task in enlisting the disciplines in an agenda of civic renewal must be to help them think through what this means in terms of their own vocabulary, priorities, and culture. And to do this we need to draw upon concepts like Harry Boyte and Nancy N. Kari's[27] "public work"—concepts that will allow the disciplines to retain some form of distinctive ownership and quality control over projects that nonetheless directly serve the common good. Here the national disciplinary societies have an especially important role to play, for it is through their own faculty and chair development efforts that the notion of civic engagement can be most effectively naturalized.

Second, and not unrelatedly, we need to develop much greater sophistication and flexibility in working with the idea of civic engagement. Here recent works like C.A. Rimmerman's *The New Citizenship: Unconventional Politics, Activism, and Service*[28] can be especially useful for they challenge us to think of civic engagement and citizenship skills in new ways. Without directly challenging R.D. Putnam[29] and his warnings of a widespread decline in "social capital"—networks, norms, and trust—that enable participants to act together more effectively to pursue shared objectives,[30] Rimmerman nonetheless characterizes his book as "a response to those who contend that the citizenry has little interest in American politics and in participating in decisions that affect the quality and direction of their lives."[31] Drawing upon studies by the Harwood Group, Rimmerman suggests that "the key to citizen participation . . . [is] the possibility of change, not the certainty of success",[32] indeed, that "At the very same time that voter turnout has been in decline, we have witnessed an explosion of citizen activism."[33]

Thus, the way to the "new citizenship" passes through opportunities for meaningful community engagement—whether or not such engagement is regarded as "political" in a traditional sense. Rimmerman sums up his case as follows:

> Underlying the development of a participatory conception of citizenship is a belief that education at all levels of society should prepare students for active participation in their communities, their workplaces, and in public policy decision-making at the grass roots. Students should think of their roles as citizens in ways that will enable them to rise above merely voting in periodic elections and venting their frustrations on call-in talk shows. A curriculum rooted in critical education for citizenship will enable students to explore these possibilities, the barriers, and how the barriers might be overcome. The goal should be to challenge the traditional political socialization process to the extent that it prevents discussion of alternative conceptions of citizenship.[34]

Putting together the new citizenship with respect for disciplinary perspectives, one can envision a curriculum where disciplines and departments actively explore the many ways in which the expertise and skills they foster can be further honed and developed in the context of public problem-solving.

But there remains a third aspect of this disciplinary strategy that must be explored and implemented. Respect for disciplinary perspectives and an expanded concept of citizenship cannot by themselves translate community service or public work into civic renewal. For this to happen, they must both be embedded in a culture of reflective practice, a culture that actively processes faculty and student involvement and turns it into civic knowledge. This practice may well be the nub of the matter, for American higher education has not shown much appetite for such self-conscious processing. However, without reflection, even effective community undertakings may never rise to the level of truly civic action or public problem-solving. Instead, they may well remain isolated "technical" interventions that arise solely out of exclusive, expert knowledge and have no implications for how we can begin to work together across social sectors to reclaim our public life.

CONCLUDING REMARKS

Having spent the last four years working on an 18-volume series on community-based work in and through the academic disciplines, I am acutely aware of the vast reserves of public concern and civic creativity possessed by our faculty and students. When this series was first conceived, part of the logic for selecting the disciplines to be represented included a desire to demonstrate that there is indeed no area of higher education where civic involvement is not called for and significant public work is not possible. Historians, philosophers, and rhetoricians have joined accountants, biologists, and engineers to make this point. Faculty and students from every sector of higher education—private research I universities through secular and sectarian liberal arts colleges through community colleges—have joined together to demonstrate just what is possible when higher education deliberately seeks to partner with the communities that surround and sustain it.

At the same time, I know from the student comments that lace these volumes just how transformative such involvement not only can be, but has been—for hundreds, perhaps thousands of students in every area of the country. From this perspective, Rimmerman's prescription for the "new citizenship" is very much on target. Still, we remain only at the threshold of this undertaking. So few faculty have had community-related work as part of their disciplinary training or general academic experience, there exists an enormous need to develop in this area models, guidelines, and venues for scholarly exchange. The monograph series itself represents a significant start, but only a start. The more faculty move from "why even bother?" to "where can I learn more?," the more serious becomes the congruence of civic engagement and faculty development.

In mapping out strategies for such development, the national disciplinary associations and their regional affiliates will, of necessity, be primary players. Already we can see significant differences in interest and momentum between those disciplines with which AAHE has collaborated in its monograph project and those where no such organizing activity has been present. For the former, creation of one peer-reviewed text tailored to a specific disciplinary constituency has led to plans for other publications, to special conference programming, to a general elevation within the discipline of the potential of such work. For the latter, alternatives to the traditional disciplinary paradigm remain little more than the private interest of individual members.

This chapter began with an American Political Science Association claim that its Task Force on Civic Education in the twenty-first century regarded as "axiomatic that current levels of political knowledge, political engagement, and political enthusiasm are so low as to threaten the vitality and stability of democratic politics in the United States." It is appropriate that we also conclude with that observation since it not only reemphasizes the magnitude of the task but is itself the result of a national disciplinary association initiative. Unless we are able to "cross reference" our efforts—working "vertically" through institutional groupings and "horizontally" through disciplinary affiliations—our efforts will lack the kind of multidimensionality we will need to impact a century-long trajectory of civic disengagement and the almost fabled inertia of academic culture.

NOTES

1. Campus Compact: A Season of Service 1997–1998. Providence, RI: Campus Compact.
2. J. Wallace, "Invisible College History," 1997 Invisible College National Gathering, Program 5.
3. D. DeZure, "Closer to the Disciplines: A Model for Improving Teaching Within Departments," AAHE Bulletin, 8, no. 6 (Feb. 1996): 9–12.
4. H.C. Boyte and N.N. Kari, Building America: The Democratic Promise of Public Work, (Philadelphia: Temple University Press, 1996).
5. B. Whilshire, The Moral Collapse of the University: Professionalism, Purity, and Alienation (Albany: State University of New York Press, 1990), 40.
6. Ibid., 45.
7. Ibid., 64.
8. P. Smith, Killing the Spirit: Higher Education in America (New York: Penguin, 1990), 130, 303.
9. Ibid., 245.
10. I.W. Lewontin, "The Cold War and the Transformation of the Academy," in The Cold War and the University: Toward an Intellectual History of the Postwar Years, ed. N. Chomsky, R.C. Lewontin, I. Katznelson, L. Nader, and D. Montgomery (New York: The New Press, 1997), 30.
11. Ibid., 27.
12. N. Chomsky, Objectivity and Liberal Scholarship (Detroit, MI: Black & Red, 1997).
13. Smith, Killing the Spirit, 237.

14. Diamond and Adam, *The Disciplines Speak: Rewarding the Scholarly, Professional & Creative Work of Faculty* (Washington, DC: American Association of Higher Education, 1995), 40.

15. Ibid., 53.

16. American Association of Colleges and Universities, *Reports from the Field* (Washington, DC: American Association of Colleges and Universities, 1990): 164.

17. B.A. Kimball, *The Condition of American Liberal Education: Pragmatism and a Changing Tradition* (New York: College Board Publications, 1995), 89.

18. Ibid., 97.

19. C. Argyris, *Reasoning, Learning, and Action: Individual and Organizational* (San Francisco: Jossey-Bass, 1982); D.A. Schön, *The Reflective Practitioner* (New York: Basic Books, 1983); D. Kolb, *Experiential Learning: Experience as a Source of Learning and Development* (Englewood Cliffs, NJ: Prentice Hall, 1984); D.A. Schön, *Educating the Reflective Practitioner* (San Francisco: Jossey-Bass, 1987).

20. B.R. Barber, *An Aristocracy of Everyone: The Politics of Education and the Future of America* (New York: Ballantine Books, 1992); T.L. Becker and R.A. Cuoto, eds., *Teaching Democracy by Being Democratic* (New York: Praeger, 1996); Boyte and Kari, *Building America*; C.A. Rimmerman, *The New Citizenship: Unconventional Politics, Activism, and Service* (Boulder, CO: Westview Press, 1997); C.D. Lisman, *Toward a Civil Society: Civic Literacy and Service Learning* (Westport, CT: Greenwood Publishing Group, 1998).

21. Accounting Education Change Commission, *Intentional Learning: A Process for Learning to Learn in the Accounting Curriculum*, Monograph, 1995, 94–95.

22. Kimball, *The Condition of American Liberal Education*, 3.

23. H. Lacey, "Listening to the Evidence: Service Activity and Understanding Social Phenomena," in *Beyond the Tower: Concepts and Models for Service-Learning in Philosophy*, ed. N. Chomsky et al. (New York: The New Press, 1998).

24. D. Bilimoria, "The Editor's Corner," *Journal of Management Education*, 22, no. 3 (1998): 265–68.

25. R.E. Rice, *Making a Place for the New American Scholar*, Working Paper Series: Inquiry #1 (Washington, DC: American Association for Higher Education, 1996): 2.

26. Diamond and Adam, *The Disciplines Speak*, 41.

27. Boyte and Kari, *Building America*.

28. Rimmerman, *The New Citizenship*.

29. R.D. Putnam, "Bowling Alone: America's Declining Social Capital," *Journal of Democracy*, 6, no. 1 (1995): 65–78.

30. Ibid., 67.

31. Rimmerman, *The New Citizenship*.

32. Ibid., 43.

33. Ibid., 46.

34. Ibid., 112

CHAPTER 18

Accounting for the Civic Role
Assessment and Accountability Strategies for Civic Education and Institutional Service

Jane V. Wellman

How does higher education assess and account for its civic teaching and community service roles? Bluntly put, not very well. Despite all the attention to assessment and accountability, the civic educational and service roles of higher education remain invisible, unreported, and largely undefined. The distinction between the institutional *service* roles—the community service, applied research, and civic activities of the institution that serve the public—and the institutional *civic teaching* roles is typically muddled, when they are separate although reinforcing strands of activities. Similarly, the preparation of students to be socially responsible is just one dimension of teaching the knowledge, skills, values, and motivation to be actively involved in political democratic processes. When assessments of civic contributions are conducted, they are of something else—of service-learning, of campus climate, of diversity, of student-faculty engagement, and of "service" to the community, sometimes reported as faculty service to the institution.

These assessments may tell something about civic contributions, but only indirectly, and never about both the teaching and community service roles. Further, there are no road maps connecting institutional civic assessments with public communication and accounting for the civic teaching and service roles. As a result, the responsibility of higher education to play a civic educational and service role is missing from public policy discussions. Since models do not exist, this chapter will forward some suggestions about how to go about assessing and accounting for civic contributions, both at the institutional and system levels.

WHY DO ASSESSMENTS?

There is only one argument for doing something; the rest are arguments for doing nothing. The argument for doing something is that it is the right thing to do.

F.M. Cornford, *Microcosmographica Academica: Being a Guide for the Young Academic Politician* (1923).

Probably the best argument for assessing higher education's civic teaching and service roles is that it will help to strengthen these roles, which is the right thing to do because it is in the public interest to strengthen the quality of civic life in this country. Assessment and accountability will also help keep the focus of the effort on higher education's social contributions, rather than just institutional improvement within higher education. Given the propensity of higher education to uncritically equate institutional interest with the public interest, assessment will help keep the basic purpose of the civic role in a better focus. Also, assessing civic teaching and service is just not a methodological or measurement challenge, but will require a deeper exploration about the goals and purposes of higher education's civic roles. The topics of "civic learning and service" contributions are so poorly understood that even finding simple activity and outcome measures will require an engaged conversation about values and purposes, definition of terms, and ways to demonstrate evidence of achievement. Having that conversation in the context of measurement can be a helpful way to avoid what otherwise can easily become overly abstracted on one hand or ideological on the other.

But institutionally based assessments—although they are a good place to start—are not going to be all that is needed to refocus institutional commitments toward the civic teaching and service roles. A designed linkage between institutional assessment and public accountability strategies is also needed to produce public evidence about higher education's civic teaching and service roles. Accountability tools are used at the system and state levels to tie together assessment with performance, not for purposes of institutional improvement but to guide state resource decisions and to enforce standards for achievement. As such, they operate as public expressions of values for what society expects in achievement from higher education. Without some effort from within higher education to put the civic role into the public accountability agenda, public and political measurement of results in higher education will continue to focus on measures of performance that are much more utilitarian, and designed to meet the demands of the current political environment and the international market economy.

THE NATIONAL ASSESSMENT AND ACCOUNTABILITY SCENE: WHAT THESE TERMS MEAN

Higher education has seen a huge increase in the last 15 years in attention to assessment and accountability. There is some tendency to discuss "assessments" as categorically different from "accountability," but they are really different ends of the same continuum. Assessments tend to be institutionally oriented and goal- and improvement-driven, whereas accountability measures are comparative, and oriented to performance and resource use. The desire to separate the two emanates from efforts to get faculties in particular to invest in institutional improvement strategies built around assessment.[1] To some extent assessment was promoted on the premise that its only legitimate use was institutional improvement, and that the data from institutional assessments would never be used for comparative purposes, or for resource allocation. Yet many states are taking institutional assessments and bundling them together at the statewide level into public report cards, which are melded with information about resource use and set in the context of statewide goals. For the most part, these "report cards" continue to respect the values of institutional individuation and improvement. Almost every state is engaged in some form of combining statewide assessment with strengthened public accountability, designed both to stimulate institutional improvement and to reward bottom-line performance. Rather than resisting assessment and accountability, it behooves the academy to think creatively about how to positively influence the agenda.

A study by the National Center for Postsecondary Improvement at the University of Michigan reports that 42 states have postsecondary assessment policies in place, and that most of them are moving from an exclusive focus on institutional assessment to linking assessment with accountability. The types of indicators of performance that are being put into accountability frameworks reveal a good deal about the indicators that are most likely to be used to define the core enterprise, as well as to distribute resources. South Carolina and Tennessee are the two states that are generally perceived to have gone the farthest (whether for good or ill) to promote accountability measures. A quick scan at the reporting format for those states shows the following measures:

> **South Carolina:** Instructional expenditures; curriculum; mission statement; plans and achievements; faculty credentials; faculty review including student, peer, and post-tenure review; faculty compensation; availability of the faculty to students outside the classroom; *community and public service activities of the faculty for which no extra compensation is paid*; class sizes; student/teacher ratios; number of credit hours taught by faculty; ratios of full- to part-time faculty; use of best management practices; ratio of administrative to academic costs;

reduction in "unjustified duplication" of course credits; amount of general overhead costs; high school class standing; GPAs and activities of students; graduation rates; employment rates; employer feedback on graduates; number of students continuing their education.

Tennessee: Performance of graduates on approved standardized tests of general education; performance of graduates on approved examinations in major fields of study; satisfaction of alumni and enrolled students; program accreditation; quality of non-accreditable undergraduate programs by external review; quality of masters' degree programs by external review; level of minority enrollment and enrollment vis-à-vis mission-related goals; graduation and retention rates; institutional success in the strategic planning process; improvement actions (correction of weaknesses identified in prior reports).[2]

It is not an exaggeration to say that civic teaching and service is scarcely on the radar screen of the national accountability agenda. Even South Carolina, which has taken a kitchen sink approach to accountability reporting, has just touched upon the topic, in a single measure of "service" that is related to faculty time, which does not "count" if it is compensated. Other forms of institutional service, including organized activities such as museums and galleries, public clinics, collaborations with schools, local economic development, and service to local government, are not mentioned; neither is any aspect of the student teaching and learning role. (A check with the officials in South Carolina show that most institutions are not completing this part of the survey form; therefore, no data are available. South Carolina has also decoupled efforts to link performance reporting with resources, so much of their plan may be going back to the drawing board).

The accountability "movement" shows no sign of going away. To the contrary, the direction seems to be toward more statewide "performance report cards," which become the basis for resource allocation, regulation, sanction, or reward. Higher education is at risk of being hoist on the petard of empiricism, and institutions which are delivering educational "product" at the lowest possible cost will look good, including most predictably vocational institutions which show good graduation and job placement rates. More important, the potential exists that those aspects of higher education's role which have yet to be objectified—in particular, the responsibility to educate students to be effective citizens, and to serve the public interest through service—will further erode, in favor of the rationalist utilitarian model. If the civil democratic role is to be protected, much less nourished and sustained, developing capacities for assessment and accountability has to be part of the national strategic agenda.

The public accountability agenda also needs to be engaged because of the erosion of funding for both public and private nonprofit higher education. The social funding compact between the state and traditional forms of collegiate higher education is predicated on the basis that there are broad-based public benefits to society from investment in higher education.[3] The investment is made in the form of direct appropriations in the public sector, and through tax exempt status in the nonprofit sector. The theory behind tax exemption for nonprofit institutions is that the privileged status is justified because of the public services that are provided which would otherwise have to be paid for by the state.

Although the state funding declines of the late 1980s and early 1990s have temporarily abated, the consensus among analysts is that the long-term trajectory for public funding for higher education is largely negative, as higher education remains in a very precarious spot within the structure of public finance.[4] At the same time, independent institutions are experiencing more threats to their tax-exempt status, particularly in loss of local property taxes, as cash-strapped municipal governments are looking for ways to bolster their revenues. And both public and independent higher education face the competition from the "new providers" of postsecondary education—the for-profit, vocational, and distance-based educational sectors.[5] These new providers claim to be able to deliver educational "product" more efficiently and effectively than do traditional colleges, and they do it without either direct tax support or tax exempt status. Yet the new providers typically lay no claim to performing a broader civic or community service role, either in the education of the students or in service to the communities. If collegiate institutions are to retain their privileged institutional positions within society, including public support and tax exempt status, more attention needs to be given to documenting the reasons why it remains a public interest to invest in institutions that are responsible not just for teaching and job preparation, but for research and service to society.

OBSTACLES TO ASSESSMENT

Even if assessing civic responsibility is "the right thing to do," it is also a tricky thing to do. Assessment will force greater institutional attention to the issue of civic roles, possibly at some cost to the institution. An aborted effort at assessment, could torpedo already fragile institutional commitments to service and civic education. Before embarking on assessment and accountability, it is therefore useful to identify some of the reasons why these issues remain subterranean in the academy, to anticipate obstacles the institution will face in assessment, and to build successful strategies to overcome them.

The Civic Teaching and Service Roles Are Not Priorities

Part of the reason that civic teaching and service activities are not assessed or accounted for is because these roles are not a high priority either for the institutions or for their patrons—students, parents, the state, and other benefactors. Effective undergraduate education, preparing students for jobs, and contributing to economic development through both basic and applied research are believed by many to be the essential purposes of higher education. Surveys of students show that the large majority of them enroll in college primarily to get a good job and "have a better life." There are not enough resources to allow institutions to do everything, and assessment and improvement of something that no one is particularly asking for can legitimately slide down the scale of priorities.

No One Has the Job Assignment Within the College or University

It may well be that civic teaching and service to the community is one of those topics which may be everyone's responsibility, but is in fact no one's *job*. Students' civic learning is presumed to be a by-product of the collegiate educational experience—a product of the fusion of the students with the faculty, the curriculum, and the cocurriculum. Likewise, many believe that the way the institution serves society is through successful teaching and research, and not a separate set of activities. Building successful assessment strategies will require both assigning the responsibility of assessment to someone in the institution, and spending some time talking through the ways in which the different pieces of the campus life contribute to civic teaching and service roles.

The Topic Is Undefined

There is no consistent existing vocabulary to use to begin to frame an assessment of higher education's civic teaching and service roles. What does civic education mean, and how should it be measured? What is the community service role, and what activities constitute pieces of it? What are the dimensions of community service responsibility for a community college, as distinct from a residential campus, as distinct from a research university? What are specific indicators of the way that this role is carried out? Without a way to talk about the topic using terms that are readily recognizable, assessments make little sense.

Civic Roles Are Hard to Separate from the Teaching and Research Roles

The civic educational and service roles are truly interdependent from the institution's teaching and research missions. More than teaching or even research, it is analytically very difficult to isolate these capacities from other dimensions of institutional effectiveness. Can an assessment of the "civic dimension" be separated from other assessments, and/or should it? Those who are familiar with typical academic approaches to measuring "joint products" between teaching and research are familiar with some of the analytic contortions that higher education is accustomed to performing around these kinds of issues. Surely there is a more straightforward way to think about civic teaching and community service, just how?

Service Activities Are Not the Administrative Responsibility of the College or University

Many of the activities that are community-oriented are not administered by the college or university, although they may depend on university employees or involve university students. Examples are some of the activities springing up in university research parks around the country, or some of the university/ community activities in some major urban centers. Whether these are properly labeled "service" or "instruction" or "research" is not clear, but what is clear is that as far as the university is concerned, they do not exist if they are not budgeted for inside the academy. Documenting these efforts as legitimate institutional activities or outcomes will require some capacity to know how to track people and their contributions, even if the money associated with them resides elsewhere.

Civic Educational and Community Service Issues Are Too Values-Laden to Be "Safe"

These are not consensus issues. Some people believe that civic education is the job of the K-12 schools, and inappropriate in higher education. Some believe that higher education is supposed to educate students to participate in the marketplace of the international economy, but not to educate students to be effective members of a democratic society. Others think that these are two sides of the same coin. And then there are those who approach citizenship education like sex education—something best left to the church or family.

GETTING STARTED: BUILDING SUCCESSFUL ASSESSMENT CAPACITIES

Institutional Assessments

One should start with institutional assessments done in the context of institutional mission and as a dimension of quality. A solid argument can be made that basic clarity about terminology needs to precede assessment, and that the first stage in the assessment agenda therefore needs to be to an investment in inquiry about the meaning of effective citizenship and institutional service. While that is intellectually right, to wait for clarity about those terms means forever delaying engaging of the agenda more directly. The more expedient way to proceed is to begin the assessment agenda at the institutional level, in the context of the institutional mission and as a dimension of quality, rather than as something wholly separate from "normal" institutional measures of quality. Integrating civic assessment into institutional quality review also gets the question squarely onto the agenda of existing quality assessments done through program review, institutional strategic planning, accreditation, and state accountability reporting. Not only does this help frame the civic role as a dimension of quality, but it will help avoid duplication of effort and excessive cost to the civic assessment strategy.

Leadership Commitment

A successful assessment strategy has to begin with a commitment by the leadership of the institution to engage the agenda. If the enhancement of the civic teaching and learning and community service roles are not priorities, then this probably is not worth it. Leadership ideally should begin with the college president, but it does not have to directly involve the president. In fact, there may well be instances where visible presidential leadership would backfire. A core of individuals who can manage the agenda is needed, including participation from the academic vice president, the budget office, faculty, and students. From that internal core of leadership, capacities to link with others to build the agenda—including as a first priority members of the governing board and community leaders—can proceed.

Test Stakeholder Perceptions and Build Awareness

The assessment process should begin with a systematic evaluation of the perceptions and values of key stakeholders to see where civic teaching and community service fall on their list of priorities for the institution, and to learn more about the language that is used by different constituencies to characterize the "civic role." This could be used to assess views within the institution—

from faculty, administrators, governing board members, and students—and from external communities, including the business community, parents, local community leaders, and statewide elected officials. Questionnaires, interviews, and focus group discussions are all appropriate vehicles for performing this assessment. The assessment instrument should be designed to capture information about both how people think and feel about the issues, and the values they have that will frame how they talk about it. Are these issues ones that are not on peoples' minds, but that—when they think about them—they feel positively about? Or do they think about them a good deal, and have passionate feelings about them? If they are not interested in the civic teaching or institutional service roles, what are their priorities for higher education?

The presumption that civic contributions are not a priority for the primary benefactors of higher education may well be wrong, but it may be the case that it is a latent rather than an explicit priority for many of them. Some preliminary assessments of the status of the civic teaching and service roles in the minds of the major institutional stakeholders is essential to developing a strategy to strengthen these roles.

Build a Strategy to Sustain a Values-Based Conversation

One of the values to the initial test of perceptions will be to learn whether there are significant differences between stakeholder groups in how they characterize "civic" and "service" issues, including the extent to which the topic is ideologically loaded for some of them. One of the unfortunate realities of our current culture is that values-based conversations are sometimes perceived as political or ideological, both of which may be problematic to parts of the campus community or to some publics. This is likely to be a bigger problem on some campuses than on others. Faith-related colleges typically find it less complicated to engage in conversation about values as a dimension of institutional missions than others, for instance. If public discussion of the civic role is perceived as having been "captured" by one group or another, or if it deteriorates into another version of the culture wars, then the conversation may be interesting, but it is not likely to be task-oriented. One of the early responsibilities of campus leadership seeking to sustain this agenda is to test the ideological issues on the campus, and seek to include diverse groups with a healthy balance of opinion in the process.

Develop an Assessment Matrix

While the assessments of civic teaching, service, and the accountability agenda are important to combine, they are sufficiently distinct in that the actual instruments should be built somewhat separately. Each should have at least three elements: goals, indicators, and measures. The data from these three pieces can be then reaggregated, and overall institutional evaluations made in the context of broad based institutional goals. An assessment matrix like the sample below can be a helpful guide to the discussion.

Sample Assessment Matrix			
Dimension	Teaching and Learning	Institutional Community Service	External Accountability
Goals			
Indicators			
Measures			

Where possible, indicators should be things that are reasonably easy to measure, and can yield information that can be monitored over time. A search for "perfect" indicators that reveal deep truths is less likely to be helpful than agreeing on ones that will be easy to measure, and will yield the ability to track a number of indicators over time. The assessments should build on existing student and institutional assessment instruments where possible to get at information which can be a proxy for aspects of the civic role. For instance, most campuses have annual questionnaires of student perceptions and interests. Others routinely survey employers to learn of their needs and levels of satisfaction with the institution's students and curriculum. And many try to conduct "exit interviews" with at least a sample of exiting seniors. All of these vehicles should be easily adaptable to yield information that can be used for civic teaching and service assessments.

Seek Partner Institutions to Help Build the Public Accountability Agenda

The public accountability agenda will be greatly strengthened if a number of institutions in a region join together in a multi-institutional assessment and accountability agenda. A multi-institutional strategy is particularly important to capture cross-institutional contributions to the student teaching role since the majority of students no longer receive their education from one or even two institutions, but are "autodidactic," and largely self-taught, and move rapidly from one organization to another. Collaboration with other colleges on this agenda will build a capacity for a public accounting that goes beyond the contributions of an individual institution. This is an issue that is particularly well suited for multi-campus treatments, in statewide reporting formats.

Keep Quality Assessments Short and Clear

Too often higher education quality assessments become so intricate that they implode from their own weight, and are not useful for either sharp-edged reviews of goals and performance, or external communication of capacities. Excessive complexity is a quite natural and predictable result of the consultative process that is typically used to develop assessment instruments in higher education. But for this kind of work is it probably better to err on the side of simplicity than complexity. To help avoid the implosion problem, knowledgeable and credible individuals who have not been directly involved in the process should be asked to critique it at different stages of development, for the explicit purpose of helping to maintain focus and if possible brevity.

Learn from Existing Research

While the civic teaching and service contributions have not been the focus of assessment or accountability measures, aspects of these functions are arguably latent in some of the assessments that have been done. Some lessons may be learned from briefly looking at the areas where the most work has been done. A short review of the places which offer the most promise for ideas follows. This is not meant to be a comprehensive review of research, but a place to get started with a particular focus on assessment and evaluation. Additional information is provided in the appendix.

Evaluations of Service-Learning

The area of inquiry where the most has been done to assess civic teaching and community service are the assessments of service-learning, where good work is being done by a number of institutions and national organizations. Some of the assessments focus on student learning outcomes from service-learning, including as examples self-reports of active learning, community in the classroom, attitudes toward service and service-learning, academic persistence, leadership, and career clarification. Others focus on the community side of the equation, and the degree to which the campus and community have healthy and engaged partnerships. The research shows that the kinds of learning outcomes which are equated with service-learning are both cognitive and affective. On the cognitive side, the research shows that service helps students learn and retain the subject matter content, and also superior capacities to synthesize information and reason analytically. On the affective side, there are positive outcomes on student attitudes and values, including positive self-esteem, personal aspirations, ability to work with others, and resistance to authoritarianism. On both the affective and cognitive sides, these learning outcomes might be good initial proxies for a discussion about goals for effective citizenship.

Assessments of Campus Climate and Campus Diversity Initiatives

Another area where interesting work has been done is the arena of campus climate and diversity, where the assessments have touched upon the goals of higher education to educate for interpersonal capacities including citizenship skills. The presumption behind much of this work is that the changing social and economic fabric of our culture will require students to be able to work collaboratively in ethnically and culturally diverse work environments. Development of respect for and sensitivity to others' values, as well as skills in problem-solving, team-building, and collaboration, are typically developed as teaching and learning goals from these initiatives. Assessment instruments have been developed to help institutional officials "take the temperature" of their campus learning climates as a way of defining goals and developing means to ensure inclusive and collaborative learning communities. In addition to institutional assessments, the research also shows positive learning outcomes for students who have been educated in diverse campus environments, particularly with respect to others and listening skills. Thus, the work on diversity and campus climate provides some clues as to how to define and measure aspects of "good citizenship," and to equate these capacities with other dimensions of educational quality.

Two recent research resources are particularly helpful: one, a recent summary of research on diversity by Daryl Smith of Claremont Graduate School and published in the Association of American Colleges and Universities (AAC&U)'s monograph *Diversity Works*, and some research commissioned by the University of Michigan contained in an unpublished brief "The Compelling Need for Diversity in Higher Education." Both reports summarize a range of research about the consequences of campus diversity on students, and Smith's study includes an annotated bibliography of pertinent research. The Michigan report includes a background study by Patricia Gurin about the relationship between student learning in diverse learning environments and what she terms "democracy outcomes." She uses longitudinal data both from national sources and from the University of Michigan. Her analyses show consistent positive correlations between education in diverse settings and democracy outcomes, including:

- growth in active thinking processes that reflect a more complex, less automatic mode of thought
- engagement and motivation
- learning of a broad range of intellectual and academic skills

- value placed on these skills
- citizenship engagement, which is the motivation to participate in activities that affect society and the political structure as well as participation in community service
- racial/cultural engagement, which is a measure of cultural knowledge and awareness and the motivation to participate in activities that promote racial understanding
- compatability of differences, which includes a belief that basic values are common across racial and ethnic groups, understanding of the potential constructive aspects of group conflict, and belief that differences are not inevitably divisive to the social fabric of society.[6]

INCH: The Index of National Civic Health

The 1997 report of The National Commission on Civic Health sounded the alarm about the deteriorating quality of the nation's civic life, and issued a multifaceted call for civic renewal including specific recommendations about roles for schools, community organizations, and churches. One of the commission's recommendations was that there be periodic assessments of the quality of civic life, to be carried out by an offshoot organization from the commission called "The Civic Monitoring Project"—to allow the public and policy makers to maintain awareness of whether civic life is improving or continuing to deteriorate. The commission developed an assessment tool to gauge national civic health, called "INCH"—the Index of National Civic Health. INCH is an average of 22 different indicators of civic health, all taken from generally available data which can be monitored over time, and combined into five categories: political, trust, membership, security, and family (please see the appendix for a more complete description of INCH).

INCH does not purport to measure anything about higher education's civic contributions, either in student teaching or community service. As a matter of fact, the role of higher education as either part of the problem or the solution to deteriorating national civic health was not on the radar screen of the National Commission. Yet INCH could be adapted to an index of higher education's civic contributions. Instead of the five categories of political, trust, membership, security, and family, categories appropriate to higher education could be developed. Decisions about what to count should be decided at the institutional or state level, but examples where measures could be devised might include student learning outcomes; student/community involvement (number of students in service-learning or other measures of volunteerism); faculty service to communities; institutional/community collaboratives (clinics, school partnerships, housing, number of individuals served by university/community activities); number served in hospitals and clinics; number of students in K-12 partnership collaboratives; children in campus run day-care centers; and measures of the use of the campus as public space benefitting the community (concerts, public debates, athletic events). The benefit of INCH is that it is designed to synthesize many complicated indicators into an aggregate index which can be tracked over time.

Research on the Institution as Citizen: Community Service

While surrogate measures of different aspects of civic teaching and learning can be teased out from the literature, there is very little to draw from for measures of institutional service to the community. This may be because so much of the assessment and accountability agendas are focused on improving the teaching and learning functions. It also may be the case that some of what might fairly be labeled institutional service gets "counted" as research rather than as service.

Research done by Fran Ansley and John Gaventa and reported in the 1997 special edition of *Change* magazine on "Rebuilding Higher Education's Civic Life,"[7] suggests that there are new models of community-university research partnership which they call "The New Research." They describe a number of new programs and centers which have emerged to tie university research to community and governmental needs. Some are designed to address particular themes or topics (for instance, the environment, urban planning, schools, or housing), and some serve as a basis for connecting faculty interested in action research with community-based organizations.

Work by Nancy Thomas for the New England Resource Center for Higher Education (NERCHE) on institutional service suggests a useful typology for categorizing different types of institutional service activities:

1. Cooperative extension and continuing education programs
2. Clinical programs and field-based learning opportunities for students in professional programs
3. Top-down administrative initiatives
4. Centralized administrative-academic units with outreach missions
5. Academically-based centers and institutes
6. Faculty professional service and academic outreach
7. Student initiatives
8. Institutional initiatives with an economic or political purpose
9. Access to facilities and cultural events.[8]

Another common form of "assessment" as it applies to institutional service are compendiums of information about university service activities. There are a number of examples of institutional efforts to catalogue their community service activities into comprehensive reports, which pull together snapshot descriptions of a whole host of activities from faculty scholarship that is community-based, to clinical activities, university extension, community government partnerships, and student internships in community-based organizations. Unfortunately, these reports tend not to synthesize the data, and stop short of reaching generalizations about how to characterize the nature of the institution's service role.

Institutions and systems also periodically develop estimates of their economic impact on their communities. Sometimes done in response to threats from local government about property tax exemptions, but also for other reasons, these surveys pull together economic impact data by counting funds expended as a consequence of the institution's many activities (employer of people, construction contractor, purchaser of goods, hospital, clinic and dormitory managers, research contractors), and estimate the "multiplier effects" of university activities on local businesses. Students are a prime example of a good "multiplier" because they live and spend money in the communities while patronizing local businesses. Impressive studies showing the considerable economic consequence of colleges and universities on their local communities are then compiled. Although these economic activity reports are poor surrogates for evaluation instruments of community service contributions, they do stimulate thinking about the many types of "organized activities," which frequently surround research universities, and about the institution's responsibility for good citizenship in all of these roles. They also may help pave the way toward thinking about areas of considerable current public and student concern, such as the use of foreign sweatshop labor to make collegiate sportswear.

College Ratings Services

The past decade has witnessed a huge increase in private college rankings services, designed to publicly rate colleges and universities on some indices of quality. Private rankings of colleges have been around for a long time, but until the early 1990s most ratings focused on graduate or professional programs. Since that time, rankings of different indicators of undergraduate colleges and universities have started to abound led by several of the national magazines' annual "rankings." Research for the Council on Higher Education Accreditation (CHEA) about the ranking services shows that most of them equate "quality" with fairly traditional peer reviews of reputation and resources, faculty credentials, and undergraduate student selectivity. But a few of them— in particular, the *Princeton Review* surveys—are designed to test student perceptions of college quality, looking at indices such student service, student activism, campus spiritual life, and diversity. A review of these guides can stimulate thinking about the kinds of things that students equate with quality, along with candid appraisals about place as a dimension of effectiveness.

One rankings service in particular is designed to assess institutional commitment to "character education," which is at least one dimension of civic education. The "Templeton Foundation Guide to College and Character" is designed to address the eroding role of colleges and universities in character education, through their "Guide to College and Character," which identifies outstanding college programs that help to foster lives of personal and civic responsibility. As their materials state: "Ample evidence suggests that too many of our nation's colleges and universities have experienced an erosion of vision regarding their responsibility to educate students who personally define and affirm a set of moral and civic commitments. The clear and pragmatic task of preparing students for a profession has pushed aside the more controversial and difficult task of inspiring students to lead ethical and civic-minded lives." Competititons are promoted in a number of areas, including identification of exemplary first-year programs, programs in civic education, service-learning, academic integrity, and presidential leadership. Criteria that are used to rank institutions include:

- a strong statement of purpose, showing the priority of character development in the institution's mission
- evidence of the active involvement in character education by the institution's leaders, including its faculty
- longevity of the programs
- evidence of a positive impact of the program on students, faculty, the campus, and community
- evidence of impact on a significant percentage of students
- the integration of the program into the core curriculum and areas of academic study
- evidence of a central campus location that provides program information, recruitment and publicity, training, and coordination
- external recognition or honors
- assessment and evidence

Research on Student Learning Outcomes

There is a considerable body of research on what it is that students actually get from college—some of which raises as many questions as answers about the specific relation of college to many student outcomes. Nonetheless it is a rich resource about ways to think about student learning outcomes and how to measure them. For instance, Alexander Astin has developed a taxonomy to characterize learning outcomes from college, which is summarized briefly below:[9]

Outcomes	**Cognitive**: Higher-order intellectual processes—knowledge acquisition, decision making, synthesis, reasoning	**Affective**: Attitudes and values, self-concepts, aspirations, personality dispositions
Measures	**Psychological**: Internal states or traits of the individual measured through tests or examinations	**Behavioral**: Direct observation of the individual

Research on the affective, psychological, and wider behavioral outcomes of college show some correlations between college attendance and a range of desirable social "civic" capacities:[10]

- individual autonomy and capacity for independence
- less tendency toward authoritarianism, dogmatism, and ethnocentrism
- interpersonal relations
- maturity and general personal development
- intellectual orientation
- extent of principled moral reasoning
- interest in service to others and friendships
- interest in current affairs, domestic and foreign politics
- cultural and aesthetic sophistication
- voting behavior

While the research is inconclusive on many of these measures—particularly about what it is in college that causes some of these outcomes—the inventory of capacities is nonetheless helpful in thinking through ways to describe and potentially document measurable citizenship skills.

SUMMARY AND CONCLUSION

Higher education does a very poor job of assessing and accounting for its civic teaching and community service roles. Yet assessment can be a critical strategic tool to strengthening the civic roles. While there are no existing models that can be adopted wholesale for civic assessments, there are a number of places where analogous work has been done that can be borrowed from. The civic assessment job should be approached as a dimension of institutional quality, and framed in the context of individual institutions. At the same time, the institutional assessments should be developed in parallel with attention to developing public accountability capacities, since external public communication is essential to the success of the agenda. This is not a narrow or technical job that can be foisted off on the institutional research office or left exclusively in the hands of the academic senate; successful assessments of civic capacities require some commitment from institutional leadership to get off the ground, and should involve individuals from across the academic community—both administrative and academic. An assessment strategy should be developed that anticipates the particular institutional hurdles that will need to be overcome, including strategies to ensure that the public conversation about goals and values does not become captured by particular ideological factions within the community. Instruments that use readily available data that can be replicated and measured over time will be most helpful.

Institutions interested in engaging the civic agenda will find the development of assessment instruments a particularly helpful way to engage a task-oriented and meaningful conversation about purpose, priority, measures, and effectiveness. There is some science to assessment, but it is not rocket science. With some commitment and good will, and some imagination, it can and should be done.

APPENDIX

American Council on Education (ACE) Higher Education and Democracy Forum can be a source of information about institutional community service activities. The American Council on Education's Democracy Forum's first meeting in June 1998, in Tallahassee, Florida, requested participating institutions to provide a listing of their institutional service activities. This compendium of information may be obtained from ACE by requesting the background papers for the conference, by contacting: ACE, One Dupont Circle, Washington, D.C. 20036, (202) 939-9331.

Association of American Colleges and Universities (AAC&U), in conjunction with the University of Maryland, has developed a comprehensive resource sharing network for information about diversity initiatives, including a database of research about evaluations of campus diversity projects. In addition to providing a starting point for learning more about the literature, this is an excellent guide to other institutions that have experimented with diversity initiatives, which can be helpful to institutions that are just getting started. Association of American Colleges and Universities, 1818 R Street, NW, Washington, D.C. 20009, (202) 884-7419, Web page: http://www.aacu-edu.org. Also, the AAC&U and University of Maryland database about campus diversity initiatives may be reached via the Web at: http://www.inform.umd.edu/diversity.

California Postsecondary Education Commission developed a "Campus Climate Assessment Instrument," which has been successfully used on campuses across California, and embraced by the Western Association of Schools and Colleges—the regional accrediting commission for California—in encouraging campuses to engage in self-assessment of campus diversity. The commission also sponsored research to measure the economic contributions of higher education to the California Economy; this material is a good starting point for other models in that genre. To learn more, contact: The California Postsecondary Education Commission, 1303 J Street, Suite 500, Sacramento, CA 95815, (916) 322-8028; and the Western Association of Schools and Colleges, P. O. Box 9990, Mills College, Oakland, CA 94610, (510) 632-5000.

Campus Compact is the national network of close to 600 colleges and universities, and 20 state networks, committed to student citizenship and values development through public and community service. Oriented both to service-learning and the civic development of students as well as to the campus as citizen, Campus Compact has developed a substantial body of research about service-learning and its consequences. In addition to having good statistical information about basic trends in service-learning, Campus Compact is a good source for information about which college campuses are involved in both service-learning and service to the community. For more information, contact: Campus Compact, Box 175, Brown University, Providence, RI 02912, (401) 863-1119, Web page: http://www.compact.org.

Corporation for National Service is the national body created by federal legislation in 1992 to promote community service in higher education. A public-private partnership, the corporation oversees three national service initiatives—AmeriCorps, Learn and Serve America, and the National Senior Service Corps. The legislation creating the corporation requires ongoing evaluation activities, including periodic efforts to define performance goals and measure performance indicators. Corporation for National Service, 1201 New York Avenue, NW, Washington, D.C. 20525, (202) 606-5000, Web page: http://www.nationalservice.org

The Council for Higher Education Accreditation (CHEA) has developed an Annual Almanac of Quality Assurance, a guide to the forms of external quality assurance review in higher education, ranging from accreditation to state licensure, state accountability reporting, and external ratings services. Copies of The Almanac can be obtained (after June 1999) from: The Council for Higher Education Accreditation, One Dupont Circle, 5th Floor, Washington, D.C. 20036, (202) 955-6126, Web page: http://www.chea.org.

Higher Education Research Institute (HERI), at the University of California, Los Angeles, is one of the best national repositories of data on student learning and college outcomes. HERI has managed the national annual survey of incoming college freshmen for more than 25 years, and has a good source of longitudinal data, as well as many current projects on aspects of this topic. For more information, contact Alexander Astin, director of the institute, and his associate Linda Sax at HERI, 3005 Moore Hall, University of California, Los Angeles, CA 90095, (310) 825-8331.

Index of National Civic Health (INCH). The five elements in INCH, and how they are weighted, is shown below. The data were compiled beginning in 1970, where the index was normed to equal 100. The National Commission on Civic Renewal's final report can be obtained via the Web at: http://www.puaf.umd.edu/civicrenewal/finalreport/america's_civic_condition.htm.

INCH Components (Each is 20 percent of the Total)	Elements and Weights
Political Components	Voter turnout (10 percent), and other political activities (signing a petition, writing to Congress, attending rallies or speeches, working for a political party, making a speech, writing an article, writing a letter to the newspaper, belonging to a reform group, and running for or holding political office (1.1 percent each)
Trust	Trust in others (10 percent) and confidence in the federal government (10 percent)
Membership	Membership in at least one group and/or church attendance (6.7 percent), charitable contributions (6.7 percent), and local participation, attending local meetings, serving on local committees, and serving as an officer of a local group (2.2 percent each)
Security Components	Youth murderers per youth population (6.7 percent), fear of crime (6.7 percent), and survey-reported crime per population (6.7 percent)
Family Components	Divorce (10 percent) and non-marital births (10 percent)

Indiana University-Purdue University Indianapolis has also been at the forefront of assessing service-learning in the context of overall institutional change strategies. Their assessments focus both at the institutional level—and on the degree to which campuses are effectively engaged in their communities—as well as the long-term impact of service-learning on students. The campus-based assessment has three stages: (1) development of a portfolio of activities; (2) rating the campus effort; and (3) recommendations for future work. In addition, they are beginning to work on a way to assess effects of long-term and intensive community work on leadership development, educational aspirations and persistence, career choice, and understanding of the nonprofit sector. Indiana University-Purdue University Indianapolis, Center for Public Service and Leadership, 815 W. Michigan Street, Indianapolis, IN 46202-5164, (317) 278-2370.

National Center for Higher Education Management Systems (NCHEMS), is located in Boulder, Colorado. Peter Ewell, vice president of NCHEMS, has been one of the leading researchers and advocates for student learning assessments as an essential dimension of institutional instructional quality. NCHEMS is just beginning a multiyear project, funded by the Pew Charitable Trusts, to develop a national assessment instrument for the "engaged student"—assessing the contributions of learning experiences and the campus environment on student learning. For more information, contact Peter Ewell, vice president, National Center for Higher Education Management Systems, 1540 30th Street, Room 173, Boulder, CO 80303, (303) 497-0301.

The **Portland State University Center for Academic Excellence** has produced an excellent handbook, "Assessing the Impact of Service Learning: A Workbook of Strategies and Methods," which focuses not just on student learning outcomes, but on ways to assess the impact of service-learning on all four constituencies—students, faculty, community, and institution. Center for Academic Excellence, Portland State University, P. O. Box 751-CAE, Portland, OR 97207-0751, (503) 725-5642.

The **Templeton Foundation Guide to College and Character** can be accessed through their Web site: http://www.templeton.org/Character.

The **Walt Whitman Center for the Culture and Politics of Democracy** at Rutgers University has been a center for study of democracy and culture. Its director, Benjamin Barber, has developed models to measure dimensions of citizenship which can be helpful in defining goals for higher education's civic teaching role. For more information, contact the center at Walt Whitman Center for the Culture and Politics of Democracy, Rutgers, State University of New Jersey, Hickman Hall, Douglas Campus, 89 George Street, New Brunswick, NJ 08901-1411, (732) 932-6861.

NOTES

1. See, for instance, the "Nine Principles of Good Practice in Assessment," from the American Association of Higher Education (Washington, DC, 1994).
2. National Center for Postsecondary Improvement, *Benchmarking Assessment: Assessment of Teaching and Learning in Higher Education for Improvement and Public Accountability: State Governing, Coordinating Board and Regional Accreditation Policies and Practices* (Ann Arbor: University of Michigan, 1997), emphasis added.
3. Carnegie Commission on Higher Education, *Higher Education: Who Pays? Who Benefits? Who Should Pay?* (New York: McGraw Hill, 1973); H. Bowen, *Investment in Learning: The Individual and Social Value of American Higher Education* (San Francisco: Jossey-Bass, 1977).
4. B. Roherty, "The Price of Passive Resistance in Financing Higher Education," in *Public and Private Financing of Higher Education: Shaping Public Policy for the Future,* ed. P. Callan and J. Finney (Phoenix: Oryx Press, 1997).
5. T. Marchese, "Not-So-Distant Competitors," *AAHE Bulletin* 50, no. 9 (May 1998): 3.
6. P. Gurin, "The Compelling Need for Diversity in Higher Education," unpublished expert report (University of Michigan, January 1999), 114.
7. F. Ansley and J. Gaventa, "Researching for Democracy and Democratizing Research," in Special Edition, *Change Magazine: Higher Education and Rebuilding Civic Life,* (January/February 1997).
8. See N. Thomas, "The College and University as Citizen," Chapter 4 of this book.
9. A. Astin, *Assessment for Excellence: The Philosophy and Practice of Assessment and Evaluation in Higher Education* (New York: Macmillan, 1990); E.T. Pascarella and P.T. Terenzini, eds., *How College Affects Students: Findings and Insights from Twenty Years of Research* (San Francisco: Jossey-Bass, 1991).
10. Pascarella and Terenzini, *How College Affects Students.*

FURTHER READING

California Postsecondary Education Commission. "Toward an Understanding of Campus Climate: A Resource Guide." Sacramento, CA, 1990.

———. "The Wealth of Knowledge: Economic Impact Assessments of the Economic Contributions of Higher Education." Sacramento, CA, 1992.

Campus Compact. *Service Counts*. Providence, RI, 1997.

Council for Higher Education Accreditation. *Almanac of Quality Assurance*. Washington, DC: The Council (forthcoming).

Ewell, Peter, ed. *Assessing Educational Outcomes*. San Francisco: Jossey-Bass, 1985.

Eyler, Janet and Dwight E. Giles Jr. *Where's the Learning in Service-Learning?* San Francisco: Jossey-Bass, 1998.

Portland State University. "Assessing the Impact of Service Learning: A Workbook of Strategies and Methods." Portland, OR, 1997.

Smith, Daryl G. and Associates. *Diversity Works*. Washington, DC: Association of American Colleges and Universities, 1997.

University of Michigan. *The Compelling Need for Diversity in Higher Education*. Ann Arbor, MI, January 1997.

CHAPTER 19

Civic Renewal in Higher Education

The State of the Movement and the Need for a National Network

Elizabeth Hollander and Matthew Hartley

INTRODUCTION

In this chapter, we argue that to reconnect higher education to its earlier and higher civic purpose a social movement is required. In the first half of the chapter, we will briefly describe the systemic and organizational reasons why colleges and universities find change so difficult. We will explain how social movement theory might inform a strategy for systemic change. Then, we will describe several initiatives and networks, which are now independently working toward civic renewal in higher education—what we believe is convincing evidence of a growing movement. In the second half of the chapter, we offer several specific strategies for building a sustained civic renewal network and outline an agenda to maximize the impact of such a network.

ORGANIZATIONAL CHANGE

Each spring at commencement, students are welcomed into "the community of scholars." This grand phrase evokes images of faculty and students laboring together in a common enterprise, grappling with the intellectual and practical matters of our time. As many have noted, the reality is often otherwise. A sense of community may have been prevalent when the small, colonial college was the exemplar, however, the fracturing of faculty into departments[1] and the "academic revolution," the rise of the research university, directed faculty members' loyalties increasingly toward their discipline and research.[2] This has drawn faculty identities

> from the local civic community . . . toward national and international disciplinary and sub-disciplinary reference groups . . . Faculty are socialized throughout their graduate school preparation to think in highly individualized and privatized terms about their work in ways that make it difficult to believe in the possibilities for effective cooperative action for change.[3]

The time faculty spend with students continues to decline. Faculty are increasingly part time. Before placing blame at the feet of the professorate, it is important to recognize that the circumstance is systemic in nature. A faculty member who aspires to follow in the footsteps of Mr. Chips must either publish or face banishment outside the ivied walls.

Further, leading change efforts in colleges and universities is difficult. It has been noted that efforts to steer a college are likely met with the same success as a driver steering "a car skidding on ice."[4] Institutions of higher learning are, by design and inclination, organizations with diffuse power. Although regents or boards of trustees are the ultimate authority, they are frequently admonished to govern but not manage. The management is left to the president, the senior administration, and the faculty (or its representative body). However, there is a price to shared governance. Each constituency has the power to veto any initiative. The president cannot modify the curriculum without the faculty's endorsement. The faculty may be disinclined to invest time and effort on "local" issues (i.e. committee work, redesigning freshman core courses) if their jobs depend upon meeting standards set by their disciplinary peers nationally.[5] Therefore, as Clark Kerr notes, colleges and universities often end up sticking with the status quo because it is the only option that *cannot* be vetoed.[6] Programs or departments continue to operate in relative isolation. The result, as Robert Birnbaum observes, is that universities become "academic holding companies"—conglomerates of semi-autonomous units with a shared brand name.[7] Or, as one wit put it, a group of academic entrepreneurs held together by a common parking policy.

These organizational characteristics make it challenging for campuses to both define their broader purposes and to then "live" their missions, including their civic missions.

SOCIAL MOVEMENT THEORY

Given the organizational characteristics that cause higher education to resist innovation and deflect faculty interest from "local" concerns, is there a strategy for change? Mervyn L. Cadwallader, in the introduction of a special issue of *Liberal Education* that was dedicated to civic engagement, called for an "academic counterrevolution."[8] He observed that for change to occur in homeostatic organizations, "something akin to a social movement has to intrude itself into and disrupt the formal rhythm and patterns of faculty life." It will be useful at this point to explore what exactly the characteristics of a social movement are.

Mario Diani, professor at Milan's Bocconi University, synthesized and distilled the work of various social movement theorists and arrived at this useful definition: "A social movement is a network of informal interactions between a plurality of individuals, groups and/or organizations, engaged in a political or cultural conflict, on the basis of a shared collective identity."[9]

The definition is derived from four characteristics that Diani identifies as being shared by most social movement theorists. First, social movements are constituted by "networks of informal interaction." These networks allow individuals and groups who share similar concerns or values to communicate with one another and to coordinate their actions. Second, a social movement "requires a shared set of beliefs and a sense of belongingness." That is, a movement must have a sense of purpose. However, Diani is careful to point out that a "homogeneity of ideas and orientations" is not necessary for the development of a collective identity. People may have very different reasons to support a particular movement. (Consider the disparate ideologies of Malcolm X and Dr. Martin Luther King Jr. Or, the idealistic and pragmatic defenses of service-learning.) Instead of rigid ideology, a social movement may coalesce around a collective agenda or shared goal. Diani's third characteristic highlights the role conflict plays in social movements. A social movement needs something to move against. Opposition is a requisite.

Although some theorists draw distinctions between social and political movements, Diani argues that these distinctions are more apparent than actual. In either case, the movement seeks to alter the political or cultural context by either promoting or opposing a particular social change. The fourth characteristic of a social movement is that its activity "occurs outside the institutional sphere and the routine procedures of social life." That is, social movements are distinct from change efforts sponsored and administered by an organization. However, Diani notes that this characteristic, which dominated social movement theory in the 1970s has been called into question. Some theorists dispute whether the extra-institutional characteristic of social movements is more correctly associated with their early stages. At some point, successful movements tend to change societal structures, including its organizations.

NETWORKS OF INFORMATION AND EXPERTISE

We believe the potential exists for a powerful civic renewal movement. Whether that movement will wash across the landscape of higher education and leave it largely unchanged, as earlier movements have, or make a significant mark is still open to question. Like all movements, civic renewal is a river fed by several streams. Among the best developed in higher education is the service-learning network, which has expanded significantly in the last decade. Service-learning is, in the words of Jeffery Howard, "a first cousin of community service. It, too, engages students in service to the community and contributes to the development of students' civic ethic." Where it differs is that an *"intentional effort is made to utilize the community service experience as a learning resource."* [10] The learning can be accomplished through a reflective component in a cocurricular service experience or by integrating service into an academic course. (For the purpose of this chapter, the data that follow about service-learning in Campus Compact schools reflect the latter practice.)

It is no coincidence that service-learning came of age as American society encountered a crisis in its civic life. Campus Compact, founded in 1985, and the Campus Opportunity Outreach League (COOL), founded around the same time, were direct responses to concerns voiced by William Bennett about a "Generation X" that had no concern for the common good. The Corporation for National Service was, similarly, a response to a desire to reengage the young in "doing for the country."

The growth of service-learning is reflected in the number of Campus Compact member campuses. There were fewer than 200 in 1989 and now there are nearly 600 at the close of 1998. [11] Another key indicator is the proliferation of service-learning courses on these campuses. In 1993, 66 percent of Campus Compact member campuses reported having at least one service-learning course. By 1998, not only did 99 percent report having at least one service-learning course, almost half (48 percent) had between 10 and 39 courses, and 1 in 5 had 40 or more courses. This growth is the result of efforts by individual presidents and faculty members who have promoted the practice on their campuses. It also reflects the now-extensive availability of faculty workshops, conferences, mini-grants, and technical assistance material made available from national Campus Compact and its 20 affiliated state offices and its special center for community colleges in Mesa, Arizona.

Many other national organizations have been an integral part of the service-learning network—including the American Association of Community Colleges, American Association for Higher Education, and the National Society for Experiential Education (NSEE). Their conferences, publications, and workshops have introduced their membership to service-learning and offered opportunities for training. The AAHE has produced a set of discipline-based monographs in service-learning under the editorial leadership of Edward Zlotkowski. NSEE has a special interest group in service-learning and, like AAHE, includes sessions on service-learning in its annual conference. In just the last few years, as noted in Edward Zlotkowski's chapter in this volume, several disciplinary associations have also taken active roles in promoting the practice of service-learning. In the health sciences, there is a particularly active network of campuses committed to community activity called the Campus Community Partnerships for Health, lead by Sarena Seifer at the University of Washington, and supported by both federal and foundation grants. The New England Resource Center for Higher Education (NERCHE) provides support for faculty engagement with community regionally.

In addition to higher education associations, the federal government has been a key supporter of the service-learning movement. The Corporation for National Service, a federal agency championed by President Bill Clinton and established in 1993 has provided seed money for hundreds of campus-based service efforts.

A second network focused on the renewal of civic life is engaged in issues of equity and diversity. Since 1988, the Association of American Colleges and Universities has been championing the cause of diversity in higher education. In 1992, through a grant from the Ford Foundation, AAC&U launched its "American Commitments" project. The project added an emphasis on democracy to the earlier initiative. It seeks to engage campuses in discussions about the important issues of diversifying faculty, staff, and students, and introducing multicultural education into the curriculum—education that not only exposes students to other cultures, but requires them to critically view issues of difference within our own society. Currently, 127 institutions are participants in the project. Hundreds more have benefited by the project's DiversityWeb, a Web site designed to share information and highlight best practices. In the fall of 1998, the DiversityWeb was receiving more than 100,000 "hits" each month.

A third network is made up of campuses undertaking community partnerships. Many campuses have had partnership programs and several organizations, including the Council of Independent Colleges, NSEE and Campus Compact had developed networks among them. The urban campuses have various vehicles to discuss their efforts. Increased networking among campuses and documentation of their efforts has resulted from the U.S. Department of Housing and Urban Development (HUD) funding of 96 schools as part of their Community Outreach Partnership program. HUD has published three directories describing various programs and brings participants together in a series of regional conferences.

In fact, there are a host of initiatives on civic engagement itself. Discussions with representatives from the majority of higher education associations yielded a wealth of examples. The National Association of Independent Colleges and Universities (NAICU) is leading an ongoing student voter registration drive with the support of many other associations. The National Association of State Universities and Land Grant Colleges' Kellogg Commission, funded by the Kellogg Foundation, recently released a report on the "engaged campus." Under the leadership of Judith Ramaley, president of the University of Vermont, this report is designed to promote a reengagement of land-grant institutions as called for in their original missions. The Council on Public Policy Education, supported by the Kettering Foundation and Pew Charitable Trust, has a project to promote "public space" which includes a network of some 29 universities.[12] The Association of American Universities (AAU) recently compiled a directory of the public service efforts of all of their members. The American College Personnel Association (ACPA) will have for the first time at their 1999 national conference a track dedicated to "civic education." In addition, they combined forces with other groups such as College Unions International to sponsor their first major conference devoted to service-learning in June of 1999. There is also a group called the Association of New American Colleges, formed in 1995, which is a consortium of some 22 private, comprehensive, mostly religious institutions who seek to model themselves after Ernest Boyer's[13] conception of the "new American university." Starting in 1997, Campus Compact started broadening its focus beyond service and service-learning to the "engaged campus," defined as a campus that seeks to engage all aspects of the campus (students, faculty, staff, and the institution) in both educating citizens and being a community citizen. And, of course there is the ACE Forum on Higher Education and Democracy, which is supporting this volume.

In addition to the networks described above, there are other networks that have the potential to play a significant role in a civic renewal movement. One such network is the growing number of campuses that are focused on "learning outcomes" and, along with it, reexamination of the quality of instruction. Funded by Title III Department of Education funds, and encouraged by AAHE and the Carnegie Foundation for the Advancement of Teaching, these campuses are focusing on evaluation of the effectiveness of teaching at their institutions. The emphasis on teaching and the learning that results has lead to the creation of new teaching and learning centers on campuses. The connection of these initiatives to the civic renewal movement is that focusing on teaching and learning outcomes provide fertile ground for the development of service-learning and civic education. Those engaged in this network share the view that the increased emphasis on research—regardless of its relevance or the expense to undergraduate teaching—is a significant problem.

Despite the existence of these networks, there is precious little communication and even less coordination among them. Again, returning to what we know best, service-learning centers are rarely linked to other community partnership efforts either on campus or nationally. As indicated earlier, since 1995, HUD has funded community outreach partnership centers from its Office of University Partnership in the Division of Planning and Research. To date they have funded 78 such centers, involving 96 campuses. Even though HUD promotes service-learning as a pedagogy by giving points to applicants that use the practice, there is little awareness of the existence of service-learning centers on campus.[14] On many campuses that belong to Campus Compact, community partnership centers operate in a different sphere from community-based service-learning centers. It is also the case that few campuses seem to connect their teaching and learning centers to their service-learning centers. On many campuses both kinds of centers are new and sparsely funded enterprises. Together these represent a staggering lost opportunity for students to learn from community outreach activities and for service-learning courses to deepen community partnerships.

In summary, the landscape of higher education looks like a prairie with a lot of unconnected silos which could, if brought together, produce a rich feed for the civic renewal movement. In Diani's terms, there is no sense of "belongingness"—no sense of common enterprise. Few envision a country to "be achieved by building a consensus on the need for specific reform."[15] R. Guarasci and G.H. Cornwell concur, noting that "colleges by and large reflect the social values, and the social and moral confusion that surround them." And in our day "liberal society has opted for a political culture in which autonomy and prosperity are its essential values."[16]

This absence of collective action prevents the outside world from noticing higher education's many efforts to rediscover their roots—to educate students for the democracy and using their knowledge and resources in the service of their communities. Its efforts are invisible, a fact all too apparent by the failure of the National Commission on Civic Renewal, co-chaired by Sam Nunn and William J. Bennett, to even mention higher education as a potential source for revitalizing democratic participation.

WORKING TOWARD A NATIONAL NETWORK

Although most efforts are occurring in isolation, some intra-network collaboration has begun to occur. The service movement, for the most part, has managed to appeal to both the political left and right's interests in democratic renewal proponents of service-learning worked together to achieve the passage of federal legislation to support student service, the legislation that created the Corporation for National Service. Included in these networks are such groups as the National and Community Service Coalition, Youth Service America, and National Youth Leadership Council.

There have also been efforts to develop a national network in civic education among higher education associations to include AAHE's efforts to embrace various forms of new "powerful" pedagogies and collaborate with Campus Compact in promoting service-learning. In addition to collaborating with its traditional allies such as AAHE, COOL, NSEE, Campus Compact began collaborating with AAC&U in 1997. Corporation for National Service funding supports a service-learning clearinghouse at the University of Minnesota, primarily devoted to elementary and secondary education. In 1998, the Pew Charitable Trust funded a senior faculty fellow at Campus Compact to help the increased engagement of disciplinary associations in service-learning move forward. That senior fellow, Edward Zlotkowski, will have the capacity to bring these associations together on a regular basis in Washington and will also have funds to give to these associations to promote service-learning in their own organizations. There will also be opportunities for campus teams to bring departmental groups to discipline-based institutes, to advance the practice on a departmental basis on their own campuses. The larger Campus Compact infrastructure will provide mechanisms to widely disseminate these efforts to other campuses. At the same time, Zlotkowski will maintain his connections to AAHE where he is general editor of a series of discipline-based monographs in service-learning. This example demonstrates the impact foundations can have in fostering collaborative activity.

There have also been some attempts to begin a national discussion on the broader idea of civic education. One effort, the Partnering Initiative, seeks to bring together elementary, secondary, and postsecondary education on the issue. In higher education, the formation of the American Council on Education's forum on the Civic Responsibility of Higher Education in 1997, under the leadership of Thomas Ehrlich and Zelda Gamson, signaled that civic responsibility had become a mainstream issue. This forum sponsored a leadership conference at Florida State University in June of 1998, on the subject of civic renewal. Those present generally agreed that there was a great need to articulate what civic education and civic responsibility mean. This volume is one response to that question. The ACE Forum planned and implemented a series of "listening to community sessions" in spring of 1999, and at Campus Compact's request, co-sponsored a presidential leadership colloquium with Campus Compact in the summer of 1999. This colloquium brought leaders of the civic renewal movement and college presidents together to formulate a call to action to higher education concerning civic responsibility and recommend concrete steps campuses can take to achieve this.

Dr. Barry Checkoway, director of the Community Service Learning Center at the University of Michigan, organized a conference at the Wingspread Conference Center in December of 1998 regarding the civic responsibilities of research universities. Leaders from a number of the networks cited earlier

attended (AAC&U, AAHE, Campus Compact). The conference strengthened the recognition that there were common interests which could be made
stronger by working together. Agreement was reached on a series of strategic
next steps, including writing a vision statement, creating new measures of
institutional civic engagement, organizing an Annual Institute for Education
in the Democracy, and identifying new scholarly fields, programs, and movements with strong civic potential and building alliances among them. The
resulting vision statement, known as the Wingspread Declaration on the Civic
Responsibility of Research Universities (1999), is being widely disseminated.
A follow-up meeting was held in July of 1999 and an annual meeting is under
discussion.

A SHARED SET OF BELIEFS

Collective action cannot occur until the various constituencies recognize the
commonalties that lie between them—what Diani calls the "shared set of
beliefs." At both conferences cited in the previous section, there was a broad
consensus among attendants that a common agenda must be articulated
around civic education. In a world where acrimonious (and interminable)
debates ensue over the presence or absence of a hyphen in the word "service-
learning," this appears a Herculean task. Much deeper debates are imbedded
in a common agenda, about the meaning of democracy and about the relationship of service to citizenship. Harry Boyte and Nancy Kari point out in their
chapter the possibility that a notion of commonwealth can move us beyond
the polarity between the communitarians and the liberals. For many, service is
not the same as citizenship.

We further believe there is a growing consensus on the two major aspects of
civic education and civic responsibility in higher education that we think are
important. The first entails the age-old desire to prepare the next generation
of active participants in the democracy, and the second to encourage campuses to act as good institutional citizens within their own communities.
Achieving these ends requires that we be able to define citizenship skills and
measure whether they have been achieved. It also requires that we have norms
for effective civic engagement by campuses with their communities. A great
deal of scholarly groundwork has already been laid to define and justify these
activities—groundwork that may form a basis for significant solidarity and
broad consensus of views.

Higher education's historical role in training the citizenry has been expli-
cated by Julie Reuben, Harkavy, Schneider, and others. There is a rich body of
literature that cogently describes what is meant by skills for democratic
society,[17] and others have devised a list of measurable civic competencies
around which it should not be hard to gain consensus. They include: tolerance

of political, religious, and racial views, sense of civic obligation to such tasks as voting and giving blood, sense of agency in accomplishing governmental/ political tasks, leadership and involvement in issues, critical thinking, public deliberation, ability to take collective action, and commitment to take action. D. Giles and J. Eyler's[18] recent work provides an objective description and analysis of student, community problem-solving capacities based on students' written work and taped conversation. Ernest Boyer and others have articulated powerful statements advocating for new and more active and engaged forms of pedagogy and scholarship.

An important finding from this work is that many of these competencies can be developed through engaging in service-learning. Astin has reported that "participation in service-learning experiences correlates positively with 35 different aspects of academic development, including academic outcomes, civic values, and life skills."[19] Surprisingly, the extent of impact on students depends upon the quality of the service experience and the depth of reflection provided. It is also important to note that service-learning courses alone, at least as currently taught, cannot achieve the outcome of helping students to overcome their alienation and cynicism about government.[20] Service-learning is but one important part of a strategy to address civic education.

In the realm of "campus as citizen," there is a growing body of literature and frameworks. This literature addresses the elements of institutionalization of the practice of service-learning, the campus as interlocutor of knowledge between campus and community, the role of faculty in both generating and sharing knowledge useful to community building as well as their own professional service in the community, and the components of effective sustained community partnerships.[21]

There is also a growing body of literature that captures the overall concepts of civic responsibility in all its aspects. Indiana Campus Compact first articulated the idea of "university as citizen" in 1998. A book titled *Colleges and Universities as Citizens* co-edited by R. G. Bringle and E.A. Malloy on this idea was recently published. Meanwhile, the National Association of State Universities and Land-Grant Colleges (NASULGC) report on the engaged campus was released in February of 1999 and provides a vision for land-grant colleges. More recently, Thomas Ehrlich and Elizabeth Hollander, with the help of a distinguished presidential committee, produced a Fourth of July "Declaration on the Civic Responsibility of Higher Education." The document was reviewed and edited at a Presidential Leadership Colloquium at the Aspen Institute June 30–July 1, 1999, sponsored by Campus Compact, ACE, and the Aspen Institute. The declaration, on the Campus Compact Web site <www.Compact.org>, has been signed by 100 presidents.

In fact, there is some evidence that finding common ground may not be the primary challenge facing the civic renewal movement. Economist Jeremy

Rifkin is making a sustained effort to gather organizations together under the banner of civic education. Rifkin has spearheaded an effort to promote what he terms "civil education" from kindergarten through college. The Partnering Initiative already has 72 member organizations representing K–12, higher education, and community service agencies such as the 4-H clubs. All have endorsed a statement promoting "civil education" which is worded to encompass the concepts of service-learning, civic education, character education, and community schooling.

> Civil Education encompasses a wide range of education reform efforts including citizen education, character education, democratic education, and service learning. The underlying theme of civil education is that students of all ages learn best when their educational experience integrates the informal education practiced in community based organizations with the more formal academic education of the classroom. Making civil education the heart of the school experience will help prepare the next generation for lifelong commitment to the values of a civil society."[22]

Unfortunately, the Partnering Initiative effort is little known in higher education or elsewhere. While Jeremy Rifkin is a powerful and popular speaker on the subject, the consortium of organizations that make up its leadership (including Campus Compact) have had a difficult time determining what collective activities the initiative can undertake to promote civil education. It is an object lesson in the difficulties of fostering "movements" in education. The presence of consensus around a set of principals is insufficient. In fact, as Diani reminds us, shared meanings evolve as a movement expands and grows. What binds people together most effectively are shared goals. Organizations also need to see a clear self-interest in collective action to sustain their interests over any length of time.[23]

SOMETHING TO MOVE AGAINST

Opposition is a powerful means of forging alliances. Indeed, Diani notes that movements *require* something to move against. Current criticism of higher education is clearly inimical to the idea of the academy as an ivory tower. There is a strong desire to see the curriculum rendered more relevant to student's lives. The curriculum ought to introduce students to the problems facing our society. Faculty ought not be penalized for pursuing community-based research. The civic renewal movement in higher education is also a reaction against the relative isolation of higher education from the pressing social problems of the day. The gap between the rich and poor grows and inhumane conditions in inner cities and rural areas of poverty persist. Problems of racism and xenophobia continue to plague the country. The uneven growth of metropolitan areas isolates people from jobs. These are just a few of the challenges of the country that are considered the purview of all caring institutions. In the words of John Gardner, "the government bodies of the cities and metropolitan areas cannot possibly solve the grave problems of these areas by themselves. They *must* work in collaboration with civic organizations, corporations, the schools, the faith community, neighborhood leaders, social agencies, and many others."[24] Gardner believes that "colleges and universities must be wholehearted participants in the life of their surrounding community. And I'm talking about an institutional commitment, not just a few scattered faculty enthusiasts." He points out that very few universities, particularly elite ones, have yet made this commitment.[25] Gardner articulates the view of those in the academy who believe that colleges and universities, as institutions, need to use their resources on behalf of community improvement in their own settings. These institutions are moving against a tendency of higher education not to be a good citizen in their own community but to surround themselves with iron gates and reach out to impoverished communities only to study their behavior.

Civic education also opposes the consumer model of education—college as a "service" that the student purchases for his or her private benefit. Instead, civic education views higher education as serving the common good. Students are expected to develop civic competencies, such as the ability to engage in civil discourse and debate, to effectively communicate, and to work with others that are different than themselves. It is a requirement because American democracy depends, and has depended since its inception, on participation by its members. A thriving democracy needs active citizens who can discern the difference between information and propaganda and who understand that our common life is influenced by the public policies we make as well as the exigencies of the economy.

Civic education is also seen as a counterweight to what some see as an excessive dominance of the market economy in all aspects of American life and the heavy price to be paid by putting competition in the global economy ahead of social investments.[26] Others are concerned about the reluctance of students to engage in informed debate—indeed, to "stand" for anything. [27] Still others want students to experience communities of difference, and learn to work with and in them, especially when so many have grown up in neighborhoods segregated by class and race. There are also those who hope to see the service-learning movement begin to ask students to not only empathize with victims of social injustice, but to develop the skills necessary to analyze social problems and craft strategies to alleviate the conditions they are witnessing.

SOCIAL MOVEMENT ON CAMPUS

Now that we have established that networks exist that could sustain a social movement, how might such a movement play out on campuses? Parker Palmer has explored the idea of social movements in the context of higher education. He eloquently describes the process by which social movements grow "outside the institutional sphere and routine procedures"—that is, how they are expressed on individual campuses. Palmer notes that a "movement response" to organizational resistance consists not of manipulating the system from within but in creating "countervailing power outside the organizational structures." Palmer identifies four stages in this process.[28]

In Palmer's first stage, individuals decide the status quo is inconsistent with their own values or ideals—what he calls "leading divided lives." In the second stage, like-minded people "discover" one another and begin to form networks of support. For example, a group of faculty may gather to discuss their teaching. Stage three consists of bringing concerns identified and expressed in stage two before the larger community—acting on their common convictions. Palmer notes that throughout the stages, participants in the movement are rewarded—their voices are heard, they experience a sense of community and a shared sense of meaning. In the final stage, "a more systemic pattern of alternative rewards emerges." A successful movement will expand in influence to the extent that rewards, formerly available only through the organization (i.e. funding and research opportunities), can be provided and legitimized by the movement itself. Eventually, Palmer asserts, the organization itself will shift to accommodate the movement. Thus, a faculty member engaged in service-learning not only has the opportunity to publish in alternative journals, but his/her institution begins to place greater emphasis on "service" and "experiential pedagogies" in the promotion and tenure decisions.

Given Palmer's framework, it is evident that many students, faculty, and college administrators have decided to no longer live "divided lives." Many faculty members are longing for a sense of renewed purpose and academic community. There is growing concern over the disconnection of higher education from social problems and civic renewal. The popularity of Boyer's *Scholarship Reconsidered*,[29] the growth of service-learning as a pedagogy, and the proliferation of "learning communities" all underscore this point. Many believe that exercising civic responsibility and learning the skills of citizenship are a core mission of higher education. Further, they have indeed "discover[ed] one another and form[ed] networks of support."[30] It was these students and their presidents who organized both COOL and Campus Compact in the mid-1980s in the struggle against widespread celebration of individualism and the self-centeredness of the "me" generation. It was such faculty who were the pioneers of service-learning.[31] In the 1990s, the community-based learning cadre grew to numbers large enough to be considered moving from "the margins to the mainstream." Today, more and more faculty members are choosing forms of pedagogy, research, and professional service designed to teach the skills of democracy to their students or serve as ways for them and their students to be civilly engaged. In its last annual survey of its members, Campus Compact found there were 10,800 faculty engaged in service-learning. The most advanced campuses were offering service-learning in as many as 25 disciplines. One in five schools (19 percent) were offering more than forty service-learning courses.

These examples suggest that one type of civic education is being "voiced in the community," as Palmer describes. Further, this network has achieved enough success as a movement to generate an alternate reward system. More than two-thirds of member schools had 10 or more departments supportive of service-learning. To support these departments, 78 percent of member schools have a community service office. Some large and prestigious campuses are working on new tenure and promotion criteria for faculty to recognize civic engagement, such as Michigan State, Kent State, and Syracuse University. [32] A few alternative, jouried journals publish research connected to service-learning—the Michigan Journal for Service Learning and NSEE Quarterly are two examples.

An indication of the extent to which faculty efforts are being recognized is the tremendous growth in the number of faculty nominees for the Thomas Ehrlich service-learning award at Campus Compact, from 35 nominees in 1996 to 81 in 1998. An even more dramatic growth has happened in the nominees for the Ernest Lynton faculty award for community engagement given by the New England Resource Center for Higher Education from 10 in 1996 to 150 in 1998. The Templeton Foundation honor roll recognizes education that emphasizes students moral and ethical growth. Approximately 2,300 programs were nominated and 1,000 applications were submitted and reviewed by the foundation. Presidents are also looking for individuals to assist them in promoting the civic missions of their campuses. In 1998, both Yale and Harvard hired vice presidents with extensive community development experience to lead their community outreach efforts.

INCREASING IMPACT ON CHANGE

Change comes slowly, however. The civic education movement has not yet significantly impacted the powerful reward systems for both faculty and institutions. These systems include the accreditation process, national rankings in such venues as *U.S. News and World Report,* and most importantly, the criteria for promotion and tenure. How can higher education associations work more effectively together to promote change and address these reward systems?

Finding the ways to increase the impact of the civic education movement in higher education is a complicated question. It will require that multiple organizations and on-campus efforts see themselves as part of a common movement and have conscious strategies to work together to forward the movement.

We believe that there are at least four things that would increase the momentum. The first is to assess the extrinsic pressures that support the current system of higher education and to identify those that might be influenced to lend greater support to civic education. A second step is to continue to build on the new efforts to create a national network of organizations that, together, are seeking to change national standards and are building external allies. The third step is to more consciously disseminate the goals and purposes of civic education and, in the process, create a stronger base for collective identity and measures for success. The fourth step is to encourage and publicize integrated efforts on campuses to foster civic education and civic responsibility.

PRESSURES FOR CHANGE

First, it is important to address whether furthering civic education and civic responsibility is likely in an era in which higher education is feeling a great deal of pressure to respond to technological and economic changes and public pressures to be more accountable. An old joke that captures this challenge is the one that asks, "How many psychiatrists does it take to change a light bulb?", and the answer is, "Only one, but the light bulb has to really want to change." We have to ask: "What will make higher education really want to change?"

The most severe extrinsic forces acting on higher education today are our rapidly changing economy, new technologies, and decreasing public revenues for higher education accompanied by increasing public pressures for accountability and efficiency. The global economy requires more education and continuous education. Already one-half of the students served by higher education are not "traditional" age. Technology is making education more and more education "virtually" accessible to these students. For-profit and corporate universities are growing to meet these educational needs and are now credible market competitors with traditional higher educational institutions.[33] Some believe[34] that the availability of distance education will force campuses to articulate the unique educational advantages of campus-based education, including the practices of service-learning and other opportunities to learn and exercise civic skills. The pressures from legislators and others on public universities and colleges to demonstrate their "public value" is certainly a strong incentive for institutions to focus on their service to the community.

These trends are likely to support an increased emphasis on civic education, but the movement needs to capitalize on these possibilities by developing strategic allies outside of higher education.

BUILDING A NATIONAL CIVIC RENEWAL NETWORK

One potential source of external allies resides in the broader civic renewal movement. A host of commissions have been organized to address civic renewal in the last five years. What is striking is how small a role these commissions envision for higher education in civic education. Some of the civic renewal leaders, like Judith Rodin, president of the University of Pennsylvania, and John Gardner, former secretary of the Department of Health, Education, and Welfare (HEW) and now at Stanford University, certainly understand the opportunities higher education has both to train citizens and be institutional citizens in their own communities. Nonetheless, higher education has not been a leader in this movement, nor is it seen as a very important player by those who have been. Evidence of this is the absence of mention of higher education in the Nunn/Bennett Commission report cited earlier, even though it was written by William Galston of the University of Maryland, and just a passing mention of the benefits of a liberal education in the Report to the Nation from the Council on Civic Society, *A Call to Civil Society: Why Democracy Needs Moral Truths*, written by Jean Bethke Elshtain of the University of Chicago Divinity School.[35]

The absence of connection between civic renewal leaders in higher education and those outside the academy is one condition that needs to be improved if the civic education movement is to succeed. Campus Compact and ACE, in concert with the Aspen Institute, took a first step in that direction by inviting leaders from the civic renewal movement to the Aspen Institute meeting of college presidents in the summer of 1999. ACE is also taking some steps to connect to community leaders in a series of spring and summer listening sessions. NSEE convened K–12 educators, civic leaders, and higher education leaders in Virginia in February of 1999. However, a much more sustained and coordinated strategy of gaining external allies is still needed.

A national strategy to identify and partner with external allies could take advantage of the unique strengths of the various national organizations. For instance, The Education Commission of the States (ECS) is in a particularly good position to make connections to governors and state legislators. Frank Newman addressed the pressing issues facing higher education, including the role of civic education full time when he stepped down from the presidency of ECS in the summer of 1999. Campus Compact is well positioned to mobilize its member presidents at both a national and state level and to gather concrete evidence of the positive impact of service-learning on students as well as the impact of community partnership activities. AAC&U has generated a wealth of wisdom on the impact of diversity initiatives through its "American Commitments" project. ACE is in a particularly good position to connect to national legislators and business leaders because of its connections in Washington, D.C. The National Association of Independent Colleges and Universities (NAICU) has established a leadership role in student voter registration that is an important element of this strategy. It is interesting to note that the latest reauthorization of the higher education act requires that all registered college students be given motor/voter registration forms.

At the time of this writing, however, there are several efforts aimed at bringing the leaders of higher education organizations together to even discuss such a strategy. At Wingspread, AAHE agreed to take the lead in coordinating the efforts of all Washington-based higher education groups on civic responsibility in higher education. ACE is helping fund this effort. AAC&U is building a Web site on civic education for everyone's use. Campus Compact will continue to seek support for the Fourth of July Resolution and will urge campuses to document the practices driven by civic assessment.

There are barriers to the long-term success of such a working group, including time and resources. Each of these leaders of the various networks we have outlined is faced with serving a range of campus constituencies and raising the funds to do so. Each is challenged to be imaginative enough in their initiatives to attract foundation and government support. Forwarding "the movement" sometimes competes with sustaining the organizations they direct. If it were easy for groups to work strategically together they would do so more often. It is certainly the case that incentives to work together are required, including both the resources to do so and a belief that working together would identify concrete actions that build on existing organizational strength and do not threaten organizational futures. In other words, a national collaborative effort is required that consciously addresses the needs of a successful collaboration. These include recognition that "In practice, the collaborative process loops back on itself, building and rebuilding trust, bringing in and developing new partners, articulating and re-articulating vision, defining and reassessing purpose, committing and recommitting to act by consensus."[36]

Collaboration also requires skilled leadership that "can create the conditions and assemble the resources that enable others to collaborate. Collaborative leaders see connections, support multiple visions, and help build consensus. They allow others to lead and take credit; they expose new and different opportunities for partnership. Able to tolerate considerable ambiguity and eager to be held accountable, they transform—and are transformed by—the relationships and structures around them."[37]

The Wingspread meetings mentioned earlier are one good model for bringing people together to think strategically about the next steps in the

movement. Dr. Barry Checkoway has structured these meetings in a collaborative way, with a broad planning committee. The meetings are designed to
find common ground and to avoid getting bogged down in hair-splitting
debate. The meetings are focused on determining next steps and then requiring that the participants take responsibility to carry out these next steps. In
doing so, organizational and campus leaders are in a position to think about
how their activities and those going on at the campus level can complement
and strengthen each other.

The Wingspread meetings are currently focused on civic responsibility in
research universities, which is important because they both have the most
influence in higher education and are the furthest behind in pursuing the civic
education agenda. However, there are just two of them currently funded. A
way should be found to continue annual meetings like this that are collaborative in nature and outcomes-focused, with sufficient funding to allow widespread dissemination of the proceedings. Additional participation should be
sought from external allies (only a few were at the first meeting), and continued participation of foundation leaders is important. Critical to the success of
a collaborative network will be collaborative leadership, and a commitment on
the part of leading national organizations to seek to work together strategically. Creation of yet another organization that competes for resources should
be avoided. Instead, responsibilities should be shared and collaborative leaders
like Barry Checkoway supported.

In addition to bolstering the civic education movement with external allies,
the national network of leaders should challenge themselves to address two
other key constituents: those who evaluate higher education, and those who
fund civic education efforts.

The next frontiers in this work are the accrediting bodies, classification
systems, and ranking systems. When each of these includes criteria about
education for citizenship and community partnerships, the movement will
have, indeed, moved into the institutional sphere. A second frontier is achieving significant investment in civic education. Some have argued that the state
of the democracy is the crisis of the new millennium, deserving the attention
the cold war received in the last.[38] We know how transformative government
and foundation investments in higher education can be.[39] As indicated earlier,
however, there are a few scattered government programs that do not seek to
purposefully reinforce each other's efforts. Corporation for National Service
funding of higher education is a small percentage of the Learn and Serve
budget ($10 million of $43 million, and has not grown since it was instituted).
There is a need for a national strategy to encourage more coordinated national
government investment. There is also a need to seek increased state funding.
A few states are currently investing in community/university partnerships
(Ohio, Florida) and more are investing in college service activities through

their service commissions and corporation for national service offices. California, Massachusetts, Minnesota, and Washington state Campus Compacts have achieved legislated state funds, and 12 Campus Compact network offices have Vista volunteers who work to promote service-learning on campuses.

Finally, foundations need to be challenged to increase their collaborative leverage to heighten the visibility and funding for civic education.

DISSEMINATING THE VISION AND PRACTICE

The vision and practice of civic education and civic responsibility must be more broadly disseminated both inside and outside higher education. As we indicated earlier, powerful statements are being written that could be used to catch the attention of allies within and without. They can also serve as the basis for institutions to look at themselves.

Experimentation with differing forms of civic engagement and civic education are proliferating on campuses. Tufts University provides free copies of the *New York Times* to freshmen in order to encourage engagement in public affairs. Gordon Gee at Brown University teaches a course on the civic responsibility of higher education. Clark University and Trinity College are engaged in major economic development efforts in their respective communities. While there are many individual efforts designed to capture and promote these practices (Kettering, NERCHE, Carnegie Foundation for the Advancement of Teaching, Campus Compact, Templeton, AAU Survey, HUD survey), there is neither a central source of information about these practices nor a survey comparable to Campus Compact's annual survey of members to capture and document practice across the country. Campus Compact is considering expanding its survey to capture more of these practices. It is certainly important to foster web links among these various efforts—it may soon be time to create a "civic education and civic responsibility" clearinghouse. The University of Minnesota maintains such a resource regarding service-learning.

Another way to both disseminate practice and consolidate the vision for civic responsibility may be to institute a prestigious campus award for civic responsibility. This award would be done in the Palmer spirit of creating "a systematic pattern of alternative rewards." It would require that a set of criteria for civic responsibility be written. Campus Compact hopes the meeting referenced above will be the important first step for such an effort. It could be a way of gathering external allies as judges of such awards. Some campuses have expressed a willingness to do self-evaluations of their own "engagement" as a way to set the stage for changing national evaluation systems (e.g., Florida State). This can be a powerful strategy, especially if some of the campuses involved are large and very influential. Self-evaluations avoid some of the pitfalls of a competition that has both winners and losers. Self-evaluation can also be a vehicle for some campuses to seek to identify and begin a dialogue on their own campus among the myriad unrelated activities, faculty, courses, and initiatives that together add up to civic education and civic responsibility.

Coordination of activity on campus is, for reasons we have identified earlier, the hardest of all. It is extremely difficult to keep track of what is going on, especially on a large campus and there is an almost knee-jerk negative response on the part of many faculty to top-down initiatives of any kind. Differential resources between departments and centers are often a source of jealousy that makes it hard for units to work together. On the other hand, like-minded faculty enjoy finding each other on a campus and cannot easily do so without someone to help them, especially on a large campus. Community partners are also grateful for mechanisms that allow them to find out what resources may be available to them and that allow them an opportunity to state their own needs. If given opportunity and incentive, groups on campus may find ways to work with more synergy with each other and their community partners, to articulate their common ground, and measure their joint impact on students and their surrounding communities.

At the campus level, the civic responsibility of higher education needs to be made manifest, and new structures, community partnerships, curricula pedagogy, and measures of student success will signal the triumph of the civic engagement "movement." Meanwhile, those of us who share this desire must continue to exercise our own best citizenship skills to work together to address what the comic strip character Pogo calls our "insurmountable opportunities."

NOTES

1. L. Veysey, "Stability and Experiment in the American Undergraduate Curriculum," in *Content and Context: Essays on College Education,* ed. C. Kaysen (New York: McGraw-Hill, 1973).

2. C. Jencks and D. Reisman, *The Academic Revolution* (New York: Doubleday, 1968).

3. H.C. Boyte, *Public Engagement in a Civic Mission* (Battle Creek, MI: Kellogg Foundation, in press.)

4. M.D. Cohen and J.G. March, *Leadership and Ambiguity: The American College President* (New York: McGraw-Hill, 1974).

5. A.W. Gouldner, "Cosmopolitans and Locals: Toward an Analysis of Latent Social Roles," *Administrative Science Quarterly,* 2, no. 3 (December 1957): 281–307.

6. C. Kerr, "Postscript 1982," *Change,* 14, no. 7 (October 1982): 23–31.

7. R. Birnbaum, *How Colleges Work: The Cybernetics of Academic Organization and Leadership* (San Francisco: Jossey-Bass, 1988).

8. M.L. Cadwallader, "A Manifesto: The Case for an Academic Counterrevolution," *Liberal Education* (1982).

9. M. Diani, "The Concept of Social Movements," *Sociological Review* 40, no. 1 (February 1992): 1–25.

10. J. Howard, ed., *Praxis I: A Faculty Casebook on Community Service Learning* (Ann Arbor, MI: University of Michigan OCSL Press, 1993).

11. Campus Compact is a coalition of college and university presidents committed to student service leading to citizenship. It was founded in 1985 by the presidents of Brown, Georgetown, and Stanford and the Education Commission of the States in response to students who rejected the self-centered values attributed to "Generation X" and wanted to serve their communities. Campus Compact focused for the first five years on co-curricular student service activity, however, that focus broadened with the growing interest in the pedagogy of service-learning. Service-learning became viewed as a more effective means for promoting citizenship and for embedding civic education in the heart of the academy.

12. Council on Public Policy Education, "The Prospects for Public Making Space in Higher Education," working draft (4 March 1998).

13. E. Boyer, "Creating the New American College," *Chronicle of Higher Education* (March 1994): A18

14. D. Cox, director of the office of University Partnerships, personal communication, (13 January 1999).

15. R. Rorty, *Achieving Our Country: Leftist Thought in Twentieth Century America* (Cambridge, MA: Harvard University Press, 1997).

16. R. Guarasci and G.H. Cornwell, "Democracy and Difference: Emerging Concepts of Identity, Diversity and Community," in *Democratic Education in an Age of Difference: Redifining Citizenship in Higher Education* (San Francisco: Jossey Bass, 1997), 6–7.

17. B. R. Barber et al.,"Democratic Theory and Civic Measurement: A Report on the Measuring Citizenship Project," Draft report (1997); H.C. Boyte and J. Farr, "The Work of Citizenship and the Problems of Service Learning," in *Experiencing Citizenship: Concepts and Models for Service Learning in Political Science*, ed. R.M. Battistoni and W.E. Hudson (Washington, DC: AAHE, 1997).

18. D. Giles and J. Eyler, *Where's the Learning in Service Learning?* (San Francisco: Jossey-Bass, 1999).

19. L. Knefelkamp and C. Schneider, "Education for a World Lived in Common with Others," in *Education and Democracy: Reimagining Liberal Learning in America*, ed. Robert Orill (New York: College Board, 1997).

20. Barber et al., "Democratic Theory and Civic Measurement."

21. Standards for effective, sustained community partnerships are emerging from Campus Compact's work with model campuses, HUD grantees, the Council of Independent Colleges' initiative for urban institutions, NSEE's campus/community work, among others. There are a number of outstanding institutional models to consider, including the "engaged campus"—a concept used by both Campus Compact and NASULGC. HUD maintains directories of effective campus/community partnerships. The most recent AAU compilation of their members' "Service to the Community" (AAU, 1998) provides information on the efforts of individual faculty members.

22. "The Partnering Initiative," The Foundation on Economic Trends, Washington, DC, 1998.

23. S. Lloyd, "Collaborating for Change in Chicago," unpublished paper, John D. And Catherine T. McArthur Foundation (December 1993), 9.

24. J. Gardner, Speech to Campus Compact Strategic Planning Committee (10 February 1998).

25. Gardner, Speech to Campus Compact.

26. Barber et al., "Democratic Theory and Civic Measurement"; Boyte et al., *Public Engagement*; R.B. Young, *No Neutral Ground* (San Francisco: Jossey-Bass, 1997).

27. C. Trosset, "The Grinnell College Study" *Change*, 30, no. 5 (Washington, DC: American Association for Higher Education, 1998).

28. P. Palmer, "Divided No More: Movement Approach to Educational Reform," *Higher Education Exchange* (Dayton, OH: Kettering, 1996).

29. E. Boyer, *Scholarship Reconsidered: Priorities of the Professoriate* (Princeton, NJ: Carnegie Foundation for the Advancement of Teaching, 1990).

30. Palmer, "Divided No More."

31. T. Stanton, D.E. Giles Jr., and N. Cruz, *Service-Learning: A Movement's Pioneers Reflect on Its Origins, Practice, and Future* (San Francisco: Jossey-Bass, 1999).

32. E. Anderson and J. Shaffer, *Service Matters: Engaging Higher Education in the Renewal of America's Communities and American Democracy*, ed. M. Rothman (Providence, RI: Campus Compact, 1998).

33. T. Marchese, "Not-So-Distant Competitors: How New Providers Are Remaking the Postsecondary Marketplace" *AAHE Bulletin*, 50, no. 9 (Washington, DC, 1998).

34. J. Wellman, Institute for Higher Education Policy, personal communication, November 1998.

35. J.B. Elshtain, *A Call to Civil Society: Why Democracy Needs Moral Truths* (New York: Institute for American Voters, 1998). *Note:* The National Council on Civic Society is a group of 24 nationally distinguished scholars and leaders who, as paid volunteers, are examining the sources of competence, character, and citizenship in the U.S. The Report is authored by Elshtain of the University of Chicago Divinity School and chairperson of the Council.

36. Lloyd, "Collaborating for Change in Chicago," 9.

37. Ibid.

38. D. Matthews, "Creating More Public Space in Higher Education." Adapted from "Character for What? Higher Education and Public Life" *Educational Record* (Spring/Fall 1997) Council on Public Policy Education, Washington, DC.

39. R.S. Lowen, *Creating the Cold War University: The Transformation of Stanford* (Berkeley: University of California Press, 1997).

FURTHER READING

Jencks, C., and D. Reisman. *The Academic Revolution*. New York: Doubleday, 1968.

AFTERWORD

Defining the Civic Agenda for Higher Education

Zelda F. Gamson

R arely does one have the opportunity in the academy to identify a problem, get it onto a national agenda, and see it define action. For this to happen in two years is nothing short of amazing—and perhaps even a bit suspicious. That is what has happened to the civic agenda in higher education. In this afterword I will place the preceding chapters in the larger context in which the civic agenda developed. I will also identify what I think are some of the problems and challenges to the civic agenda for higher education.

GETTING "CIVIC LIFE" ON THE AGENDA OF HIGHER EDUCATION

As a sociologist whose specialty is higher education and former director of the New England Resource Center for Higher Education (NERCHE), which works with hundreds of colleges and universities in New England, I have considered it my professional responsibility to keep track of the major policy discourses that are likely to affect higher education. One of those policy discourses concerns the decline of civic life in the United States, to which many of the authors in this volume refer. In reading the reports of commissions, books, and articles, I was struck by the absence of discussion of the academy, whether it was part of the solution or part of the problem. I noted that many of those who were sounding the alarms about the decline of democracy and community in America were faculty members in our leading universities—M.J. Sandel and R.P. Putnam at Harvard, Jean Bethke Elshtain at Chicago, and R.N. Bellah and his colleagues at Berkeley. Yet unlike Harry

Boyte at Minnesota, Benjamin Barber at Rutgers, and Ira Harkavy at Penn, who were writing at the same time, they did not make the connection to higher education.

I decided to take on the challenge of making the connection intellectually and of encouraging the development of a national movement to strengthen the academy's contribution to civic life. As one of three executive editors of the higher education magazine *Change*, I had promised its editor, Ted Marchese, that I would edit a special issue on a topic related to higher education's role in society. The opportunity presented itself during a sabbatical in the fall of 1997. I invited Peter Kiang, a younger colleague of mine at the University of Massachusetts in Boston, to join me as a co-editor. A former community organizer, Kiang could bring to my knowledge of higher education and the national discourse about civic life his extensive experience with activism in cities around the country.

As we talked about what should go into the special issue, Kiang and I knew that there was a lot of activity around the country and that the sense of crisis among commentators and commissions applied more to voting behavior and participation in traditional organizations than to contemporary community life. We learned from research carried out by the sociologists Carmen Sirianni of Brandeis and Lewis Friedland at Wisconsin that participation in community and local problem-solving activities, as well as citizen activism on political campaigns, has been increasing in the last decades. Many of these activities evinced a creativity and freshness that Sirianni and Friedland term "civic innovation." Authors of one of the articles in the special issue of *Change,* they were joined by other authors who made the same point: people involved in the activities they had uncovered could be viewed as learners whose curriculum is the community and whose pedagogy is active engagement in the problems of their communities.

But where were the colleges and universities in the very communities where these wonderful things were happening? They were there, we knew, but invisibly. From projects at NERCHE carried out since the early 1990s, I knew that many faculty, staff members, and students were involved in civic activities of many sorts. Most of these activities were seen by the faculty, staff, and administrators who engaged in them as personal rather than professional and, even if they viewed them as professional, as unrelated to their jobs. Students who were doing volunteer service and internship activities off-campus did so through programs that were not in the mainstream of the typical college or university.

Occasionally, we found that some colleges and universities had made a deeper commitment to engaging civic issues through the leadership of a president or through outreach units of various kinds. In Chapter 4 of this book, Nancy Thomas describes some of these efforts across the country. But these efforts, whether individual or institutional, are isolated, uncoordinated, not strategic, and unassessed, as Jane Wellman points out in Chapter 18.

The task I set for myself was to bring the issue of higher education's role in civic life to national higher education leaders and observers. Soon after the *Change* issue appeared in January 1997, I attended an invitational conference called by the American Council on Education (ACE), the major national organization representing higher education as a whole, and the Carnegie Foundation for the Advancement of Teaching. ACE had a new president, Stanley Ikenberry, who wanted ideas for ACE's policy agenda. He responded with some interest when I suggested that ACE take on for higher education as a whole the renewal of civic life. From this meeting, another followed quickly to plan what would turn out to be the ACE Forum on Higher Education and Democracy, which has sponsored and published this book. The Forum, co-directed by Thomas Ehrlich and myself and staffed by Jane Wellman, held a conference in June 1998 at Florida State University, which brought together college presidents, faculty, program heads, and students from a variety of colleges and universities across the country, along with representatives from several higher education associations. A few weeks later, I attended a collo-quium organized by the Kettering Foundation, which has been devoted for a long time to strengthening civic life in America, that focused on the academy's role in civic life. Kettering's president, David Mathews, outlines in his chapter for this book the current thinking at Kettering about the academy's role.

SOME PROBLEMS IN THE CIVIC AGENDA

The Forum and the Kettering colloquium revealed several problems I will describe briefly. They include: (1) the challenges from student activism to the definition of what constitutes civic activity; (2) the role of communities in defining the agenda for higher education; (3) the role of the liberal arts in supporting civic learning and activity; (4) the incentives for civic engagement; and (5) the institutional requirements for civic engagement.

Challenges to the Definition of Civic Activity by Student Activism

One of the speakers at the Florida State University conference was Jeremy Smith, the chair of the board of the Center for Campus Organizing (CCO), a national organization that supports progressive campus activism. As a member of the board of CCO, I am concerned about the lack of connection between the civic agenda and the considerable campus activism going on across the country, activism that seems to be growing. While the media do not accord student activism the attention it received during the high protests of the

Vietnam War era, students on campuses across the country have been protest-
ing attacks on affirmative action programs and lack of support for
underrepresented groups. They have brought to the attention of their campuses the exploitation by American global corporations of children and women
in sweatshops that supply campus clothing. They have organized study groups
and teach-ins on environmental issues. They have acted in concert with poor
communities to hold their institutions accountable for their impacts on those
communities.

Is student activism on campus part of the civic agenda? If the answer is no,
then a significant proportion of student leadership is excluded. This leadership
will, rightly, believe that "civic" is a way of domesticating students' impulses
for social justice, a way of channeling them into "nice" volunteer and service
activities. If the civic agenda does not involve social change, as President
Gregory Prince of Hampshire College put it at the Florida State conference,
what is the point of it?

The Role of Communities in Defining the Civic Agenda

While this volume does not focus much on the role of communities and their
leaders in helping to shape the civic agenda for higher education, the Tallahassee conference devoted a good bit of time to communities and higher
education. There was much agreement that colleges and universities have
much to learn from communities, not only about the problems and issues that
are most important to tackle but about civic life as a source of learning. These
ideas led to the formation of the Listening to Communities project by the
Forum on Higher Education and Democracy. Chaired by Nancy Thomas,
Listening to Communities brings together community leaders, politicians, and
business and labor representatives with college and university people in
regions across the country. The purpose of the project is to jointly define the
civic agenda and to identify the resources within colleges and universities in a
region to work on that agenda.

The Role of the Liberal Arts

At the Tallahassee conference, Stanley Ikenberry talked about the crucial role
of the liberal arts and of campuses as crucial sites for promoting the civic
learning of students and the university as citizen. These are the features of
traditional colleges and universities that distinguish them from online degree
programs and for-profit institutions. If colleges and universities compete with
the latter by weakening the liberal arts and the role of the campus as a
gathering place, as many have done, it is likely that they will lose the

competition with providers with fewer fixed costs and a profit mentality. But if they take seriously their historic civic role by encouraging the creativity that enlivens the traditional liberal arts disciplines described by Carol Schneider (Chapter 5) and other authors in this volume, they are more likely to succeed—especially if they involve their communities. Of course, this is a tall order given the pressures in the disciplines and in the organizational structure of universities toward specialization and isolation.

The Incentives for Civic Engagement

What could be a more powerful incentive for institutions to encourage civic engagement than competition from for-profit institutions? If that is not enough, what could be more powerful than declines in financial support and attacks on the internal workings of colleges and universities, such as the tenure system, teaching loads, and curricular decisions? There are some who believe that higher education has become interested in the civic agenda for public relations reasons only, and there is some truth to this assertion. However, if self-interest is all there is the game will become dangerous. Public proclamations of commitment to civic improvement that are not backed with real resources and activities will further erode public support for higher education and only deepen the considerable cynicism about the sincerity of college presidents and others in the academy.

What could colleges and universities do to demonstrate that they are committed? They would have to seriously listen to communities and make the campus available as a space for public discourse of the sort that the Kettering Foundation promotes, as described by David Mathews in Chapter 7. They would seek joint funding for projects of interest to both communities and themselves and share the power and resources equally. And perhaps most important, they would encourage all constituencies of their campus to engage in public discourse about the policies of their own institutions.

Institutional Requirements for Civic Engagement

Which leads me to the last problem. If higher education is to become a serious participant in rebuilding civic life, it will need to make some serious internal changes. In an era which rewards careerists and masters of the sound-bite, we must ask our college presidents and senior administrators to do more to defend the historic civic mission of higher education. Many either do not understand this historic mission or reject it. More than a few have given away the store by not defending academic freedom and the tenure system on which it depends in the face of attacks from without and abuses from within. They have given in too easily to politicians and business people who pressure for accountability and increased work loads (without asking the same of themselves) and to ideologues who want to shape admissions policies, student life, and curricula.

It is not surprising, then, that the gap between administrators and faculty is wide and growing wider. At the same time, faculty members grow more isolated from one another because of generational, disciplinary, gender, and racial differences laid on top of increasingly stressful work conditions. Not much can happen without dealing with the breakdown of community in most colleges and universities. The first step in rebuilding civic life outside the academy is to rebuild civic life within the academy. Our ways of handling power differences and diverse points of view and cultures should be models of the civic life we wish to engender in our communities. Encouraging the articulation of differences, and then finding areas for collaboration, should be the norm rather than the exception.

Strengthening the civic life of higher education depends on the representation of most of the population of the nation in our student bodies. This means fighting for maintaining and expanding the representation of underrepresented populations and helping them succeed, as Alexander Astin argues in Chapter 6. Only with these populations fully present on campuses can we work on building the kind of diverse communities that exist in the larger society. As Schneider, Boyte, and Benson and Harkavy tell us, colleges and universities should do more to integrate the contemporary world into the curriculum, especially general education courses. This means understanding what animates our students, as Sax (Chapter 1) and Eckert and Henschel (Chapter 10) remind us, and recognizing that John Dewey's advice to overcome the split between "skills" and "content," between the liberal arts, and that professional preparation is even more timely at the end than it was at the beginning of the twentieth century. It also means paying as much, if not more, attention to how we teach and how students learn than to what we, as educators, teach and learn.

Finally, a point that cannot be made too often: Colleges and universities need to liberate themselves from the stranglehold of the research culture that has sapped the vitality of most of our colleges and universities. As Zlotkowski, Boyte and Kari, Sullivan, Benson and Harkavy, and others argue in this book, the domination of the research culture has had negative epistemological, professional, organizational, and cultural effects. In particular, the denigration of applied research and problem-solving has eroded higher education's connection to the world. The fetishism of much academic writing—and speech—has contributed to the unintelligibility of academic discourse. This book is an exception and a model of another way to engage in the academic life.

INDEX

by Kay Banning